O9-BTL-893

THE COMMON COURAGE READER

Essays for an Informed Democracy

Edited by

Kevin Griffith

Common Courage Press

Monroe, ME

Copyright © 2000 by Common Courage Press.
All Rights Reserved.
Cover design by Erica Bjerning.

Cataloging-in-Publication Data

The Common Courage reader : essays for an informed democracy / edited by Kevin
  Griffith.
    p. cm.
  Includes index.
  ISBN 1-56751-203-8 (cloth) -- ISBN 1-56751-202-X (paper)
    1. Social problems--United States. 2. Social problems. 3. Critical thinking.
I. Griffith, Kevin.

HN59.2.C62 2000
361.6'1'0973--dc21

                                                                    00-031754

Common Courage Press
PO Box 702
Monroe, ME 04951

(207) 525-0900; fax: (207) 525-3068
orders-info@commoncouragepress.com

www.commoncouragepress.com

First Printing

Contents

Chapter II: Analyzing the Media

Chapter III: Corporate Greed and Crime

Chapter IV: Health and the Environment

Chapter V: Washington Politics and Religion

For Jordan and Clare

Special thanks to my wife, Judy Petrou, for her feedback and comments and to Dana Blanke for her assistance in assembling the manuscript of this reader. Thanks also to Bev Matteson.

Introduction for Teachers

As Howard Zinn states in *The Future of History*, "The textbook publishers want to play it safe. They don't want to say anything which might raise an eyebrow anywhere." *The Common Courage Reader* will, I hope, raise a few eyebrows. This reader, unique in its unapologetically progressive perspective, is designed to stimulate students who, for the most part, have been bombarded for much of their lives by propaganda messages from the conservative mainstream media. Designed for use in both first-year and advanced composition courses, this anthology of excerpts from recent Common Courage Press books encourages students to think critically about the political and social scene, to confront issues of class, sexuality, gender and race, and to become more active participants in progressive social and political causes.

The chapters are organized thematically (see the "Table of Contents") and the readings represent topics from across the college curriculum: psychology, journalism, media studies, business, politics, health, and international studies. My principle for selecting the readings was guided by the knowledge that most first-year college students were born in the early 1980s and their knowledge of and connection to the Reagan administration, Iran-Contra, and even Desert Storm is often vague and hazy at best. Therefore, I have tried to include the most accessible and up-to-date readings I could find that represent a broad range of topics in subjects relevant to college students. *The Common Courage Reader* begins with the prologue "How Social Change Happens" from *The Future of History* by Howard Zinn. I included this prologue so that students and their instructors can discuss social change, and the level of commitment it requires. The reader then proceeds with a chapter on adolescence, a topic with which students can readily identify. The book then progresses through topics which require increasing levels of thought and background knowledge. Each reading is followed by several questions for class discussion, and the end of each chapter includes suggestions for paper topics based on the readings. Of course, instructors should understand that the discussion questions and reading suggestions are not all-inclusive. Good instructors, the kind who will use this reader, should feel free to create variations on the questions and the writing assignments.

Even though many composition instructors are actively engaged in progressive causes, most composition readers are designed to offend no one—with material that is as apolitical as possible. The articles and excerpts the students encounter here are written by authors who are passionately committed to a cause and actively engaged in working for a better, more sane society. The writing in Common Courage books is certainly writing with a purpose—writing that raises students' eyebrows, challenges their assumptions, and motivates them to think critically about society and politics.

Students should experience the range of emotions that I do when reading Common Courage books: anger, awareness, enlightenment. I can assure you that none of the readings will fail to answer the "So What" question. And isn't that the type of writing we want from our students?

Introduction for Students

Apathetic, ignorant, unmotivated—the list of adjectives used to describe you and your peers could go on and on. For those of you who are smarter and more savvy than you're given credit for—for those who crave writing that challenges mainstream assumptions and sparks critical thought about our society—the The Common Courage Reader is designed for you. While most composition readers follow the same old formula, The Common Courage Reader presents writing that will shock you at one moment and have you laughing at the next. None of the writing you are about to read will bore you, I hope. In fact, all of the readings in presented here are written by people who are passionately committed to improving our society. What you are about to read is truly writing with a purpose—whether that purpose is to expose the dark side of capitalism, the way power and wealth control the media, or the way our own government terrorizes its own citizens and the citizens of neighboring nations. The purpose of The Common Courage Reader is not to indoctrinate you into any particular way of thinking, but to provide an antidote to the culture we are all a part of, a culture that promotes political passivity and apathy. We live in a society in which others who have more wealth and power than we do will gladly do our thinking for us—unless we choose to think critically for ourselves.

As you make your way through this anthology, remember that some of the readings will be more accessible to you than others. As a member of an educated citizenry, you should be aware of recent history and keep up with your local and national news. These readings will not insult your intelligence—but they do *expect* your intelligence. The road to knowledge is a two-way street. Don't back down if a reading makes a reference to a historical event or to a country or person about which you know little. Ask your professor or look it up. Your rewards will be great: you'll be a better writer and a more informed citizen.

Prologue

In this chapter from *The Future of History*, Howard Zinn, Professor Emeritus of History at Boston University and author of the ground breaking book, *A People's History of the United States*, discusses with interviewer David Barsamian how issues of class conflict are often absent from the college and university curriculum, and how students, teachers, and citizens can work toward social change.

How Social Change Happens

Howard Zinn

The Future of History: Interviews with David Barsamian

December 16, 1996

David Barsamian: *I was just looking at a book of poetry of Langston Hughes. You had an opportunity to meet while you were at Spelman College in Atlanta. Do you remember that?*

Howard Zinn: Do I remember that? I'm the one who told you about that! I could have pretended to your audience that you just know all these things. But I told you that I met Langston Hughes, because I tell everybody I've met important people, whether I've met them or not. I actually did meet Langston Hughes. Not a serious meeting. It's not like when you and I sit down together and have cappuccino at the Cafe Algiers in Cambridge. This wasn't like that at all. I was teaching at Spelman. They invited him down to the Atlanta University Center. I was dispatched to pick him up at the airport, which I think I've told you is my claim to being a revolution- ary. I pick people up at the airport. Sometimes even bring them back to the airport. So I picked him up at the airport and spent a little time with him, a great guy. I love his poetry. Class-conscious, simple, clear, strong. I quote it whenever I can.

DB   *He was an ally of the anti-fascist forces in Spain as well. He went to Spain.*

That's right. There are pictures of him speaking in Spain. He suffered because of his left-wing connections. They put a lot of pressure on him and so he had a hard time. I think at one point in his life he relented and tried to move away from that to protect himself. He was vulnerable in many ways. His personal life made him vul- nerable.

DB   *Because he was gay?*

Exactly, because he was gay. It's bad enough in our time, but in that time to be gay, forget it.

DB   *You've used "Ballad of the Landlord."*

"Ballad of the Landlord" is one of my favorite poems because it's so ferociously class-conscious. Maybe you'd like to read it. Do you know that this is the poem that got Jonathan Kozol fired from his job here in Boston? I guess that's what attracted me to the poem. I said, Any poem that can get anybody fired is worth paying attention to.

DB   *Jonathan Kozol, a National Book Award winner and noted educator, was fired for reading the poem?*

Yes, he got fired. College professors can be fired for what they do, but it's always done very indirectly because universities are supposed to be places of free inquiry. But elementary schools and middle schools and high schools make no pretense. They are totalitarian places, and they don't make any claim to anything else. After all, they say, these are very young minds. We mustn't expose them to class conflict. We mustn't make them think that the country is run by the rich. We mustn't give them the idea that you should oppose your landlord and fight eviction, which is what happens in this poem.

DB   *Do you want to read it?*

I'll tell you what. Let's both read it. We'll have a duet. You read one and I'll read the other.

DB   *"Ballad of the Landlord," by Langston Hughes.*

Landlord, landlord, my roof has sprung a leak.
Don't you 'member I told you about it way last week?

Landlord, landlord, these steps is broken down.
When you come up yourself it's a wonder you don't fall down.

Ten bucks you say I owe you?
Ten bucks you say is due?
That's ten bucks more'n I'll pay you
Till you fix this house up new.

What? You're gonna get eviction orders?
You're gonna to cut off my heat?
You're gonna to take my furniture
And throw it in the street?

Um-huh! You talking high and mighty.
Talk on till you get through.
You ain't gonna to be able to say a word
If I land my fist on you.

Police! Police! come and get this man!
He's trying to ruin the government

And overturn the land!

Copper's whistle! patrol bell! arrest

Precinct station.
Iron cell.
Headlines in press:

*MAN THREATENS LANDLORD
TENANT HELD. NO BAIL.
JUDGE GIVES NEGRO
90 DAYS IN COUNTY JAIL.*

What an incendiary poem. It's a poem about civil disobedience. Challenging a law, but so obviously you being right and them being wrong. So you don't want young kids to hear that. So if a teacher reads that to young kids, or has them read it, he's got to go. So Jonathan Kozol went. But he had his revenge. He wrote this book (*Death at an Early Age*) which brought this to the attention of an awful lot of people.

DB   *His subsequent books on education,* Savage Inequalities *and* Amazing Grace, *are very powerful works.*

He's a wonderfully eloquent and passionate person about poverty and inequality and racism. That connection between him and Langston Hughes was a good one.

DB   *Perhaps Langston Hughes' most famous poem is "Raisin In the Sun. A Dream Deferred." Why don't you read that?*

I think I quote that. I shouldn't say that, "I *think* I quote that." We always say that in modesty. I *know* I quote that in A *People's History of the United States* when I start talking about the movement of the 1960s and how much led up to it in black poetry and literature. Some of the people know that title "Raisin In the Sun" because there's this famous play by Lorraine Hansberry and Sidney Poitier starred in this famous movie and on television and all that, but not a lot of people know that it came from Langston Hughes.

What happens to a dream deferred?

Does it dry up
like a raisin in the sun?
Or fester like a sore—
And then run?

Does it stink like rotten meat?
Or crust and sugar over—
like a syrupy sweet?

Maybe it just sags like a heavy load.

Or does it explode?

His language is so simple but so powerful. That image of all of that pent-up explosion. Richard Wright sort of did the same thing. Richard Wright always talked about that pent-up anger in the black population. In *Black Boy*, in which he talks about growing up in the South and what he went through and the humiliation and looking around him and seeing all the black people are toeing the line out of necessity, out of self-protection, but thinking, "Something's going to happen here."

DB   *Speaking of something that's going to happen here, Hughes asks, "What happens to a dream deferred? Does it explode if that dream is not realized?" In late October in Boulder you said that, "We can't go on with the present polarization of wealth and poverty."*

I don't know how long we can go on, but I know we can't go on indefinitely. That growing gap between wealth and poverty is a recipe for trouble, for disaster, for conflict, for explosion. Here's the Dow Jones average going up, up, up and there are the lives of people in the city. The Dow Jones average in the last fifteen years has gone up 400%. In the same period, the wages of working people, of 80% of the population, have gone down 15%. 400% up, 15% down. Now the richest 1% of the population owning 43%, 44% of the wealth. Up from the usual maybe 28%, 30%, 32%, which is bad enough and which has been a constant throughout American history. In fact it's been so constant that when they did studies of the tax rolls in Boston in the seventeenth and eighteenth centuries, they concluded that 1% of the population owned 33% of the wealth. If you look at the statistics all through American history, you see that figure, a little more, a little less, around the same. Now it's even worse and worse. So something's got to give.

DB   *Given that enormous growth in income and wealth, the inequality, if you were a member, let's say, of the ruling class, I know you're not, that's why I say if—*

How do you know I'm not?

DB   *You're just a historian, retired, professor emeritus. But let's say if you were, wouldn't this trend toward increasing polarization give you cause for concern? Because for you to keep your power and privilege you need stability. You don't need unrest and upheaval.*

That's true. But there's always this conflict within the ruling class. The people who know this from a long-term point of view say, "Hey, we'd better do something about it." That's why you see people up there in the ruling class, that's your phrase, "ruling class." I would never use a class-conscious phrase like that. But you used it, so I can use it. The ruling class. There have always been some members of the ruling class who wanted reforms, who wanted to ease things, who worried about a future explosion. These are the people who supported Roosevelt. They were members of the ruling class who supported Roosevelt and the New Deal reforms because they knew that they couldn't let things go on the way they were, with the turmoil of the 1930s, that there was a revolution brewing. So there have always been people like that. I think of Felix Rohatyn, who's this big banker. He says," Let's not go on like this. This polarization of wealth is going too far." But on the other hand, there are all those other greedy ones. They want it now. They think of the short term, "OK, maybe there'll be rebellion against my grandchildren…" It shows how their family values operate. They don't care if the rebellion takes place against their grandchildren. "But now I'm going to haul in as much as I can." And that's what they're doing.

DB   *I'm saving the easy questions as we proceed into the interview. How does social change happen?*

Thanks. I can deal with that in thirty seconds. You think I know? We know how it has happened, and we can sort of extrapolate from that, not that you can extrapolate mathematically, but you can sort of get suggestions from that. You see change happening when there has been an accumulation of grievance until it reaches a boiling point. Then something happens. When I say, "look at historical situations and try to extrapolate from that, what happens in the South in the 1950s and 1960s?" It's not that suddenly black people were put back into slavery. It's not as if there was some precipitating thing that suddenly pushed them back. They were, as the Southern white ruling class was eager to say, making progress. It was glacial progress, extremely slow. But they were making progress. But it's not the absolute amount of progress that's made that counts. It's the amount of progress made against what the ideal should be in the minds of the people who are aggrieved. And the ideal in the minds of the black people was, "We have to be equal. We have to be treated as equals." The progress that was being made in the South was so far from that. The recognition of that gap between what should be and what is, which existed for a long time but waited for a moment when a spark would be lit. The thing about sparks being lit is that you never know what spark is going to ignite and really result in a conflagration. After all, before the Montgomery bus boycott there had been other boycotts. Before the sit-ins of the 1960s, there had been between 1955 and 1960 sit-ins in sixteen different cities which nobody paid any attention to and which did not ignite a movement. But then in Greensboro, on February 1, 1960, these four college kids go in, sit in, and everything goes haywire. Then things are never the same. You never know, and this is, I think, an encouragement to people who do things, not knowing whether they will result in anything, and you do things again and again and nothing happens, that you have to do things, do things, do things, you have to light that match, light that match, light that match, not knowing how often it's going to sputter and go out and at what point it's going to take hold, at what point other people, seeing what happens, are going to be encouraged, provoked to do the same. That's what happened in the civil rights movement and that's what happens in other movements. Things take a long time. It requires patience, but not a passive patience, the patience of activism.

When I was in South Africa in 1982, I was invited there to give a lecture to the University of Capetown. At the time, apartheid defined the country, Mandela was in Robben's Island, the African National Congress was outlawed, people were being banned. We know about books being banned, there, it was people who were banned. They couldn't speak. They couldn't go here or there. The secret police everywhere.

Just before I arrived at the University of Capetown the secret police of South Africa had just broken into the offices of the student newspaper at the University and made off with all of their stuff. It was the kind of thing that happened all the time. The atmosphere was an atmosphere of terror. You would think perhaps, only seeing that, nothing is going to happen here, like you would think in the South in the early 1950s. You don't see any sign of a civil rights revolution in the South in the early 1950s. But having come from that experience in the South, I became aware, just talking to people, going to meetings, going to a huge rally outside of Johannesburg, where everybody did everything illegal, where they sang the anthem of the African National Congress, raised the flags of the African National Congress, where banned people spoke. I suddenly was aware that underneath the surface of total control things were simmering, things were going on. I didn't know when it would break through, but we saw it break through not long ago. Suddenly Mandela comes out of Robben's Island and becomes president of the new South Africa. We should be encouraged. We shouldn't be discouraged. We should be encouraged by historical examples of social change, by how surprising changes take place suddenly, when you least expect it, not because of a miracle from on high, but because people have labored patiently for a long time.

DB *Do you think it's important to rethink the way we think about time? Everyone's in a hurry. Well, this change you're suggesting, Professor, I'm a very busy guy. I've got about fifteen minutes.*

It's true. We have to rethink the whole question of time. We have to get used to the idea that the great society—I'm sorry to use that phrase. All those phrases were OK: the Great Society, the New Frontier, the New Deal. They weren't realized. We have to get accustomed to the idea that it may not come in our lifetime. We will see changes in our lifetime. Who knows what we will see? Think of Mandela, in prison for decades. Think of people in the South living in humiliation for a hundred years, waiting. I'm not saying it will take a hundred years or it will take decades. I don't know how long it will take for important changes to take place. You never know. But when people get discouraged because they do something and nothing happens, they should really understand that the only way things will happen is if people get over the notion that they must see immediate success. If they get over that notion and persist, then they will see things happen before they even realize it.

DB *Was your job at Spelman College in Atlanta the first job you got when you got out of the university?*

I call it my first "real" teaching job. I had a number of unreal teaching jobs. By unreal I mean I was teaching part-time at Upsala College in New Jersey.

DB *Now bankrupt, incidentally.*

Because I taught there?

DB *This just happened. Literally, colleges are now going bankrupt.*

I said patience. It took a while after I was there to reap the fruits of my being there and go bankrupt. I wouldn't be surprised if every other place that I've touched goes bankrupt. I have written articles for a number of magazines. Those magazines are now defunct. I'm warning you about what will happen to *Alternative Radio* after this interview. You never know.

DB *I'll take my chances.*

I taught at Upsala College. How do you know about all these defunct places? Do you have a list? Anyway, I did teach there part-time. Maybe it's defunct because it was very Lutheran. So strict. It was like being back in the time of Luther, back in the sixteenth century. But in any case, I had a part-time job there and a part-time job at Brooklyn College. But Spelman College was my first full-time teaching job. I immediately catapulted from graduate student at Columbia University to chair—I want you to take full cognizance of that—of a department. Four persons in the department. Like being head waiter in a two-waiter restaurant. Not just history. Four persons included everything: history, political science, sociology, philosophy. Four people doing all of that. We were renaissance people.

DB *What year was that?*

That was in 1956 when my wife Roz and my two kids Myla and Jeff—mind if I mention their names? I want to give them air time—all trundled into our old Chevy, went down.

DB *I assume it was in terms of your socialization a rather radicalizing experience for you. I presume you lived in a black neighborhood near the college.*

Actually, the first year we were there—we were there a total of seven—we lived in a white, working-class neighborhood on the edge of Atlanta, which was an interesting experience in itself. We weren't far from Stone Mountain, which is a Ku Klux Klan gathering place. We were living in this first house we'd ever lived in. We had always lived in the slums in New York or in low-income housing projects. Here we were in a little house like the other little houses on this block of working-class white people. One of the first things that happened when we were there is we hear all this noise. We go outside. There was a main street about a block from our house. There was a parade of people with white hoods, KKK, marching to Stone Mountain.

We spent a year there. It was sort of inconvenient traveling back and forth. We moved to the Spelman College campus, which was surrounded by a black community. We lived essentially in the black community for the next six years. You say radicalizing experience? I guess so. Of course I like to think that I was a radical even before I came to Spelman College. But we all like to pretend that we were radical at the age of three, right? You might say I had been radicalized by working in the shipyards, but maybe a little more radicalized by being in a war. But probably that time at Spelman College was the most intense experience of learning in my life. I think it's fair to say that. Talk about social change, I could see social change happening all around me and then writing about it, observing it, participating in it, seeing my

Spelman College students so controlled in that old guard atmosphere of the old South in which students, especially young black women, were being trained to take their obedient places in the segregated society. Trained to pour tea and wear white gloves and march into and out of chapel and really to be kept inside this kind of nunnery. Then suddenly to see them break out of this when they look at television and watch the sit-ins taking place in Greensboro and Rock Hill, South Carolina and Nashville and to see them gathering. Julian Bond across the street at Morehouse College meeting with Lonnie King, the football captain at Morehouse College, gathering people from Spelman and getting together and planning the first sit-ins in the spring of 1960 in Atlanta. My students literally leaping over that stone wall that surrounded the Spelman campus and doing what they weren't supposed to do. Seeing this remarkable change in them, this growth of courage and getting arrested, going to jail. Marian Wright Edelman, my student at Spelman, going to jail. A photo of her appearing in the newspapers the next day showing this very studious Spelman student behind bars reading a book which she had brought along with her so she wouldn't miss her class or homework. Seeing the South change in that time, seeing white Southerners change, seeing white Southerners get used to the idea that the South is going to change and accepting it.

DB *What I meant by radicalizing you, I was thinking in terms of being a witness to an oppressive mechanism, segregation, U.S.-style apartheid, Jim Crow, and then watching the resistance to it grow.*

Anybody who was in any way in the U.S. socially conscious knew vaguely that there was racial segregation. But to be right there and to witness it in action, to talk to my students about their early lives, about the first time they realized that they were black and being considered different and treated differently. To participate in sit-ins and to see the atmosphere around us in Rich's Department Store suddenly change from friendly to hostile when four of us, two black and two white, my wife and I and two black students from Spelman, sit down in this lunch counter at Rich's. Suddenly it's as if a bomb had been dropped or plague had been visited on it. The people gathering around us and shouting and cursing. Getting an inkling, being white people, just an inkling, of what it is to be black and be subject all your life to the thought that if you step one foot out of line you'll be surrounded by people who are threatening you. That's a learning experience. Learning comes in layers. There's something you think you know? You don't know it until you see it very up close, penetrating you. So it was a learning experience.

I learned a lot about teaching, too. I learned that the most important thing about teaching is not what you do in the classroom but what you do outside of the classroom and what you do to bring the lessons of books and the writings of thinkers and the facts of history, what you do to make a connection between that and the world outside. To go outside the classroom yourself, to bring your students outside the classroom, or to have them bring you outside the classroom, because very often they do it first and you say, "I can't hang back. I'm their teacher. I have to be there with them." And to learn that the best kind of teaching is the one that makes this connection between social action and book learning.

DB   *Why do you think so many of your colleagues, and I think this is a fair state-ment to make, really want to just busy themselves with their scholarship and turning out papers and attending conferences? I'm not saying that doesn't have any value. But when it comes to "out there," to being engaged with what's happening in the streets, in society, they don't feel it's appropriate.*

There's a powerful drive in our society for safety and security. And everybody is vulnerable because we all are part of a hierarchy of power in which unless we're at the very, very top, unless we're billionaires, or the President of the U.S., or the boss, and very few of us are bosses, we are somewhere on some lower rung in the hierarchy of power, where somebody has power over us, somebody has the power to fire us, to withhold a raise, to punish us in some way. Here in this rich country, so prideful of the economic system, the most prominent, the most clear-cut thing you can say about this great economic success is that everybody is insecure. Everybody is nerv-ous. Even if you're doing well, you're nervous. Something will happen to you. In fact, the people who are doing fairly well, the middle class, are more nervous than the people at the bottom, who know what to expect and have smaller expectations. There's this nervousness, this insecurity, and this economic fear of saying the wrong thing, doing the wrong thing, stepping out of line. The academic world has its own special culture of conformity and being professional. All the professions have the cult of professionalism, even in your profession, radio broadcasters. Being professional means not being committed.

DB   *Not having an agenda.*

Right. There are people who might call you unprofessional, because sometimes I suspect you have an agenda. Sometimes I suspect you care about what's going on in the world. Sometimes I suspect that the people you interview are the people whose ideas you want to broadcast. You're not supposed to do that. It's unprofessional. It's unprofessional to be a teacher who goes out on picket lines, or who even invites stu-dents out on picket lines. It's unprofessional to be a teacher who says to students, "Look, instead of giving you a final exam, your assignment for the semester is to go out into the community and work with some organization that you believe in and then do a report on that instead of taking a final exam of multiple choice questions asking you who was president during the Mexican War." So that's unprofessional. And you will stand out. You will stick out if the stuff you write is not written for scholarly journals but is written for everybody to read, because certainly the stuff written for scholarly journals is not written for everybody to read. It's deliberately written in such a way that not everybody can read it. Very few people can read it. So if you write stuff that the ordinary person can read, you're suspect. They'll say you're not a scholar, you're a journalist. Or you're not a scholar, you're a propagandist, because you have a point of view. They don't have a point of view. Scholarly articles don't have a point of view. Of course, they really do. They have an agenda. But they don't say it. They may not even know they have an agenda. The agenda is obedience. The agenda is silence. The agenda is safety. The agenda is, Don't rock the boat.

DB *One of the criticisms of Alternative Radio that I hear from program directors around the country is that it's "not objective." It's not balanced. These are terms of abuse in order to actually limit the possibility of people actually hearing dissenting voices such as yours.*

This business of "balance" is very funny. What is balance? The *MacNeil/Lehrer NewsHour* is balanced, right? They have people on the far right balanced by people on the not-so-far right balanced by people in the middle balanced by one person two degrees to the left of the middle. That's balanced. If you said to *MacNeil/Lehrer*, "Why don't you have Noam Chomsky on as a regular commentator to balance all the Assistant Secretaries of State and the Secretaries of Defense and the Congressmen, just one person to balance hundreds of others?" They would say, "No, that's not what we mean by balance."

The fact is, things are already unbalanced. The pretense is that things are balanced and you want to keep them that way. But of course they're already so far out of balance, we would have to put an enormous amount of left-wing weight onto the scales in order even to make the scales move slightly towards balance.

DB *You just mentioned that MIT professor Noam Chomsky. When did you first meet Chomsky?*

I first met Noam—do you mind if I call him Noam? I call you David.

DB *Very familiar.*

Very familiar. Unprofessional. I first met Noam, I had moved not long before to Boston from the South. It was the summer of 1965. I had vaguely heard of him from somebody who talked about him as a linguist. I knew there was a guy named Chomsky at MIT and that he was brilliant in the field of linguistics. That's all I knew about him. I didn't know that he had any interest in politics. This is a funny thing to say. If somebody said today about Noam Chomsky, "Oh, I didn't know that he was interested in politics"—well! And then, something was happening. I moved out of the South but I was still in touch with things in the region. A lot of people were being arrested in Jackson, Mississippi, black people, SNCC [the Student Nonviolent Coordinating Committee] people, and being held in the big compound because there were too many of them to fit into the jails. It was decided to send a delegation of people from the Boston area down to take a look at things and make a report. Bob Zellner, one of the original SNCC people, one of the few white people in SNCC, a white Southerner from Alabama, a fantastic person, organized this and asked me to come. I said OK. I found myself on a plane going south sitting next to a guy who introduced himself as Noam Chomsky. A very immodest statement, don't you think, for him to say, "I'm Noam Chomsky?" So we talked all the way down. Then we talked while we were there and we talked on the way back. We became friends. I became aware of the fact that he was a guy who wasn't just interested in linguistics— although he had a slight interest in linguistics—but he was very, very deeply concerned about what was going on in the country and the world and it occurred to me, talking to him, that he was very smart. So from then on, and then of course with the

Vietnam War escalating just about that time, the two of us found ourselves on the same platform again and again at the same rallies. So we got to know one another.

DB   *You've said that you were often the opening act for Chomsky.*

Like rock and roll groups. I was the warm-up. I had a lot of emotional statements surrounding several facts. Noam would come on with one vaguely emotional statement and 7,000 facts. It seemed to me a good combination.

DB   *As you know, he's not a flamboyant, charismatic speaker. He would be the first to acknowledge that. What accounts for the enormous crowds that he attracts, not just in the U.S. but all around the world?*

You say, "Not just in the U.S." He attracts bigger crowds in Canada and in Europe and now lately in Latin America. I just talked to him today. He just returned from Latin America. Everywhere he goes there are huge crowds. Everywhere I go to speak, five hundred people show up. They inform me quietly, "Noam Chomsky was here two weeks ago. Two thousand people came to hear him." Is this a message they're trying to give me? I'm inadequate? The reason so many people turn out to hear him is that they've heard about him. I guess he's famous. It's interesting that he should be famous, because all the organs of power in the U.S. are trying their best not to make him famous, to shut him up, not to publish him, not to pay attention to him, not to put him on national radio or TV. But his message has been so powerful and so outrageously true and so backed up by information and so very often ahead of everybody else. Look, he was the first one in this country to talk about East Timor. Now the East Timor rebels get the Nobel Prize. As I go around the country, wherever I go Noam has already spoken or is about to speak there. Plus he speaks at a lot of places where I don't speak. I have run into so many people all over who say that they went to hear him speak and it had an amazing effect on them, as you say, without him being flamboyant. Just the power of what he says, the information that piles up, so devastating and so obviously true, and with such documentation. It amounts to a powerful indictment of our society, of our economic system, of our political system, of the hypocrisy, of the failure of the press to report what is going on in the world. To me it's a very encouraging thing that wherever Noam speaks huge crowds turn out. It shows me that there is an enormous population in this country that is hungry for information that they don't get in the major media.

Another encouraging thing to me is the alternate radio and alternate media. I can't tell you how many people have said to me—I know you think I'm buttering you up, yes, I guess I am buttering you up. Call it margarine, it's the New Age. People say to me, "Hey, I heard the talk you gave." And they mention some radio station somewhere that I never heard of and apparently you have this satellite that's floating around. You bounce a talk by Noam Chomsky or by me or by Barbara Ehrenreich off these satellites and they go out to radio stations. You notice how technologically astute I am in my accurate description of exactly how this thing works? It bounces off the satellite, goes to these radio stations and then into people's homes? Isn't that how it works exactly?

DB *So despite what the pundits are telling us about the population being passive and quiescent, you think there's an audience there for dissidence?*

Absolutely. I talk very often to captive audiences. Not prisoners, I mean people who turn out to hear me talk, and I imagine this is even more true of the larger crowds that turn out to hear Noam. These are not the radicals of the community. Five hundred people come to hear me in Duluth, Minnesota. There are not five hundred radicals in Duluth, Minnesota who have come to hear me tell them what they already know. I don't know why they're there. Maybe there's not a lot to do in Duluth that night. That seems like an insult to Duluth. There are a few things to do. Who knows why? What I'm trying to say is they're not people who are already aficionados of the left and of radical messages. They come maybe out of curiosity. Their interest has been piqued by an article in the newspaper or whatever and they come to hear me. Then I deliver what I believe is a radical message: this is what's wrong with our economic system. It's fundamental. This is what's wrong with our political system. It's fundamental. We need to redistribute the wealth in this country. We need to use it in a rational way. We need to take this enormous arms budget and not just cut it slightly but dismantle it because we have to make up our minds we're not going to go to war any more. We're not going to militarily intervene anymore. If we're not going to go to war any more, then we have $250 billion. Then we don't have to worry about Medicare, Social Security, child care, universal health care, education. We can have a better society. I say things which if you mentioned them to *MacNeil/Lehrer* they would say, "That's a little too much for our listeners." It's not too much. I think this is what Noam does, too. You tell people what makes common sense, it makes common sense that if you're a very, very rich country nobody in the country should be hungry. Nobody should be homeless. Nobody should be without health care. The richest country in the world. Nobody should be without these things. We have the resources but they're being wasted or given somewhere to somebody. It's common sense. So there are people all over this country, millions of people, who would listen to such a message and say, "Yes, yes, yes." The problem is to organize these people into a movement.

DB *Mike Moore, the celebrated film director of* Roger and Me *and of* TV Nation *very effectively uses humor to convey political ideas, as does Molly Ivins and Jim Hightower and yourself. Do you feel that humor is a way to maybe hook a larger audience and to make left, progressive ideas more attractive?*

I don't like to think of it that way. I don't go home and say, "I think we've got to reach people, so I'll try to get humorous." Rather, it's a way of having a little fun with the world in a world that is not giving us a lot of fun, that's giving us tragedy, pictures of hungry people and pictures of war. Maybe it's something I learned from being in the South and being in the black community, to see how much humor there was among people who you might say have no right to laugh. There's nothing to laugh about, and these people are laughing and having fun. Or people in the army, people at war. They've got to have humor. They've got to have fun. They need to laugh. We've got to have fun even while we're dealing with serious things. We've got to represent in the present what we want in the future. I suppose that's why we do that. It's not a planned conspiracy.

DB   *Have you noticed any changes in your profession, history? I hesitate to use the term "revisionist," because it smacks of the Soviet era. But along the lines of A People's History, your book, there's James Loewen's book* Lies My Teacher Told Me. *Have there been some changes in this area?*

No question there have been changes. Obviously not enough to say, "The teaching of history has changed." But obviously enough changes to alarm the right wing in this country, to alarm the American Legion, to alarm senators, to alarm Lynne Cheney, Robert Dole, William Bennett, Gertrude Himmelfarb, and to alarm all these people who are holding on to the old history. They're alarmed because there have been changes. The story of Columbus has changed now, not in the majority of schools around the country, but in thousands. This is alarming. What? Young kids are going to begin to think of Columbus as not just an adventurer, but as a predator, a kidnapper, an enslaver, a torturer, a bad person and think maybe that conquest and expansion are not good things and that the search for gold is not something to be welcomed? Kids, be happy! Gold has been found! No, greed is no good. And maybe, let's take a look at the Indian societies that Columbus came upon. How did they live? How did they treat one another? Columbus stories that are told in the schools don't usually include stories of how the Indians were living on this continent.

Somebody sent me a letter reminding me of the work of William Brandon. He has done research for decades about Indians and their communities on this hemisphere before Columbus came and after. His research was in the French archives because he works in France. The reports came back from the French missionaries, the Jesuits, on how the Indians live. It's an amazing story and one that would make anybody question capitalism, greed, competition, disparate wealth, hierarchy. To start to hint about that, telling a new kind of Columbus story, a new kind of Native American story, is subversive of the way things are. Also, the Reconstruction period is being told in a new way. Eric Foner's book *Reconstruction* is marvelous. It's a very different treatment of Reconstruction and the books on Reconstruction that existed when I was going to graduate school in the 1950s, where incidentally they did not put on my reading list W.E.B. Du Bois' *Black Reconstruction*, which you might say is an earlier version of Eric Foner's book, at least a vital predecessor to it. So a lot of history teaching has changed. Not enough yet. We need to do a lot more. But just enough to frighten the keepers of the old.

DB   *We had an opportunity in late October to visit the new maximum security prison in Florence, Colorado. It was a rather extraordinary trip.*

Don't deny the fact that you drove the getaway car. Also the get-there car. I didn't have a car at my disposal, I was speaking in Boulder, and I had this old friend of mine in prison, in this maximum maximum, they call it "ad max" security federal prison in southern Colorado. It was good that we had a lot of fun on the way, because when we got there it was no fun. Grim. Frightening. Something out of some fantasy of totalitarianism. New. Technologically admirable. But holding these prisoners in such a tight grip. The man that I visited I've known for twenty-five years, and he is actually an extraordinary human being. There are some extraordinary human beings behind bars. Sure, there are mad killers and rapists. There are those. But there are also extraordinary people behind bars who shouldn't be there. He is one of them. I could not shake hands with him when I visited. We were separated by this glass wall. We had to talk through these phones. So there's no contact. It's called a no-contact visit. Yet, although there is no contact, there's all this between us, before he comes out to see me he is strip-searched by the guards. After he sees me he is strip-searched again by the guards. That's humiliating, taking all his clothes off, inspecting all the cavities of his body. Assuming that I, Houdini-like, have managed to slip things through the glass to him which will enable him to escape from there. It was a nightmare. What was amazing was that not everybody commits suicide in a situation like that, that somebody like my friend Jimmy Barrett, and I think it's because of his social consciousness, has the strength to withstand that. You talk about patience. Jimmy says, "Patience. Things will change. I will get out of here and things will be different."

DB   *I was wondering also about the larger societal message that a building like that sends. I was sitting in the lobby while you were inside talking to your friend. What do I see? An incredible building costing a lot of money, with tiled inlaid floors, high ceilings, huge glass windows, smiling photos of Clinton and Janet Reno and the prison warden and assistant warden. You see in the back "Florence ADX. First in Security." While I was sitting there waiting for you I had a very mischievous thought that I'd like to connect the words "in" and "security" together. What struck me was that about the same time that we were there the New York Times, a well-known source of radical information, reported that kids in the New York City public school system, the largest one in the country, were meeting in gymnasiums, cafeterias, and locker rooms because of overcrowding. That contrast was startling.*

I remember you pointing that out to me on our way back, which was not as fun-filled as our way there. Those ironies, those contrasts, are such as to make one think very, very hard about our society. To think that there are more young black people in prison than in college, or to think that the state of California spends more money on prisons than on schools. Or to think that it costs more to house one person in a prison than to send one person to Harvard, room and board, tuition and everything. Maybe we should have a prisoner exchange, Harvard students and prisoners, just for a little while, and see what happens.

Discussion Questions

1. What does Zinn mean when he says that schools are "totalitarian" places?

2. Do you agree that discussions of class conflict are absent from the school curriculum? Why are they absent?

3. Why does Zinn admire Langston Hughes' poems "Ballad of the Landlord" and "Raisin in the Sun. A Dream Deferred"?

4. How does social change happen, according to Zinn?

5. Why was Zinn's time as a professor at Spelman College "the most intense learning experience" of his life?

6. What does Zinn mean when he says "Being professional means not being committed"?

7. Why does Zinn believe that there is an audience for dissidence?

8. What point is Zinn trying to make about our society by discussing his trip to a prison?

9. Have you ever participated in an act of dissidence or protest? What was the outcome?

Writing Suggestion

What are some changes that you would like to see in our society? Why? What could you or others do to achieve those changes?

Chapter I

Childhood and Adolescent Myths

In this chapter, you will be asked to consider how children and teens get treated by adults. In a country that supposedly promotes family values, many adults rarely hesitate to give children, even preschool children, mind-altering drugs when they do not conform to impossible standards regarding how a child should behave. When those children become teenagers, they're often blamed for many of society's problems—from crime to unwanted pregnancies. In "Myth: Today's Youth Are America's Worst Generation Ever," a chapter from his book *Framing Youth*, Mike Males analyzes some of the common stereotypes about today's teenagers. In "Of 'Faggots' and 'Butch Dykes' and Other 'Unfit' Children," from her book *Of "Sluts" and "Bastards,"* Louise Armstrong recounts the story of a gay child and his struggles in the foster care system. The rest of the chapter considers the use of Ritalin and other drugs used to "tame" children diagnosed with attention deficit disorders. Peter R. Breggin and Ginger Ross Breggin point out how quickly our culture has taken to over-prescribing Ritalin to its children in "Born to be Disruptive," from *The War Against Children of Color*. In "The Kind of Adults Our Children Need Us to Be," from *Talking Back to Ritalin*, Peter Breggin offers parents advice on how altering their own behavior can ease many of the symptoms of their children's attention deficit disorders.

Myth:
Today's Youth Are America's Worst Generation Ever

Mike A. Males

Framing Youth: 10 Myths about the Next Generation

Flanked by three past presidents and bipartisan luminaries in a bombed-out north Philadelphia neighborhood one fine April Sunday, President Clinton keynoted the official abandonment of America's impoverished youth.

Volunteers, not "more government," will be called on mentor the impoverished young to become "good citizens," Clinton said at the 1997 President's Summit for America's Future. Moderate Republican Colin Powell and liberal Democrat Bill Bradley, White House prospects both, echoed that private initiatives must help kids, not more taxes and Big Government.

Some might say that private initiative combined with vanishing government, the Washington-aided business and industrial flight which devastated the economy of north Philadelphia and left inner cities charred wastelands of silent factories and broken neighborhoods, had done quite enough already. As sociologist William Julius Wilson pointed out in *When Work Disappears*, half the inner city job loss and subsequent growth of severely impoverished, primarily black populations could be traced to private abandonment:

> In the twenty-year period from 1967 to 1987, Philadelphia lost 64 percent of its manufacturing jobs; Chicago lost 60 percent; New York City, 58 percent; Detroit, 51 percent. In absolute numbers, these percentages represent the loss of 160,000 jobs in Philadelphia, 326,000 in Chicago, 520,000—over half a million—in New York, and 108,000 in Detroit.[1]

"You've got to go to work or be in school, you've got to pay your taxes and—oh, yes—you have to serve your community to make it a better place," Clinton lectured from his stadium microphone to youths living amid the rubble.

The Big Government deplored by Clinton and Republicans was perking along fine, still the vital solution to the problems of Americans who count. Powell did not call for an end to the $250 billion defense budget or offer to rely on private donors to equip the next march on Baghdad. Clinton did not announce that the $400 billion Social Security and Medicare programs would be slashed and volunteers recruited to care for seniors. Bradley did not suggest cutting the yearly $200 billion in economically purposeless "big government" subsidies and tax breaks to business.[2] All insinuated that the Aid to Families with Dependent Children program, costing about $20 billion per year and slated for shredding under bipartisan welfare reform, was a big cause of social malaise. Yet no one called for the nation's wealthiest 5 percent of homeowners to be "good citizens" by giving up their $30 billion in annual federal "welfare" subsidies doled out under home mortgage interest tax deductions.[3]

The assemblage did not visit the inner-city schools they recommended. Nor did they entreat lawmakers to force rich suburban districts to yield funds to their upgrading. Jonathan Kozol did both, citing the industry-abandoned city of Camden, New Jersey, a 10-minute drive across the Ben Franklin Bridge.

Camden is America's post-industrial national monument. Its devastation has to be seen to understand the particular cruelty that is post-Reagan America. Looming, vacant factories backdrop mile after mile of once-prosperous working-class blocks now chock-full of falling-down row houses. If Camden were a ghost town, abandoned, it would be tolerable. But the city of no jobs, no newspaper, no grocery store, no lodging save a burned-out hulk, is inhabited by 100,000 people—and growing. Average age by census count is 23, though the visitor could be excused for thinking from visual assessment it couldn't be more than 12.

Camden teachers told Kozol they did "not have books for half the students in their classes." Tiles fell from splotched ceilings. The high school had no lunchroom. The lab had no equipment. The typing room had no computers. In the nation's third richest state, spending on Camden students, 98 percent black and Latino, averaged half that of nearby suburban schools.[4]

Before departing the Volunteer Summit, Clinton and other dignitaries made it clear who they blamed for the lamentable social conditions of America's young:

> The president, First Lady Hillary Rodham Clinton, Vice President Al Gore and his wife Tipper, helped paint over black, green and red graffiti—including the names of local gangs—with tan paint.[5]

None of Clinton's 1997 Summiteers answered the question posed by Paul Goodman 40 years ago in *Growing Up Absurd* to a gubernatorial call for volunteers and programs to lure New York City's youth of 1955 away from gangs: "Does the governor seriously think he can offer a good community that warrants equal loyalty?"[6]

A Democratic president, Republican chieftains, a full spectrum of liberals, an academic and business establishment, allied in self-aggrandizement. "The forces of organized greed," Franklin Roosevelt lambasted their like back in an era when presidents exhorted the young to fight back.[7]

Not today. Imperious moral tone blared over the burned-out shell of inner Philadelphia and its shattered neighborhoods, boarded storefronts, vacant factories, vanished jobs, crumbling schools and segregation enforced more stringently by 1990s mercantilism than 1950s Bull-Connor cattle prods. Even Kozol, relentlessly optimistic since Jim Crow days that America's goodness would finally overcome its "savage inequalities," sounds weary: "I have never lived through a time as cold as this in the United States," he concluded in *Amazing Grace*. "I don't know what can change this."[8] What, then, is there to be hopeful about as America approaches the new millennium?

Plenty, it turns out. But not due to the attitudes or policies of those at the upper ends of America's age and power scales.

The Superpredators Are...White Adults?

When America's elders screw up big time, expect them to trash the younger generation with a vengeance. Such happened during the Depression, after a decade of economic and personal indulgence combined with puritanical Prohibition rhetoric wrecked American economy and society. Such is happening in the 1990s, largely for the same reasons. Today, national leaders skillfully meld racism and fear of the young into a potent political crusade that menaces the fabric of American society in new and complex ways.

Americans are becoming aware that we are evolving toward a nation without a racial majority in the next half-century. No other industrial culture has faced this challenge. The initial phase involves abject lying about the young, the leading edge of the diverse tomorrow. But that is not the whole story. The rapidly deteriorating behavior of American grownups (particularly aging Baby Boomers) in both personal and social realms has led to a crisis of adulthood in which youth is the target of displaced anxiety and fury.

"For the past decade," historians Neil Howe and Bill Strauss wrote in *13th Gen: Abort, Retry, Ignore, Fail?*,

> 13ers ["Generation Xers"] have been bombarded with study after story after column about how bad they supposedly are. Americans in their teens and twenties, we are told, are consumed with violence, selfishness, greed, bad work habits, and civic apathy. Turn on the TV, and it's hard to see a bad-news-for-America story—from crime to welfare to consumerism—in which young bodies and faces don't show up prominently in the footage.[9]

Howe and Strauss's excellent 1993 cultural history provides pages of vitriol by elder America on the young people *it raised*—including many statements which are not just pejorative excess, but bizarrely shallow. Do Allan Bloom and his followers seriously regard the snobby name-calling against the younger generation in *The Closing of the American Mind* an example of seasoned intellect? Can it be that columnist Ellen Goodman and fellow liberals, whose 40–50-something generation set rocketing records for lavish personal consumption, really puzzle over where their kids get consumerist values? Do the mass of professors and teachers blasting the stupidity of today's students realize Baby Boom kids sported lower test scores? Did former New York Mayor David Dinkins and the legions of grownups who wonder "who taught our children to hate so thoroughly and mercilessly" ever visit a hospital emergency room to appraise the numbers of battered kids and drug-addicted parents of the over-30 generation?

No, indeed. From the most august of authorities and media, we routinely hear clichéd lies such as the following: yesterday's kids ran in halls and shoplifted; today's kids gun and slaughter. The press headlines recent school shootings in Pearl, West Paducah, Jonesboro, Edinboro, Springfield, which killed a total of 11 youths over an eight-month period. None of the anguished commentary on these school tragedies mentioned that is the average number of children murdered by their parents in *two days* of domestic violence in the United States. In a society in which Simi Valley, Daly City, Riverside (California), Weston (West Virginia), Kerrville (Texas)—a few examples of many communities where multiple killings of children (totalling 16 dead in these cases) by parents recently occurred—were as well-known to the public and as deplored by officials as Jonesboro or Springfield, what we call "youth violence" would be better understood. We are further from that understanding in 1998 than ever.

True, the average teenager of the mid-1990s is 0.00025 times more likely to commit murder than the average teen of the 1950s. A small proportion of young people display worse rates of violence, primarily murder and robbery. Most of these are directly traceable to rapidly deteriorating urban conditions. Homicide has risen among a fraction of impoverished youth living in inner-city moonscapes, but not middle- or upper-class kids. Today, 1,999 of 2,000 youths will not commit murder at any time during their adolescence. Normally, a society would characterize its young people by the vast majority who are not murderous.

If we did, there would be generous things to say. As a group, today's American youth are less criminal than those of the 1970s or 1980s. The decline in serious youth crime has occurred while major crime among their parents, the 30–40-agers, has risen sharply. By a wide variety of measures, kids today act more maturely than kids of the past and more responsibly than adults today.

In the mid-1990s, 12–19 year-olds comprise:

- 14 percent of the population ages 12 and older (according to the Bureau of the Census).

They account for:

- 18 percent of the nation's violent crime, and
- 15 percent of murders (estimates from Department of Justice crime clearance and conviction rates);

- 9 percent of violent deaths,
- 14 percent of gun deaths,
- 15 percent of murder victims,
- 7 percent of suicides, and
- 2 percent of drug deaths (according to the National Center for Health Statistics);

- 14 percent of highway deaths and
- 9 percent of drunken driving deaths (according to the National Highway Traffic Safety Administration); and

- 12 percent of births (only 4 percent when both the mother and father are under age 20), and

- 15 percent of HIV infections (practically none if both partners are under age 20) (according to the NCHS and Centers for Disease Control).

In short, teenagers do not account for a high percentage of America's social problems. Teens' share of problem-causing does not even exceed their share of the 12-and-older population in most cases. Conversely, what experts and the media aren't saying about the deteriorating behaviors of adults is even more incredible. If that sounds exactly the opposite of what the press and authorities proclaim, well, [check out the rest of *Framing Youth*].

Table 1 shows why officials might be reluctant to discuss what groups are displaying the largest, most astonishing crime increases. (California crime figures are cited because, unlike national figures, they are the nation's most completely and consistently tabulated over the last two decades and because they separate Euro-whites from Latinos. Where they are comparable, California trends appear to be a couple of years ahead of, but otherwise similar to, national crime trends). The truth, abundantly obvious from official crime reports over the last one to two decades, is that it is not minority teenagers, but adults over the age of 30—*white* adults, most specifi-

---

Table 1

Who's showing California's biggest crime increase?
White adults over age 30.

Felony crime increase, 1980–97:

Rate, violent crime	age 10–19	20–29	30+
White	+6%	+47%	+148%
Latino	-12	+20	+75
Black	-16	-5	+56
Asian	+58	+61	+137
Total	-2	+33	+111

Rate, all felonies	age 10–19	20–29	30+
White	-42%	+23%	+138%
Latino	-18	+12	+62
Black	-27	-19	+63
Asian	+51	+84	+118
Total	-27	+13	+102

Rate is per 100,000 population ages 10–19, 20–29, and 30–69, by race.
Source: California Department of Justice, Crime & Deliquency in California, 1980, 1997 update.

Table 2

**California's secret: serious crime plummeting among
nonwhite youths, exploding among older white grownups**

Change in California felony arrest rates:

	White adults over age 30	Nonwhite youths
1997 vs 1976	+160%	-32%
1997 vs 1980	+138	-32
1997 vs 1985	+74	+5
1997 vs 1990	+21	-28

Rate is per 100,000 Euro-whites ages 30–69 and per 100,000 black, Asian and Latino youths ages 10–17. Felony arrests include all violent, property, drug and other felonies. The year 1976 is the first for which consistent statistics by age and race are available and which is not confounded by 1975's drug law reforms changing marijuana possession to a misdemeanor.
Source: see Table 1.

cally—who consistently display the largest increases in serious (felony) violent, property, and drug-related crime rates.

Note that it isn't even close. Youths display decreases in felonies, 20-agers small increases, and over-30-agers large increases—with whites over 30 showing by far the largest rise. The pattern of these trends is consistent for felony violent crime (shown above), property crime, and drug offenses regardless of what years are constrasted (ie, comparing 1997 with 1975 or with 1985, etc.). Nor are we talking small numbers. There were 72,000 more annual felony arrests among California whites over age 30 in 1997 than in 1980, versus 19,000 FEWER among teenagers.

Yet not a single major criminologist seems to have noticed. Examining California's extremes—the poorest population everyone *thinks* is causing rising crime (nonwhite and Latino youths) versus the richest population no one thinks of as crime-prone (white adults over age 30)—reveals trends both consistent and suprising (Table 2).

The upshot is too startling to immediately comprehend: In the late 1970s, whites over age 30 comprised 40 percent of California's population and 7 percent of its felony arrests; in the late 1990s, 37 percent of the population but one-fifth of felony arrests. In what must be a criminological first, aging whites accounted for a larger share of California's felony crime increase (40 percent) than they contributed to its population increase (30 percent). In two decades, the proneness of over-30 whites to serious criminality *tripled* compared to that of younger age groups and nonwhites!

What does this mean? About six impossible things before breakfast, the first of which is: for 20 years, *crime trends have been dramatically and diametrically the opposite of what California officials and the media have been saying.* Except for a rise from 1985 to 1990, serious crime trends among nonwhite teenagers have been on the decline for 20 years—but major crimes among white adults have been surging steadily upward. Nonwhite adults show lesser increases in felony rates than white adults (up 38 percent from 1976 to 1997), and white youths show the largest decreases of all (down 53 percent over the last 20 years).

Similar trends are going on nationwide. The FBI lists eight serious felonies (murder, rape, robbery, aggravated assault, burglary, larceny/theft, motor vehicle theft, and arson) as "index crimes." These have been tabulated reasonably consistently for the last three decades. The FBI's annual *Uniform Crime Reports* provides two measures of these serious crimes: offenses known to police, and arrests. The first measure tells how much crime is reported. The second tells how many persons were arrested by age for each offense. Examining the two measures together allows us to factor out whether crime is really increasing or police are just making more arrests to solve ("clear") reported crimes [see Chapter 1 of *Framing Youth* for method].

Using these two measures of crime, it is evident that the rate of serious offenses committed by youths—that is, index crimes divided by the youth population ages 13–17—has *declined* by 5 to 10 percent over the last two decades. However, the index crime rate of their parents, age 30–49, has *risen* by 30 percent. It is hard to believe such dramatic trends could have gone unnoticed among experts whose job it is to monitor crime statistics—and who have had 20 years to get used to the new and astonishing developments.

Why the silence, then? The first reason may simply be genuine disbelief. That America's most affluent, aging population should show the largest rise in serious offenses fits no known theory of crime. So much of modern criminology, as it has for decades, consists of defining and studying crime as a young-male problem[10] that authorities may be adrift when confronted with graying misdeed.

I presented the above figures (in the form of a "news story" the media ought to be running, headlined, "Rising crime by white grownups, not minority teens, drives California's serious crime wave") to the May 1998 Children Now conference in Los Angeles. The theme of the conference was negative media images of youth of color, documented by a new Children Now survey showing kids of all races felt black, Latino, and Asian kids were depicted as criminals "doing bad things."[11] Engaged in earnest soul-searching over media unfairness to minority youths were top reporters from the *Washington Post, Dateline NBC,* CNN, MTV, Associated Press, *Time, Fox News, Los Angeles Times,* ABC News, CBS News, and *TV Guide.*

Well, I suggested in my 15 seconds of panel time, the media might try this novel strategy: tell the truth. The facts provide ample basis for refashioning a stunningly positive image of black and brown kids showing healthy crime declines even as privileged white elders are running amok. Oddly, none of the Big Media representatives at the conference seemed the slightest bit interested in *examining real crime reports and telling the truth about kids.* Perhaps they thought I was making a bizarre joke or pulling a lies-and-damned-lies crime statistics shenanigan such as equating parking tickets with drive-bys. What I suspect is that Big Media and other luminaries have so much invested in hyping youths as the American terror that their idea of image-busting was a few more profiles on Hmong teenage violinists or Rastafarian female center fielders.

Second, of course, any statistic may not show what it appears to show. Perhaps it is not a real violence increase, but growing attention to domestic violence, including new laws mandating arrests of offenders, that produced the skyrocketing rate of arrests of over-30 adults for violent crime. Even if true, this development would be unsettling. It would show that homes are much more violent than previously thought. It would show that adults do not "age out" of violence-prone younger years so much as they take their fury indoors. Since domestic violence represents the chief violent crime (including murder) threat to children under age 13 and to women of all ages, the surge in arrests should indicate that household, not street, violence is our biggest menace. Whatever the explanation, authorities' refusal even to talk about the sharp increase in adult violence arrests remains deeply puzzling.

Further, the concomitant leap in property and drug felonies among over-30 adults, particularly whites, indicates that something more is afoot than simply better enforcement. This age group is becoming more criminal in lots of ways. There is no way to avoid the fact that it is adult behavior, particularly among the 30- and 40-age Baby Boomers, that has deteriorated sharply, endangering children and disrupting families and communities. This deterioration has occurred without economic decline to explain it.

However, beyond the growth in aging adults' rising, record levels of drug abuse and criminality lies the politics of the crime debate. The only issue of interest is this: who would benefit from talking about rising adult crime, particularly white-adult crime? No prominent entity would. The art of successful politicking of wedge issues requires blaming vexing national problems on unpopular groups *outside* of the constituencies candidates wish to flatter. By definition, no major political interest would be crazy enough to blame the cohort most known for Big Voting—over-30 adults, whites, "soccer moms"—for the worsening state of what this same cohort calls the Big Issue—crime.

White Hot Fear

Still and all, why is there an attack on young people today, and why is it so hard to redirect? "Today's young people are scapegoated by an adult generation that is abandoning them," declares Lori Nelson, youth and education director for Los Angeles's National Conference on Communities and Justice. "Race is a big reason. The kids people are scared of are kids of color."[12]

Fear of racial transition appears a powerful factor. The Census Bureau reports that 80 percent of America's adults over age 40 are whites of European origin (Euro-white). Thirty-five percent of children and youths under age 18 are nonwhite or of Hispanic (Latino) origin, a proportion that has doubled since 1970.[13] In most of America's big cities, white elders govern nonwhite kids. In California, two-thirds of the elders are Euro-white; three-fifths of the youths are nonwhite or Latino. As California and the cities are, so America is becoming.

In growing multi-racial and -ethnic areas, outspoken fear of young people mixes with unspoken fear of racial transition. "Whites are scared," reports Stanford professor Dale Maharidge of his interviews and study for his moderate book on "California's eruptions," *The Coming White Minority*. "The depth of white fear is underestimated and misunderstood by progressive thinkers and the media." Maharidge points to research showing that when the minority share of the population reaches one-third, most whites express negative opinions and desires to escape.[14] That proportion has been exceeded among American youth, harbingers of the multi-racial future. Figuratively as well as actually, then, aging whites and more prosperous minorities who identify with them are "moving out" of children's "neighborhoods."

Thus, one aspect of aging America's hostility toward its young derives from reflexive racial and ethnic discomfort: the kids don't look like the parents. It is no accident that political authorities, scholars, and the media now ascribe to adolescents the same prejudices once hurled at nonwhites—violent, hypersexed, irrational, volatile, dangerous.

Second, racial fear is building at a time when racism is impolitic to openly express. The increase in (white) adult crime is most inconvenient for politically-adept interests courting that dominant constituency, and so it has been swept aside in an obsessive focus on violent crime by inner-city youth. But trumpeting that violent crime increased only among minority, not Euro-white, teens would insult major Democratic voting blocs. Thus, New Democrats led by President Clinton have developed racialist code words such as "youth violence" and "teen pregnancy," which are modernized versions of the 1960s "law'n'order" and pre-'60s "Negro question" ("nigger-baiting," or "niggering," in plain stump talk) employed by traditional southern politicians.[15] The function of modern crypto-racism is more refined than that of its cruder past: to simultaneously flatter majority constituencies, avoid antagonizing key minority groups, and assuage aging America's fears of the rising population of nonwhite youth. Because racial coding cannot be admitted today, it is hidden behind a false image of an entire generation out of control, from meanstreet to megamall.

For the crassest of political reasons, then, an utterly unreal symbol of American crime has emerged: the violent teenager, white, black, brown, threatening inner-city and affluent suburb alike. The most intensive headline and feature stories target the wealthy killer kid who, by definition, hails from an adoring family and went bad strictly from surrender to his personal darkside. The twisted affirmative-action remedy for media demonizing of dark-skinned kids was not accurate reporting of the adult-created reality of violence and abandonment inflicted on the young, but to demonize more white kids.

The Clinton regime is not unique among American presidencies in its propensity to lie, but it is singular in its willingness to warp statistics and studies wholesale to lend a liberal-sounding, scientific veneer to its lying. For moderates and liberals, "racism" is officially deplored with a formulaic clubbiness codified in the President's Initiative on Race, in which older African Americans recount the brutality of Sheriff Clark apartheid and shake their heads as rainbow coalitions of '90s students lament high school lunchroom segregation. In such a climate, carefully scrutinizing why black and Latino youth homicide rose in the 1980s would raise socioeconomic issues of the sort candidate handlers rate as fearful and loathesome on the '90s campaign trail. And so, by popular default, "moral values" became the winner.

Third, while the race-transition argument has been cited by a growing number of progressives to explain California's and America's astonishing hostility toward the young (following Maharidge, former *Sacramento Bee* editor Peter Schrag buttresses it in his 1998 work, *Paradise Lost*[16]), it explains only a part of the older generation's fear. Like Cub Scouts around a nighttime forest campfire terrifying themselves with embellished slasher tales, latter-day grownup America delights in horror stories about suburban stone-killer kids. *Within* white, black, and Latino populations, there is growing anger and disowning of youth by elder. Wealth differences are paramount. In every group, kids are poorer than older adults, and the affluence gap between young and old is mushrooming. Growing numbers of well-off minority middle-agers join their white golfing buddies in fear of youths, from gang shootouts downtown headlined on News at 11 to the suburban devil-worshipping killers festooning *People*.

Crumbling Adulthood

Politicians and interest groups have caught hold of public anxieties and bent them to profit. The attack by the Clinton administration, the Republican Congress, and major media and institutions against America's young people marks the most anti-youth period in American history. Fear of the young is enthusiastically embraced by modern economic and political interests busy dismantling the public sector, promoting unprecedented concentration of wealth, and building an enclave/prison society to manage the inevitable conflict such inequality creates. Practically nothing that today's top officials and the media declare about teenagers is true. The magnitude of the falsehood is in direct proportion to how stridently and often it is repeated.

Are teenagers "ruining America"? The fairest summary of "kids of the 1990s" I could muster would be the following:

- Despite being worse off economically on average, the *average* youth today is better behaved than the *average* youth of 25 years ago and the *average* adult of today.

- Because of being *much* worse off economically, the *most troubled 1 percent* of youth today are *more* troubled than the *most troubled 1 percent* of youths 25 years ago—but not as bad off as today's most troubled adults. It takes a lot of killer kids to equal one Timothy McVeigh, thousands of 'hoodsful of teenage robbers to do the damage of a single S&L looter.

Before making my case for the above convolution, let me say that "today's most troubled adults" should mean those in positions of government, institutional, and corporate leadership whose selfish, shortsighted policies have exploited younger and poorer people to the point that this powerful country's future is in severe jeopardy. More skilled polemicists than I have covered that point well. My purpose is to show that even using conventional measures of "troubled"—violent crime, criminal arrest, drug abuse, alcohol abuse, suicide, AIDS, other risky behavior—what popular authorities and news media say about kids today just ain't so. Not even nearly so.

The unadmitted reality of youth and adult behavior is bad for the immediate needs of politicians and their institutional support networks, but it is a hopeful one for the future of America's larger, noble experiment. Despite being poorer, despite suffering the most violent, addicted, and disarrayed parent generation in knowable history, today's children and teenagers are holding up remarkably well. Notwithstanding the drumbeat of fear organized by varied enterprises and spread in the media, adolescents display declining rates of crime, drug abuse, alcohol abuse, and suicidal behaviors. The elders should be doing so well.

It is an adult generation at loose ends that spreads false fear and slander against the young. The attack on youth has grown ever more shrill as interests compete for support in the cold, penurious '90s of tightened pursestrings and slashed sympathies. Liberal moralism flowed in part from the fund-raising and political difficulties liberal groups weathered in the hostile 1980s and '90s. Well-intentioned youth services justified overstatement on the grounds that modern funders would not turn loose the bucks unless grantees could present evidence of a serious teenage menace. To survive in a hardening climate, sex education, drug and alcohol abuse prevention, gun control, media reform, mental health, and other progressive services wildly hyped youth misbehaviors. Only we, programmers intoned, stand between your wealthy fundee's pleasant suburb-ville and the legions of gnashing superpredators downtown.

More led to more, and today, there appears no limit to the extremity of untruths that the most august of authorities will proclaim in pursuit of attention, funding, and poll points. In the most abysmal example, leading crime experts fan anti-youth phobia with predictions of a "coming crime storm" by rising hordes of "adolescent superpredators" in the new millennium. The regression by top criminologists to long-debunked "demographic" theories (that crime is caused by the composition of the population) represents academic laziness at its worst. And not incidentally, charging that certain race/ethnic/age groups are just naturally crime-prone serves to insulate crime policies from criticism. Today, the demographic scapegoat is the Adolescent. Standard crime and census reports clearly show the presence of more teenagers in the population has nothing to do with violent, property, drug, or any other kind of crime. It is aging Baby Boomers, not adolescents or young adults, who drive today's crime numbers.

In 1980, the FBI reported 450,000 Americans ages 30–49 arrested for serious violent, property, or drug crimes. In 1996, 1.5 million. Adults age 30–49 accounted for nearly three-fourths of the nation's crime rise. Both violent and property felony rates have risen among the parent-age group, indicating a rapid increase in criminality among these adults even as crime among other groups has declined.

What is causing an increased crime rate—made up of dumb stuff, like aggravated assault, burglary, and car theft—in a privileged, aging population? It turns out that the increase in major crimes committed by adults closely tracks skyrocketing drug abuse among aging Baby Boomers. Among 30- and 40-agers, the number of hospital emergency cases involving drug overdose rose from 60,000 in 1980 to over 200,000 in 1995. Heroin and cocaine cases soared from 10,000 to 100,000. Other measures of drug abuse also mushroomed in this age group.

Unlike the increase in homicide and robbery among the poorest fraction of the teenage population from a mid-'80s trough to an early-'90s peak, the increase in 30-40-ager crime and drug woes is larger, more broadly-based, and more persistent. It has occurred among all races over the last 25 years. Paradoxically, it has accompanied *rising* middle-aged wealth. While the cyclical teenage homicide and robbery increases appear socioeconomic in origin, the sustained Baby Boom crime boom appears to result from rising drug abuse. This, in turn, creates more family instability and, in further turn, leads to negative views of kids among adults unwilling to face their own misbehaviors.

It does not take Sherlock Holmes to deduce that parents involved in drugs and crime are more likely to have trouble parenting. Normal family functions become more difficult. Conflicts routinely settled in healthy households produce spousal warfare and parent-child alienation. Divorce and separation explode; modern marriages last only seven years, on average. Kids seem more trouble to raise.

As parenting competence, and American adulthood itself, declined, parents' movements of the 1980s and '90s arose to demand that government and private interests step in to manage their kids. "Often," wrote a veteran California Appeals Court judge of the avalanche of youths shoveled into institutional management, the child "was a minor nuisance some inadequate parent was trying to fob off on the court...He usually just did not get along with his parents and, when one met the parents, this was often completely understandable."[17] The director of Montana's state juvenile prison had a remedy: "In most cases, we should leave the kid home and send the parents to Pine Hills."[18]

Woes of low-income parents and families, increasingly isolated in abandoned inner cities and depopulating rural areas, continued to be ignored. But more affluent, politically-connected Baby Boom parents got attention. Government and private enterprise were happy to intervene when kid and progenitor did not get along.

Beginning in the mid-1970s, kid-fixing services erupted to meet the market. They were of two kinds. Prison gates opened wide in the 1980s to receive tens of thousands more poorer teens, three-fourths of them nonwhite. Confinement of minority youths in prisons increased by 80 percent in the last decade. Imprisonment of Euro-white youth did not rise.[19]

At the same time, mental health and other treatment centers raked in huge profits therapizing hundreds of thousands more health-insured children of the affluent, nearly all white.[20] The *annual* growth rate in private youth correctional facilities "has been a staggering 45 percent over the last decade," *Youth Today* reported in May 1998. Youth treatment is now a $25 billion per year business with "a record of steady profit growth:"

> The wave of tough anti-drug laws and the public's lock-'em-up attitude for juvenile offenders is now sweeping along for-profits that focus on young people. Equitable Securities Research, in what it terms a "very conservative" forecast, looks for a six percent annual growth rate for juvenile residential programs and an eight percent rate for non-residential programs. That would mean 93,000 youths locked up by 2004, up from about 52,000 in 1995. By 2004, more than 107,000 teens are likely to be in for-profit non-residential programs, compared with 51,000 in 1995.[21]

Yet, as is documented in later chapters [of *Framing Youth*], teenage drug abuse, suicide, crime, and other maladies have generally been declining over the last 25 years. Serious problems are concentrated in a shrinking, not growing, proportion of the youth population. No matter. With a 20-year construction and maintenance investment of $1.5 million per bed, private treatment facilities will have enormous interest in planting a steady drumbeat of bad news in the pliant media about "rising" teenage woes to ensure a steady flow of clientele. Just as the psychiatric industry hawked a "teenage suicide epidemic" in the 1980s to fill empty beds in its overbuilt private hospitals [see Chapter 7 of *Framing Youth*], today's teen-fixing entrepreneurs can be counted on to generate maximum hysteria.

Thus, there are political and profit-driven reasons for drug and alcohol abuse, law enforcement, political, and media authorities to trumpet a succession of unprecedented "teenage" behavior crises. All of these combine with psychological solace. Authorities who morally condemned the sins of poorer parents for their bad kids benignly excused, and serviced, the failings of more affluent parents. It was not parents', or adults', values and behaviors, but demons lurking in "popular culture" and "drugs" corrupting a teenage generation just naturally eager to embrace any and every evil. If every kid was bad, parents by definition were not to blame. "Blaming drugs for kids' troubles also worked within the family just as demonizing individuals' drug use worked in wider society," wrote drug-war chronicler Dan Baum: "it obviated concern for 'root causes' and let parents take their own behavior off the hook."[22] Not just parents, but an entire parent generation, had a lot of behaviors to take off the hook.

The rising cascade of bad news about teenagers tracked growing disarray of Baby Boomers, a generation also becoming the nation's wealthiest. A chunk of this wealth accumulated from the lavish public subsidies of Baby Boomers combined with their refusal to support their children. An aging, self-preoccupied America was in no mood to share its time or lucre with the young—not personally following divorce and family breakup, not privately through providing job opportunity, not publicly through taxes. Rationales for abandonment abounded: today's kids are so rotten that they don't deserve our hard-earned money, so dissolute that resources invested in them would be wasted anyway. Statistics of disownment abound and are cited throughout [*Framing Youth*], evidencing how little today's adults value kids compared to the way our parents valued us. A typical one, lamented by Kozol: in 1970, New York City employed 400 school physicians; today, fewer than two dozen.[23]

What "kids these days" need, adult respondents to a 1997 Public Agenda poll declared, is stern values sermons and tough discipline. Faithful to the public ire they helped inflame, experts and the media combed the country for sensational teenage murder, drunken driving crash, heroin overdose, welfare mother, devil cult, just plain badness. Most in media demand are evil young wastoids, preferably white and suburban, from "good families" to prove that all kids everywhere fit the "satanic" label applied by *Toughlove*'s rotten-parent emeriti Phyllis and David York. More common, worse adult incidents and trends are ignored or downplayed. Today's result is a weird climate in which authorities, liberal and conservative, refuse to discuss the most obvious implications of their most obvious studies and clearest statistics.

Major institutions from the conservative American Medical Association to the liberal Carnegie Corporation jumped in front of the public mood. They assembled blue-ribbon panels to issue a stream of reports (actually, recyclings of the same report) depicting a peace-loving, healthy adult society besieged by barbaric brats.

Drastic measures were proposed, many enacted. Nighttime and daytime curfews so strict that (as endorsed by President Clinton) teenagers could legally be in public only a couple of hours on most days. Mass drug-testing, forced strip-searches of students, and draconian punishments for runaways and curfew violators evidence grownups' anti-youth frenzy. California's 1998 governor's race kicked off with the top Democrat candidate demanding random drug-testing of students, his chief challenger backing capital punishment for 14-year-olds, and the leading Democrat for lieutenant governor on record favoring execution of 13-year-olds. (What's left for Republicans—random executions of fifth graders?)

Left Meets Right

The response by liberals to the attacks of Clinton and the Right has ranged from ineffective to disastrous. When conservatives and New Democrats attack youth, liberals respond not with fundamental challenges to repressive assumptions, but with traditional arguments designed to advance their own agendas. The emergence of the Cultural Left, which leftist theorist Richard Rorty points out has "collaborated with the Right in making cultural issues central to public debate," amiably pillow-fights with Bill Bennett's Virtuecrats over TV violence, consumerism, and pop culture sins. "It is as if," Rorty added in *Achieving Our Country*,

> sometime around 1980, the children of the people who made it through the Great Depression and into the suburbs had decided to pull up the drawbridge behind them. They decided that although social mobility had been appropriate for their parents, it was not to be allowed for the next generation. These suburbanites seem to see nothing wrong with belonging to a hereditary caste and have initiated what Robert Reich (in his book *The Work of Nations*) calls "the secession of the successful."[24]

The Cultural Left's war against sin has abetted this secession, a double calamity for the young. On the one hand, the Cultural Left rarely talks about tangible realities such as child abuse, rape of young girls, parents abusing drugs, parents damaging their kids' health with passive smoke, or the menaces to kids caused by grownups' rising crime and addiction. In fact, the Cultural Left talks less and less about youth poverty and socioeconomic attrition. Instead, the secondary symptoms of powerlessness and poverty, such as drinking or gun possession, have been elevated into *primary causes* of malaise. Like the Right, the Cultural Left claims that personal morality is the problem, teenagers' natural depravity the base chemistry, evil pop culture the catalyst. Endless, moral tongue-clucking that a bare butt on *NYPD Blue*, a candy ad, corporate "messages," or an explicit website deprave kids to violate sacred Baby-Boomer values emanates from both ends of the political spectrum.

The conservative fear lobby paints a dire statistical picture of hordes of black and Latino "adolescent superpredators" born of ghetto teenage moms. Liberals smartly respond with anecdotes to prove that white, suburban kids are just as criminal. Conservatives hype a "drug crisis" among teenagers. Liberals rejoin that teenage alcohol disaster is worse. The Right blames teenage miscreancy on immoral kids seduced by internet porn, Tupac Shakur, and Marilyn Manson. The Liberal/Left blames stupid kids enthralled by Joe Camel, Channel One, and media-fed consumerism. The Right warns of a teen AIDS plague created by *Our Bodies, Ourselves*, the Left about teen alcoholics spawned by a Budweiser bullfrog. Conservatives hawk censorship, purity lectures, and prison. Liberals push censorship, purity lectures, and behavior education [see Chapter 8 of *Framing Youth*].

The Leftist stance fit into Rightist campaigns that emphasized "personal morality" (for certain people) over social equality. When race and poverty were taken off the table, "values" and "responsibility" became the issues. The result was that the two most important influences on teenage behavior—family and socioeconomics—were buried in an avalanche of punitive moralizing. As the more sophisticatedly exploitative Clinton era unfolded, any semblance of perspective winged into the sunset.

Interests seeking profit, funding, and popularity pumped ever-scarier prevarications about terrible teens. The self-reporting survey, the weakest, most easily manipulated of social science tools, was deified, replacing more reliable statistical measures. Pump those numbers up! In truth, teenage suicide rates are low, so rephrase the question to whether they ever *thought* of killing themselves. In fact, teenage heroin and cocaine use is practically nil, so ask if they *know* anyone who *ever* used a hard drug. In fact, the teenage drunk driving toll is minuscule compared to adults', so recalculate it as a function of some absurd index such as *miles driven drunk*. Hell, just make something up: All teenagers lead secret lives of debauchery! 135,000 bring guns to school every day! All kids snort smack! Two-thirds of fifth graders approve of rape! Sixty percent of high schoolers are suicidal! Your kids have sex in your bed! Your child will kill you!

The eruption of rash statements such as the above, using numbers to give scientific veneer, splashed in the press and political arenas to create pressure for funding. Mark Twain had a handle on such proprietary statistics in his 1901 anti-colonialism essay, "To the Person Sitting in Darkness:"

> He presented the facts—some of the facts—and showed these confiding people what the facts meant. He did it statistically, which is a good way. He used the formula: twice 2 are 14, and 2 from 9 leaves 35. Figures are effective; figures will convince the elect.

Some of the weirder figures on teenagers tossed out by the most luminous of expert in the most august of forum are just that chimerical. To believe proprietary statistics purveyors is to wonder why every teenager in America isn't dead twice over.

In a Gresham's Law by which bad information drives out good, ridiculous proprietary numerology has all but eliminated the most carefully gathered and explicitly defined statistics (the latter of whose limitations and errors are much better understood). Today, it is all but impossible to induce a leading authority to examine teenage *and adult* death, birth, or crime statistics in the *complete context* of what they show and *don't* show. It is much more profitable to bellow about the phony Top Ten School Problems of Today (drug abuse, alcohol abuse, pregnancy, suicide, rape, robbery, assault, etc.) versus the Top Ten School Problems of 1940 (talking, gum-chewing, making noise, running in halls, getting out of line, wearing improper clothing, not putting paper in wastebaskets). I defy anyone to produce the "study" behind these statements, which are treated as gospel from "Dear Abby" to *Congressional Record*. There is no study. It was made up.[25] Who cares?

In the cold '90s in which hysteria, not humanitarianism, generates bucks and acclaim, humane groups joined the shouting. Funds flowed—for a while. But now the bill for two decades of unfounded shrieking about adolescents has come due. Washington and the public are fed up with young people and their intractable evil. An angry electorate and political system has thrown up its hands and declared the next generation hopeless, not worthy of investment in anything except sermons and cagings. The Clinton/Republican litany of convenience holds that liberal solutions were tried, so earnestly, and just didn't work.

As of this writing, in August 1998, the low point is low indeed. The scholar-and-statistics brandishing Clinton presidency legitimized official, scholarly, and media falsification of adolescent issues. Making things up. Maintaining silence on the growing mass of inconvenient information that did not advance immediate political or monetary profit. Public emotings about "caring for kids" after polls, focus groups, and professional handler strategies pinpointed how craftily to exploit them. It is no accident that a New Democrat, far more effectively than Reagan or Bush, finally destroyed Roosevelt's future-directed policies of power disbursement and replaced them with regressive measures of concentrated wealth and police control. "When it comes to corporate welfare or policing powers, Clinton, like Reagan, adores big government and only derides its role in helping the poor," Alexander Cockburn understates.[26] Clinton's capitulation to popular Republicanism is so complete that even the most courageous thrust of his presidency—universal health care—has disintegrated to endorsement of the Patient Access to Responsible Care (or "Bill of Rights") Act of 1998. This Republican-whooped "I've-got-mine" travesty, even conservative professor James Pinkerton laments, will "make health care more of a perk" by rewarding the already insured with better coverage while pricing the poor and young who can't afford insurance "out of the market."[27]

When crime, public health, education, and other standard sources are examined, popular statements about teenagers not only evaporate, they turn out to be outrageously false. Dismayingly, it doesn't make any difference. The shame of academia, institutions, and the media is that few of prominent status challenge official lies about young people. The institutions charged with questioning authority in a democracy could weakly justify their past acquiescences by lack of good information. Today's luminaries, however, refuse to examine the wealth of information available.

Many of today's adults seem to *want* young people to feel hopeless and self-hating. A May 1998 poll by *USA Today*'s tabloid *USA Weekend* of a quarter-million teenagers in grades 6–12 reaffirms how trapped the media are in their own concocted image of the miserable '90s wastrel.[28] The poll's questions and youths' responses are as follows:

- "In general, how do you feel about yourself?" GOOD, 93 percent; BAD, 7 percent (VERY BAD, 1 percent).

- "Do you consider yourself healthy?" YES, 89 percent.

- "About how often do you have a conversation with one of your parents that lasts longer than 15 minutes?" A FEW TIMES A MONTH to EVERY DAY, 83 percent; ALMOST NEVER, 17 percent.

- "Do you have an adult you can confide in, inside or outside the family?" YES, 80 percent.

- "How pressured do you feel to do the following…?" NOT AT ALL: drink alcohol, 77 percent; smoke, 77 percent; take illegal drugs, 84 percent; have sex, 72 percent; look a certain way, 45 percent.

- "How much influence does each of the following have on your life?" A LOT: parents, 70 percent; religion, 34 percent; teacher, 25 percent; girlfriend/boyfriend, 24 percent; other kids, 21 percent; celebrities, 21 percent; TV shows, 8 percent; advertising, 4 percent.

- "Which do you think describe you…?" Kind, 78 percent; honest, 75 percent; good sense of humor, 69 percent; smart, 66 percent; self-confident, 65 percent; creative, 63 percent; good at sports, 53 percent; not influenced by others, 53 percent; attractive, 40 percent; tough, 40 percent; popular, 32 percent; rich, 10 percent.

Note that the eight most-claimed teenage traits are those of personal achievement while the four least-claimed are of dubious, and/or outside-awarded, distinction. Boasting or not, kids are proud of themselves. Even when the poll deliberately tried to elicit negative responses, such as by the following questions…

- "Two million teens suffer from severe depression, according to one estimate. Do you ever feel really depressed?"

- "Have any of your friends ever tried to commit suicide, or discussed it?"

…only 16 percent of the youths reporting feeling depressed "often." Even though youths may be aware of the grapevine news on hundreds of students in school, only one-third had ever heard of a peer who discussed or tried suicide. When asked directly "which of the following would make you feel better about yourself," teens did volunteer some shortcomings: half wanted better grades, a third wanted to look better and to get along better with their parents. Imagine in all cases what 40-age adults, given sodium pentathol, might answer to the above questions.

USA Weekend would have to bend its poll results completely out of shape to present a negative image of youths. Warp it did. Here is how it headlined the findings: "Teens tackle their identity crisis…teens are riddled with self-doubt about everything from their looks to their relationships with adults…Looks are key…Teens find lots of imperfections…Depression is common…Families aren't communicating…" Ironically, the most abruptly negative response about grownups was to the question, "do you think adults generally value your opinions?" Thirty-six percent said "no." I'd like to know if that percentage shot up after they saw how the newspaper relentlessly negativized their positive poll responses.

Pop media, luminous expert symposium, all the same. At the State of the World Forum in San Francisco in November 1997, I ask my fellow "Global Portrayal of Youth" panelists if young people are vilified in their home countries as they are in the United States. Represented are Mexico, Peru, Slovenia, United Kingdom, Singapore, South Africa, Russia, Thailand, China, Australia, Nigeria, and Pakistan. They look puzzled. The young man from Slovenia takes the microphone: "We do not see in our press or official discourse at home the kind of negative statements about young people that we see in America's." The man from UK seconds that view. The rest of the panelists nod. Two hours later, they will be treated to yet another dismality, as the Forum's All-American roundtable on drugs winds up its session with a sensationally idiotic denigration of teenage drinking and marijuana use—just before a glitterati dinner at the luxurious Nob Hill digs in which booze flows like Niagara. Pompously billed as the international conference that will accomplish "paradigm shifts" in international thinking about youth, the State of the World's U.S. participants vie to peddle their own wares with misleading claims and and stale programmatic solutions.

New Calvinist "Messages"

What has emerged from the jockeying of interest groups is an abysmally upside-down notion of "prevention" which seeks to blame virtually all major social and health problems on young people. Since, as noted, youths actually cause very few of society's serious problems, an unreal world in which adults don't exist has been constructed.

A 1995 study by the American Medical Association warns that one in 12 drunken driving instances involves a person under age 21 (uh…who're involved in the other eleven-twelfths?). The 1994 Surgeon General's report blamed smoking entirely on the character flaws of young people. The Carnegie Council on Adolescent Development blamed bad adult health on time bombs set by bad youth habits. Expert America agrees: the dark force that walks among us is Youth Culture. Even when obliged to admit the existence of widespread drug, drinking, smoking, violence, and crime among adults, the claim is that "prevention" policies must impose draconian restrictions on young people to forestall them from setting off a new cycle. Adults who smoke or take drugs are hopelessly habituated, says former cabinet secretary and current drug-war general Joseph Califano Jr. So leave the grownups alone and take drastic steps to nip any and all wrongheaded teenage habits in the bud.[29]

This prevention theory might be called New Calvinism. Instead of infant damnation, "teenage damnation" preaches that adults exist simply as embodiments of the worst courses they locked onto in adolescence. A convenient enabler for party-on adults, no question. But this youth-obsessed concept of "prevention" has such serious flaws it is no wonder nations with more successful health strategies don't go near it:

It is *cruel*. The policy of clamp-down-on-teens while going-easy-on-grownups effectively "writes off" the suffering caused by addiction in the adult generation. As is shown in subsequent chapters [of *Framing Youth*], kids who grow up in families with addicted parents risk severe health damage, violent abuse, and fatality.

It is *self-defeating*. Addiction does not "begin with teenagers." It is a circular process from parent generation to youth generation. As documented in later chapters [of *Framing Youth*], kids who grow up in families and communities where adults abuse drugs, alcohol, and tobacco are many times more likely to abuse these substances in adolescence and adulthood than youths in communities where addiction is low.

It is *derelict*. This concept of prevention challenges the very notion of adulthood itself. It defines "adult" not by the responsibility to be mature, but by the *privilege* to engage in immature behavior. Child raising is no longer seen as the art of setting good example, but of "monitoring" and "referral."

It is *arrogant*. The condescending, superior tone of prevention programmers toward youths, especially toward teens trapped in addicted and abusive families, leads to the absurd notion that "prevention" consists of "sending messages." The 1994 Surgeon General report's petulant complaint that some teenagers (the report made it sound like all) *still* take up smoking despite the "messages" health officials send betrays a common prejudice: that programmers' golden words should magically reform a youth away from years of day-to-day exposure to unhealthy adult behaviors that officials, for political gain, pretend do not exist.

This is a crock. Adult behaviors set the standards for society. It is adults who decide how, when, where, and at what price products may be used. Adults govern how products will be produced, sold, taxed, and regulated. Adults impose their smoking, drinking, drug habits, and rewards and consequences thereof upon children and youths in their homes. For adults to blame young people and their supposed attraction to media debauchery for the persistence of bad habits in society belies the maturity and responsibility adults claim to represent.

But for the above reasons, teen-obsessed policy is also *popular*. Alcohol control policies that assessed individual capacities to drink safely would curb the drinking rights of many prominent adults (legislators, to be blunt), but a policy based solely on preventing persons under age 21 from drinking does not threaten adult habits. This dereliction of adulthood is manifested by the variety of interest groups which now reap solace and profit from the Clinton message of exonerating grownups and demonizing kids. Not surprisingly, the worst punishments have fallen on poor, mostly nonwhite youths who were the conservative targets in the first place.

And so, America of the 1990s is an extraordinarily difficult society to grow up in. Consult this morning's (May 31, 1998) paper. President Clinton, moralizing on school prayer, implores that "children" should be "spiritually grounded" because they are exposed to "images of immorality." Many of those images derived from the grotesquely immoral behavior of Clinton and legions of cronies in a White House that aspires to no higher grounding than poll-driven popularity. Republican Senator Christopher Bond of Missouri declares that "illegal drugs are a terrible influence on our young people," failing to mention that Republicans' own elected legislative chief, House Speaker Newt Gingrich, was a prominent illegal-drug user and adulterer.[30] California Governor Pete Wilson, who personally benefitted from free university education in the 1960s, raised college tuitions through the roof in the '90s to avoid taxing his wealthier constituents. The nation's sternest welfare-reformist, anti-single-mom crusader is California (formerly Wisconsin) social services director Eloise Anderson, herself a former single welfare mother. As columnist Molly Ivins pointed out, a parade of 1996 GOP presidential aspirants condemned single mothers as the killers of civilization, excepting their own former wives whom they made single mothers.[31]

Flip on the radio to hear high-toned morals-doctor Laura Schlessinger holler, "How could you do that?!" and demand rigidly disciplined civility from dissolute America. She who derides callers as "moral slime, bimbos, bums, jerks, manipulators, idiots, scum, sluts, whores and bitches." She who is divorced, angrily estranged from her own mother and sister, so hostile to her family she calls herself an "orphan."[32] Spin the dial and arrive at right-wing black radio host Larry Elder, denouncing affirmative action, dismissing racism, browbeating poor kids who stumble in school as losers, kicking single mothers. He who checked the "race" box on his own college application in order to win admission to Brown University under affirmative action guidelines in 1970 despite his own below-par grades. He who himself is bitterly divorced.[33] On TV, there is Geraldo, whipping up the audience to a rage against teenage mothers, labeling a 14-year-old girl in big screen letters: "WANTS TO BE A SEXUAL SLUT JUST LIKE HER SISTER." He of super-slutdom who, in a 1989 *Playboy* interview, bragged of having boffed "thousands of women, literally thousands." He whose 1991 autobiography did not admit that his own unsafe sex produced a son, which he admitted only after it was disclosed in a *People* profile.[34] *Rolling Stone* founder/publisher Jan Wenner waxes piously sarcastic against teenage drinking and sex. He whose once-reasonably-honest, now-money-glam-worshipping rag sloshes with liquor, cigarette, lavish fashion, and nude starlet grabbers. Gary Hart concubine Donna Rice rails hysterically against internet porn seducing children. Rich, celebrated, indignantly defended as a right, Baby Boom hypocrisy never ends. The parent generation message is not lost on teens: self-discipline counts for nothing; stridently voiced values and morals to be imposed on others is everything.

The young are held up as symbols of all that has gone wrong with America even in exemplary liberal works. Boston University sociology professor Charles Derber's *The Wilding of America* adroitly details how the looting of the economy by the wealthy, corporate, and politically powerful contributes to the "ungluing of society" far more than sensational street crimes. Derber focuses most of his appropriately broad-brush attack on the greedy and amoral government-business skulduggeries of the Reagan and post-Reagan eras. He cites rising community and family disintegration. When it comes to the sins of the old, his attack is on individual villains and villainies, of which there are plenty. But young people are attacked in their entirety as a *demographic group* (that is, a group defined by race, age, sex, or ethnicity). Derber cites anecdotes and the typical kinds of bile elders of every era express toward juniors to paint a picture of faceless, violent, indifferent, materialistic, television-hooked young.[35] The biases routinely expressed against youth as a group would be offensive if, say, "blacks" or "women" were substituted for "youths" or "adolescents" in the sentences of many modern liberal commentaries.

Today's angry barrage against adolescents appears unique to the United States. Other societies, even our aging peer countries, don't seem enraged and terrified of their kids. In [*Framing Youth*], Europeans, Canadians, Australians, and Japanese will be lauded for the humanity of their nations' social insurance systems, the higher standards their governments enforce in health and welfare, their more enlightened views of youth, their more relaxed perspective on vice, their low crime and behavior problems. European health and social policy focuses not on age but on harmful behavior. The U.S. has much to learn from Europe's social policies, even though powerful movements in those nations, apparently envious of America's copious poverty, murder, and prisons, would dismantle their entitlement and employment systems.

But we have much to un-learn from Europe as well. European nations tend to be monocultures. Their borders are drawn to promote ethnic and religious homogeneity. A hundred million or so dead this century testifies to how badly Europeans handle ethnic disparities. The multicultural United States faces a more difficult domestic challenge than other Western societies. That challenge is presaged in multi-ethnic states such as Hawai'i, California, and New Mexico, and in most urban centers—led by New York and Los Angeles.

At present, America's grownups in the Clinton era are not up to the challenge. Moralizing, coded fears and harmonious platitudes cover policies of division and repression. By every measure, public and private, today's wealthier adults are not giving today's youths the same chance to succeed as the poorer parents and grandparents of previous generations afforded us. Children and adolescents of the new millennium are raised by the most self-fixated adult generation in known history, one which seems unwilling to fulfill either its parenting or public policy obligations toward the young. It is adults whose crises are troubling and inexplicable.

The hopeful news is that 1990s children and adolescents are behaving far better than we have a right to expect. The next generation shows signs of stability and strength reflected in surprising statistics. And so [Framing Youth] is essentially just one repeating chapter. Whether the issue is violence, crime, suicide and self destruction, drugs, smoking, drinking, risk, or attitude, the sequence is the same. Teenagers are universally denigrated when, in reality, they are behaving well amid severe stresses.

Indeed, the 1997 Public Agenda poll's sermonizing adult hostility against children and teenagers included an tragicomic comeuppance. The teenagers surveyed revealed considerable warmth toward the very adults who castigated them en masse. Adolescents responding to the poll judged their elders as individuals rather than as faceless demographic stereotypes. They liked most of us. But at some point, if this society is to survive, their tolerance for the 1990s Raw Deal must wear thin.

Growing Up in a State of Extremes

By conventional logic, America's most extreme state should have been burned to its ungrounded foundations by adolescent superpredator mobs. California's teenage population is rising faster than in any other state—up half a million since 1990 with another million and a half, lurking in grade school, on the way. The reversal of fortunes among California youth has been more cataclysmic than that of teens elsewhere even as adults remain richer than their national counterparts.

In the last quarter century, California's young have fallen from among the nation's richest to its among its poorest. Poverty doubled among youths, exceeding 25 percent by 1997.[36] Per-pupil funding of schools plummeted from among the top five states in 1965 to among the bottom 15 in 1998. Today, the state consistently has the most crowded classrooms and fewest teachers and school personnel per student of any state. University tuition rose from free in the Sixties to $4,000-plus in the '90s. Cities have lost hundreds of thousands of industrial jobs.

The economic and social disaster that has befallen California youths and young families is set against the sunny fortunes of its aging Euro-whites and prospering non-whites. Poverty has declined among Californians over 40. Median household incomes top $50,000 per year. Seventy percent own their own homes (and nearly all younger people's, too).

Baby Boomers are the apex of California affluence. Yet average tax rates have fallen by one-quarter, with special windfalls accruing to wealthy senior homeowners. Lush communities of opulence grace coastal and hilltop retreats, sprouting gates, guards, and surveillance. "Welcome to post-liberal Los Angeles," writes urban historian Mike Davis, "where the defense of luxury lifestyles is translated into a proliferation of new repressions in space and movement…the militarization of city life."[37]

Yet what has transpired among California's diverse populations in the last 25 years is so unbelievable that a whole new social theory may evolve to explain it. Reactionary to Marxist, conventional logic holds that extremes of violence, personal degradation, rage, anomie, poisonous apathy, and every other malaise *should be* pushing California's young to new depths of debauchery. Meanwhile, middle-agers *should be* basking in tiptop granola health and serenity. In standard determinism, scholars and media portray California exactly as orthodoxy says it should be: the Golden State of grownups versus the Gundown State of adolescents.

Eminently logical—except that's not what is going on at all.

Consider a mega-metropolis of 10 million, fountainhead of super-lethal permutations of heroin, cocaine, speed, and pharmaceuticals. One million teens age 10–19 live in this sprawling conurbation. Imagine now its drug overdose death toll for an entire year: adults, 562; teens, zero.

That would be real Los Angeles County, 1994.

Imagine a mega-state of 32 million that accounts for one-fourth of the nation's heroin deaths. Three million teens, 750,000 in families with annual incomes of less than $15,000, inhabit it. Imagine now its heroin overdose toll for a year: adults, 528; teenagers, zero.

That would be California, 1994.

A state whose adult drug abuse toll tripled from the 1970s to the 1990s—but whose teenage drug death toll fell by 90 percent. Where an exhaustive report would find a record 36,000 emergency hospitalizations for cocaine and heroin abuse in 1995—fewer than 2 percent of whom were teenagers.

Imagine that in this state, teenage suicide and self-destructive deaths—drug overdoses, gunshot accidents, hangings, drownings, car wrecks, other self-dispatch—declined by 50 percent in the last two decades.

Where teenage population increased by half a million and youth poverty doubled from 1975 to 1997. But where 80,000 *fewer* teenagers were arrested every year in the mid-'90s than in the mid-'70s. Where teenage felonies were down 35 percent. Teenage misdemeanors down 23 percent. Teenage drug offenses down 35 percent. Even an august crime commission appointed by the Republican governor would scratch its head over the youth crime decline, burying that finding in its final report so as not to disturb the lucrative political issue of "youth crime."

Where murder decreases among teenagers from 1990 to 1997 read as follows: Euro-whites, down 49 percent. Blacks, down 70 percent. Latinos, down 50 percent. Asians and Native Americans, down 52 percent. Especially strong teenage murder declines occurred in Los Angeles, where no coherent city law enforcement strategy could have caused it: 251 youth homicides in 1990, 75 in 1997.

Imagine how much interest these utterly unbelievable statistics generated among academic scholars, agency officials, politicians, or the news media (who, Mark Twain might say, worship "some of the facts"). That would be zero as well.

The Writing on the Wall

Once a month or so, I take the Blue Line urban train from Long Beach to downtown Los Angeles. The train smoothly whisks through the city's ripped backsides: silent industrial yards and dilapidated stucco blocks of Artesia, Compton, Watts, Firestone, Florence, Slauson, 18th Street, into the diseased and bustling Garment District.

After a few trips you, too, may find yourself monitoring the pitched battles between Southcentral's fleetfooted black, brown, "Asian/other" (and a few white) graffitists and taggers versus the plodding pastel paintover patrols. Graffiti first appears below the railway bridge on the cement banks of the Los Angeles River, a story in itself. Writes University of California, Irvine, doctoral graffitologist Faye Docuyanan:

> The history of the L.A. River is a particularly poignant example of the relationship between the proliferation of graffiti in urban environments and an abandonment of the public sphere in favor of more predictable and seemingly secure spaces such as "fortified enclaves" and "normalized" gated communities.[38]

In 1930, the renowned Olmsted and Bartholomew urban design firm recommended that the L.A. River connect "a unified system of beaches, parks, playgrounds, and mountain reserves" through the heart of the expanding city, designed to serve lower income working-class families.[39] Instead, at the behest of the Southern Pacific Railroad and allied cut-and-fill octopi, the river was paved from source to mouth to facilitate private development. The city shut out poor communities and created an immense canvas for their later retaliation.

On the train, I join the ghosts of Olmsted and Bartholomew in irony at the sight of the shaded, accented, wildstyle flourishes and murals adorning miles of river wall. Public displays along freeway and train vistas extend for blocks. Factories, vacant and broken-windowed, are enameled story above story. Scrawly three-letter tags appear on impossibly angular freeway bridges, defacing 50-foot razor-wire-defended signs no mortal could scale or depend. Graffiti galleries flank the river, where cavernous vaults of cement are enameled two to three stories high. These are not for public view, but trade admiration. Parked beside the Blue Line route, I see heavily spray-painted freight cars, descendents of Southern Pacific rolling stock, ready to spread L.A. tagger messages from sea to shining sea.

Reversing the trends of larger society, the police enforcers of beige are hopelessly outflanked and outcanned. Caltrans says it spends $3 million per year to erase graffiti from its freeway walls, train stations, and signs, 20 times more than a decade ago. Yet colorful murals and ugly curlicue tags abound, mile after mile. Even the brightly lit Firestone station's barricades are graffiti-blanketed, pastel-painted-over, then re-enameled.

Consider this blaze of energy amid what William Julius Wilson's *When Work Disappears* tells about the psychology of chronic inner-city unemployment.[40] "None of the other industrialized democracies has allowed its city centers to deteriorate as has the United States," Wilson writes. Where industries have shut down and unemployment is widespread, "lack of self-efficacy" takes over. Jobless adults, in the shadow of abandoned factories, spend lost days and months in which "they are unable to recall anything worth mentioning." Men loiter in unlimited time, talking aimlessly, drinking on corners, trapped in "emotional depression," surrendering to futility and paralyzing apathy. Where predatory manufacturing industries depart, predatory intoxicant industries (legal worse than illicit) infiltrate.

Yet selves are gloriously efficating in southcentral L.A. The eruption of adolescent spraycan exuberance annoys, infuriates, challenges at visceral range. "We paint trains even though they don't run," rues graffitist theoretician William Upski Wimsatt in *Bomb the Suburbs*.[41] Someone, thousands of ones, give up comfortable blunt and malt-liquor lounging to venture out for nights of creative wallwork. They wage what Mayor Richard Riordan calls "a constant assault on the psyches of Angelinos."[42]

Apropos, the angriest, most bitingly articulate rejoinders I've ever received were to my 1994 *Coast Weekly* editorial, "In Defense of Graffiti:"

> Whatever taggers' good, bad, or ugly intentions, spray-paint vandalism serves to remind us of a vital point: we alleged adults don't *deserve* to bask complacently in pretty vistas as we motor and stroll through a nation whose children's future we have unconscionably wrecked.
>
> …So taggers, just as Washington and Sacramento target your young age groups for yet more legislated attrition, do America's future a favor by targeting your lost and avaricious elders for graffiti-canings right where it hurts us most—smack in our material souls. Colorize Winnebagos. Decorate country clubs. Claim fortress architecture as a challenge (it was built to keep your kind out—forever). Prioritize upscale Prop-13-happy suburbs for a field night. Enamel the Capitol.
>
> Just maybe, as we wrathfully behold your superficial sprayings, a few of us old folks might start thinking about how our devastating intergenerational economic and social vandalism has uglified the lives of millions to come.[43]

The reactions of the Winnebago, suburban, fortress, country-clubbing, and capitol folks whose environs I volunteered to bear the burden of intergenerational redress can be imagined. Said a Monterey property owners' association letter-writer in a more thoughtful response: "I doubt that the kids who are applying graffiti" are doing so "to punish the over-40 group for being irresponsible and selfish."[44]

Unbeknownst to me at the time, some are. Reported the *Bay Guardian's* A. Clay Thompson in 1998…

Grease and Solid…are graffiti writers, armed with spray paint, and they are on a continuing mission—a battle against the new San Francisco, a sanitized city purged of grimy homeless lowlife and housing project problem children.

For Grease and Solid, graffiti is direct action against gentrification, part of a campaign not on any politician's agenda: to curb property values by keeping the city seedy.[45]

…so the poorer young can afford to live in the new Boutique City by the Bay, 1998, average house price $271,000, in the post-Proposition-13 world. "I hope my graffiti annoys yuppies," Grease, age 20, said. "If we all get pushed out of this city (due to gentrification), I'll still come back and write graffiti. Just for retaliation. Just to leave a piece of me here." Adds colleague Light:

I'm more or less pissed at the world, the government, laws. The laws aren't there to treat people fairly—they're totally biased racially, economically. You have to be rich to have a real voice. Graffiti is a choice to have an impact. Rich people have huge advertismements and billboards. We have walls.

Good for their psyche assault. It is apathy in the young we should fear. The biggest failing of adolescents, Franklin Roosevelt told the jobless young in 1936, is that they lose idealism, are not rebellious enough. Kids need adults and adults need kids. Yet we are disinheriting them, and we are doing it with our eyes wide open.

"Young people," writes Luis Rodríguez in *La Vida Loca*, "can only satisfy their needs through collective strength—against the police, who hold the power of life and death, against poverty, against idleness, against their impotence in society."[46]

The sheer volume of graffiti, more than the dramatic artism of its pieces, inspires awe. This is energy, power. More than cops and curfews can contain. I feel nervous in cities where there's no graffiti, nothing to gauge what the indigent young are about. Outrage at the smug lies of the privileged old, amazement at the frenetic energy of the disowned young, are why [*Framing Youth*] was written.

A Note on Presentation

There seem to me five banes of 1990s public discussion of youth (and probably many other) issues that I attempt to avoid:

- **The Gut-Grabbing Neverland Anecdote.** Rush Limbaugh's got stories, Jim Hightower's got stories. Anecdotes and cases give a human face to cold statistics. "Jimmy" (non-existent eight-year-old heroin addict), Becky Bell (teenage abortion death), Polly Klaas (murder provoked Three Strikes), Willie Horton, Jonesboro, and Ryan White all stimulated larger debate and action good, bad, and disastrous. But whether an anecdote is true, and whether it illustrates a general problem or an exceptional case is crucial when considering whether to enact sweeping new laws and policies. In order to inflate the importance of news stories, extremely rare cases (such as school shootings or teenage heroin deaths) are irresponsibly depicted as "alarming new trends." In [*Framing Youth*], anecdotes are used to illustrate general cases, not rare exceptions.

- **The Dangling Statistic.** Liberals and rightists uniformly pick and choose only the few statistics which buttress their case and ignore the avalanche that refute it. Proprietary statistics, many simply manufactured, are a '90s epidemic evidencing how little today's interests care what conditions and behaviors really affect kids. In [*Framing Youth*], I attempt to present complete statistics and major studies that bracket the issue discussed.

- **The Secondary Source.** By now, any Ph.D. has said just about anything, "experts" quote whatever the quoter wants, and studies can be found to buttress any cockamamie notion. I attempt to cite primary sources (original statistics) rather than what someone said about original statistics. This is the most fun part. Lots of kings are wearing barrels.

- **The Great Unread.** Both liberals and conservatives cite sound bites from studies pleasing to their agendas—but which they never read. Lots of studies, when examined, do not show what they claim to show or even claim what they are claimed to show. Studies of tobacco advertising and other media effects, and all "blue ribbon" reports, are particularly egregious, yet they are universally cited by interests who have never even read them. It is impossible to fully apprise every study cited, but I attempt to read and evaluate the major studies on opposing sides of the points discussed and to present the flaws therein.

- **False Egalitarianism.** The Right claims racism is dead; any impoverished minority kid can succeed on equal terms with a more affluent white kid today. Liberals claim advantaged white kids cause just as much murder, pregnancy, and drug abuse as poorer nonwhite kids. Baloney and baloney. Socioeconomics is a crucial determinant of behavior (and official response to behavior), and it remains intimately intertwined with race. Conservatives' lionizing of against-the-odds successes of individual minority youths does not relieve larger society of its obligation to take much stronger actions to compensate for racism. Liberals' demonizing of white kids with Gut-Grabbing Anecdotes does not make up for demonizing minority kids with Dangling Statistics. It is flatly untrue that most nonwhite youth have opportunity even remotely approaching that of most white youth. It is flatly untrue that white teenagers suffer even nearly as much homicide, violent crime, or AIDS as nonwhite youth. These two facts are interrelated. I attempt to treat race and economic inequality bluntly rather than fitting them to false egalitarian agendas.

Finally, a note about racial/ethnic references: America is undergoing a period of realignment in racial terminology, good for society but hell on communicating the topic. No terminology seems right. Referring to African Americans, Latinos, Asians, and Native Americans collectively as "nonwhites" is objectionable because it combines disparate groups into a word denoting what they aren't. "People of color" is awkward to use in many sentences, does not wear well in repitition, and seems to me little more than a rephrasing of the old term of segregation, "colored people."

"Minority" no longer means anything in most cities and in California, where all races/ethnicities are minorities. Listing each race/ethnicity seperately each time is cumbersome. Since there are many circumstances in this book in which people of color/nonwhites as a group endure conditions and present characteristics different from those of whites as a group (and since, unfortunately, statistics are gathered most reliably by racial categorization), some use of collective references is needed. I use the term "nonwhite," and where it applies, "minority," since these are at least accurate and simple with regard to who is being talked about. Finally, consistently hyphenating every racial/ethnic reference (Asian-American, Latino-American, European-American, etc., to parallel African-American), gets old quick, and so I use the simpler terms denoting color (black, white) or ethnicity (Latino, Asian). I apologize to readers in advance who may find those terms inappropriate, and suggestions are welcome.

Notes

1   Wilson WJ (1996). *When Work Disappears: The World of the New Urban Poor.* New York: Vintage Books, pp 29–30.

2   Shapiro RJ (1994, January). Cut-and-Invest to Compete and Win: A Budget Strategy for American Growth. Washington, DC: Progressive Policy Institute, p 4. See also Hage D, Black RF (1995, 10 April). "America's other welfare state; Getting business off the dole." *US News & World Report,* pp 34–38.

3   Albelda R et al (1996). *The War on the Poor.* New York: Center for Population Economics, p 39.

4   Kozol J (1991). *Savage Inequalities: Children in America's Schools.* New York: Crown Publishers, pp 137–156, 236.

5   Shogren E (1997, 28 April). "Clinton sounds call for citizens to volunteer." *Los Angeles Times,* pp A1, A8.

6   Goodman P (1956). *Growing Up Absurd: Problems of Youth in the Organized Society.* New York: Vintage Books, pp 42–44.

7   Maharidge D (1996). *The Coming White Minority: California's Eruptions and the Nation's Future.* New York: Times Books, p 293.

8   Kozol J (1995). *Amazing Grace: The Lives of Children and the Conscience of a Nation.* New York: Crown Publishers, p 230.

9   Howe N, Strauss B (1993). *13th Gen: Abort, Retry, Ignore, Fail?* New York: Vintage Books, pp 17 (quoted), 18–28.

10 Blumstein A (1995, August). "Violence by young people: Why the deadly nexus?" *National Institute of Justice Journal,* p 3.

11 Children Now (1998). *A Different World: Children's Perceptions of Race and Class in the Media.* Oakland, CA: Children Now.

12 Males M (1998, 29 April). "Five myths about teenagers and why adults believe them." *The New York Times,* Special Section, Adolescents.

13 Bureau of the Census (1997). *Statistical Abstract of the United States 1996.* Washington: U.S. Department of Commerce, Table 23.

14 Maharidge D (1996), op cit, pp 11, 129.

15 See Chester L, Hodgson G, Page B (1969). *An American Melodrama.* New York: Viking Press, pp 307–13; Williams TH (1969). Huey Long. New York: Alfred A. Knopf, Inc.

16 Shrag P (1998). *Paradise Lost: California's Experience, America's Future.* The New Press.

17 Presiding Justice (Gardner). *In re Ronald S.* California Court of Appeals, Fourth District. 69 Cal.App.3d 866, 138 Cal.Rprtr. 387.

18 Davis A, in Males M (1989, 18 October). "Youth crime is tied to earlier abuse." *Bozeman Daily Chronicle*, p 3.

19 Office of Juvenile Justice and Delinquency Prevention (1996). *Juvenile Offenders and Victims: A National Report*. Washington, DC: U.S. Department of Justice, p 144.

20 See discussion and references in Males M (1996). *The Scapegoat Generation: America's War on Adolescents*. Monroe, ME: Common Courage Press, pp 242–53.

21 Kearns R (1998, May). "Finding profit in at-risk kids." *Youth Today*, pp 1, 10–11.

22 Baum D (1996). *Smoke and Mirrors: The War on Drugs and the Politics of Failure*. Boston: Little Brown, p 155.

23 Kozol (1995), op cit, p 107.

24 Rorty R (1998). *Achieving Our Country: Leftist Thought in Twentieth-Century America*. London: Harvard University Press, pp 14, 86.

25 Males M (1992, September). "Top 10 school problems are myths." *Phi Delta Kappan*, p 54.

26 Cockburn A, Silverstein K (1996). *Washington Babylon*. London: Verso, p viii.

27 Pinkerton JP (1998, 13 August). "Clinton turns 180 degrees away from Clintoncare." *Los Angeles Times*, p B9.

28 Rhule P, Soriano CG (1998, 1–3 May). "Teens tackle their identity crisis." *USA Weekend*, pp 6–18.

29 Califano JA Jr (1995, 16 September). "Adult smoking victims all started young." *New York Times*, p A14.

30 Rosenblatt RA, and AP (1998, 31 May). "Clinton sees no need for school prayer measure. Drugs behind youth crimes, senator says." *Los Angeles Times*, p A4.

31 Ivins M (1995, 27 March). "Illegitimacy ratio—another idiotic GOP policy." *Liberal Opinion Week*, p 4.

32 Wiscombe J (1998, 18 January). "I don't do therapy." *Los Angeles Times Magazine*, p 12.

33 Mitchell JL (1998, 31 May). "Larry knows best." *Los Angeles Times Magazine*, p 15.

34 Young CM (1997, 18 September). "Geraldo Rivera." *Rolling Stone*, 769, pp 118–19.

35 Derber C (1996). *The Wilding of America: How Greed and Violence Are Eroding Our Nation's Character*. New York: St. Martin's Press.

36 Children Now (1998). *Report Card 1997: Spotlight on California's counties*. Oakland, CA: Children Now, p 5.

37 Davis M (1990). *City of Quartz: Excavating the Future in Los Angeles*. New York: Vintage Books, p 223.

38 Docuyanan F (1998, March). *The heavens, the lake, the river, and the pit: Graffiti and the politics of space in urban Los Angeles*. Irvine, CA: University of California, summary of poster presentation to the Environmental Research Design Association, St. Louis, MO.

39 Davis M. *How Eden lost its garden*, cited in Docuyanan (1998), op cit.

40 Wilson WJ (1996), op cit, pp 73–78.

41 Wimsatt WU (1994, October). *Bomb the Suburbs*. Chicago: The Subway and Elevated Press Co, p 66.

42 Docuyanan F (1998, 4 February). *Inscribing at the Crossroads of Culture and Crime: A Study of Urban Graffiti Writers in Southern California*. Irvine, CA, University of California, School of Social Ecology: Dissertation Proposal, Literature Review, p 33.

43 Males M (1994, 7 July). "In defense of graffiti: There's worse ugliness than tagging." *Coast Weekly* (Monterey-Seaside, CA), p 8.

44 Appel C (1994, 28 July). "Letters." *Coast Weekly*.

45 Thompson AC (1998, 11 March). "The writing on the wall. A nighttime bicycle tour of S.F.'s graffiti galleries." *Bay Guardian*, pp 24–27.

46 Rodriguez LJ (1993). *La Vida Loca: Gang Days in L.A.* New York: Simon & Schuster, p 250. English title: *Always Running*.

Discussion Questions

1. Why is private enterprise not the answer to youth problems?
2. How are youth portrayed in the news and in TV programs?
3. What information about youth crime and violence do Tables I and II reveal?
4. Why, in spite of statistics that illustrate the contrary, does the news still portray teens as criminals?
5. What is causing the rise of crime rates among adults 30–49?
6. How have both liberals and conservatives conspired to stereotype adolescents?
7. What are the dangers of using self-reported surveys as indicators of teen behavior?
8. What are the "new Calvinist" messages?

Writing Suggestion

How does your own experience or observation support or discredit Males' assertions? Do you see problems with teens that he does not consider?

Of "Faggots" and "Butch-Dykes" and Other "Unfit Children"

Louise Armstrong

Of "Sluts" and "Bastards":
A Feminist Decodes the Child Welfare Debate

The place where I am to meet Lawrence is a New York City walk-in storefront facility for homeless kids called Streetwork. These are the truly down-and-out. They are kids who've been kicked out of other youth shelters; runaways who choose to stay out of the system; some kids who—having hooked to survive—now have AIDS. The facility offers counseling, it offers help in locating jobs, it offers food and an opportunity to do laundry and somewhere, during the day and evening, at least, to safely sit down.

When I arrive, the place is in what I presume to be its usual state of controlled chaos: kids coming, kids slumped in chairs, kids going; kids vying for counselors' attention, for particular items, particular needs. One girl is seventeen and seven months pregnant. With her is her "fiancé"—they mean to get married; at the moment, however, that's the least of their concerns. They have been sleeping in the Port Authority bus terminal.

Tall, rangy, Lawrence slinks in. He's black, nineteen, and a self-described queen: in his word, "flamboyant." We find ourselves a small, glass-partitioned office in which to talk—only barely removed from the ongoing clamor of phones and kids' talk.

Lawrence is an "okay-'kay?" talker, gesturing continuously with his long-fingered, slim hands. He reminds me, to begin with, of a character who might be portrayed to you by Whoopi Goldberg. Here is Lawrence, censored for only some of the liberally sprinkled "likes" and "whole bits."

"My mother was fourteen years old when she had her first child [Lawrence] and then she was fifteen when she had the second child. When I'd see her, I'd say, 'I can't believe you're my mom.' She looked so young, you know. She's real hyperactive; she drinks, she does drugs and the whole bit like that.

"My sister—she's still in a foster home. But me—my life has been from one scandalous part to another.

"I don't remember all the foster homes because there's been so many. The first real influential foster home was when I was six. That had the greatest impact on me. Me and my sister were there together. They used to play roles against us: 'I like the little girl so much more. She's so cute. Who wants that big-lipped black guy?' And I was only six, and so—bed-wetting and things like that were a problem. And I literally received beatings that were unbearable. That left like a ton of bruises all around my body. I was really scared.

"The lady, she was a reverend, her name was Sister Porter. I remember we used to go to church all the time—and little things really hurt me. Riding with her it would take us like forty minutes to get to church, which was five blocks away. All of us cram-packed in a car and she would drive ten miles per hour and if I speak up like, 'Can't we go any faster?' I would get a backhand across the lip: 'Why don't you shut up?' And my lip is bleeding and I'm sitting in church with a big bloody lip and little kids, like, 'What happened to you?' 'Oh. I fell down.'

"And I remember she used to make me sleep on the floor beside her bed, which I used to hate. Because my sister and the other foster kids slept upstairs. She had me sleep downstairs because, 'Oh, you stole this.' Or, 'Oh, you stole that.' She's like, 'I left this chicken in the refrigerator and now it's gone.' And the kids would be like, 'Oh, Lawrence took it.' Because I was a 'problem' child: it was very easy to say I had done it.

"There were four other foster kids. And she had like four kids of her own. And the kids would say, 'Oh, Lawrence done it.' And she would beat me senseless. And make me sleep on the floor: 'I'm gonna watch you and make sure you don't get up and go steal any of my food.' 'It wasn't me that took it.' 'You're lying. Yes you did. My kids aren't liars. I sent them to church.' And, 'They were here first and I know my kids more than I know your crummy little ass.' "

Lawrence remembers the move to the next foster home (but not the reason for it).

"Miss Spanner. Now she was really fab. We stayed with her about four years. Now at this point I was so jealous of my sister because everybody said she was so much better and because of me being accused of everything.

"But at this home we were treated differently. Like, 'No one gets more than the other.' And then I started school first, so I learned to read. I had always been a very smart child. That has helped to my advantage."

At this point, Lawrence's stutter begins to appear. It starts almost imperceptibly, and since he is talking so rapidly, for a moment or two I think it to be my inability to hear and register so quickly.

"Let's s-see. I guess I'm about ten now. I was becoming aware of my sexuality. I knew I was gay. Little kids at school were calling me, 'He acts like a sissy. He acts like a girl.' The foster parents, they denied it. 'He's not gay. He just acts like a little girl because of he feels like little girls get more attention than little boys. So the way to get attention is to act like a little girl.' So I guess becoming feminine, the way I am now, with my feminine characteristics, was wanting to get the things that my sister has.

"Because I was a little boy—just got me in trouble. Play outside, play in the dirt. 'Oh, look at you! You're absolutely filthy! I just washed your clothes…' And, 'We're gonna wash you down in bleach.' And they literally poured bleach and tried to wash me. I remember that. When I had a scratch or a sore—from playing in the dirt? With the bleach it just made it burn—beyond belief.

"So when I got to Margaret Spanner's house—she took us in—she'd bathe us. She really did us good."

Margaret Spanner, however, decided to take on an infant whose mother didn't want her. It turned out to be a child with enormous medical problems, and, with Lawrence and his sister at each other's throats all the time, a choice between the sick child and the older children was forced. At that point, Lawrence and his sister were placed separately. As Lawrence says, "Because this problem of fighting was out in public, out in school. It came down to an actual denial of relationship: 'Oh, that's not my brother, that little faggot.' And I was saying, 'Oh, that's not my sister, that little baldheaded girl.' Because my foster mother, you know, she had to cut my sister's hair because the previous home had permed my sister's hair and the perm had made her hair fall out in patches. So she had to cut it all off. And I was, 'Ha-ha, you have no hair. You're not a little girl.' And she was real insecure about that. Because in foster homes, each family has their idea of how they want their little girl to look: 'I want my little girl to have a perm, curls in her hair.' And then the other foster mother: 'I want my child to look natural.' 'I want my child to have dreadlocks.' Then another foster home: 'Well, I want my child to be bald.' "

Kids who come into state care at infancy, and are then bumped around, are forced—almost heroically—to invent themselves. If any further evidence were necessary that sexuality does not come in a package marked "optional," Lawrence's story should clinch it: Is there anyone in this whole universe who would *choose*, growing up as Lawrence did in the South, to invent himself as a black effeminate foster child?

Lawrence's sister went to a foster home he describes as "fab." "I went to a nastier foster home than the one I came from—another churchgoing people. And they had their kids. And I'm alone. S-s-s-so it's no good. So—me being jealous of my sister again—I got myself in trouble."

Lawrence was moved again.

"With a reverend and his wife. They were an older couple. They had no kids. It was fab. But he used to make like sexual advances at me. And I'm, 'Oh no you don't.' Like, 'Come and lie on top of me.' Like, 'Here's a quarter, your ice cream money.' And if I didn't do anything with him, you know, I had no ice cream money.

"Because I was in f-f—f-f-f-foster care, I got the f-f-f-free lunch, you know. School was my only release. From my body. I could study. I could learn things. I could read. When I'm in a book, it was my state. I would read-read-read-read-read. Then, 'Why you always got your face in a book?' I would hold the book up t-t-t-to ignore her and she'd snatch the book: 'Don't you hear me talking to you? Don't ignore me that way!' And slap me. 'You've always got your face in a book. You're really dumb. You never talk to me. You're stupid, you're really stupid. You don't know shit. You're never gonna be nothin' in your life.' It used to really hurt my feelings. 'That's right, look at the little sissy cry, now, look at him cry.' It's like, 'Well, if you're gonna cry, I'll give you something to cry for.' She'd spank me. I'm like, 'For what? For reading a book? That's how it all started?' "

By this time, Lawrence's sister had moved again (into the foster home where she currently lives): her fourth home. Lawrence is then on his fifth (that he can remember)—and about to move again.

"The neighbors started complaining. I'd be in the backyard and they'd see my foster mother slap me hard, knock me across the yard. So they reported."

The next home, Lawrence says, was a better one. They were, by his standards, people of means, childless. In short order, however, the couple decided they preferred being childless, and became part of whatever statistic presently speaks to foster parent churn and turnover. It is easy enough to see why people would drop out. It is also possible for them to simply drop out because…they feel like it (or don't feel like it). Being a foster child, then, is this knowledge: There is not even the illusion of a place where, when you go there, they have to take you in. And certainly no place where, once you're in, they have to keep you.

From there, Lawrence moved in with a woman whom he describes as "a real fruitcake." The social worker discovered serious negligence and—Lawrence went to his first group home.

To begin with, everything was "fab."

"I was given appreciation for the good things I did. Which I had never received. I became a little snobbish, a little snottyish: 'I'm so fab now because I did good in school.' My good grades, you know. 'Oh, he's a wonderful child!' 'Thank you.' I'd go into school and get one of these little certificates for my report card: if you get A, you go shopping for free.

"But then I was starting to go through puberty and being aware of myself and, 'No, I don't like girls.' So I was kind of flamboyant—because I was out, and I could be myself.

"But now schools were another issue altogether. I would get in fights. They'd throw things at me. 'Look at the faggot.' That was down south—where homosexuality is not accepted in no way, shape, or form. When cars drove by, they'd throw bottles at you. And then I was going to therapy. The therapist said, 'Just ignore them. As long as you're comfortable with yourself that's all that matters.' That's what I was led to believe. That's what I did. But it wasn't true at all.

"I found that out the hard way. 'I'm gonna be myself.' That just caused the kids to go off."

No matter how quixotic the foster care system may appear, in one area it reveals a stunning predictability. Gay kids face the culture's full wrath. Certainly, they face the biases other kids have picked up from adults. But majorly compounding that are the biases within the system itself that mitigate against the placement of kids with gay couples—the presumption that it is in *that* circumstance the kids would be molested. In reality, Lawrence was molested by a heterosexual, church-going foster father.

It is mysterious. Over the past decade we have heard the testimony of tens of thousands of men and women who were molested as children by fathers and stepfathers within the apparently heterosexual nuclear family. And certainly, as one travels around the world of foster care, reports of children molested by foster fathers—again, men part of a standard nuclear unit—are entirely common. Yet there continues to be this ferocious bias against placing children with same-sex couples. It is evidence of a Victorian Superpop mindset that has lurked in the system all along—well before being given full cry by mid-1990s reactionaries. It is a mindset based on suffocating stereotypes which would equate licentiousness, deviance, and perversion. It is the system's fourth bias—on top of gender, race, class. In a sense, it is the last straw. Because if gay couples are most prevalently perceived as unfit parents, it is as though gay kids are perceived to be unfit children.

Joyce Hunter is director of social works services for the Hetrick-Martin Institute, which serves lesbian, gay and bisexual youth in New York City. She says, "What happens to the kids who are openly gay or effeminate is that they wind up in diagnostic centers where they're supposed to be evaluated and processed. What happens is they wind up *staying* in diagnostic centers in lieu of foster care. So what you find is that kids are living in diagnostic centers—for years. These are the kids that wind up getting lost through the cracks. They're in one center, they go to another one, and eventually they drop out of the system—with no employable skills or independent living skills. This happens in a lot of cities around the country, and I don't think it's just the major cities. I've been a consultant on a case in the Midwest where this kind of problem exists as well.

"I think this is homophobia at its core. The kids are perceived as a 'problem' because they're perceived only in sexual terms. And they are seen as 'not being able to fit in.' These foster care placers will say, 'Well, this kid will pose a problem for all the other kids.'

"The *kid* becomes the problem, not the attitude of the staff, not the attitude of the other kids in the group home. This is discrimination. So not knowing what to do with these young people, and not really having programs for them, these kids are denied access to quality care, and the right to a stable living situation. I am having such trouble finding homes for these kids. It is so hard. And it doesn't help if they are black or Hispanic either because—then, the racism. It's a double whammy for these youngsters. But the homophobia is the overriding theme.

"If you get a gay couple who is a family willing to go through a foster care screening and they come out really good, you're gonna have two people who really want to be parents. And I think that lesbian and gay people should be able to take children in."

"Particularly," I say, "when your alternative is placing them in what are effectively detention centers."

"Exactly. Can you imagine growing up in a diagnostic center? I have kids who spend two or three years in those places. It is not conducive to getting any sense of who you are, your sense of self; developing any kind of interpersonal skills. No sense of family or anything. Because kids are coming and going at a diagnostic center—and the gay kid sits there."

It is a poignant image: the child, effectively permanently sidelined, watching as other kids are selected for placement. To this child—whatever the reality of those placements may be—the fact that others are placed and he or she is not is what signifies. The child takes it as evidence that he is an unfit child. Even were he to understand that it is not himself but what he *represents* that is being rejected, what effect would this have except to impress on him that his primary identity is his sexual orientation?

"And for girls, it's even more difficult," Joyce Hunter says. "I have a difficult time with boys, but sometimes I can get them placed. But with girls, it's very, very hard."

What happens when kids do find placement?

In an article in the journal written by foster kids, *Foster Care United*, Carlford Wadley reports on a boy named Shantur. "I would leave in the morning for school," Shantur says. "When I came back to go to my room, somebody had spray painted the word FAGGOT on the door…

"Bottles were thrown and people would shoot at me…My clothes were burnt, things that were precious to me were stolen or broken…The staff didn't do nothing much but laugh when I told them."[1] Wadley reports on Polee, a seven-year veteran of the system, who says, "When it got out that I was gay, people around the neighborhood decided to beat me stupid. When I went back to the group home and told the staff, they said that I should learn to take care of myself." [2]

Joyce Hunter says, "So these kids wind up being homeless, turning to the streets, living in the subways and at risk for antisocial behavior, also at risk for prostitution and drugs. And AIDS. These kids on the street are very knowledgeable about that issue. Some of them can even personalize their knowledge and their vulnerability. But they don't care. Their sense of self is so low. 'Well, I don't care. I'm going to hell anyway. I'm gonna die anyway. Who cares?' If you've talked to these kids, you know that a lot of them are really, really neat kids—and just had a lousy break. I think the society has failed them. Social services have failed them."

As you listen to Lawrence, then, know that his story is not only far from unusual—it is not even close to worst-case.

"It was," Lawrence says, "like I started dreading school. I really started s-s-s-slipping. I was gonna turn into a total fuckup now. They put me in special ed. And I pictured myself as 'Hey, honey, I am *smart*. I'm not retarded.' It's just that I hated school, to be taunted and tantalized just because of my sexual preference."

By tenth grade, Lawrence had been moved again, to a family group home. Once again, he was "taunted and tantalized." By eleventh grade, things were so "scandalous" that he was moved to another group home—and then another.

"School was still hell. No one wanted to sit near me in the cafeteria. No one wanted to talk to me. I was treated like I had leprosy or AIDS. I was the freak kid. Kids would say, 'Oh, hi, Lawrence.' And I would speak back. And, 'Oh my God, you sound just like a girl.' Guys wanted to pick fights. People would say just a whole bunch of v-v-v-vulgar things to me. Every day I'd come home from school cryin'. Kids would yell from the school bus, 'Faggot!' Throw stuff out the window. Made me hate kids, hate school, hate life."

Lawrence discovered his first gay bar. He discovered drag. He'd leave the home in his regular clothes and change in a men's room somewhere. Then, if he was drunk, he'd say the hell with it, not change back; go back to the home as he was. He didn't care. " 'Cause I was ready to give up on life anyway."

He left the group home, moved in with some queens he had met. Lawrence figured that with the part-time job he had he could make out. His housemates then involved him in some kind of check-forging scheme with the fantasy that "we could quit our jobs, quit society, just have fun." They all went to jail for thirty days.

When he got out of jail, he tried going to live with his mother, whom he had been in touch with off and on. When she told him, "I wish you were never born. You're a little faggot," Lawrence suspected it was not going to work out. When she said, "I don't want you here. Get out," it was clear.

Lawrence was working. But now he had nowhere to live. "And my boss would complain, 'You're dirty. You're smelly. You're wrinkled. Where are you staying?' I'm like, 'I'm stayin' nowhere. My mom kicked me out.' In Virginia they have no men's shelters. So if you're out there on the streets, you're just out there on the streets. So that's where I was. I was an eighteen-year-old bum."

With his last paycheck he bought a bus ticket to Atlanta, hoping to stay with some friends. "The friends I *thought* I had—'I'm sorry, honey, we have no room. You've burnt your bridge here with your smart mouth and your little flaming ways.' " He stayed awhile at the Salvation Army. Then he was out on the mall. "And people ridiculing me. So here I am cryin'. Hungry. Nothin' to eat. No motivation to do anything because—who wants to hire someone that's smelly and dirty? Hasn't had a bath in weeks. And gay. Who desperately needs a haircut, a shave. No one's gonna hire that person. And no one did."

Some guy appeared who had been given a round-trip ticket at a place in New York called The Mission, and was willing to trade Lawrence his ticket back to New York for Lawrence's last seven dollars. "That was about seven o'clock. Nine o'clock I was on that bus to New York. No money. No clothes. Nothing to my name. Didn't have a thought of where I was goin' or nothing."

Some guys on the bus who'd just been released from prison gave him a change of clothes. In the bathroom at Port Authority he washed up, changed; found a comb, combed his hair. The guys on the bus had told Lawrence he could get help in Greenwich Village.

"I'm nineteen now, no place to go, no food. All I had was just, 'Go to the Village.' I went to the Village—no luck. I didn't know what to do. Just walk the streets. In case someone would pick you up and say, 'Hey, come home with me. You look like you need to be fed.' I'd heard about prostitution. But I thought you stand on the corner with-a-with-a-with-a miniskirt on and flash your leg, and they get out of a car, 'Hey, babe, stop.' That was my idea of prostitution. How wrong I was!

"New York then—it was snowing, it was cold. I did not have a coat. But I found a coat in a garbage can, shook it out. It was four sizes too big, but—wonderful, I'll use it as a blanket and a coat. And I went looking for jobs and all, filled out applications. I was so surprised at how friendly the people were. 'Sure, you can have an application. No problem.' I'm like, 'Well, I'm gay.' 'So what? Who isn't?' Oh fab! That was when I really came out of the closet. *I'm gay!* I don't care. I was starting to feel good—still hungry."

Lawrence found a gay bar. "I thought they'd go, 'Oh, he stinks, he needs a shave, he needs to cut his hair.' But there was one guy there, he said, 'I'm staying at Covenant House. Why don't you come stay there? You're not from New York. Someone's gonna grab you and kill you. New York is dangerous.' I went with him. It was fab. They fed me. I hadn't eaten in three days. All I'd had was—sh-shit I could find. They fed me, took me to the doctor for my asthma medication. They gave me plain clothes. They took me for a haircut. They gave me classified ads. Some tokens. Everything was fabulous. I found a job and the whole bit.

"So now I have money. A place to stay. Now I want to go see the sights of New York. I've never seen the Statue of Liberty. I've never seen Twin Towers, Rockefeller Center. Now's the chance to do it. That's the way I felt. I was doin' all that, I got kicked out. 'Lawrence, you violated the rules. You can't do this. You gotta be in at seven-thirty. To sign in. And then you gotta be in by nine-thirty.'

"I'm like, 'Well, wait a minute. Clubs don't open until ten o'clock. I'd have to be *in* before they open. I don't want that. I have my money. I'm makin' money on a job. I'll go out and get an apartment.' So I went out and got a hotel—which cost me twenty-one bucks a night. Fab. I'd party, stayed out all night. Doing drugs. Had a bad time. I was workin' as a messenger."

Wait, wait, "You could afford twenty-one dollars a night?"

"Yeah. I got a two-hundred-dollar paycheck. The first time I paid off a hundred—and the other hundred I could blow. Fab. But the money ran out. I started to get hungry again. I moved to this place on Saint Marks. Where I got hooked into the wrong crowd. Doing drugs. Having fun. Because I was doing good again.

"How fab. I'm gay. I'm in the Village. What more could I ask for? The piers were right there. And kids were teaching me how to trick. That you just go t-t-t-to the piers and snatch someone's glasses away. And tell 'em, 'You can get your glasses back if you give me twenty bucks.' The man wants his glasses. So he'll cough up the money. So five people for twenty or fifty bucks—you got a large sum of money. So I was able to go out and buy drugs, go out and drink. Go dance the night away and have a really fab time.

"And then the kids started teaching me how to mop clothes."

"Mop?"

"That's like—pull a girdle over the top of your pants—you gotta wear a long coat. Put a girdle on. You stand at the rack. You wear the girdle around your knees. You rip the tags off the stuff and put the stuff in your girdle. Then you pull the girdle up as high as it will go, and you walk out of the store fab. Then you go to Forty-second Street, and you sell them to the girls that be strippin' and stuff. 'Honey, *look* at these stockings. These are twenty-five-dollar stockings. They're yours for only three dollars.' 'God, these are the stockings I've been *dying* for! I'll give you fifty dollars for everything you've got in that bag.' I had two hundred dollars' worth of clothes and I sold them for fifty. No problem. 'Cause tomorrow I could get more. And more, more, more. A lot of kids now—that's the only way to survive—is doin' that. Goin' out and moppin' clothes.

"At this point, I got kicked out of Saint Marks—drinkin' and drug issues and shit like that. So I went back to Covenant House. And they were like, 'Well, we're sorry. You had your chance. We tried to help you. Now you have to prove yourself. You don't hang out. You don't go moppin'. You don't do this. You don't do that. You don't go bum and borrow and beg.' "

By this point, however, Lawrence had "got involved with this child" who had forged a check. "Another check-forgery thing I didn't need, right?" Whatever the complications involved (and I found them hard to follow), Lawrence now owed money. "Now I owe a hundred twenty-five and the only thing I can do is mop clothes. And two of my friends—they got caught stealing and they're in jail. So what can I do? You don't want to go mopping alone. 'Cause you want someone to cover you.

"So I went to the men's shelter in Brooklyn. And it's really horrible. Most of the guys there just got out of jail, where they were facing twenty years. They haven't seen their girlfriend in ages. There's rapes there. Just yesterday this guy was stabbed in the bathroom. Six buildings. And in Building One there was two murders there. Within a year. All these constant fights and beating-ups, and death threats.

"And I've been beaten up on the train. So many times it isn't funny, you know. 'He's a fag. Look at those faggots. Get 'em.' I got socked around pretty bad. I don't mind trains at night, b-b-b-b-b-but I was told..."

Suddenly, Lawrence looks alarmed: "What time is it?"

I tell him it's 7:35. We both look through the partition toward the storefront window. Since it's spring, it's still light, but getting on. Lawrence clearly is terrified of going back to the men's shelter after dark. And so, the wrap:

"Basically, what I'm doin' is tryin' to get my life together. Tryin' to get out of the shelter. I called my sister and I told her—we've had like casual contact—and she's like, 'Well, I'm sorry. I wish you the best of luck. Hang in there.' She's still in the foster home after I've been through jail, and through foster homes, and through beatings on trains. And she's in a little mommy-daddy foster home and having fun.

"Now I'm basically surviving day to day. And I risk going to jail by hopping trains. Because I don't have any money. That's why the Streetwork project—they don't provide housing—but they feed you, do your laundry, counsel you, help you find jobs."

Lawrence tells me he's just started school today, taking "cashier technology." ("They teach you travel agent, banking, ticket sales.")

"I just don't have any training in any specific field. Plus, it's kind of hard when they ask you, 'Well, where do you live? Where can we call you?' 'Well, I stay in a shelter, you know. The shelters don't have phones.' 'Well, we're sorry. We want somebody who's gonna be dependable. Who can come in when we need them.'

"The only thing I see facing me now is going back to the shelter and having to get back and forth every day to Manhattan—hopping the turnstile and risking going to jail. Hopefully, if I can just do that for the next three months I will be able to keep skimping and scraping and sliding by. Until I graduate. And get a job, and can afford to live near my job."

I had thought, to begin with, to buy Lawrence dinner. Now I feel badly. He clearly is frightened of traveling after dark. For all his "tricking" and "mopping," in this town (in this country?), Lawrence is less predator than prey.

I pull out twenty bucks. "Listen," I say, "I really meant to buy you dinner. You buy yourself something to eat. And the rest," I say sternly, "is to be doled out in small increments to the Transit Authority."

Notes

1. Carlton Wadley, "From the Frying Pan Into the Fire," *Foster Care Youth United*, Jan./Feb. 1994, p. 1.
2. Ibid, p. 4.

Discussion Questions

1. What does Lawrence's story illustrate about the traumas faced by gay children in the foster care system?

2. Do you believe lesbian and gay couples should be allowed to adopt children? Why or why not?

Writing Suggestion

Research further the issue of adoption by gay parents. Why do some people oppose this adoption? Do you think their reasons are legitimate?

Born to Be "Disruptive"?: Diagnosing and Drugging America's Children and Youth

Peter R. Breggin, M.D. & Ginger Ross Breggin

The War Against Children of Color:
Psychiatry Targets Inner City Youth

The past 25 years has led to a phenomenon almost unique in history. Methodologically rigorous research…indicates that ADD [attention deficit disorder] and hyperactivity as "syndromes" simply do not exist. We have invented a disease, given it medical sanction, and now must disown it. The major question is how we go about destroying the monster we have created. It is not easy to do this and still save face…

> —Diane McGuinness, "Attention Deficit Disorder:
> The Emperor's New Clothes, Animal 'Pharm,'
> and Other Fiction" (1989)

Diagnosis is too often antithetical to the interests of a particular youngster.

> —Jerome G. Miller, *Last One Over the Wall* (1991)

Zac is a small, blond-haired boy with blue eyes that shine with mischief and intelligence. At nine years old, his teachers and community have already decided his future for him. He fits all the profiles—restless, easily distracted, smart but doing just average in school, and too often into trouble. Chances are he'll be one of those boys who picks up "tagging" in the neighborhood by the time he is twelve. At fifteen he'll be known by the police, and if drugs don't get him, alcohol will.

How can they be so sure about his future? Because they've read about attention deficit-hyperactivity disorder (ADHD) in newspapers and magazines, and seen reports about it on TV.

Zac's school counselor and the teacher will have a chat about Zac and then invite his mother to a meeting to inform her that he has ADHD. His mother, who has already heard about the "disorder," will feel some relief even before she gets her son to the psychiatrist.

No one seems equipped or willing to deal with Zac's real problems—an absent father, a distracted and overwhelmed mother, an impatient teacher with an overcrowded classroom, and Zac himself with a wondrous abundance of energy that doesn't fit well into his world. So the psychiatrist prescribes Ritalin for Zac, and within an hour of taking the first dose, the boy is sitting much more quietly in class. His teacher is happy because her classroom is more peaceful. His principal is happy because the school can receive extra money for a special education class for Zac. His mother—who didn't know what to do about her son—now feels she is doing everything she can for him. And it *is* much more peaceful at home. She makes sure he takes his medicine every morning before leaving for school. The nurse at school has a bottle with Zac's name on it for the noontime dose.

Zac's story is being repeated around the United States. Every day during the school year, a million kids take their Ritalin. I discuss this massive drugging of America's children in *Talking Back To Ritalin* (1998). Hundreds of thousands more are taking other drugs, such as lithium and Prozac.

Recently *Newsweek* asked, "Where do the great minds come from? And why are there no Einsteins, Freuds or Picassos today?"[1] There is a tragic possibility: they are being psychiatrically diagnosed and drugged. Any biography of Einstein, Freud, or Picasso will demonstrate enough childhood "pathology" to warrant diagnosis and drugging with the inevitable suppression of his unique contribution to life.

How Could They Get Away with It?

The government's plans for an inner-city violence initiative shocked many Americans. How could the National Institute of Mental Health [NIMH] have thought it would get away with plans aimed at drugging tens of thousands of inner-city children? In reality, the government had no reason to anticipate taking flak. NIMH has been pushing drugs for children for many years all across America, and there has been no public outrage. The media seem uncritically accepting of the diagnosing and the drugging of children, as psychologists and psychiatrists join hands with parent groups devoted to managing children medically.

Throwing "The Book" at Children

Periodically, committees of the American Psychiatric Association update the association's *Diagnostic and Statistical Manual of Mental Disorders (DSM)*. The current version is the third edition, revised, published in 1987 and called *DSM-III-R* (See Breggin, 1998, for a discussion of *DSM-IV*).

In psychiatry, diagnoses tend to be used very loosely, with considerable reliance on subjective impressions. Hardly any psychiatrists can recite the association's more or less official requirements for the diagnoses they routinely use, and rarely do they turn to the manual itself to make sure a patient meets all the standards. The standards themselves are controversial even within the profession. But they are important in setting clinical and research trends, and they tell us a great deal about official psychiatric dogma. Their very existence creates a strong, if misleading, impression of validity for diagnosing in general.

The diagnosing and drugging of America's children is rationalized on the basis of the *DSM*. Frederick Goodwin's plans for the inner city and most of NIMH's research funding were based on its diagnoses.

The same diagnoses influence how millions of parents and teachers view the children in their care. Anyone who deals with kids has heard of "hyperactivity," or ADHD, and many non-professionals are sure they can diagnose it.

The DBDs

The children we're concerned with are usually diagnosed as suffering from one or another of the disruptive behavior disorders—the DBDs. The DBDs are divided into attention deficit-hyperactivity disorder (ADHD), or sometimes just attention deficit disorder (ADD); oppositional defiant disorder; and conduct disorder. These diagnoses often overlap each other, and NIMH often refers to them as one group, the DBDs.[2]

The *DSM-III-R* states that DBD children are "characterized by behavior that is socially disruptive and is often more distressing to others than to the people with the disorders." The "illness" consists of being disruptive to the lives of adults—a definition that seems tailored for social control.

Oppositional Defiant Disorder

To be diagnosed as having oppositional defiant disorder a child must meet five of the following nine criteria:

1. often loses temper
2. often argues with adults
3. often actively defies or refuses adult requests or rules, e.g., refuses to do chores at home
4. often deliberately does things that annoy people, e.g., grabs other children's hats
5. often blames others for his or her own mistakes
6. is often touchy or easily annoyed by others
7. is often angry and resentful
8. is often spiteful and vindictive
9. often swears or uses obscene language.

What child with any spunk would not qualify—at least at some time in his or her life? And once diagnosed, the label sticks. And while some children might fit only two or three of the criteria, that would not prevent them from being diagnosed. After the *DSM-III-R* committee designs the official criteria, individual mental health professionals freely indulge in their own subjective impressions.

It doesn't matter that the child has good reasons for being angry or upset. The diagnostic manual specifically states that these children feel justified about being angry or resentful toward the adults around them. To make matters worse, the displays of anger and resentment may exist in only one situation, such as home or school.

Any child in serious conflict with adults would surely end up fitting the diagnosis. Children—especially little ones—aren't equipped to handle conflict with adults by staying cool and acting mature. They aren't equipped to handle their painful emotions without showing them. Since the diagnosis can include "mild" cases that cause "only minimal or no impairment in school and social functioning," it encompasses every kid in the world who's got any gumption.

It's as if the committee members added up all the things their own kids ever did to aggravate them and then took revenge. At best these so-called disease criteria are a hodgepodge of things that boys (as discussed below most DBD kids *are* boys) do that particularly annoy adults.

Who's Got the Problem?

If the list of criteria for oppositional defiant disorder has any use, it identifies children who have lost respect and trust for the adults around them. This shouldn't red flag the children. It should red flag the adults.

When a small child, perhaps five or six years old, is persistently disrespectful or angry, there is always something wrong in that child's life—something over which the child has little or no control. Typically, the child is not being respected, because children learn more by example than by anything else. When treated with respect, they tend to respond respectfully. When loved, they tend to be loving. While the source of the child's upset may end up being more complicated than that—perhaps the parent is too afraid or distracted to apply rational discipline and lets the child run wild—the source always lies in the larger world. Children do not, on their own, create severe emotional conflicts within themselves and with the adults around them.

Diagnosing a child as suffering from oppositional defiant disorder is a means of denying adult responsibility and shifting blame to the wounded child.

Children aren't "spoiled" or "unruly" by nature; but this stigmatizing label implies they are. These children are usually more energetic, more spirited, and more wonderful than their parents and teachers can handle. Yet they are being called "mentally ill"—a label that can follow them into adulthood to ruin their future lives.

Conduct Disorder

For Goodwin and other biopsychiatrists, conduct disorder is a genetic and biological precursor to adult antisocial personality disorder, criminality, and physical aggression. The goal of the violence initiative—and a raft of related research being carried on at NIMH—is to identify and treat these children before they become a menace to society.

The *DSM-III-R* states, "In *Conduct Disorder* all of the features of Oppositional Defiant Disorder are likely to be present..." It is a continuum from labeling the child "pretty bad" to labeling him "very bad."

In the old authoritarian system, supposedly bad kids were yelled at and spanked. In the new authoritarian psychiatry, "mentally ill" children are given drugs and hospitalized. While we do not advocate yelling at kids or spanking them, these methods can be less damaging and demoralizing than a psychiatric label, drugs, and a mental hospital. Nowadays it is safer to be labeled bad than mentally ill.

To be labeled "conduct disorder," a child must meet a mere three of thirteen criteria. It's not worth repeating the criteria word for word, but we can catch the flavor of the first five: (1) stealing on the sly ("without confrontation of a victim") at least twice, (2) running away from home "overnight at least twice," (3) "often lies," (4) fire setting, and (5) "often truant."

The APA diagnostic manual remarks that the first three items are the most "discriminating"—the most consistently effective in making the diagnosis. Yet these three criteria simply reflect a child in conflict with adults.

Why Do Children Lie?

In order for lying to qualify as a criteria for conduct disorder, the child must lie "other than to avoid physical or sexual abuse." Yet it is impossible for any psychiatrist to know why a child is lying, and whether the child is being threatened with physical or sexual abuse. And why focus on physical and sexual abuse? Children can react at least as fearfully to purely emotional threats, such as abandonment or loss of love. Probably the single most common reasons children lie is that they don't trust their parents or authorities to be fair, empathic, helpful, or benign.

The *DSM-III-R* must make believe that psychiatrists can discern whether or not children have good reasons for lying. If children do have good reasons to lie, then it looks absurd and unjust to label them mentally ill.

Children who lie are almost always afraid and distrustful; they believe they are lying in self-defense. Instead of reflexively resorting to punishment or psychiatric diagnosis, it is better for their parents to focus on earning their children's trust.

Attention Deficit-Hyperactivity Disorder

The official standard for ADHD requires any eight of fourteen items. The first five items are described as the most useful or discriminating, in descending order, and include:

1. often fidgets with hands or feet or squirms in seat (in adolescence, may be limited to subjective feelings of restlessness)
2. has difficulty remaining seated when required to do so
3. is easily distracted by extraneous stimuli
4. has difficulty awaiting turn in games or group situations
5. often blurts out answers to questions before they have been completed.

The remaining nine in abbreviated form are: (6) difficulty following instructions, (7) attention problems, (8) jumping from one thing to another, (9) "has difficulty playing quietly," (10) "often talks excessively," (11) interrupts others, (12) "often does not seem to listen," and (13) "often loses things."

The public has been taught to think of ADHD as a specific "mental illness" with a genetic and biochemical cause. But as the list of criteria demonstrates, it's just one more DBD—another way a child gets labeled disruptive. As observed by Gerald Golden, a professor of pediatrics and neurology in Memphis and an advocate of the diagnosis, "The behavior is seen as being disruptive and unacceptable by parents and teachers…"

A dean of ADHD ideology, psychologist Russell Barkley, says, "Although inattention, overactivity, and poor impulse control are the most common symptoms cited by others as primary in hyperactive children, my own work with these children suggests that noncompliance is also a primary problem."[3] But who can blame children for being noncompliant with Barkley? Not only does he want to drug them, but he blames nothing on the parent and everything on the child. As he puts it, "there is, in fact, something 'wrong' with these children" (p. 4). As for the parents, he continually makes clear there's nothing wrong with them. That's how he has become so popular with so many parents.

Talking Back to Ritalin (Breggin, 1998) describes recent *DSM-IV* changes in the diagnosis, including separating ADHD from the DBDs. The committee found that while disruptive behavior and attention problems "often occur together," "some" ADHD children are not hyperactive and disruptive.[4] The drugs, however, continue to be used for behavioral control.

Diagnoses Tailored to Social Caste

ADHD tends to be a middle-class diagnosis. Most ADHD kids could as easily be called oppositional defiant disorder or conduct disorder. But because they come from "good families" in a "good neighborhood," they get called ADHD. In the inner city, the same behavior in an ethnic minority child is more likely to earn a label of mental retardation (MR) or severely emotionally disturbed (SED).

Instead of the relatively interesting high-tech teaching programs offered to some children labeled ADHD, inner-city children are likely to be shunted into special education.[5] Many will be lied to and told that passing the general- equivalency-diploma (GED) exam is as good as getting a real diploma, and they'll drop out of school.

Cruel Diagnoses

A variety of ADHD scales are given to parents and teachers to rate their children and pupils. One of the most popular, the Revised Conner's Questionnaire, was recently brought to me by a parent who was being urged to drug her child. The forty-eight items include "sassy," wanting to "run things," "daydreams," "shy," pouting, "feelings easily hurt," "childish… clings, needs constant reassurance," not getting along with siblings, bragging, and getting pushed around—or pushing around—other kids.

One of the items of the Conner's scale simply states "cruel." Two of its items are "Basically an unhappy child" and "Feels cheated in the family circle." We think it's cruel and unjust to label such a child mentally ill instead of examining the problem in the family.

The Conner's Abbreviated *Teacher* Questionnaire, with only ten items, is even more simplistic and potentially abusive. The criteria include restlessness, overactivity, failing to finish things, fidgeting, and so on. It's an inventory of the ways children can annoy and frustrate their teachers.

A Disease That Goes Away When Kids Get Attention

The symptoms or manifestations of ADHD often disappear when the children have something interesting to do or when they are given a minimal amount of adult attention. This is agreed upon by all observers and even indirectly finds its way into the *DSM-III-R* The manual specifies that the symptoms may not be apparent while the child is playing a videogame or in a "novel setting" or even being examined by the doctor.

Supposedly "impossible" ADHD kids usually do wonderfully during the two hours or so that they are around my home office—playing around the back yard, visiting with my wife in the house, or talking seriously in a family session about how to get more attention from their parents. Most advocates of ADHD as a diagnosis also note that it tends to go away during summer vacation.

Whose Disease Is This, Anyway?

Most so-called ADHD children aren't getting enough attention from their fathers, who are separated from the family, too preoccupied with other things, or otherwise impaired in their ability to parent. This is so typical that in *Toxic Psychiatry* I proposed calling the diagnosis DADD—dad attention deficit disorder.

The "cure" for these kids is more rational and loving attention from their dads. Young people are nowadays so hungry for the attention of a father that it doesn't even have to be their own. A whole bunch of seemingly impulsive, hostile children will calm down when a caring, relaxed, and firm adult male is around.

Arlington High School in Indianapolis was canceling many of its after-school events because of student unruliness, when a father happened to attend one of them.[6]

> That evening there was an odd quietness on [the father's] side of the auditorium. It turned out that when he would tell his group to settle down, some students would second him. One said: "That's Lena's father. You heard him. Be quiet; act right." Since then the school has begun to enlist volunteer dads for its after-school events.

At other times, the so-called disorder should be called TADD: teacher attention deficit disorder. The problem is almost always rooted in parents and teachers who feel overburdened, unable to reach out, or frustrated in trying to impose discipline.

Whose disease is ADHD?

Whose disease is oppositional defiant disorder?

Whose disease is conduct disorder? These are not our children's problems, they are ours.

Every Therapist Needs a Magic Wand

Recently an eight-year-old girl showed astonishment after sitting for only a few minutes with her parents and me in my office. She practically yelled, "Wow, is this different."

"How?" I asked her.

"Have you ever tried to talk to a wall with ears and a pad?" She pointed at the wall behind me. Humor, anger, and pain came together as she repeated her impression of her previous psychiatrist, "Like that wall, only with ears and a pad."

If possible, I try to meet new clients—children and their families—in my back yard by the fish pond. I want the youngster to know right away that this is going to be different—an experience aimed at making them comfortable and providing for their basic needs. I want the parents to realize the same thing.

Often it's obvious in a few minutes that there are serious family conflicts. As the little boy eagerly leans over the pond, Dad may be standing back as if he has no idea how to play or to enjoy himself. Mom may be dragging on her son's arm to "keep him from falling in." Dire warnings may be issued concerning the child's malicious tendencies. Meanwhile, I'm standing by thinking to myself, "This looks like a really nice kid. How can he stand this?"

Recently a ten-year-old boy, Tommy, came to me with his parents. At the pond, Mom seemed relaxed and in touch with her son, but Dad was so aloof I assumed he was a new stepfather. In the session, when I spoke of him as the stepfather, his wife said, "See, I told you, you don't even act like his real father."

In the office, I asked Tommy if he'd been told why he was here.

"Yeah," he said, "You're the doctor who doesn't believe in drugs for my ADHD."

Tommy even knew the acronym for attention deficit-hyperactivity disorder.

"It's worse than that," I kidded him. "I'm the doctor who doesn't even believe in ADHD."

I then explained to Tommy that there was nothing at all wrong with him and that I wouldn't make any diagnosis. Instead, I would help his parents understand how to meet his basic needs and help all of them learn how to resolve their daily and frequently severe conflicts.

Later in the session, I gave Tommy a "magic wand"—a long clear plastic tube filled with colorful sparkles. With his parents' agreement, he could point the wand at them and ask them to change anything about the way they relate to him. The wand, I said, would ensure that they would pay attention to his requests. They might not want to or be able to comply, I added, but they would listen, and we would take seriously whatever he said.

Tommy of course realized there was no magic in the wand. He knew exactly what was going on. We were empowering him to express himself.

Tommy pointed the wand at Dad and said, "I'd like you to spend more time with me. Not going along shopping or stuff like that—fun time."

Tommy's parents told him that we had already come to the same conclusion— that he had DADD, dad attention deficit disorder. Tommy thought that was very funny and right on the mark. We went on to discuss what Tommy meant by fun and arrived at agreements on activities that he and Dad could enjoy sharing. We talked about how Dad seldom played—not even grown-up entertainment like golf or going to the movies—and how it would be beneficial to him to learn to play with his son.

We then talked about the conflicts that were spoiling life in the family—how to deal with them in a non-punitive, empathic fashion. We were able to narrow down disciplinary issues to two or three minimum areas—everyone in the family treating each other with respect, and Tommy learning to take over doing his homework and going to bed at agreed-upon times.

Singing All the Way Home

Later Tommy's parents told me that he was singing in the car on the way home. He hadn't done that since he was a small child. Yet how many children leave a psychiatrist's office singing? None, after a diagnosis and drugs.

Within a few weeks, Dad had transformed his relationship with his son—spending more time with him, more openly expressing affection toward him, and limiting discipline to the most minimal essentials that the entire family had agreed upon. He had given up punishing Tommy and instead relied on a caring relationship to ensure cooperation. Tommy was "one hundred percent better."

Tommy's parents are well-meaning, mature people. They needed help in relating to their son. Other parents may also need help in getting their school to address the basic needs of their children, and sometimes the therapist may have to confer directly with teachers. In my experience, when parents and teachers are well-motivated, the children "get better" within a very short time. When parents and teachers aren't well-motivated, it's unjust and perhaps criminal to drug the child as an alternative.

Do Psychiatrists Have Magic Wands?

Psychiatrists, pediatricians, neurologists, and medical professionals in general do not necessarily have special gifts with children. They have no special capacity to love kids. They have no guaranteed capacities for relating to parents, sizing up family situations, or figuring out what's wrong in school.

What these professionals do have is the talent for getting accepted into highly competitive, scientific training programs, and then for graduating from them. They have had to distinguish themselves as bookworms and lab moles, and if they are well suited to being with children, it is a quality they have preserved despite their training.

Becoming a medical specialist is so long and arduous that it often discourages people who delight in human relations, children, and family life. Now that psychiatry is obviously dominated by biology and behaviorism, young doctors who choose to enter the field are likely to be especially aloof and insensitive.

The medical training experience itself flattens the child within every adult by suppressing the imaginative, playful, intuitive side of the future professional. Psychiatrists must learn to categorize people as if they are defective devices, and to lock them up and drug them against their will. They must also agree to give shock treatment or end up getting fired from their training programs. The experience pushes them toward becoming power-oriented and authoritarian, and hardens them to the suffering they cause. It makes them comfortable in suits and lab coats, and uncomfortable getting down on the floor with a child.

Many psychiatric residency programs no longer provide extensive training in talk therapy. Despite the public's misconceptions, they do not require the future psychiatrist to undergo psychotherapy or even to attend an occasional workshop in human relations. What do they learn? The *DSM* diagnoses, genetic and biochemical theories, and drugs. Parents who have read a few self-help or parenting books, and have perhaps attended a few human relationships seminars, probably know more about modern psychology than most psychiatrists, pediatricians, or neurologists. And by natural bent, the average parent is likely to be more intuitive and empathic as well.

The selection and training of psychiatrists especially tends to discourage the development of those all-important qualities.

By selection and training, a psychiatrist is among the least likely persons to help a child or a family with its problems. Now that the profession is so thoroughly dominated by the medical approach, a psychiatrist is likely to do more harm than good.

Professionally Discredited

We are not alone in believing that ADHD and other childhood "disorders" do not exist as genuine medical or psychiatric syndromes.[7] In 1993 Fred Baughman, Jr., a neurologist in La Mesa, California, noted that studies have failed to confirm any definite improvement from the drug treatment of these children. He concluded his critique with these neglected questions:

> What is the danger of having these children believe they have something wrong with their brains that makes it impossible for them to control themselves without a pill? What is the danger of having the most important adults in their lives, their parents and teachers, believe this as well?

Baughman cites estimates of the frequency of ADHD that vary from one in three to one in one thousand. He therefore asks, "Is attention deficit-hyperactivity disorder, after all, in the eye of the beholder?"

The eye-of-the-beholder theme echoes the thoughts of Diane McGuinness, who has systematically debunked ADHD as the "emperor's new clothes." But psychiatry in general shows no inclination to admit that it's parading around naked when it comes to diagnosing children.

A Physical Basis to ADHD?

A 1990 study led by NIMH's Alan Zametkin received a great deal of publicity for finding increased brain metabolism in positron emission tomography (PET) scans of adults with a history of ADHD in childhood. However when the sexes were compared separately, there was no statistically significant difference between the controls and ADHD adults. To achieve significance, the data was lumped together to include a disproportionate number of women in the controls. In addition, when individual areas of the brains of ADHD adults were compared to the same areas of the controls' brains, no differences were found. It is usually possible to massage data to produce a particular result, and Zametkin's study is a classic example of such massaging.

Since ADHD is not a disorder but a manifestation of conflict, we doubt that a biological cause will ever be found. In 1991, Gerald Golden put it simply:

> Attempts to define a biological basis for ADHD have been consistently unsuccessful. The neuroanatomy of the brain, as demonstrated by neuroimaging studies, is normal. No neuropathologic substrate has been demonstrated...

No Specific Drug Treatment

Contemporary experts agree that Ritalin affects all children in the same way—not just "hyperactive ones."[8] Within an hour after taking a single dose, any child will

tend to become more obedient, more narrow in his or her focus, more willing to concentrate on humdrum tasks and instructions. Parents in conflict with a little boy can
hand him a pill, knowing he'll soon be more docile.

It is commonly held that stimulants have a paradoxical effect on children compared to that on adults. In the past, I've accepted that view; but I've now begun to
believe it isn't true. The drug probably affects children and adults in the same way.
At the doses usually prescribed by physicians, children and adults alike are "spaced
out," rendered less in touch with their real feelings, and hence more willing to concentrate on boring, repetitive tasks.

The British are much more cautious about using stimulants for children. The
1992 *Oxford Textbook of Clinical Psychopharmacology and Drug Therapy* suggests that
stimulants may work in children the same way they impact on rats, by "inducing
stereotyped behavior in animals, i.e. in reducing the number of behavioral responses…" Stereotyped behavior is simple, repetitive, seemingly meaningless activity, and
is often seen in brain-damaged individuals. The textbook states somewhat sugges-
tively, "It is beyond our scope to discuss whether or not such behavioral control is
desirable."[9]

At higher doses, both children and adults become more obviously stimulated into
excitability or hyperactivity. It's a matter of relative dose, but people vary in their
drug responsiveness, and a number of children and adults will become "hyper" and
more inattentive at the lower doses as well.[10]

Toxic Psychiatry

One way to understand the routine effect of any psychiatric drug is to look at its
more extreme or toxic effects. The clinical or "therapeutic" effect is likely to be a less
intense expression of the toxic effect. In discussing Ritalin's "cognitive toxicity,"
James M. Swanson and his co-authors summarized the literature:

> In some disruptive children, drug-induced compliant behavior may be accompanied
> by isolated, withdrawn, and overfocused behavior. Some medicated children may seem
> "zombie-like" and high doses which make ADHD children more "somber," "quiet,"
> and "still" may produce social isolation by increasing "time spent alone" and decreas-
> ing "time spent in positive interaction" on the playground.[11]

Meanwhile, as they confirm, there's no evidence that Ritalin improves learning
or academic performance.[12]

The Long-Term Effects "Remain in Doubt"

Parents are not told that years of research and clinical use have failed to confirm
any positive long-term effects from Ritalin in behavior or academic performance. As
NIMH succinctly stated, "The long-term effects of stimulants remain in doubt."[13]
The FDA-approved information put out by the drug company CIBA-Geigy admits
"Long-term effects of Ritalin in children have not been well established."[14] Yet
Ritalin is typically advocated as a long-term treatment.

NIMH further states that studies have demonstrated short-term effects such as
reducing "classroom disturbance" and improving "compliance and sustained atten-

tion." But it recognizes that the drugs seem "less reliable in bringing about associated improvements, at least of an enduring nature, in social-emotional and academic problems, such as antisocial behavior, poor peer and teacher relationships, and school failure."

While estimating that "between 2 and 3 percent of all elementary school children in North America receive some form of pharmacological intervention for hyperactivity," NIMH continues to encourage giving Ritalin to increasing numbers of children.

Ritalin and Amphetamines

Parents are seldom told that Ritalin is "speed"—that it is pharmacologically classified with amphetamines, has the same effects, side effects, and risks. Yet this is well-known in the profession. For example, the American Psychiatric Association's tome *Treatments of Psychiatric Disorders* (1989) observes that cocaine, amphetamines, and methylphenidate (i.e., Ritalin) are "neuropharmacologically alike." As evidence, the textbook points out that abuse patterns are the same for the three drugs; that people cannot tell their clinical effects apart in laboratory tests; and that they can substitute for each other and cause similar behavior in addicted animals.[15] The *DSM-III-R* confirms these observations by lumping cocaine, amphetamine, and Ritalin abuse and addiction into one category. The Food and Drug Administration (FDA) classifies Ritalin in a high addiction category, Schedule II, which also includes amphetamines, cocaine, morphine, opium, and barbiturates.

Before it was replaced by other stimulants in the 1980s, Ritalin was one of the most commonly used street drugs.[16] In our home town of Bethesda, youngsters nowadays sell their prescribed Ritalin to classmates, who abuse it along with other stimulants. In working with various community groups, I often hear anecdotal reports of individuals who have graduated from using medically prescribed Ritalin to alcohol or street drugs, and I have seen some cases of this in my own practice.

Like any addictive stimulant, Ritalin can cause withdrawal symptoms, such as "crashing" with depression, exhaustion, withdrawal, irritability, and suicidal feelings. Parents will not think of a withdrawal reaction when their child gets upset after missing even a single dose. They will mistakenly believe that their child needs to be put back on the medication.

While it is true that doctors don't often report these and many other Ritalin side effects, harmful reactions are probably far more common than the literature suggests. Except when a drug is brand new, doctors almost never report or publish negative side effects. Many physicians do not know there is a mechanism for informing the drug companies and the FDA.[17] In addition, advocates of psychiatric drugs for children have proven themselves especially unwilling to examine or underscore their dangerous effects.

More Facts Withheld from Parents

Parents are not told that Ritalin, as a stimulant, can cause the very things it is supposed to cure—inattention, hyperactivity, and aggression. When this happens, the child is likely to be given higher doses of the drug, or an even stronger agent, such as the neuroleptics Mellaril or Haldol, resulting in a vicious circle of increasing drug toxicity.

Rarely are parents informed that Ritalin can cause permanent disfiguring tics. I've recently seen the case of a young boy in whom routine dosage produced frequent, disfiguring muscle spasms and tics of the head, neck face, eyes, and mouth.

It is sometimes explained to parents that Ritalin can suppress growth (height and weight), but the explanation is usually given in a manner calculated not to frighten them. Much of the brain's growth takes place during the years in which children are given this drug; but doctors don't tell parents that there are no studies of the effect of this growth inhibition on the brain itself. If the child's body is smaller, including his head, what about the contents of his skull? And if size can be reduced, what about more subtle and perhaps immeasurable brain deformities?

Parents are infrequently informed that like any form of speed, Ritalin can often make children anxious and sometimes cause them to behave in bizarre ways that seem "crazy."

Most surely, parents will not be told about any danger of permanent brain damage from long-term exposure to Ritalin. But how then to account for the following: no consistent brain abnormalities have been found in children labeled ADHD, but one study has found brain shrinkage in adults labeled ADHD who have been taking Ritalin for years.[18] The authors of the study suggested "cortical atrophy may be a long-term adverse effect of this [Ritalin] treatment."

Whenever researchers claim to find a biological defect supposedly caused by mental illness, they rush to the media and garner publicity. But when a researcher finds evidence that psychiatric drugs are producing detectable brain damage, no one is listening, no one cares, no one even bothers to investigate further.

Finally, parents will not be told by their doctor that there are almost guaranteed non-drug methods of improving the conduct of nearly all so-called DBD children— through more interesting, engaging schools and through more rationally managed, loving family relationships.

Parents frequently contact me because their child's private or public school is insisting upon drug treatment. Sometimes the school has referred the parents to a specific doctor who is inclined to prescribe drugs. Sometimes the school threatens to take punitive measures if the parents don't go along with a prescription of Ritalin. There are instances of public schools refusing to allow children to continue until they have been placed on drugs.

Ritalin for African-American Children

When I travel around the country for speeches and workshops, I frequently hear stories about African-American parents being pushed or coerced into accepting Ritalin for their children, sometimes with very harmful results.

Poor, minority parents are especially vulnerable to pressure from the schools. They may be afraid to challenge professional advice, for fear of endangering their resources, such as school programs or welfare payments. They don't have the where-withal to get second opinions. Many live in single-parent households without an effective male presence and may be thankful for any offer of help. For example, they are aware of how many inner-city boys turn to or fall victim to violence and they will try almost anything to prevent that eventuality.

Is ADHD an American Disease?

ADHD is rarely diagnosed in countries with more evident concern for children, such as Denmark, Norway, and Sweden, where psychiatric drugs of any kind are hardly ever given to children. A doctor working in Britain's National Health Service is not allowed to give Ritalin in routine practice because it is not on the approved drug list of the *British National Formulary*. The doctor could prescribe amphetamines, which have a similar effect, but this is discouraged and rarely done.

Data from the International Narcotics Control Board for 1991 showed that the United States, closely followed by Canada, uses proportionally much more Ritalin than most other countries.[19] If Ritalin use is a comparative measure of national attitudes toward children, North America is the most pedist region in the world.

Is ADHD a Boy's Disease?

Males are far more frequently given DBD diagnoses than females.[20] Aside from feeling bored or in conflict with adults, why would boys ordinarily tend to act resentfully and rebelliously toward the authority of their mothers and female teachers? A partial answer is that they are trained to be that way toward women in general. In fact, most grown men in the world today resent being told what to do by women.

A multiplicity of factors contribute to the conflicts and confusion in little boys: how boys are trained to suppress their tender ("feminine") side and encouraged to be competitive, dominating, and hostile toward women; how these lessons are imprinted through TV and the entertainment media, and reinforced in sports and on the playground, as well as in the family and almost everywhere else in society.

It's a wonder that *any* boys learn to restrain themselves in the presence of women or to respect their mothers and female teachers. Add to this the boring, oppressive atmosphere of most schools, and it's a miracle that female teachers are able to manage young boys at all.[21]

Female DBDs?

If DBD is an extreme expression of being socialized as a boy, what's an extreme expression of being socialized as a girl? The female equivalent of DBD would be "compulsive *obedience* disorder." Its most common subcategory would be "compulsive *attention* disorder."

Girls are too often trained to sit still and listen to almost anything an authority says to them. They feel especially compelled to pay attention to everything almost any male says, even while the male is paying no attention whatsoever to them.

Why doesn't the *DSM-III-R* offer any diagnoses for children who are compulsively obedient or attentive? Because it is an instrument of social control and there's no need to suppress already overcontrolled girls and young women—or overcontrolled young men for that matter.

In our modern society, in which girls receive increasingly confusing messages about assertiveness, more and more young girls are being diagnosed with one or another DBD and are being drugged or hospitalized.[22] Often they are girls with potential leadership qualities.

Into the Loony Bin

In the suburbs, psychiatric hospitals have become what jails are for the inner city—alternatives to crumbling society and failing families and schools. In her 1993 book *And They Call It Help*, Louise Armstrong describes the combination of economic and social pressures, and flawed values, that has led escalating numbers of suburban white parents to dump their protesting children in psychiatric hospitals. She cites newspaper headlines aimed at exposing the abuse:

CAGED KIDS: Behave or Mom and Dad Will Put You in the Nuthouse.

TREATING TEENS IN TROUBLE: Can the Psychiatric Ward Fill In for the Family?

COMMITTED YOUTH: Why Are So Many Teens Being Locked Up in Private Mental Hospitals? [pp. 3–4]

Armstrong points out that 270,000 children under eighteen were hospitalized for psychiatric reasons in 1985—double the number from 1971. This is a disaster for our children, since the hospitals are humiliating and stigmatizing, and often do more harm than good. Isolation and physical restraint are common, and drugs are the norm. Visiting privileges and phone calls are heavily restricted, isolating the children from their families and communities. Frequently, the children are medicated with agents that can cause permanent brain damage or that have been largely untried on children and youth.

The psychiatric incarceration of children impacts on all children in the community. Among those who frequent our home, a few have been hospitalized, and everyone knows who they are and what they went through. Children who haven't been locked up still know enough to live in fear of it, especially when their parents raise it as a threat during family conflicts.

CH.A.D.D

Founded in 1987, Children with Attention Deficit Disorders (CH.A.D.D.) is an organization of parents who have children labeled with attention deficit disorders. CH.A.D.D.'s official policy views these children as suffering from genetic and biological problems. In the words of CH.A.A.D. president Sandra F. Thomas, "Our kids have a neurological impairment that is pervasive and affects every area of their life, day and night."

The politics and drug company financing of CH.A.D.D. are discussed and updated in more detail in *Talking Back to Ritalin* (Breggin, 1998).

CH.A.D.D. leaders claim that their children's emotional upset and anger is in no way caused by family conflicts, poor parenting, or inadequate schools. A recent CH.A.D.D. brochure headline announces: "Dealing with parental guilt. No, it's not all your fault." After stating that ADHD is a neurological disorder, the brochure goes on to explain:

Frustrated, upset, and anxious parents do not cause their children to have ADD. On the contrary, ADD children usually cause their parents to be frustrated, upset, and anxious.

CH.A.D.D. has followed the model of its adult counterpart, the National Alliance for the Mentally Ill (NAMI).[23] NAMI parents usually have grown offspring who are severely emotionally disabled, and they promote biochemical and genetic explanations, drugs, electroshock, psychosurgery, and involuntary treatment. NAMI also tries to suppress dissenting views by harrassing professionals who disagree with them.[24] Now NAMI has developed an affiliate, the National Alliance for the Mentally Ill—Child and Adolescent Network.[25] NAMI-CAN, like CH.A.D.D., believes in BBBD— biologically based brain diseases.

Power Sources

CH.A.D.D. and NAMI parents have developed enormous influence by joining forces with biologically oriented professionals, national mental health organizations, and drug companies. CH.A.D.D.'s National Professional Advisory Board, for example, includes NIMH biopsychiatric stalwarts Alan Zametkin and Judith Barkley, as well as C. Keith Conners and Barbara Ingersoll.

Where is the money coming from to support high-pressure lobbying, media campaigns, and upscale national conventions at hotels like the Chicago Hyatt Regency? CH.A.D.D.'s 1992 convention program, "Pathways to Progress, states:

> CH.A.D.D. appreciates the generous contribution of an educational grant in support of our projects by CIBA-Geigy corporation.

CIBA-Geigy manufactures Ritalin, the stimulant with the lion's share of the ADHD market.

NAMI has had equal success with its political efforts. It too is closely aligned with biological psychiatry and takes money from the drug companies.[26]

The combination is potent: parents who resort to the biomedical management of their children; professionals who make their living researching, promoting, and practicing it; and the drug companies who profit from selling their products. *There has been no corresponding national organization to protect children from psychiatric diagnosis and biomedical control, largely because there is no corresponding power base for more caring empathic approaches.* The International Center for the Study of Psychiatry and Psychology is trying to fill this vacuum by opposing the widespread psychiatric diagnosis and drugging of children.

Stifling All Rebellion

A recent CH.A.D.D. *Educators Manual* [27] was written with the collaboration of professionals, including Russell Barkley. It makes clear the intention to diagnose and drug children who won't conform to strict discipline:

> Attention Deficit Disorder is a hidden disability. No physical marker exists to identify its presence, yet ADD is not very hard to spot. Just look with your eyes and listen with your ears when you walk through places where children are—particularly those

places where children are expected to behave in a quiet, orderly, and productive fashion. In such places, children with ADD will identify themselves quite readily. They will be doing or not doing something which frequently results in their receiving a barrage of comments and criticisms such as "Why don't you ever listen?" "Think before you act." "Pay attention."

Children Are Not Adults in Small Bodies

Children, from the time they come into this world as infants, have an infinite number of tasks to learn and developmental goals to attain. Fortunately, nature has built in the impulses needed for the child to grow. For example, as an emerging toddler, a fourteen-month-old baby, newly walking, needs lots of time to practice that activity. Even as the baby is becoming mobile, he or she is also becoming curious about everything—from magazines to the dog's tail, from overflowing wastebaskets to the roll of toilet paper, the sooty fireplace to the broken paper clip you dropped a day ago.

This baby has a brain to develop, and is being helped in this task through natural curiosity. Young parents will often feel worn out when their child suddenly starts cruising through the house, looking for new excitement. But the baby's behavior is normal and absolutely essential for proper development and growth.

Instead of lamenting a highly active child, parents need to rejoice in this sign of vitality and intelligence, and to nurture it by providing lots of opportunity for their baby to explore, move about, and grow. But in the face of all the media coverage for ADHD, some parents will wonder if their child is "hyperactive."

Making a Home for Our Children

Children need to have their homes tailored to their needs. Author and educator Thomas Gordon, who developed Parent Effectiveness Training, puts it this way:

> Most parents...say they believe [their family home] is exclusively their home; the children, therefore, must be trained and conditioned to behave properly and appropriately. This means a child must be molded and scolded until he painfully learns what is expected of him in his parents' home. These parents seldom even consider making any major modifications in the home environment when a child is born into the home....

Gordon goes on to describe how he asks parents what changes they would make in their home if one of their parents was suddenly wheelchair-bound and needed to live with them. A long list of accommodations results from these discussions. Parents who think this through find they are then more willing to make changes in the home environment for their little child.

A home requires many accommodations for a small child—from locking up the poisons to installing baby gates and putting breakables well out of reach. As the child grows older, the changes need to evolve. A ten-year-old isn't going to pull books off a shelf and rip pages, but he may drag a chair around the kitchen and repeatedly climb up on it to reach the peanut butter. We realized at one point that our children were having to hop up on the counter to reach the dishes, so we rearranged the kitchen, placing dishes, snack foods, and other essentials on low shelves.

Parents ought to be thankful for every bit of spunk and spirit their children possess. It demands energy, attention, and involvement on our part as parents, but it will
result in bright, creative, spirited, and secure young adults.

Like Shining Stars

Our children relate to us mostly through home and school. In both places we
need a new devotion to their basic needs rather than to our old attitudes and ways.
Above all else, our children need a more caring connection with us, the adults in
their lives. This is now being realized in school systems throughout America as they
begin to abandon the large, factory-like facilities of the past in favor of "small is
beautiful."

There are many advantages to smaller schools, but the biggest one is this: they
allow teachers to get to know their students well enough to better meet their basic
educational and emotional needs. At the same time, small schools and classes meet
the teachers' basic needs for a satisfying, effective professional identity. Conflict can
be resolved more readily as it ideally should be—through mutually satisfying solutions—rather than through suppression.

The result of smaller, more caring schools? *The DBDs are disappearing.* There is no
better evidence for how the environment powerfully shapes the behavior that results
in children being psychiatrically diagnosed.

In a July 14, 1993, *New York Times* report entitled "Is Small Better? Educators
Now Say Yes for High School," Susan Chira reports:

> [S]tudents in schools limited to about 400 students have fewer behavior problems, bet-
> ter attendance and graduation rates, and sometimes higher grades and scores. At a
> time when more children have less support from their families, students in small
> schools can form close relationships with teachers.

Teachers in these schools have the opportunity for "building bonds that are particularly vital during the troubled years of adolescence."

Even students from troubled homes respond to smaller, more caring schools.
"They are shining stars you thought were dull," said New York City teacher Gregg
Staples. "If you're under a lot of pressure and stress, they help you through that," said
student Joy Grimage. "They won't put you down or put you on hold."

What a difference from "Behave...or else!" It's not that we don't know what our
children need. They need more of us—us at our best. The question is, "Are we willing to develop more meaningful relationships with them?"

Environment Molds the Child's Brain and Abilities

Ironically, while there is no convincing evidence that genetic brain disorders
cause abnormalities such as disruptive or aggressive behavior, there is increasing evidence that the developing brain has "plasticity" and is permanently influenced by
environmental conditions.[28] William Greenough of the University of Illinois at
Champaign-Urbana, for example, has found that rats exposed to an enriched environment with toys, food, exercise, and playmates have 25 percent more brain cell
connections on autopsy than animals raised in typical drab laboratory cages.

Craig Ramey of the University of Alabama has found similar results in children whose IQs and social skills are permanently raised by early enrichment programs. He also finds that PET scans demonstrated increased efficiency.[29] According to Ramey, "Early intervention appears to have had a particularly powerful preventive effect on children whose mothers had low IQs—while also benefiting other children from economically, socially or educationally disadvantaged backgrounds." Early enrichment programs are costly, but through prevention they end up saving money. Ramey also related his findings to violence prevention: "There's no real mystery about this. When you have high concentrations of people who don't have basic social skills— and being able to succeed in school is a universally required basic social skill—you have chaos."

The implications of brain plasticity are profound. If we don't provide a nurturing, enriched environment for children, they may be permanently disadvantaged by relatively undeveloped brains; while if we do provide the proper surroundings, children show more brain development and better social and academic skills. Under no circumstances should this rule out giving help to older children or adults who have grown up under deprived circumstances; human beings can always benefit from improved opportunities. But it argues strongly for the special importance of early environmental interventions, such as Head Start (research cited in Breggin, 1998).

"Curing the Child Without Treatment"

Children respond so quickly to improvements in the way adults relate to them that most children can be helped without being seen by a professional person. Instead, the professional can counsel the parents, teachers, and other concerned adults (Breggin, 1997b and 1998).

Many psychotherapists, for example, routinely practice "child therapy" without actually seeing any children. They help their adult patients become more loving or disciplined parents through the routine work of psychotherapy, indirectly transforming the lives of their children. The children "get better" sight unseen. These therapists, many of whom work only with adults, may not see themselves as child psychiatrists or child therapists. But they are doing more good for children than the professionals who see and diagnose them, and then give drugs.

Children don't have disorders; they live in a disordered world. When adults provide them a better environment, they tend quickly to get their lives together.

Children can eventually become so upset, confused, and self-destructive that they internalize the pain or become compulsively rebellious. They may need the intervention of a therapeutic—unconditionally caring—adult to help them overcome their inner suffering and outrage. Sometimes these children can benefit from learning how to help ease the conflicted situation. But they should never be given the idea that they are diseased or defective or are the primary cause of their conflicts with their schools and families.

Children can benefit from guidance in learning to be responsible for their own conduct; but they don't gain from being blamed for the trauma and stress that they are exposed to in the environment around them. They need empowerment, not humiliating diagnoses and mind-disabling drugs. Most of all, they thrive when adults show concern for and give attention to their basic needs as children.

Notes

1. Begley. S. (1993, June 28). "The puzzle of genius." *Newsweek*, p. 46.
2. The DSM-III-R (American Psychiatric Association, 1987) observes. "Studies have indicated that in both clinic and community samples, the symptoms of these disorders covary to a high degree." A recent NIMH study of DBDs (Kruesi et al., 1992) similarly observes, "'Pure' conduct disorder or 'pure' opposition disorder are relatively rare in clinical samples, with most cases also qualifying for an attention-deficit disorder diagnosis."
3. Barkley, R. (1981). *Hyperactive Children: A Handbook for Diagnosis and Treatment*. New York: Guilford Press., p. 13.
4. Fasnacht, B. (1993, September 3). "Child and adolescent disorders get fine-tuning in DSM-IV." *Psychiatric News*, p. 8.
5. See Gaines, D. (1991). *Teenage Wasteland: Suburbia's Deadend Kids*. New York: HarperPerennial, concerning special education.
6. Smith, B. D. (1993, August 1). "Relaxed, firm dads save school events." *The New York Times: Education Life supplement* p. 5.
7. According to Richard E. Vatz of Towson State University, "Attention-deficit disorder (ADD) is no more a disease than is 'excitability.' It is a psychiatric, pseudomedical term." Frank Putnam, a director of one of NIMH's research units, recently applauded "the growing number of clinicians and researchers condemning the tyranny of our psychiatric and educational classification systems." Putnam finds that it is "exceedingly difficult to assign valid classifications" to children, and yet "children are by far the most classified and labeled group in our society." He warns against "the institutional prescriptions of a system that seeks to pigeonhole them."
8. For example, Golden, G.S. (1991, March), "Role of attention deficit hyperactivity disorder in learning disabilities." *Seminars in Neurology*, 11 (1):35 41, says "the response to the drug cannot be used to validate the diagnosis. Normal boys as well as those with ADHD show similar changes when given a single dose of a psychostimulant."
9. Grahame-Smith, D.G., and J. K. Aronson (1992). *Oxford Textbook of Clinical Pharmacology and Drug Therapy*. Oxford: Oxford University Press.
10. Compare this to the more familiar range of variability in response to coffee. Some people seem more relaxed after a cup or two; others quickly get too "hyper."
11. Citation numbers removed from the quote.
12. Reviewed in Breggin, P. (1991a). *Toxic Psychiatry: Why Therapy, Empathy and Love Must Replace the Drugs, Electroshock and Biochemical Theories of the 'New Psychiatry'* New York: St. Martin's Press; Coles, G. (1987). *The Learning Mystique: A Critical Look at "Learning Disabilities."* New York: Pantheon Books; McGuinness, D. (1989). "Attention deficit disorder: The emperor's new clothes, animal 'pharm,' and other fiction." In Fisher, S., and R. P. Greenberg (eds.). *The limits of biological treatments for psychological distress*, pp. 151-188. Hillsdale, NJ: Lawrence Erlbaum Associates; and Swanson, J. M., D. Cantwell, M. Lerner, K. McBurnett, L. Pfiffner, and R. Kotkin (1992, fall). "Treatment of ADHD: Beyond medication." *Beyond Behavior*, 4(1):13-22.
13. Regier, D. A., and A. I. Leshner (1992, February). *Request for applications: cooperative agreement for a multi-site, multimodel treatment study of attention-deficit hyperactivity disorder (ADHD)/attention-deficit disorder (ADD)*. MH-92-03. Washington, D.C.: Department of Health and Human Services; Public Health Service; Alcohol, Drug Abuse and Mental Health Administration; and NIMH. Discussed later in chapter.
14. *Physicians' Desk Reference* (PDR) (1993). Montvale, NJ: Medical Economics Company.

15. American Psychiatric Association (1989). *Treatments of pychiatric disorders: A task force report of the American Psychiatric Association.* Washington, D.C.: APA, p. 1221. Also see Breggin, 1991a. Advocates of Ritalin point out that addiction is rarely if ever reported in the literature, but the same literature also fails to emphasize any Ritalin side effects, including withdrawal symptoms, which are relatively common in clinical practice.

16. Spotts, J. V., and C. A. Spotts (1980). *Use and abuse of amphetamine and its substitutes.* Rockville Maryland: National Institute on Drug Abuse. DHEW Publication No. (ADM) 80-941. Some of the medical reports in the compendium point out that taking Ritalin once a day to deal with personal problems or conflicts constitutes an abuse.

17. Goodman, A. G., T. W. Rall, A. S. Nies, and P. Taylor (1991). *The Pharmacological Basis of Therapeutics, 8th edition.* New York: Pergamon Press, p. 78, observe, "Over 40% of physicians are not aware that the FDA has a reporting system for adverse drug reactions...." Also see Breggin, P. (1993a). "News and views on psychiatry: The FDA—More harm than good?" *The Rights Tenet* pp. 3-5, and Breggin, P., and G. Breggin (1994). *Talking Back to Prozac.* New York: St. Martin's Press.

18. Nasrallah, H., J. Loney, S. Olson, M. McCalley-Whitters, J. Kramer, and C. Jacoby (1986). "Cortical atrophy in young adults with a history of hyperactivity in childhood." *Psychiatric Research,* 17:241-246.

19. John George provided us with these figures. Within the United States in 1991, the dozen states and territories with the highest per capita use of Ritalin, in descending order, were Idaho, Michigan, Utah, Ohio, Iowa, Alaska, Montana, Georgia, Indiana, Wisconsin, Maryland, and Virginia. The lowest in descending order were New York, South Dakota, California, Hawaii, Maine, Puerto Rico, Guam, and the Virgin Islands.

20. According to the *DSM-III-R,* ADHD occurs in boys up to six to nine times more frequently than in girls and conduct disorder occurs in 9 percent of boys and 2 percent of girls.

21. About schools, see Kozol, J. (1991). *Savage Inequalities—Children in America's Schools.* New York: Crown Publishers; and Armstrong, L. (1993). *And They Call It Help: The Psychiatric Policing of America's Children.* New York: Addison-Wesley Publishing Co.

22. For girls who grow up to become caricatures or exaggerations of the expected female role, psychiatry has proposed a controversial adult diagnosis: self-defeating personality disorder. This is an extension of Freudian ideas of "women's masochism" into modern psychology. It blames the tendency to fail on the women themselves when failure is in reality desired and even demanded of them by the male-dominated society. We shall never have a *DSM-III-R* diagnosis of "male dominator syndrome."

23. Breggin, 1991a.

24. Documented in Breggin, 1991a.

25. Armstrong, 1993.

26. See Breggin, 1991a. For example, NAMI's national director is officially invited to attend the closed board meetings of the American Psychiatric Association, and NAMI lobbies and promotes "mental health" in partnership with the association.

27. Fowler, M. (1992). *Educators manual: A project of the CH.A.D.D.* National Education Committee. Plantation, FL: CH.A.D.D.

28. Material for this section was taken from Kotulak, R. (1993, December 14). "Why some kids turn violent." *Chicago Tribune* p. 1. I have attended scientific conferences in which unpublished research presentations have confirmed these findings.

29. The brain scan findings require confirmatory research.

Discussion Questions

1. Why do the authors begin their chapter with a discussion of the nine-year-old Zac?

2. Why doesn't the public fight against the widespread use of Ritalin and other drugs used to control children?

3. What are the symptoms of ADD, "Conduct Disorder," and ADHD? How are these symptoms typical of "normal" children?

4. What is the real cause of ADHD, according to the authors? How should parents address these causes?

5. What are the dangers involved in taking Ritalin?

6. Why is the diagnosing of ADHD prevalent in America? What does this diagnosing have to say about the way we treat our children?

Writing Suggestion

Consider your own experience. Have you or someone you have known ever taken Ritalin? Why? How do you evaluate its effectiveness?

The Kind of Adults Our Children Need Us to Be

Peter R. Breggin, M.D.

Talking Back to Ritalin:
What Doctors Aren't Telling You About Stimulants for Children

I do not think people realize the tremendous impact that one person can have on another person's life. I know that when I became a mother, I wanted to give my children everything that I did not have. I knew in my heart that everything was not right with me. I knew that my emotions and behaviors were often out of my control, but I was sure I could cover all this up and be a good parent. I wanted so much in my heart to be a real mother to my children. I read every book I could get my hands on and watched other mothers so I could learn how to care properly for my son...I was considered to be a good person and a responsible parent by most of the people I know. However, when my son started to have problems in school, I was faced with a problem and was not sure how to solve it. I was drawn down the avenue of Ritalin.

—"Mrs. Blair" (1997)

Mrs. Blair, the mom who was trying so hard, took her son off Ritalin after a few months. Her mistake, she decided, was her belief that she "knew everything there is to know about loving children." She obtained help in improving her parenting.

No one knows everything about family life, parenting, or love. There are always turns and twists in our family relationships and often we need guidance to find the right path. With counseling, Mrs. Blair learned about herself:

Each problem that I had with my son was traced back to problems in my life. I do not find that easy to say, but it is the truth. It is also an awesome responsibility to know that our behavior can affect another person so much. It is also a great blessing to know that we can influence those around us in a healthy way. It is also a wake up call for us to take responsibility for our own lives so we can be a positive influence to others.

While Mrs. Blair's emphasis on her own responsibility is admirable, I don't want to suggest that ADHD-like behavior is primarily the result of faulty mothering. Many of the diagnosed children have nothing at all wrong with them. Others cannot conform to unrealistic expectations at home or at school. Many have excellent parents like Mrs. Blair who need to reconsider some of their parenting ideas and practices. And when children do have problems due to unmet needs or conflicts in the family, they often require more quality attention from their fathers. Mrs. Blair's failure to mention the boy's father suggests that his absence may be contributing to the family problems.

Mrs. Blair is a deeply religious woman who raises the question, "If God created us in his own image, why do so many people believe that most of our problems are genetic?" Mrs. Blair believes that giving Ritalin is an aspect of modern materialism:

> I was at the checkout at the Wal-Mart today and almost every front cover said something about body and beauty and how to improve everything that was external. But what about the inside? Why do we not feed our souls? If every child on Ritalin had more attention given to their emotional and spiritual growth, I wonder how many would still need the medicine. But first the parents have to recognize this need in themselves. Instead of turning to reasons and solutions outside of ourselves, maybe we should look internally for our answers because they are there, and they work.

You don't have to be religious to reject the idea of blaming the brains of children for the difficulties they face in adjusting to our adult world. You don't have to believe that children are created in God's image to know not to play God by drugging them into conformity with our expectations. From a religious or secular perspective, children should be treasured as unique beings with basic psychological or spiritual needs that we, as adults, are obligated to identify and to satisfy.

Why have we become so seemingly poor at treasuring our children and attending to their needs?

What's Really Needed

This is worth repeating: Knowing that a child fits into the diagnosis called ADHD gives us very little useful information about the child's inner life or about the child's home and school life. That the child fits the ADHD category tells us next to nothing about the child's real needs. To recognize each child's needs and to respond to them requires time, effort, patience, wisdom, and love. Even if a child displays the whole range of ADHD symptoms to a severe degree, it tells us nothing about what to do next except to carefully evaluate the source of the child's problem.

What's needed is a careful, informed, and loving evaluation of each individual child's needs. The following vignettes or sketches are very simplified but they reflect reality:

- The "over-active" or "hyperactive" child who may have more abundant energy than other children, and who needs more challenging outlets for physical and emotional self-expression;

- The "rebellious" or "negative" child who may have more autonomy and determination than most kids, and who needs a strong guiding hand that doesn't crush that gift;

- The "impulsive" child who may be unusually exuberant and daring, and who needs consistent discipline combined with imaginative guidance to channel all that vitality;

- The "day-dreamer" child who has a poetic soul and who needs especially creative nurturing and artistic outlets;

- The "sensitive" child who is shy and somewhat fearful, and needs an adult who is sensitive enough to respond to the child's needs in an empowering fashion;

- The "undisciplined" child who has a great deal of potential but lacks the patience and discipline to master it, and who needs a kind but firm role model of discipline;

- The "bored" child with a restless spirit who is especially bright and creative, and who needs more inspired learning opportunities;

- The "slow" child for whom ordinary expectations are frustrating and sometimes overwhelming, and who needs patience and more individualized educational opportunities;

- The "immature child" or "late bloomer" who is taking his or her time growing up, and who needs acceptance along the way;

- The "troubled child" who is undergoing a great deal of stress in a conflicted or disorderly home, and who needs his parents to get help for themselves;

- The "learning disabled" child who has difficulties with specific aspects of the school program, and needs individualized educational help, perhaps including tutoring, and a lot of reassurance that there's nothing wrong;

- The medically ill child who suffers from the effects of an old head injury, lead poisoning, thyroid disorder, medication side effects, or some other physical problem, and who needs a real medical evaluation, rather than a concocted diagnosis of ADHD;

- The severely abused or deprived child who suffers from an extreme lack of nurturing, abandonment, various kinds of abuse, or malnutrition, and who needs a social service intervention by appropriate agencies.

To these groups we may add "all school-age children," because all children need small classrooms, interesting educational materials, inspired teachers, and devoted parents. They all need a carefully balanced mixture of unconditional love, rational discipline, inspiring educational activities, and play. They all need good role models.

These are the types of children who get diagnosed as suffering from ADHD and who get subdued with stimulants and other medications. Do we *really* believe that drugs are the solution to the challenges that they present us, our families, and our schools?

Have You Ever Been A Child?

"I was a child once, were you?" It's a naive question, of course. We were all children. Yet so many of us seem to think and to act as if we cannot feel empathy for children—cannot put ourselves into a child's perspective.

It's a most remarkable phenomenon. All of us were children yet all of us tend to become impatient and critical with children as if there's no accounting for their irrational behavior. Despite our common ancestry as children, we all sometimes treat children as if they are as alien to us as an extra-terrestrial.

Being a child is always incredibly difficult. To start with, everyone seems bigger than you—and in the beginning, they are. For another thing, everyone seems to know more than you—and in the beginning they do. Everyone seems to have more power than you—more control over what happens—and of course they do.

And there's so much to learn—everything from how to talk to how to behave. Then there's the alphabet and reading, and numbers and math to master. As a child, it seems impossible to learn everything you're supposed to learn—and it is impossible. None of us ever catch up on everything we need to learn and to know as adults.

It's impossible to be a child without feeling bad about yourself at times. You make so many mistakes. You do so many dumb things. You cause embarrassment to your parents and even lose things and break things without meaning to. Then sometimes you just can't seem to help it—you do or say stuff that makes your parents seem to hate you. At least, it feels that way, like your parents wish you weren't around—and sometimes they do wish you weren't around. It makes you feel very badly about yourself, like maybe you shouldn't be around.

There are fights. Fights with your mom and dad. Fights with your annoying little brother. Fights with your mean big sister. From your perspective as a child, you *never* seem to win any of the fights. You're sure of it. You've never won any of them. Meanwhile, Mom and Dad act as if you're always getting away with things.

If all goes well, there are a lot of good times for the first few years: Mom reading to you, Dad doing things with you, running around in the back yard, chasing pigeons in the park, feeding the ducks at the pond, playing with friends, visiting the aunt and uncle who love you so much.

And then there's school. All of a sudden, everything changes. You're not home with your family, you're surrounded by *a lot of other children you don't know* and adults you never saw before. You don't get to play a lot. You sit a lot. You're supposed to pay attention a lot. If you get hungry, tired, or have to go to the bathroom, you're too embarrassed or afraid to let the teacher know. You'd rather be watching TV or, if you've already had the chance, playing computer games. You'd much rather be playing with your friends or maybe feeding the ducks.

"It's Unfair"

At a relatively early age, the idea of unfairness enters a child's mind. Especially in our consumer culture, the child almost always wants many more things than he or she can have. Every child is told "no" so often that life begins to take on an aura of unfairness.

Feelings of unfairness are also generated in the child's relationships. An older child is given more freedom than we are. A younger child "gets away with everything." Mom blames us for things we didn't do; Dad gets angry for no reason at all.

It is probably impossible to get through childhood without feeling that we're victims of unfairness. But it's such a painful feeling, and expressing it can get us in so much trouble, that we usually suppress the feeling. Instead, we end up suppressing the idea of injustice, and many of our basic needs along with it. We decide that there's something the matter with us.

"Something's Wrong With Me"

Do any children grow up without feeling that there's a lot wrong with them? I doubt it. In a sense, there is a lot wrong with all of us—as children and as adults. We all have feelings we can't handle, unsatisfied desires we can hardly contain. Sometimes we hide our frustrations, sometimes we lash out with them. We all behave in ways that end up embarrassing us or hurting someone else. We all seem to have trouble learning one thing or another. I don't know anyone who isn't sensitive or even mortified about some personal characteristic or failing.

To become more psychologically attuned and available to the children in our care, we need to become more aware of the injuries we received in childhood. We cannot readily empathize with a child if we cannot empathize with ourselves as adults and as the children we once were.

Are We Ready To Be Parents?

Being a parent may not be as hard as being a child, but it's close. I've never met anyone who was truly ready to be a parent. In my clinical practice, I sometimes have the fun of following a couple through their first pregnancy and birth, and then the early stages of childrearing. Invariably, the new mother and father end up feeling that being a parent is far more taxing than they could have imagined.

An Obligation To Ourselves And To The Children In Our Care

Nothing will benefit a parent or teacher more than gaining sympathy for their own personal journey through childhood. Sometimes we forget what it was like being a child because it's too painful and humiliating to remember. Forgetting childhood also seems to be a natural part of the process of growing up. Perhaps there's a physiological component to how little we remember of childhood. The brain goes through drastic changes during the early years, perhaps erasing some of the earliest memories.

Despite our difficulty remembering childhood, we must become comfortable with ourselves as children to become comfortable with the children in our lives. Once again, the starting point is to transform ourselves, rather than the children in our care—to make ourselves more able to relate, to understand, and to care about them.

If we don't wish to go through the pain of recalling the more difficult aspects of our childhood, we can find other ways to increase our awareness of what children go through. We can pay attention to the children around us and read books about childhood that will help us to understand.

There are a number of books that can fine-tune our skills in relating to children, including Thomas Gordon's (1970) *P.E.T.: Parent Effectiveness Training*, Haim Ginott's *Between Parent and Child* (1969), and my own *The Heart of Being Helpful* (1997b). Books by E. Sue Blume (1990), John Bradshaw (1988), Susan Forward (1989), Jane Middleton-Moz (1989), and Alice Miller (1983)—as well as many others on the shelves of bookstores—can help to put you in touch with your own childhood and to appreciate what many children face in growing up. You may not find that you or the children in your care have suffered as much as the children in these books, but the reading will almost surely heighten your sensitivity. One way or another, we owe it to the children in our care to come to an appreciation of the difficulty of being a child. But no one book, no one person can fully grasp the complexities of childhood or parenting. We need to be talking among ourselves as adults and parents.

As mentioned earlier in the book, parents should get together in discussion groups to study and to share. Groups can be started in your schools, churches, or service organizations. Or you can find existing parenting groups. People not only need to inform themselves about the difficulties of parenting and teaching, they need to provide each other moral support in rejecting the ADHD/Ritalin lobby in favor of more child-oriented approaches.

Empowering Ourselves To Help Children

Here are some of the major principles to remember in taking responsibility for the children in our care:

- First and foremost, we can empower ourselves as parents and teachers to help children without resorting to psychiatric diagnoses and medication.

- We can create reading and discussion groups for ourselves as adults in which to share problems and solutions, and to empower ourselves.

- We can develop our own abilities as parents and teachers through workshops on classroom techniques and educational materials, family counseling, and parent training groups.

- We can join reform groups to provide mutual support in resisting the pressure of the ADHD/Ritalin lobby, and to encourage the schools and government to understand a more child-oriented viewpoint.[1]

- When our children are having difficulty, we do not have to send them to medical doctors, such as pediatricians and psychiatrists, or to ADHD/Ritalin advocates. Medical doctors are useful in ruling out genuine physical diseases, such as lead poisoning or head injury, but do more harm than good when they diagnose and treat "ADHD."

- When in need of professional help, we can seek educational consultants, tutors, counselors, psychologists, social workers, family therapists, and other professionals who understand family life and child development, and who won't make psychiatric diagnoses and prescribe drugs.

- Children diagnosed with ADHD need exactly what all children need—adults in their lives who will put the necessary time and effort into identifying and fulfilling their basic needs for love, rational discipline, inspiring education, and fun. We do not have to treat an "ADHD child" differently from any other child, except to recognize that ADHD-like symptoms often signal that the child needs more quality attention from us and other adults.

- To offer help to children, we must be ready to love and to understand them, to pay genuine attention to them, to help them feel secure and valued, and to identify and fulfill their basic needs within the family and school. Being able and available to offer love is not easy; it requires constant work and renewal. Sometimes we can get help from "how to" books, personal counseling, parent training groups, refresher courses in teaching, or self-help groups that we create for ourselves.

- To help a child, the most important step is to create a relationship in which the child feels safe, appreciated, understood, loved, and treasured. Everything good flows from a caring relationship; and nothing good can come from a relationship that's lacking in respect and love for the child.

- Within the caring relationship, we can discover and meet the child's unique needs as expressed in the family or school. There is no substitute, no short cut, no quick fix, to building relationships with children and to using these relationships to meet the child's psychological, social, recreational, and educational needs.

Parenting and teaching are awesome responsibilities and sacred trusts. Nothing else on earth requires as much devotion, patience, self-understanding, and love. Once we have assumed the role of parent or teacher, we cannot and should not turn our backs on the needs of the children in our care. We must do whatever it takes to provide for their well-being.

While parenting and teaching may be the toughest jobs in the world, they are also among the most fulfilling—when we fully devote ourselves to them with the determination to become the kind of adults that our children need us to be.

Notes

1   The International Center for the Study of Psychiatry and Psychology (ICSPP) is one group that advocates a non-medical, child-oriented approach to the problems that children face in the home and school. See Appendix B [in *Talking Back to Ritalin*] for more information, including how to become a member.

Discussion Questions

1.   How is giving Ritalin to children "an aspect of modern materialism"?

2.   Why does Breggin go to such lengths to describe all the types of children who suffer from ADHD?

3.   Is it really so difficult to be a child?

4.   How would you assess your parents' or guardian's effectiveness in raising you?

Writing Suggestion

Do you agree with Breggin that many of the problems associated with Attention Disorders are caused by the parents? Why or why not?

Writing Suggestions for Chapter One

1. Using the readings in the chapter as a basis for your essay, examine more closely the issue of the rise of materialism and greed in our culture and its effects on parenting and attitudes toward children and teens. Do you see a clear relationship?

2. What do you think are the greatest problems of children and/or adolescents? Why? Use the readings and your own personal experience to support your views.

3. Using the readings in Chapter One as a starting point, argue that adults face many more problems and cause many more problems in our society than children do. Why do you think the media emphasizes the problems of children and teens?

4. Follow the news in your local paper or on your local television station for a week. What stories did you find regarding children and/or teens? Was the news mostly positive or negative?

Chapter II

Analyzing the Media

How does the media control and shape reality? In this chapter, that question will be examined by authors who, in most cases journalists themselves, turn their investigative lens on their own profession. In "Media, Knowledge, and Objectivity" from *Keeping the Rabble in Line*, Noam Chomsky examines the problems arising from the increasing concentration of media outlets, and what average citizens can do about it. In three selections from *The Habits of Highly Deceptive Media: Decoding Spin and Lies in Mainstream News*, Normon Solomon points out how the news media privileges certain stories over others, slanting information to accommodate the interests of those in power. Laura Flanders then discusses the role of women and women's issues in the news media in two selections from her book *Real Majority, Media Minority: The Cost of Sidelining Women in Reporting*. In " 'It's Just a Cartoon,' " from *The Trouble with Dilbert: How Corporate Culture Gets the Last Laugh*, Norman Solomon illustrates how the cartoon strip *Dilbert* promotes the agendas of big business while simultaneously encouraging passivity and acceptance on the part of employees. Finally, in "Burning Books Before They're Printed" from *Toxic Sludge is Good For You: Lies, Damn Lies and the Public Relations Industry*, John Stauber and Sheldon Rampton expose how the public relations industry works aggressively to control or silence sources of information that could be beneficial to consumers' health.

Media, Knowledge, and Objectivity

Noam Chomsky

Keeping the Rabble in Line: Interviews with David Barsamian

June 16, 1993

David Barsamian: *It's about 7:00 a.m. here in Boulder, 9:00 where you are in Lexington. What is your morning routine like? Do you start off with reading the* Boston Globe *and the* New York Times?

Noam Chomsky: Yes, and the *Wall Street Journal*. The *Financial Times*. Whatever.

DB *Is the morning a good time for you to work or are you interrupted with a lot of phone calls like this one?*

Usually, quite a lot.

DB *The* Boston Globe, *your daily newspaper, has just been acquired by the* New York Times. *The* Globe *is one of the last major papers in the country not owned by a chain. What are your thoughts on that?*

It's a natural continuation of a tendency that's been going on for a long time. Ben Bagdikian, for example, has been documenting it year after year. It's a natural phenomenon. Capital tends to concentrate. I frankly doubt that it would make much difference in the nature of the newspaper, at least for a few years. However, over time it probably will.

DB *There is a well-documented trend in the concentration of media ownership. Do you see any countertrends?*

What you are doing right now is a countertrend. It's just like everything that's going on in the world. There's a trend toward centralization of power in higher and higher levels, but there's also a countertrend towards regionalization, including what's called "devolution" in Europe, creation of grassroots movements, construction of alternatives. The new electronic technology, in fact, has given opportunities for lots of spreading of alternatives. Cable television offers alternatives. So things are going in both directions. Institutionally, the major tendency is centralization. The other tendency in the opposite direction, which is the only hopeful one, in my opinion, is much more diffuse and has nothing much in the way of organized institutional forms. But it's certainly going on at every level.

DB *There are also computer networks.*

They offer lots of possibilities. There are tens of thousands of people hooked up, maybe hundreds of thousands hooked into various networks on all kinds of topics and lots of discussion goes on and lots of information comes through. It's of varying quality, but a lot of it is alternative to the mainstream. That's still pretty much of an elite privilege at this point.

DB *I recently got a letter from a listener in Lafayette, Colorado, a few miles from Boulder. He heard your talk "Manufacturing Consent," which you gave at the Harvard Trade Union Program in January. I thought the listener's comments were telling. He said after hearing the program that it left him feeling "as politically isolated as the PR industry would have us." He asked, "How do we get organized? Is everybody too tied down by monthly bills to care?" So there are multiple questions and concerns there.*

How do we get organized? There's a simple answer: you go ahead and do it. People have gotten organized under much more onerous conditions than these. Suppose, for example, you're a peasant in El Salvador in a Christian base community which tries to become a peasant cooperative. The conditions under which those things took place are so far beyond anything we can imagine that to talk about the problems we face seems superfluous. Sure, there are problems. People are weighed down with bills, they have personal problems. But most of us live under conditions of extraordinary privilege by comparative standards. The problem of getting organized is a problem of will.

DB *Isn't one of the functions of the media to marginalize people like this listener who wrote and to convince them that affairs must be left to the experts and you stay out of it.*

Of course. But notice that it's done differently in El Salvador. There they send in the death squads. Here what they do is try to hook you on sitcoms. It's true that both are techniques of control, but they are rather different techniques.

DB *You're a scientist. Talk about the notions of objectivity and balance in the media and in scholarship. Who determines those kinds of things?*

There's a big difference between the sciences and humanistic or social science scholarship or the media. In the natural sciences you're faced with the fact of nature as a very hard taskmaster. It doesn't let you get away with a lot of nonsense. At least in the more well developed areas of the sciences, it's difficult for error to perpetuate. Theoretical error, of course, can perpetuate because it's hard to detect. But if a person does an experiment and misstates the results, that's likely to be exposed very quickly, since it will be replicated. There's a fairly stern internal discipline, which by no means guarantees that you're going to find the truth. But it imposes standards that are very hard to break away from. There are external conditions that determine how science proceeds: funding, etc. But it's qualitatively different from other areas, where the constraints imposed by the outside world are much weaker. Much less is understood. The empirical refutation is much harder to come by. It's much easier to simply ignore things that you don't want to hear.

So let's go back to your opening comment about the *Times* taking over the *Globe*. The east-coast press has been flowing with praise for this and saying that because of the *Times'* high journalistic standards there's no concern that this will have any danger. There are thousands of pages of documentation in print which demonstrate that the *Times'* journalistic standards are anything but high. In fact, they're grotesque. But it doesn't matter, because the critical analysis can simply be ignored. It has the wrong message. Therefore you ignore it. That's the kind of thing that's very easy in journalism or any of the other ideological disciplines. You just ignore what you don't like, and if you are on the side of the powerful, it's easy to get away with it.

The other day I read a summary article in the *Washington Post* by a good reporter who knows a lot about Central America, the lost decade in Central America. His article expresses all sorts of puzzlement about why Central America is worse off than it was in 1980 despite the enormous amount of American aid that went into the region. It asks whether this American aid was well-spent, whether it was well-designed, whether it went in the right areas. He asks what went wrong with our enormous effort to bring democracy and social development to Central America.

The author (Douglas Farah) of that article, at least when he's not writing for the *Post*, knows the answer perfectly well. The U.S. led a devastating terrorist war throughout the region to try to prevent democracy and social development. These billions of dollars of aid that he talks about were billions of dollars spent to destroy these countries. That's why they are worse off than before. But the *Post* can't say that. No matter how overwhelming the evidence is, it's perfectly possible simply to disregard it and to go on with fantasies that are much more pleasing to powerful interests and to oneself. In journalism, or in a good deal of what's called "soft scholarship," meaning outside the hard sciences, that's quite easy to do. The controls are very weak, and it's very easy simply to ignore or to deflect critical analysis. In the hard sciences it just won't work. You do that and you're left behind. Somebody else discovers things and you're out of business. Years ago C. P. Snow talked about what he called the two cultures of the humanities and the hard sciences. He was much criticized for that. But there's something to it. They are rather different in character. There are further blurring comments that have to be made, but roughly speaking the difference is real.

So to answer the question, within the more developed natural sciences, although nobody has any illusions about objectivity, there is a kind of peer-pressure control that reflects the constraints imposed by nature. In the other areas, work is commonly considered objective if it reflects the views of those in power.

DB   *The concept of objectivity in journalism definitely seems to be something that's situational and mutable.*

If you look at serious monographic work in diplomatic history, the situation is somewhat different. Although there, choices and focus and concentration and framing are themselves often quite ideological and can hardly fail to be. More honest people will recognize that and make it clear. The less honest will make it appear that they're simply being objective.

DB   *But of course one of the central myths of the media is that they are objective and balanced.*

Sure. That's part of their propaganda function.

It's obvious on the face of it that those words don't mean anything. What do you mean by balanced? What's the proper measure of balance? There's no answer to that question. If the media were honest, they would say, "Look, here are the interests we represent and this is the framework within which we look at things. This is our set of beliefs and commitments." That's what they would say, very much as their critics say. For example, I don't try to hide my commitments, and the *Washington Post* and *New York Times* shouldn't do it either. However, they must do it, because this mask of balance and objectivity is a crucial part of the propaganda function.

In fact, they actually go beyond that. They try to present themselves as adversarial to power, as subversive, digging away at powerful institutions and undermining them. The academic profession plays along with this game. Have a look at academic conferences on the media. One I went through in detail was held at Georgetown University. It was run by a dovish, rather liberal-leaning Quaker. It was about media coverage of Central America and the Middle East. The way the conference is framed is this: First came a series of statements opening the discussion by people who said the media and journalists are overwhelmingly biased against the government. They lie. They try to undermine the U.S. government. They're practically communist agents. After these bitter attacks on the media for their adversarial stance, another set of papers were presented which said, "Look, it's pretty bad, we agree. But it's not quite as bad as you say. That's our job, to be subversive, and that's what you have to face up to in a democratic society." Then these two positions were debated.

There is obviously a third position: the media are supportive of power interests. They distort and often lie in order to maintain those interests. But that position can't be expressed. In fact, in the conference I'm talking about, one hundred percent of the coverage on Central America was within the bounds I've described. On the Middle East, where the media are just grotesque, it was only ninety-six percent within those ludicrous bounds. The reason was that they allowed one statement by Eric Hoagland, a Middle East scholar who made an accurate statement, and that's the four percent, which nobody ever referred to again. That's the way the media like to present themselves, naturally, and that's the way the academic profession likes to see them presented. If you can present the media as being critical, antagonistic to power, maybe even subversive, that makes an enormous contribution to the propaganda function. Then they say, "Look how critical of power we are. How could anyone go beyond us?"

DB *In an article about the acquisition of the* Boston Globe *in the* Times *a few days ago, it was pointed out that the* Globe *was one of the first papers in the United States to lead the crusade against U.S. intervention in Vietnam. You were reading this paper throughout that period. Is that accurate?*

Yes, it's very accurate. They published the first editorial calling for withdrawal from Vietnam. The editor at that time was a personal friend and I followed this quite closely. They did a big study to determine if it would be possible to publish this editorial and still get away with it. They finally agreed to do it. My recollection is that that was in late 1969, that is, about a year-and-a-half after Wall Street had turned against the war. I think it's probably true that that was the first mainstream call for withdrawal of U.S. forces. Of course, it was not framed in terms of a call to withdraw the U.S. forces that had attacked Vietnam, but rather, "We should get out, it doesn't make sense," etc. That tells you something about the U.S. media. What it tells you is a year-and-a-half after the business community determined that the government should liquidate the effort because it was harmful to U.S. economic interests, about that time the courageous press timidly began to say, "Well, maybe we ought to do what the business community announced a year-and-a-half ago," without even conceding the simple truth: that it was a war of U.S. aggression, first against South Vietnam, then all of Indochina. Some elementary truths are too outrageous to be allowed on the printed page.

DB *Do you see knowledge as a commodity? Is it something that's traded and purchased and sold? Obviously it's sold: one sells oneself in the marketplace.*

I'd be a little cautious about the knowledge part. What passes for knowledge is sold. Take, say, Henry Kissinger as an example. He certainly sells himself in the marketplace. But one should be very skeptical about whether that's knowledge or not. The reason is that what's sold in the marketplace tends to be pretty shoddy. It works. It's knowledge or understanding shaped or distorted to serve the interests of power. Or, to go back to the hard sciences, their knowledge is certainly sold. Take American high-tech industry, or the pharmaceutical industry. One of the ways in which the public subsidizes the corporate sector is through university research labs, which do straight research. But the benefits of it, if something commercially viable comes out of it, are handed over to private corporations. I don't know of any university departments which contract out directly to industry, but there are things not too far from that.

DB *Would you say information is a commodity?*

People make such statements. I'm a little leery about them. When you say that information is a commodity, it can certainly be sold, traded, in elementary ways, like a newspaper joins Associated Press and purchases [articles] or you go to a bookstore and buy a book. Information is sold. That's not a deep point, I don't think.

DB *What about ways of acquiring knowledge outside of the conventional structures, the colleges and universities?*

First of all, even within the conventional structures, colleges, universities, the *New York Times*, etc., if you read carefully, you can learn a lot. All of these institutions have an important internal contradiction: On the one hand, they wouldn't survive if they didn't support the fundamental interests of people who have wealth and power. If you don't serve those interests, you don't survive very long. So there is a distorting and propaganda effect and tendency. On the other hand, they also have within them something that drives them towards integrity and honesty and accurate depiction of the world, as far as one can do it. Partly that just comes out of personal integrity of people inside them, whether they're journalists or historians. But partly it's because they won't even do their job for the powerful unless they give a tolerably accurate picture of reality. So the business press, for example, often does quite good and accurate reporting, and the rest of the press too, in many cases. The reason is that people in power need to know the facts if they're going to make decisions in their own interests. These two conflicting tendencies mean that if you weave your way between them you can learn quite a lot.

To get back to your question: Outside these institutions there are all sorts of things people can do. Let's go back to the article I mentioned in the *Washington Post* about Central America. Central American activists in Boulder or plenty of other places, when they look at that article just collapse in laughter. They know the facts. They didn't find out the facts from reading the *Washington Post*, for the most part. They found them out through other sources. The Central American solidarity movements had access to extensive information and still do, through direct contacts, through alternative media, through people travelling back and forth, that is completely outside the framework of the mainstream media. For example, one thing that this article states is that the United States compelled the Marxist Sandinistas to run their first free election in 1990. Everyone in the Central American solidarity movements, and plenty of other people, knows that that's complete baloney and that there was a free election held in 1984, except it came out the wrong way, so therefore it was wiped out of history by the U.S. In fact, the author of this article certainly knows it as well. But for him to say it in the *Washington Post* would be like standing up in the Vatican and saying Jesus Christ didn't exist. You just can't say certain things within a deeply totalitarian intellectual culture like ours. Therefore, he has to say what he says, and maybe even believes it, although it's hard for me to imagine. Everybody has to say that. But people in the popular movements know perfectly well that it's not true and know why it's not true, because they've found other ways to gain understanding of the world.

In case you heard a big bang in the background, that was one of the piles of books in my study collapsing on the floor, as happens regularly.

DB *I can see you surrounded by mountains and stacks of papers and books.*

Occasionally they decide that the laws of physics won't handle it and they fall on the floor, which is what just happened.

DB *You commented to a friend that the amount of material that you lose is "awesome," but it seems to me that the amount of material that you retain is awesome as well.*

It doesn't feel that way to me. I feel mostly the loss. As I see it disappearing it's agonizing. I know if I don't write about something within a couple of years it will be gone, lost in these piles. The trouble is, all of us feel like this. You're so far out of the mainstream that the few people who follow these issues closely and who write about them know that if they don't deal with something it's out of history. For example, the Nicaraguan election is in history, at least for people who care, primarily because Edward Herman did some very good research on it. It doesn't matter to the *Washington Post*. For them it's out of history, period, because those are the orders from those who are on high. But for people who want to know, you can look at Herman's work.

Discussion Questions

1. What are the trends in the "concentration of media ownership"? Can you think of any recent examples?

2. What countertrends does Chomsky point out, and why does he find hope in them?

3. Who determines what the "notions of objectivity and balance" in the media?

4. What does Chomsky mean when he states that "the media are supportive of power interests"?

5. How do we acquire knowledge outside of "conventional structures" like colleges and universities?

Writing Suggestion

Research recent media mergers and acquisitions and then argue for or against the idea that the media is growing more controlled by the interests of the wealthy and powerful.

If a TV News Anchor Talked Straight

Norman Solomon

The Habits of Highly Deceptive Media:
Decoding Spin and Lies in Mainstream News

Warren Beatty's movie *Bulworth* has caused quite a stir. The plot features a successful politician who begins to speak with absolute candor—a notion so outlandish that it's apt to sound incredible.

But the scenario might seem even more far-fetched if the film's blunt protagonist were a TV news anchor instead of a U.S. senator. Imagine how astonished you'd be if you turned on a television and found a newscast like this one:

"At the top of the news tonight—well, never mind. As usual, the script on my TelePrompTer is a scam. It's written to make money, not sense.

"Tonight, I'm supposed to say more about sorrow in the wake of the latest school tragedy. Yes, the sorrow is genuine. But the chances of your kid getting hit by a bullet at school are very small. During an average month in this country, four children die after being shot at school—while about 400 kids are killed by gunshots away from school grounds. Overall, poverty is a big risk factor.

"Meanwhile, television offers little to young people other than mediocre programs and a lot of commercials. As for TV news coverage: If it bleeds, it leads. But if it challenges social inequities, it rarely gets air time. We'd much rather run more footage of yellow police tape, grieving relatives and moralizing politicians.

"From the somber tone of some news stories, you might think that our network is appalled by violence. Don't make me laugh. This network adores violence. We broadcast plenty of it—in prime time—with guns often presented as the way to solve problems. And the conglomerate behind this network also owns a movie studio that puts out a continual stream of films glorifying murder and mayhem.

"During the last few years, White House conferences and newsmagazine covers have hailed scientific discoveries about the importance of the first years of a child's life. Duh. What did we think—that we could keep kicking kids around from year one and not have it affect them in crucial ways?

"While we've cheered the ascending stock market, children have seen us short-changing their futures. I've been around long enough to know that lip service is meaningless compared to how we use our money.

"In many public schools, the students get little or no counseling—because, officials say, there's no money to hire more counselors. As for higher education, the Justice Policy Institute points out that government decision-makers 'have been robbing our universities to pay for prisons we don't need.'

"Back in 1995—while media outlets were busy distracting us with endless reports about O.J. Simpson—state governments made history by collectively spending more to build prisons than colleges. Prison construction went up by $926 million, to $2.6 billion, while university construction fell by $954 million, to $2.5 billion. How's that for planning a future for our kids?

"The Census Bureau recently found that 11.3 million Americans under age 19 had no health insurance (even though 92 percent of them had at least one working parent). Meanwhile, a study by the Center on Hunger, Poverty and Nutrition Policy at Tufts University calculated that more than 30 million Americans are going hungry—an increase of 50 percent since 1985.

"Today, among all the industrialized countries, the United States has the largest gap between rich and poor. But we're not going to spend much time talking about such facts on our newscasts. Why should we?

"It's not rocket science: To watch out for my career, I've kept a lid on—playing it safe—going along to get along with people more powerful than me. After all, I don't really work for journalists. I work for business executives. And the day I upset their apple cart is the day I'm looking at a pink slip with my name on it.

"Most of the news we put on television reminds me of the story about the emperor's new clothes—the royal guy parades around without a stitch on, but no one wants to take the risk of saying so out loud. Maybe you yell at your TV set. But believe me, the studio walls are just about soundproof. We can barely hear you. And we won't, unless you shout a whole lot louder."

May 27, 1998

Only Some Babies Dazzle News Media

Norman Solomon

The Habits of Highly Deceptive Media:
Decoding Spin and Lies in Mainstream News

When Bobbi McCaughey gave birth to septuplets, she became an instant heroine. Fame and fortune arrived with her babies. The news media went nuts. And the gifts poured in.

It's been one heck of a baby shower. In the words of the Associated Press, the seven McCaughey infants "have received, among other things, a free van, groceries for a year, a lifetime supply of diapers, college scholarships and free cable for seven years—one year for each baby."

Newsweek's special contribution came in the form of free dental work on its cover, where the smiling mom's teeth were straightened and whitened by computer. A spokeswoman for the magazine later conceded that "perhaps" the photo technicians "reconstructed too much."

A few days after the McCaughey family boosted Iowa's population by seven, the news broke that a mother who gave birth to six babies earlier in the year had not fared nearly as well. Jacqueline Thompson, the first black woman with sextuplets born in the United States, was living in obscurity as she struggled to raise her children in Washington, D.C.

The disparity between the McCaugheys' fame and the Thompsons' oblivion surfaced just before Thanksgiving. Suddenly, the hard-working mother and her blue-collar husband were buoyed by a flash flood of charity. General Motors gave the Thompson clan a minivan—for presentation on a nationally syndicated TV show. A Ford dealer came up with a slightly used blue Aerostar.

In recent days, plenty of baby clothes, diaper-rash ointment, teething gel and strollers have arrived, along with a lot of small checks. A foundation set up by a mortgage investor announced that it will give the Thompsons a house.

While such generosity is all well and good, it's very likely the media interest and the public response would have come much sooner for the Thompson newborns if they'd been white. That kind of tacit racism is only one of the problems with the media's mania for multiple births.

In this country, thousands of babies are born into dire poverty each week—and the news media commonly depict their mothers as problematic rather than heroic. Evidently, if a low-income mom gives birth to half-a-dozen babies at once, she merits journalistic concern and strong community support. But if she gives birth to several babies one at a time, she's apt to be seen as an intractable social problem.

Politicians and media pundits often speak as though the typical beleaguered mother with scant income doesn't deserve much of anything. She certainly doesn't get her teeth whitened or straightened on any magazine covers.

While *Newsweek* was putting the finishing retouches on Bobbi McCaughey's teeth, the London-based *Financial Times* reported a grim story on its front page, under the headline "Reform May Push U.S. Poor Into Squalor."

The article was blunt: "Large numbers of Americans risk destitution when the law requiring people on welfare to take jobs comes fully into effect 18 months from now." Citing the results of a national survey by the U.S. Conference of Mayors, the newspaper sketched a bleak picture.

"A key problem was that welfare recipients were heavily concentrated in inner cities when vast numbers of retail and low-skill jobs had migrated to suburban shopping malls and industrial parks," the *Financial Times* said. "Public transport did not reach them and most welfare recipients lacked cars."

Of course, few of the low-income parents in such situations will be receiving free minivans.

As for medical care, there's more bad news: The mayors estimate that only 27 percent of "low skill" jobs offer health insurance. For many families, when welfare disappears, so will health coverage. Meanwhile, child-care subsidies are so meager that mothers with young children often have few realistic options for working outside the home.

The news media can be very effective at showing us what's poignant and laudable about one family with limited resources. But the focus gets hazy when considering millions of those families: The coverage tends to become quite abstract.

Eager to report on upbeat examples of generosity, numerous stories about septuplets and sextuplets tell us that our society is committed to taking care of children. Maybe we're trying to convince ourselves, despite all the evidence to the contrary.

November 26, 1997

Orwellian Logic 101— A Few Simple Lessons

Norman Solomon

The Habits of Highly Deceptive Media:
Decoding Spin and Lies in Mainstream News

When U.S. missiles hit sites in Sudan and Afghanistan, some Americans seemed uncomfortable. A vocal minority even voiced opposition after the attacks in late August [1998]. But approval was routine among those who had learned a few easy Orwellian lessons.

When terrorists attack, they're terrorizing. When we attack, we're retaliating. When they respond to our retaliation with further attacks, they're terrorizing again. When we respond with further attacks, we're retaliating again.

When people decry civilian deaths caused by the U.S. government, they're aiding propaganda efforts. In sharp contrast, when civilian deaths are caused by bombers who hate America, the perpetrators are evil and those deaths are tragedies.

When they put bombs in cars and kill people, they're uncivilized killers. When we put bombs on missiles and kill people, we're upholding civilized values.

When they kill, they're terrorists. When we kill, we're striking against terror.

At all times, Americans must be kept fully informed about who to hate and fear. When the United States found Osama bin Laden useful during the 1980s because of his tenacious violence against the Soviet occupiers in Afghanistan, he was good, or at least not bad—but now he's really bad.

No matter how many times they've lied in the past, U.S. officials are credible in the present. When they vaguely cite evidence that the bombed pharmaceutical factory in Khartoum was making ingredients for nerve gas, that should be good enough for us.

Might doesn't make right—except in the real world, when it's American might. Only someone of dubious political orientation would split hairs about international law.

When the mass media in some foreign countries serve as megaphones for the rhetoric of their government, the result is ludicrous propaganda. When the mass media in our country serve as megaphones for the rhetoric of the U.S. government, the result is responsible journalism.

Unlike the TV anchors spouting the government line in places like Sudan and Afghanistan, ours don't have to be told what to say. They have the freedom to report as they choose.

"Circus dogs jump when the trainer cracks his whip," George Orwell observed, "but the really well-trained dog is the one that turns his somersault when there is no whip."

Orwell noted that language "becomes ugly and inaccurate because our thoughts are foolish, but the slovenliness of our language makes it easier for us to have foolish thoughts." And his novel *1984* explained that "the special function of certain Newspeak words...was not so much to express meanings as to destroy them."

National security. Western values. The world community. War against terrorism. Collateral damage. American interests.

What's so wondrous about Orwellian processes is that they tend to be very well camouflaged—part of the normal scenery. Day in and day out, we take them for granted. And we're apt to stay away from uncharted mental paths.

In *1984*, Orwell wrote about the conditioned reflex of "stopping short, as though by instinct, at the threshold of any dangerous thought...and of being bored or repelled by any train of thought which is capable of leading in a heretical direction."

Orwell described "doublethink" as the willingness "to forget any fact that has become inconvenient, and then, when it becomes necessary again, to draw it back from oblivion for just so long as it is needed."

In his afterword to *1984*, Erich Fromm emphasized "the point which is essential for the understanding of Orwell's book, namely that 'doublethink' is already with us, and not merely something which will happen in the future, and in dictatorships."

Fifty-two years ago, Orwell wrote an essay titled "Politics and the English Language." Today, his words remain as relevant as ever: "In our time, political speech and writing are largely the defense of the indefensible."

Repression and atrocities "can indeed be defended," Orwell added, "but only by arguments which are too brutal for most people to face, and which do not square with the professed aims of political parties. Thus political language has to consist largely of euphemism, question-begging and sheer, cloudy vagueness."

National security. Western values. The world community. War against terrorism. Collateral damage. American interests.

August 26, 1998

Discussion Questions

1. Why don't news anchors talk straight? Who does Solomon say they work for?

2. How is the news reminiscent of the tale of "the emperor's new clothes"?

3. Why didn't Jacqueline Thompson, mother of sextuplets, fair as well as the McCaugheys?

4. In what ways is the issue of welfare reform connected to the McCaughey's story?

5. What is doublethink? What are some current examples of it?

6. What are the Orwellian lessons we learned when U.S. missiles hit targets in Afghanistan and in Sudan?

7 . How does the U.S. use terrorists to its own advantage sometimes?

Writing Suggestion

Examine news coverage of a recent national or international news event and analyze the use of Orwellian logic.

Women ARE the News

Laura Flanders

Real Majority, Media Minority:
The Cost of Sidelining Women in Reporting

In 1990, the executive editor of the *New York Times* responded to a critical study of his paper by saying, in effect, that when women were making the news, they would be in it. But women are making news daily. Usually, they *are* the news, yet Frankel and his colleagues, as Jane O'Reilly would say, still "don't get it."

When young women organize against rape and claim their right to sex on their own terms, *Newsweek* calls it "Sexual Correctness," and asks, "Have We Gone Too Far?" When Antioch College supported a student initiative to promote consent-seeking rather than blame-assigning in sex, it becomes a media laughing-stock.

On the medical front: According to the *New York Times*, some 194,000 people in the U.S. have died of AIDS since 1980; 450,000 have died of breast cancer. Yet when ABC in September produced a special on breast cancer, it was called "The Other Epidemic." When women organized for increased federal funding for research into breast cancer, the *New York Times*' Gina Kolata reported (10/20/93), "The question is not whether breast cancer is worthy of research. Instead, it is whether the nation benefits when vocal advocacy groups get their way."

As for lesbians, the media's favorite minority of 1993: Where were *Vanity Fair* and *Newsweek* in 1992, when an African-American woman was burnt alive in her home by skinheads? Hattie Mae Cohen's death received barely a murmur. In September, Sharon Bottoms had her two-year-old taken away from her by the Virginia supreme court because she made her family with another woman. "The mother's conduct is illegal and immoral and renders her an unfit parent," said Judge Duford M. Parsons. Is this what the media call "Lesbian Chic"?

And as '93 came to a close, the biggest headlines had to do with genital mutilation. Not the kind that affects more than 100 million women in parts of Africa, the Middle East and Asia who are ritually mutilated before adolescence. The mutilation that became a media magnet this autumn was the castrating act of Lenora Bobbitt. She hacked off her husband's privates and newspapers from coast to coast picked up the sordid story. In New York's *Daily News*, a full-page headline screamed the brilliantly incisive, "It Really Hurt." Cutting off a penis is a crime—but so is this coverage.

The same outlets that present feminists as hysterical whiners and lesbians as having all the fun routinely shut women's perspectives out of most of their reporting. Women are made invisible, along with all our differences, our difficulties and our points of view.

Consider almost any major issue up for debate today—you'll find that women are at the heart. Take NAFTA: Women are the workers already employed in huge majorities by the transnational corporations most likely to expand in Mexico. They're also the ones last-hired, first-fired in the textile and electronic factories most likely to be displaced here in the U.S.

When you talk about welfare and the poor, you're talking predominantly about women; 90 percent of the adults on welfare are female. Those who most use the health system and are most devastated by it—women, the elderly; the education system—the same. They are precisely the voices that, according to Fairness and Accuracy in Reporting's [FAIR's] studies, are often excluded—even from discussions addressing issues, like abortion or family leave, that have been deemed legitimate "women's" affairs.

On Oct. 18, the *New York Times* ran a story on a massive demonstration protesting U.S. and UN actions in Somalia. The accompanying picture featured a woman at the head of the demonstration. Writer Douglas Jehl explained that the thousands-strong demonstration was made up "mostly of women and children." Did Jehl think to speak to a woman? All the named sources were male; all but one, a U.S. or UN official. The women were seen, but never heard.

When FAIR complains about the coverage of women, we're not looking for special coverage or special supplements—where advertisers can sell us things to keep us young, content and in the home. We're calling for accurate coverage of what's actually going on, and that includes women. Not just as the acted-upon, but as actors and as analysts: not just as those who have experiences but among those who have expertise.

To *Newsweek*'s question, Have We Gone Too Far? Yes. Way too far to go back.

January/February 1994

Super Bowl Success Sparks Good Ol' Boys' Backlash

Laura Flanders

Real Majority, Media Minority:
The Cost of Sidelining Women in Reporting

Shortly before the start of the Super Bowl on NBC this January, viewers saw a public service announcement that warned: "Domestic violence is a crime." For some, the PSA came as a surprise, but not for those involved in the campaign to get 30 seconds of airtime donated to the ad. The moment (worth roughly $500,000 to advertisers) was the result of many weeks of work by FAIR and a coalition of anti-violence groups in negotiation with executives at NBC and NBC Sports.

Workers at women's shelters, and some journalists, have long reported that Super Bowl Sunday is one of the year's worst days for violence against women in the home. FAIR hoped that the broadcast of an anti-violence PSA on Super Sunday, in front of the biggest TV audience of the year, would sound a wake-up call for the media, and it did.

"Since the Super Bowl it seems as though public awareness has increased dramatically on this topic," the executive director of a women's shelter in McKeesport, Pennsylvannia wrote to FAIR. "We believe you've played a major role in bringing domestic violence out in the open."

But a handful of reporters and editors decided to "debunk" the story. These journalists, mostly men, apparently felt affronted by FAIR's success in getting NBC to dedicate 30 seconds, in between the beer ads and the car commercials, to a crisis that, according to the National Coalition Against Domestic Violence, claims thousands of women's lives per year.

The "debunkers", led by Ken Ringle of the *Washington Post* (1/31/93), claimed that FAIR, in coalition with women's groups, slanted the facts in their effort to get NBC to run the PSA. Ringle (and journalists at AP, the *Boston Globe* and the *Wall Street Journal*) asserted that the coalition had claimed "national studies" linked Super Bowl Sunday to increased assaults. No such claims were made. In fact, FAIR made the point repeatedly that domestic violence is understudied and prevention work is gravely underfunded.

Critics charged that the coalition was forced to "acknowledge" that its evidence was largely "anecdotal." "Anecdotal" was the word used in countless interviews by FAIR; stories from women on the front lines were something that made the campaign stronger, not something anyone was forced to "acknowledge."

In the *Washington Post*, Ringle attacked those who fought for the NBC public service spot as "causists" who "show up wherever the most TV lenses are focused." The article painted a picture of a feminist mob strong-arming the networks with myth and false statistics.

But it was Ringle who distorted the facts. *Post* readers would not know that of the four experts cited by Ringle, only one agreed with the article's thesis that there is no "evidence that a link actually exists between football and wife-beating."

Ringle quoted psychotherapist Michael Lindsey to defend his point that the Super Bowl PSA campaign was misguided: "You know I hate this," Ringle quotes Lindsay saying. But Lindsey told FAIR that he was referring to Ringle's line of questioning, not the anti-battering campaign. "He was really hostile," Lindsey added. On the same day as Ringle's "debunking" story, Lindsey was quoted in the *New York Times*, saying, "That PSA will save lives."

Ringle claimed triumphantly that a speaker at a press conference co-hosted by FAIR had "misrepresented" a study by Old Dominion College on violence and sports. FAIR interviewed the authors. While due to the small sample involved, they chose not to express the study results in percentage terms as the activist had, they did not see this as misrepresentation. "We have not accused anyone of distorting the results of our study," the authors stated.

Following the lead of the *Washington Post* and editorialists at the *Wall Street Journal*, Rush Limbaugh jumped into the act on his TV show (2/16/93). He berated the PSA as "just a bunch of feminist bilge" because the man it featured is not a credible batterer: "Like people who beat their wives wear ties," Limbaugh scoffed.

The backlash articles bore all the traits of typical coverage of domestic violence: They belittled the victims, minimized the crisis and missed the point—which is that, according to FBI averages, a woman is battered every 18 seconds. That is enough to deserve attention all year long.

FAIR's goal was to open up debate. We did. The PSA was seen by more people than any anti-battering message in history. Weeks later, TV news and talk shows were still covering the issue intensely and constructively.

The fact that some good ol' boys managed to miscast the campaign came as no surprise. Some journalists' determination to undermine the Super Bowl effort was just a reminder of how many in mainstream media typically disbelieve women when they talk about the violence in their lives.

April/May 1993

Discussion Questions

1. How are women made invisible by the media?

2. Can you name any headlines from recent news that dealt specifically with a women's issue?

3. Consider all the media attention to the sex drug Viagra. Do you think there is any correlation between that attention and the dominance of men in the news?

4. Do you think it was wise to include a public service announcement concerning domestic violence during the Super Bowl? Why was there so much resentment from certain journalists?

Writing Suggestion

Examine several newspaper stories taken at random from your local newspaper. How many sources are women? What is the ratio of quotations from women versus those from men?

"It's Just A Cartoon..."

Norman Solomon

The Trouble with Dilbert:
How Corporate Culture Gets the Last Laugh

There are many ways to defend *Dilbert*:

- It's clever.
- It's funny.
- It's just a cartoon.
- It's a witty spoof of daily life at the office.
- It uses humor to make people feel better about workplace predicaments.
- It's a force for workplace sanity.
- It lowers blood pressure.
- It exposes the management stupidities and absurdities that millions of people face at work.
- It shouldn't be taken too seriously.
- And anyway, different people read it different ways.

———

It's true that *Dilbert* is sometimes clever. And funny.

And the essays by Scott Adams include some imaginative writing.

Yet cleverness and imagination are not abstract qualities. They're tied to content...attitude...and values.

These days, *Dilbert* is hardly "just a cartoon." By 1997, United Feature Syndicate was calling it the most widely distributed comic strip in the United States. And *Dilbert*'s reach is global; the syndicate claims that it appears in 1,700 newspapers worldwide, in seventeen languages and fifty-one countries. The publisher of *The Dilbert Future* says that every day "*Dilbert* is currently read by more than 150 million readers."

Dilbertization has just begun. With *Dilbert* hardcovers in the million-seller range, plenty more are on the horizon; in early 1997, *Entertainment Weekly* magazine reported that "HarperBusiness will publish four more hardcover books in the next five years, and Andrews & McMeel hopes to roll out calendars and softcover collections of strips for the next seven." Meanwhile, across the planet, *Dilbert* cartoons are appearing on calendars, coffee mugs, cards, clothes and scads of other products.

Perhaps most significantly in the long run, *Dilbert* has become a mass-marketed attitude—a public way of coping—while we encounter the tightening vise of corporatization. The *Dilbert* phenomenon is part of a process making people more accustomed to a stance of ironic passivity.

To say that the proliferation of *Dilbert* lacks social importance or impact is to claim that mass culture doesn't matter much—that it doesn't affect how we perceive or act on our perceptions—that it doesn't influence how we talk and think and live. In fact, how we use words is a marker and pointer for our outlooks. As George Orwell observed, everyday language "becomes ugly and inaccurate because our thoughts are foolish, but the slovenliness of our language makes it easier for us to have foolish thoughts."

Certainly no advertising exec can afford to underrate the consequences of words, images and marketed attitudes. The ad industry deals in hard numbers and empirical results. Billions of dollars get spent every season in the USA on the well-tested assumption that what keeps flashing before our eyes and ears has major effects on what we buy. And buy into.

Mega-marketing requires, more than ever, a capital-intensive blitz. To saturate the grassroots, mass-mediated "popular culture" needs a nod from a big-money suite somewhere. In the nationwide amphitheater, would-be creators are to remain in their seats unless summoned to the stage by someone with appreciable monetary clout. The audience does not create. The audience consumes.

As Thomas Frank puts it: "No longer can any serious executive regard TV, movies, magazines, and radio as simple 'entertainment,' as frivolous leisure-time fun: writing, music, and art are no longer conceivable as free expressions arising from the daily experience of a people. These are the economic dynamos of the new age, the economically crucial tools by which the public is informed of the latest offerings, enchanted by packaged bliss, instructed in the arcane pleasures of the new, taught to be good citizens, and brought warmly into the consuming fold."

———

So what is *Dilbert* selling, along with comics, books and other Dilberphernalia? When we buy it—literally and psychologically—what are we accepting?

To praise *Dilbert* as an uplifting or positive force is to ignore the contexts of present-day corporate theology. The sight of CEOs and office workers singing from the same *Dilbert* hymnal should give us pause, especially as Scott Adams essays increasingly claim to explain the meaning of modern work and the proper options ahead for corporate management.

The spring 1997 issue of *Office Depot Business News* reported that the *Dilbert* comic strip "caught the imagination of millions of white-collar workers fed up with 'downsizing,' 'rightsizing,' 're-engineering' and other examples of corporate ineptitude masquerading as efficient management."

Unfortunately, the "imagination" that *Dilbert* caught was already problematic. To the extent that we accept the limits of mass-marketed imagination, they become our own. And no major changes for the better can come about unless we break through the limitations that often go unrecognized because they've become so familiar.

Adams conveys no interest in solidarity between men and women, or between people of different races. Sexism and racism seem to bother him not at all. In *The Dilbert Future*, he lists "mandatory sexual harassment training" and "mandatory diversity training" among half a dozen "Productivity-Thwarting Activities."

In *Dilbert* comics, feminists assert themselves by doing things like wielding a crossbow or physically pounding men. In a 1994 episode, Dilbert's date sits at the restaurant table and tells him: "I'm a '90s kind of woman. I demand equality but the man must pay for dinner. And recent surveys show that many women my age think it's okay to slap a man."

Believing that *Dilbert* provides incisive satire about our situations as human beings in the late 1990s is an exercise in devotion. As a set of satiric theses nailed to the Corporate Church door, *Dilbert* cartoons and books retain the essential faith. It is a belief based on a truncated sense of possibilities for the creation of popular art that could resonate deeply and profoundly, in personal and social terms.

Cute little jokes, mass produced, can dominate a sparse field of corporatized dreams. Funny and meaningful. But compared to what?

Okay, *Dilbert* is irreverent—compared to most comic strips in daily papers, which have little to say and keep saying it. Irreverent in *style*, *Dilbert* is substantively reverent toward the essential elements of corporate domination. Amid all his wisecracks, Adams quibbles about how to revise that domination.

Throwing stark light on unpleasant absurdities without the slightest hope of solutions for the common good, Scott Adams digs the readers into a deepening trough. In his estimation, the only way out is an individual escape—a point that Adams has emphasized since leaving his mid-level phone company job in 1995.

"The gutsiest professionals are already quitting their jobs and going it alone," Adams gloats in *The Dilbert Future*, "but they're the exception. Most professionals are like sheep." On another page he declares: "I'm convinced that my job situation is a model of the future."

Adams appears to be sharing his insights—combining his humor with helpful tips for the average reader. In this way, *Dilbert* books may indeed seem to be aiding workplace sanity, suggesting better alternatives for office employees who feel trapped.

But few people will strike it rich on their own—in cartooning or any other venture—and most will find the go-it-alone dream to be as disappointing as a mirage. For each successful entrepreneur, many more fail. Meanwhile, the vast majority of distressed workers will do their best to hang onto their cubicle jobs in the first place—not, as Adams implies, because of a shortage of brains or zest for life, but rather because that's how the system is structured.

The sharp *Dilbert* tone that routinely slices into middle management—and grows duller on the rare occasions that it swipes at corporate higher-ups—is a double-edged blade that cuts deeply against the rank-and-file office worker. And against the lowly human being in general. The *Dilbert* tenor is often contemptuous of garden variety people—mockingly dubbed "Induhviduals" in *The Dilbert Future*.

Ha ha. Get it? Most people are so dense that "duh" may as well be their middle names. Adams confers special dispensation on those who read *Dilbert* books, of course; their wisdom is attained by willingness to fork over money in his direction. As a clever marketer, Adams recognizes that the paying customers must be kept out of his nonstop line of fire.

> "There are two types of people in the world: the bright and attractive people like yourself who read *Dilbert* books, and the 6 billion idiots who get in our way. Since we're outnumbered, it's a good idea not to refer to them as idiots to their faces."
>
> —Scott Adams, *The Dilbert Future*, p. 1

Even so, Adams doesn't always restrain his sweeping contempt. (Only a few pages of *The Dilbert Principle* go by before his notification to readers, "I don't underestimate your intelligence. I mean, how could I?") At every moment, the venom threatens to splatter on those who are savoring the spectacle of it falling elsewhere.

Despite his image as a breaker of conventional molds, Adams operates in the dispiriting spirit of most TV comedy. Media critic Mark Crispin Miller's apt description of televised humor applies to *Dilbert*: it offers "not a welcome but an ultimatum—that we had better see the joke or else turn into it."

Adams' ridicule of "Induhviduals" may be enjoyable for those who feel out of range of his nasty spit. *Dilbert* invites us to appreciate that *finally* a successful cartoonist/author is showing just how contemptible some people really are. His depictions of the obnoxious and the asinine plainly apply to the jerks who try our patience and waste our precious time because they're so dumb—and, even worse, because they're our co-workers or even our supervisors. Later it might dawn on us that we fall within his big circle of disdain.

Discussion Questions

1. What is the "stance of ironic passivity" that Dilbert encourages in its readers?

2. How are movies, TV, etc. more than "simple entertainment"? What values are they really promoting?

3. Why does Solomon find it disturbing that both CEOs and employees sing the praises of "Dilbert"?

Writing Suggestion

Examine certain comic strips that run in your local mainstream newspaper and/or your alternative newspaper. Are they as harmless as they seem? What values are they promoting?

Burning Books Before They're Printed

John Stauber and Sheldon Rampton

Toxic Sludge Is Good for You!:
Lies, Damn Lies and the Public Relations Industry

Who kills a Man kills a reasonable creature, God's Image; but he who destroys a good Book, kills reason itself, kills the Image of God.

JOHN MILTON
Areopagitica

"All documents...are confidential," warned the September 7, 1990 memo from Betsy Gullickson, senior vice-president at the giant Ketchum public relations firm. "Make sure that everything—even notes to yourself—are so stamped...Remember that we have a shredder; give documents to Lynette for shredding. All conversations are confidential, too. Please be careful talking in the halls, in elevators, in restaurants, etc. All suppliers must sign confidentiality agreements. If you are faxing documents to the client, another office or to anyone else, call them to let them know that a fax is coming. If you are expecting a fax, you or your Account Coordinator should stand by the machine and wait for it. We don't want those documents lying around for anybody to pick up."[1]

Gullickson, a 1969 graduate of Northwestern University's prestigious Medill School of Journalism,[2] understood perfectly the need for secrecy. If word leaked out, the media might have had a field day with Ketchum's plan to scuttle a groundbreaking environmental book even before it went to press.

The stakes were high for Ketchum's client, the California Raisin Advisory Board (CALRAB), the business association of California raisin growers. In 1986, CALRAB had scored big with a series of clever TV commercials using the "California Dancing Raisins." The singing, dancing raisins, animated through a technique known as "claymation," were so popular that they had transcended their TV-commercial ori-

116 THE COMMON COURAGE READER

gins. Fan mail addressed to the Raisins was forwarded to Ketchum, along with phone inquiries from the media and public clamoring for live public performances. Ketchum obligingly supplied live, costumed characters dressed as the Raisins, who performed at the White House Easter Egg Roll and Christmas Tree Lighting, Macy's Thanksgiving Day Parade, and "A Claymation Christmas Celebration" on the CBS television network.

In the summer of 1988, the Raisins were sent out on a 27-city national tour, beginning in New York and ending in Los Angeles. Along the way, they performed in hotel lobbies, children's hospitals and convalescent centers and supermarkets. In several cities, they were greeted by the mayor and given keys to the city. They visited historic landmarks, singing and dancing their version of "I Heard It Through the Grapevine." They performed at a charity benefit honoring singer Ray Charles and his claymation counterpart, "Raisin Ray." Over 3,000 people joined the California Dancing Raisins Fan Club, and a research poll found that the Raisins were second in popularity only to comedian Bill Cosby.[3]

For CALRAB, of course, the real payoff came in raisin sales, which had risen 17 percent since the Dancing Raisins were first introduced. Behind the scenes, however, trouble was brewing, and Gullickson's secret memo outlined Ketchum's plan to "manage the crisis."

The "crisis" was a science writer named David Steinman. In 1985 while working for the LA Weekly, Steinman had written a story about fish contaminated from toxic waste dumped near his home in the Santa Monica Bay area, and was shocked when a test of his own blood showed astronomical levels of both DDT and PCBs. Steinman had read the research linking these chemicals to higher rates of cancer and other diseases, and started "wondering how many other poisons were in the food I ate. It started me asking why government officials, who had known about the dumping for years, had withheld the information for so long." In his search for the answers to these questions, Steinman began a five-year investigation, using the Freedom of Information Act to obtain obscure government research reports. Based on this research, he had written a book, titled Diet for a Poisoned Planet, scheduled for publication in 1990.

Steinman's investigation had uncovered evidence showing that hundreds of toxic carcinogens and other contaminants, mostly pesticides, are found routinely in US foods from raisins to yogurt to beef. For example, government inspectors found "raisins had 110 industrial chemical and pesticide residues in sixteen samples." Diet for a Poisoned Planet recommends that people avoid any but organically-grown raisins raised without pesticides.[4]

By compiling this information in book form, Diet for a Poisoned Planet enables readers to make safer food choices. But before shoppers can use the information, they must first hear about the book, through media reviews and interviews with the author during a publicity campaign in the weeks after the book is published. And the California Raisin Advisory Board wanted to make sure that Steinman's book was dead on arrival.

PR firms, of course, are the experts at organizing publicity campaigns. So who better to launch an anti-publicity campaign, to convince journalists to ignore Steinman and his book?

For Spies' Eyes Only

Our copy of Betsy Gullickson's memo came from an employee of Ketchum PR. Despite the risk of being fired, conscience drove this corporate whistleblower to reveal Ketchum's campaign aimed at concealing the possible health risks from high pesticide levels in California raisins and other foods.

"I find it very discouraging when I read in the paper that cancer among children has increased dramatically, and they don't know why," our source explained. "I believe that people have the right to know about the little Dancing Raisins and the possibility that they might be harming children. There is a new censorship in this country, based on nothing but dollars and cents."

According to the 1994 *O'Dwyer's Directory of PR Firms*, Ketchum is the sixth largest public relations company in the United States, receiving net fees of over $50 million per year. Headquartered in New York City, Ketchum represents a number of corporate food clients, including Dole Foods, Wendy's, the Potato Board, Oscar Meyer Foods, Miller Brewing, Kikkoman, H.J. Heinz, the Beef Industry Council, the California Almond Board, and the California Raisin Advisory Board.[5] In addition to writing press releases and organizing news conferences, Ketchum aggressively markets its services in "crisis management," a growing specialty within the PR industry. In a profile written for *O'Dwyer's PR Services Report*, Ketchum boasted of its experience handling PR problems ranging "from toxic waste crises to low-level nuclear wastes, from community relations at Superfund sites to scientific meetings where issues like toxicology of pesticides are reviewed."[6]

Gullickson's PR expertise is in "food marketing strategic counsel,"[7] and Steinman's book is the type of "crisis" that she was hired to manage. Her memo outlined a plan to assign "broad areas of responsibility," such as "intelligence/information gathering," to specific Ketchum employees and to Gary Obenauf of CALRAB. Months before the publication of *Diet for a Poisoned Planet*, Ketchum sought to "obtain [a] copy of [the] book galleys or manuscript and publisher's tour schedule." Gullickson recommended that spokespeople "conduct one-on-one briefings/interviews with the trade and general consumer media in the markets most acutely interested in the issue...The [Ketchum] agency is currently attempting to get a tour schedule so that we can 'shadow' Steinman's appearances; best scenario: we will have our spokesman in town prior to or in conjunction with Steinman's appearances."[8]

To get this information, Ketchum used an informant involved with the book's marketing campaign to tell them when and on which talk shows Steinman was booked. "They called up each and every talk show," explained our source inside Ketchum. A "list of media to receive low-key phone inquiries regarding the Steinman book" included specific journalists at the *New York Times*, the Larry King Show, and the *Washington Post*. The callers from Ketchum argued that it would be unfair to allow Steinman on the show without the other side of the issue, or tried to depict him as an "off-the-wall extremist without credibility."

Ketchum wasn't the only PR firm working to cripple Steinman's book publicity efforts. Jean Rainey of Edelman Public Relations contacted the *Today Show*, providing anti-Steinman material and offering to make available "the president of the American Dietetic Association" to counter Steinman. Apparently she succeeded in bouncing him from the program. *Today* interviewed Steinman, but never aired the segment.[9]

Government Moves to Suppress

Gullickson's memo also suggested possible "external ambassadors" who might be recruited into the campaign, including Republican California Governor Pete Wilson and Democratic Party fundraiser Tony Coelho. Thanks to a pesticide industry front group with deep Republican connections, the stealth campaign against Steinman's book even reached into the White House and other arms of the US government.

Elizabeth M. Whelan is a prominent anti-environmentalist who heads the American Council on Science and Health (ACSH), a group funded largely by the chemical industry. The ACSH is also a client of Ketchum PR. On July 12, 1990, Whelan wrote a letter to then-White House Chief of Staff John Sununu warning that Steinman and others "who specialize in terrifying consumers" were "threatening the US standard of living and, indeed, may pose a future threat to national security." Whelan's letter was copied to the heads of the government's Food and Drug Administration, Department of Agriculture, Department of Health and Human Services, Environmental Protection Agency, and the Surgeon General. Whelan also contacted her friend, former Surgeon General C. Everett Koop, whom she calls a "close colleague."[10] Dr. Koop joined the attack against Steinman's book, calling it "trash" in a statement mailed nationwide.[11]

In September 1990, before Steinman's book was published, the USDA initiated its anti-book campaign through the Agriculture Extension Service. The federally-funded effort was led by government employees Kenneth Hall, Bonnie Poli, Cynthia Garman-Squier and Janet Poley. According to a government memo, the Department of Agriculture group felt that "communications with the media by concerned parties have been effective in minimizing potential public concern about issues in the book." Attached to the memo is a "confidential analysis" of Steinman's book written by the National Food Processors Association, a food and pesticide trade group. The memo warns recipients that this information is "for internal use and should not be released" to the news media.[12]

Dr. William Marcus, who was then a senior science advisor to the US Environmental Protection Agency, wrote the introduction to *Diet for a Poisoned Planet*. Marcus' views were his own, but they greatly angered Whelan. She asked White House Chief of Staff Sununu to personally investigate the matter, and exerted pressure to have the introduction removed from the book. Marcus refused, and was later fired from the EPA.[13] Government policy has now been changed to prohibit officials from writing book forwards.

Deciding What You'll Swallow

You are probably going to eat some food today. It is possible, in fact, that you are in the process of eating *right now*.

You have the right to eat. You have the right to eat wholesome foods. You have the right to read, even while you are eating. You have the right to read *about* the foods you are about to eat. Neither Ketchum Public Relations nor the White House has any right to interfere with your access to good food or good reading materials.

You have never voted for a politician who campaigned on a pledge that he would work to limit your access to information about the food you eat. You never voted for Ketchum PR, and, if you are like most people, you've never even *heard* of them. You never gave your consent for them to become involved in your life, and in return, they have never bothered to *ask* for your consent. After all, they're not working for *you*. They're working for the California Raisin Advisory Board.

One of the most cherished freedoms in a democracy is the right to freely participate in the "marketplace of ideas." We value this freedom because without it, all our other freedoms are impossible to defend. In a democracy every idea, no matter how absurd or offensive, is allowed to compete freely for our attention and acceptance. Turn on the TV, and you'll find plenty of absurd and offensive examples of this principle in action. On the Sunday public affairs shows you'll find Republicans, Democrats, Republicans who love too much, and Democrats who love Republicans. On *A Current Affair* or *Oprah Winfrey*, you'll find self-proclaimed werewolves, worshippers of Madonna, and doomsday prophets from the lunatic fringes of American society.

Unfortunately, what you *won't* find can kill you.

Diet for a Poisoned Planet is a serious, important contribution to the public debate over health, the environment, and food safety. It fell victim to a PR campaign designed to prevent it from ever *reaching* the "marketplace of ideas." And it isn't alone. Here are some other examples:

- In 1992, John Robbins was promoting his book, *May All Be Fed*, which advocates a strict vegetarian diet. He became the target of an anti-book campaign by Morgan & Myers PR, working on behalf of the world's largest milk promotion group, the National Dairy Board. Based in Jefferson, Wisconsin, Morgan & Myers is the nation's 42nd largest PR firm, with about sixty employees and a 1993 net fee intake of $3.7 million. Within its field of specialization—representing agribusiness interests—Morgan & Myers ranks fifth in the United States. Its clients include Kraft, the Philip Morris subsidiary that buys and sells most of America's cheese; Upjohn, a major producer of antibiotics used on livestock; and Sandoz, a manufacturer of atrazine herbicide, a carcinogen that contaminates thousands of water wells.[14]

  As with Ketchum's California Raisins campaign, Morgan & Myers used behind-the-scenes contacts to undermine Robbins' publicity tour, thereby limiting his book's public exposure and readership. A Morgan & Myers memo of September 17, 1992, states that "M&M currently is monitoring coverage of Robbins' media tour," to counter his advice that readers cut back their consumption of dairy products. The memo was widely distributed to key dairy industry contacts. It contained the schedule of Robbins' book tour and provided this tactical warning: "Do not issue any news release or statement. Doing so only calls attention to his message...Ideally, any response should come from a third party, uninvolved in the dairy industry."[15]

- The September 22, 1981, *Washington Post* reported that "a single telephone call from a DuPont public relations man to the Book-of-the-Month Club financially doomed an unflattering history of the DuPont family and its businesses." The book by author Gerard Colby Zilg, titled *DuPont: Behind the Nylon Curtain*, was a "relentlessly critical" exposé of the business and personal affairs of the wealthy DuPont family. After a copy of the manuscript found its way into the hands of the DuPonts, they deployed PR representative Harold G. Brown Jr., who phoned the Book-of-the-Month Club editor to say that several people at DuPont considered the book "scurrilous" and "actionable."

  The Book-of-the-Month Club had already contracted with Prentice-Hall, the publisher, to feature *DuPont* as a November selection of its Fortune Book Club, but a few days after Brown's phone call the club called Prentice-Hall to back out of the deal. Apparently intimidated by the implied threat of a DuPont lawsuit, Prentice-Hall made no effort to enforce its contract with the Book-of-the-Month Club or to seek money damages. Instead, the publisher reduced the book's press run from 15,000 to 10,000 copies, and cut its advertising budget from $15,000 to $5,500, even though the book was getting favorable reviews in major publications. The *Los Angeles Times*, for example, called it "a vastly readable book and...a very important one." Peter Grenquist, president of Prentice-Hall's trade book division, ordered the book's editor, Bram Cavin, not to discuss the matter with the author. In October, three months later, conscience finally drove Cavin to disobey Grenquist's order and inform the author of the phone call from DuPont. Cavin was later fired for being "unproductive."[16]

- PR firms also campaigned against the book *Beyond Beef*, by activist Jeremy Rifkin. *Beyond Beef* recommends that people stop eating beef for ethical, health and environmental reasons. Its message has been loudly denounced by both the Beef Council and the National Dairy Board, clients of Ketchum and Morgan & Myers, respectively. Rifkin's enemies hired an infiltrator to pose as a volunteer in his office. The spy—Seymour "Bud" Vestermark, whose infiltrations of other organizations are detailed in chapter 5 of *Toxic Sludge is Good for You!*—obtained Rifkin's book tour itinerary, after which all hell broke loose.[17]

  In *The War Against The Greens*, author David Helvarg reports that Rifkin's spring 1992 national book tour "had to be canceled after it was repeatedly sabotaged. Melinda Mullin, *Beyond Beef*'s publicist at Dutton Books, says...radio and TV producers who'd scheduled Rifkin's appearance began receiving calls from a woman claiming to be Mullin cancelling or misrepresenting Rifkin's plans. Finally, Mullin had to begin using a code name with the producers. Liz Einbinder, a San Francisco-based radio producer who had had *Beyond Beef* on her desk for several weeks, was surprised to receive angry calls and an anonymous package denouncing Rifkin within hours of placing her first call to Mullin. This led to speculation that Dutton's New York phones might be tapped."[18]

Making the World Safe from Democracy

The public relations or "PR" industry did not even exist prior to the twentieth century, but it has grown steadily and appears poised for even more dramatic growth in the future. No one knows exactly how much money is spent each year in the United States on public relations, but $10 billion is considered a conservative estimate. "Publicity" was once the work of carnival hawkers and penny-ante hustlers smoking cheap cigars and wearing cheap suits. Today's PR professionals are recruited from the ranks of former journalists, retired politicians and eager-beaver college graduates anxious to rise in the corporate world. They hobnob internationally with corporate CEOs, senators and US presidents. They use sophisticated psychology, opinion polling and complex computer databases so refined that they can pinpoint the prevailing "psychographics" of individual city neighborhoods. Press agents used to rely on news releases and publicity stunts to attract attention for their clients. In today's electronic age, the PR industry uses 800-numbers and telemarketing, advanced databases, computer bulletin boards, simultaneous multi-location fax transmission and "video news releases"—entire news stories, written, filmed and produced by PR firms and transmitted by satellite feed to hundreds of TV stations around the world. Video news releases are designed to be indistinguishable from genuine news, and are typically used as "story segments" on TV news shows without any attribution or disclaimer indicating that they are in fact subtle paid advertisements. "Most of what you see on TV is, in effect, a canned PR product. Most of what you read in the paper and see on television is not news," says a senior vice-president with Gray & Company public relations.[19]

The PR industry also orchestrates many of the so-called "grassroots citizen campaigns" that lobby Washington, state and local governments. Unlike genuine grassroots movements, however, these industry-generated "astroturf" movements are controlled by the corporate interests that pay their bills. On behalf of the Philip Morris tobacco company, for example, Burson-Marsteller (the world's largest PR firm) created the "National Smokers Alliance" to mobilize smokers into a grassroots lobby for "smokers' rights." Deceptive PR has become so cynical that sometimes it staggers belief. To fight former Attorney General Ed Meese's Pornography Commission, *Playboy* and *Penthouse* magazines had Gray & Company PR create a front group called "Americans for Constitutional Freedom," to "assist in countering the idea that those who opposed the commission's efforts were motivated only by financial self-interest" or were "somehow 'pro-pornography.'"[20] To defeat environmentalists, PR firms have created green-sounding front groups such as "The Global Climate Coalition" and the "British Columbia Forest Alliance."

In defense of these activities, the PR industry claims that it is simply participating in the democratic process and and contributing to public debate. In reality, the industry carefully conceals most of its activities from public view. This invisibility is part of a deliberate strategy for manipulating public opinion and government policy. "Persuasion, by its definition, is subtle," says another PR exec. "The best PR ends up looking like news. You never know when a PR agency is being effective; you'll just find your views slowly shifting."[21]

Today's PR industry is related to democracy in the same way that prostitution is related to sex. When practiced voluntarily for love, both can exemplify human communications at its best. When they are bought and sold, however, they are transformed into something hidden and sordid. There is nothing wrong with many of the *techniques* used by the PR industry—lobbying, grassroots organizing, using the news media to put ideas before the public. As individuals, we not only have the *right* to engage in these activities, we have a *responsibility* to participate in the decisions that shape our society and our lives. Ordinary citizens have the right to organize for social change—better working conditions, health care, fair prices for family farmers, safe food, freedom from toxins, social justice, a humane foreign policy. But ordinary citizens cannot afford the multi-million-dollar campaigns that PR firms undertake on behalf of their special interest clients, usually large corporations, business associations and governments. Raw money enables the PR industry to mobilize private detectives, attorneys, broadcast faxes, satellite feeds, sophisticated information systems and other expensive, high-tech resources to out-maneuver, overpower and out-last true citizen reformers.

Talking Back to the Flacks

Although the public relations industry is a twentieth-century phenomenon, the art of influencing opinion has a long history, dating in fact to the days of ancient Athens, the first recorded western democracy. Aristotle's *Rhetoric* remains one of the most insightful books ever written on the subject. Aristotle argues that rhetoric is an "art" as opposed to the sciences, which are governed by logic. The sciences deal with measurable quantities, known facts, and principles of proof based on propositions which can definitely be labeled "true" or "false." In social life, however, people are often confronted with situations in which many of the facts are unknown and unknowable. In addition, competing sectors within society have conflicting interests. It is often impossible to say for sure whether a proposition is "true" or "false," and scientific logic is incapable of evaluating statements whose degree of truth can only be approximated using concepts like "maybe," "probably," or "probably not." Instead of logic, therefore, people turn to *rhetoric*, the art of communication and persuasion.

Aristotle recognized that rhetoric could be used to mislead as well as to enlighten the public. Persuasive speakers could lead their audience into unwise choices. For this reason, he argued that rhetoric should be widely taught and understood, so that the wise members of society would be able to contend effectively with the rhetoric of the unwise. Society would be best served if the public could choose from a range of contending arguments, and if people were trained in the skills necessary to recognize manipulative uses of rhetoric.

Aristotle's analysis is over 2,300 years old, but it offers the best solution that we have found to the problem of democracy in our own age—the age of public relations. Today's opinion manipulation industry is a powerful giant, but like Goliath, it is a giant with a fatal weakness. When the public is educated about its techniques, it often loses its ability to mislead and manipulate. In Nevada, for example, Don Williams, president of Altamira Communications and widely known as a Nevada "political king maker," attempted in 1992 to persuade the state to serve as a national storage site for nuclear waste. When the nuclear industry's PR activities were exposed in Nevada newspapers, public opinion turned decisively *against* the plan.[22]

The founders of the American revolution argued that the price of freedom is eternal vigilance. "Every man ought to exercise the faculties of his mind, and think and examine for himself, that he may be the less likely to be imposed on, and that he may form as accurate an opinion as possible of the measures of his ruler," wrote one farmer who campaigned against the British. Christopher Gadsen, another American revolutionary, argued that it was easier to stop the work of "crafty, dissembling, insinuating men" *before* rather than *after* they "carry their point against you."[23] The price of democracy is the same today as it was in the days of Samuel Adams and Thomas Jefferson, and the PR industry is a haven for many of the "crafty, dissembling men" we need to guard against.

The PR industry is a little like the title character in the 1933 Claude Rains movie, *The Invisible Man*. Rains plays an evil scientist who attempts to rule the world, committing crimes such as robbery and murder and using his invisibility to evade detection. *The Invisible Man* was an early special effects film, using hidden wires and other tricks to make ashtrays, guns, and other objects float in mid-air as though they were manipulated by an invisible hand.

Instead of ashtrays and guns, the PR industry seeks to manipulate public opinion and government policy. But it can only manipulate while it remains invisible.

We like to think of our book as the literary equivalent of a nice, big can of fluorescent orange spray paint. We are spray-painting the Invisible Man in order to make him visible again. We want the public at large to recognize the skilled propagandists of industry and government who are affecting public opinion and determining public policies, while remaining (they hope) out of public view.

In a democracy, everyone needs to know who is really in charge, who makes the decisions, and in whose interest. Democracies function best without Invisible Men.

Notes

1. Ketchum Public Relations Confidential Memo to CALRAB Food Safety Team, Sept. 7, 1990.
2. *O'Dwyer's Directory of Public Relations Executives 1995*, p. 178.
3. David P. Bianco, ed., *PR News Casebook: 1000 Public Relations Case Studies* (Potomac, MD: Phillips Publishing, 1993), pp. 120–121.
4. David Steinman, *Diet for a Poisoned Planet: How to Choose Safe Foods for You and Your Family* (New York: Harmony Books, 1990).
5. *O'Dwyer's Directory of Public Relations Firms 1994*, pp. 96–97.
6. *O'Dwyer's PR Services Report*, Vol. 8 No. 2, Feb. 1994, p. 42.
7. *O'Dwyer's Directory of Public Relations Executives 1995*, p. 178.
8. Ketchum Public Relations Confidential Memo to CALRAB Food Safety Team, Sept. 7, 1990.
9. Jean Rainey, Memo for Roland Woerner Regarding David Steinman Booking on Today Show. (no date)
10. Elizabeth M. Whelan, American Council on Science and Health, to John Sununu, Chief of Staff, White House, July 12, 1990.
11. Daniel P. Puzo, "The New Naturalism: Controversy Eats at *Diet for a Poisoned Planet*," *Los Angeles Times*, Nov. 29, 1990, p. 27.

12. Kenneth N. Hall et al., U.S. Dept. of Agriculture, to Food Safety Contacts, Oct. 29, 1990.
13. Ken Miller, "Meltdown in EPA Watchdog Office Puts Millions at Risk, Workers Say," Gannett News Service, May 4, 1995. See also "EPA Reinstatement, Compensatory Damages Awarded Toxicologist Removed by EPA," BNA *Chemical Regulation Daily*, Dec. 11, 1992.
14. *O'Dwyer's Directory of Public Relations Firms 1994*, pp. 124–125.
15. Carol Ward Knox, Morgan & Meyers, to dairy industry representatives, Sept. 17, 1992.
16. John F. Berry, "Suit Says Du Pont Co. Pressured Publishers; Author Alleges His History of Family Was Financially Doomed," *Washington Post*, Sept. 22, 1981, p. A2.
17. Interview with Dan Barry.
18. David Helvarg, *The War Against the Greens* (San Francisco: Sierra Club Books, 1994), pp. 365–366.
19. Susan B. Trento, *The Power House: Robert Keith Gray and the Selling of Access and Influence in Washington* (New York: St. Martin's Press, 1992), p. 233.
20. Ibid., p. 196.
21. Ibid., p. 62.
22. James Flynn, Paul Slovic and C.K. Mertz, "The Nevada Initiative: A Risk Communication Fiasco" (unpublished manuscript), May 6, 1993, pp. 6–8.
23. Peoples Bicentennial Commission, *Voices of the American Revolution* (New York: Bantam Books, 1974), pp. 114–116.

Discussion Questions

1. Why were California raisins considered so dangerous?

2. What strategies did Ketchum PR use to cancel information about the dangers of California raisins?

3. How was the U.S. government involved in Ketchum's actions?

4. Why, according to the authors, is it important for the PR industry that its activities remain "invisible"?

Writing Suggestion

Visit the *PR Watch* web site, www.prwatch.org, and report on recent abuses of public relations firms. Or argue for the value of public relations in promoting positive change in society.

Writing Suggestions
for Chapter Two

1. Using the readings in this chapter as an analytical frame, spend a week watching various national and local news broadcasts. What stories dominate? Why? Do you think the stories deserve the coverage they are receiving? What important issues, in your opinion, are being neglected by the news?

2. Analyze the advertising in a week's worth of newspapers or television broadcasts of the news. What kinds of ads are most popular? What do the ads say about the readers/viewers of the news?

3. Using further research, examine the growing dominance of corporate sponsorship of public television. How has that sponsorship changed over the years? Is there now such a thing as "commercial-free" television?

4. What are your peers' attitudes to the news? Do you or your classmates read the paper or watch the news regularly? Why or why not?

Chapter III

Corporate Greed and Crime

W hat is good for business is good for America, we often hear. But are there times when big business goes too far, when the hunt for profits and the relentless drive for growth ceases to benefit our communities? In this chapter, the readings will ask you to consider what happens when capitalism runs rampant and exploits and undermines the very population it depends upon for its profits.

In three selections from *Corporate Predators: The Hunt for Profits and the Attack on Democracy* ("The Corporate Takeover of Public Space," "Wal-Mart and the Strip-Mining of America" and "Destroy the Dummy, Destroy the Child"), Russell Mokhiber and Robert Weissman discuss how corporations attempt to intrude on both our private and public space, and how they often neglect to consider issues of safety in their quest for dollars. The use of prison labor is examined by an author who is himself a prisoner in "Microsoft 'Outcells' Competition," from *The Celling of America: An Inside Look at the U.S Prison Industry* edited by Daniel Burton-Rose, Dan Pens and Paul Wright. In "A Tale of Two Inner Cites," from *Field of Schemes: How the Great Stadium Swindle Turns Public Money into Private Profit*, Joanna Cagan and Neil deMause examine the social and economic costs of building professional sports stadiums and arenas. Jennifer Vogel probes the drawbacks of the gambling industry in "Disneyland with Dice: Cannibalizing the Economy Under the Guise of Entertainment," from *Crapped Out: How Gambling Ruins the Economy and Destroys Lives*.

In "From Tiny Tim to Jerry Lewis: Charity and Economic Rights on a Collision Course," from *Beyond Ramps: Disability at the End of the Social Contract*, Marta Russell questions our current system of charitable giving and how that system benefits the wealthy. In " 'Rent to Own': The Slick Cousin of Paying on Time," from *Merchants of Misery: How Corporate America Profits from Poverty*, Michael Hudson reveals the exploitative tactics of the rent-to-own industry. Finally, in "The Ideology of Competitiveness: Pitting Worker Against Worker," from *Corporations are Gonna Get Your Mama: Globalization and the Downsizing of the American Dream*, edited by Kevin Danaher, James Rinehart illustrates how companies, in their drive for profits, play employees off of one another.

The Corporate Takeover of Public Space

Russel Mokhiber & Robert Weissman

*Corporate Predators: The Hunt for Mega-Profits
and the Attack on Democracy*

February 6, 1998

It wasn't always the case that the market intruded into every aspect of our lives.

Not long ago, for example, you could go to the museums at the Smithsonian Institution in Washington, D.C. without being bombarded by corporate advertisements. Not so today. Today, major Smithsonian exhibits are sponsored by big corporations. Corporate advertisements fill brochures. And credit card companies are hawking their cards inside the museums.

The sign at the credit card table inside the Air and Space Museum last month read "Free T-Shirt." But the T-shirt wasn't free—you had to sign up for the credit card before you got the T-shirt.

It used to be that you could watch public television and listen to public radio without being hit with a barrage of commercials from companies such as Archer Daniels Midland (ADM) and Pepsi.

It used to be that corporations and their markets had private commercial places, and individuals with their communities had their public places.

Today, it is difficult to find a public place that commercial culture hasn't infiltrated.

The airport? Try and find anywhere, outside of the restrooms, in a modern American airport where you can sit and read without being infected by a television or billboard commercial. The new National Airport outside of Washington, D.C. has been transformed from an airport to a shopping mall, with more than 50 upscale shops. If you get up from your chair in the waiting area to get away from the GAP television commercials on CNN, you run right into the GAP store itself. And once you get on the airplane, the television plops down in front of your face.

The public highway? Littered with billboard ads. Some estimate 500,000 billboards pollute the nation's highways. We don't know the exact figure, because the powerful billboard lobby has defeated legislation requiring official billboard counts.

In the 1960s, the industry, represented by the Outdoor Advertising Association of America (OAAA), pushed through the perversely named Highway Beautification Act, to regulate the industry. OAAA supported the law because it realized that regulation was better than an outright ban on billboard advertising. The law has led to a proliferation of what has been called "litter on a stick."

Rural America? If you are fed up with the rampant commercialism that has swamped the cities and suburbs, fleeing to the country won't do you any good. Rural areas are being overrun by industrial corporations looking for compliant populations to accept their toxic pollution and waste, by prison corporations and by ugly strip mall developers and fast food outlets that have paved over suburbia and are looking to convert ever more of the natural landscape into neon America.

Public schools? Millions of public school children are force fed Channel One. In exchange for video and satellite equipment, public schools are required to make their children sit through Channel One's daily news program—including the ads. Corporations are flooding cash-strapped public schools with study guides, magazines, posters and books. Some schools even sell ad space on the public school buses.

James Howard Kunstler, author of *The Geography of Nowhere*, believes that America has evolved from a nation of coherent publicly spirited communities to a national living arrangement that "destroys civic life while imposing enormous social costs and economic burdens."

Kunstler argues that "amidst the tides of cultural sewage now overflowing our national life there is a growing recognition that we desperately need something better, more worthy of the human spirit."

The Baltimore-based comedian Bob Somerby, in his persuasive and funny one-man show, "Material World," claims that "products have taken over the planet." Somerby blames much of our unhappiness and social problems on the commercialism that has swamped every aspect of our society.

There is a time and place for everything. The place for corporations is in the market, out of the public's space. The time to begin again to enforce the separation is now.

Wal-Mart and the Strip-Mining of America

Russel Mokhiber & Robert Weissman

*Corporate Predators: The Hunt for Mega-Profits
and the Attack on Democracy*

October 23, 1998

Walk into any Wal-Mart and marvel. One near us is open 24 hours. Never closes. Consumer goods as far as the eye can see. Quality product at a low price. Friendly workers greeting eager consumers at the door.

In 1997, Wal-Mart had sales of $118 billion and is on course to become, within 10 years or so, the world's largest corporation.

Wal-Mart is three times bigger than Sears, its nearest competitor, and larger than all three of its main rivals (Sears, Target and Kmart) combined.

Wal-Mart now has 3,400 stores on four continents. "Our priorities are that we want to dominate North America first, then South America, and then Asia and then Europe," Wal-Mart's President and CEO David Glass told *USA Today* business reporter Lorrie Grant recently.

And given the history of steady rise of the Bentonville, Arkansas retailer, who would doubt it?

Certainly not *USA Today*, which last week ran Grant's glowing review of Wal-Mart's worldwide operation under the headline: "An Unstoppable Marketing Force: Wal-Mart Aims for Domination of the Retail Industry—Worldwide."

But Bob Ortega, a *Wall Street Journal* reporter, reveals a different side of the Wal-Mart phenomenon in his recently released book, *In Sam We Trust: The Untold Story of Sam Walton and How Wal-Mart Is Devouring America* (Times Business, 1998).

Ortega documents how Sam Walton—perhaps the most driven corporate executive ever to walk the face of the planet—built his empire. Wal-Mart has used Asian child labor to make blouses for sale under "Made in America" signs in his stores. When he began his operation in Bentonville, Arkansas, Sam Walton hired a union-busting attorney to quash worker organizing. Outer city Wal-Marts have steamrolled inner city shopkeepers.

Ortega speaks to Kathleen Baker of Hastings, Minnesota, who was fired after talking with other workers about asking for a pay raise.

He speaks to Mike and Paula Ianuzzo, of Cottage Grove, Oregon, who blamed Wal-Mart for wiping out their photo-shop business.

In Guatemala, he interviewed Flor de Maria Salguedo, a union organizer who arranged for Ortega to talk with workers making clothes for Wal-Mart and other giant retailers.

Salguedo, whose husband was murdered during an organizing drive in Guatemala City, was herself kidnapped, beaten and raped shortly after Ortega left Guatemala City. After the attack, one of her attackers told her, "This is what you get for messing about with foreigners."

Ortega documents how communities around the country have revolted against Wal-Mart's plans to plunk down giant superstores in their communities, ripping apart the fabric of small town life.

In Oklahoma, the owner of a television and record store adversely affected and eventually closed down after a Wal-Mart moved into the area, told reporters, "Wal-Mart really craters a little town's downtown."

Shelby Robinson, a self-employed clothing designer from Fort Collins tells Ortega that she "really hates Wal-Mart." Why?

"Everything's starting to look the same, everybody buys all the same things—a lot of small-town character is being lost," Robinson says. "They dislocate communities, they hurt small businesses, they add to our sprawl and pollution because everybody drives farther, they don't pay a living wage, and visually, they're atrocious."

James Howard Kunstler, an ardent Wal-Mart foe from upstate New York, talks about what he calls the $7 hair dryer fallacy.

Kunstler argues to Ortega that "people who shop at a giant discounter to save $7 on a hair dryer don't realize that they pay a hidden price by taking that business from local merchants, because those merchants are the people who sit on school boards, sponsor little league teams and support the civic institutions that create a community."

Kunstler calls Wal-Mart "the exemplar of a form of corporate colonialism, which is to say, organizations from one place going into distant places and strip-mining them culturally and economically."

Ortega documents how communities around the country are rising up to slap down Wal-Mart's plans at expansion.

But Ortega questions whether, given the amazing popularity of Wal-Mart among consumers worldwide, anything will stop this juggernaut.

As Ortega points out, consumerism has not always held sway on this soil. Back 200 years ago, in the United States, "one did not shop for pleasure."

"The very idea of coveting goods ran counter to a broad Puritanical streak in American society, and to its proclaimed values of living simply, working hard (the famous 'work ethic'), being thrifty, and seeking salvation through faith," Ortega writes.

Ortega closes the book with a story of how Tibetans believe, depending on their past actions, people can come back to other realms besides this one.

"Among the worst of the realms is the realm of the hungry ghosts—a place reminiscent of certain neighborhoods of Dante's Inferno," he writes. "The hungry ghosts are the reincarnations of people who were covetous or greedy in this life. In the realm of the hungry ghosts, they are constantly ravenous but can never be satisfied. They despoil and devour everything around them. They consume endlessly and insatiably. It struck me immediately as a metaphor for our own mass culture."

On April 6, 1992, Sam Walton died one of the wealthiest men in America. Ortega says that he cannot presume to know where Walton went after he passed on. "But I can't help but think, at times, that his hungry ghost is still with us, in the form of Wal-Mart itself."

Destroy the Dummy, Destroy the Child

Russel Mokhiber & Robert Weissman

Corporate Predators: The Hunt for Mega-Profits and the Attack on Democracy

May 1, 1998

On October 15, 1995, Robert Sanders lost his seven-year-old daughter, Alison. Alison Sanders was riding in the front passenger seat of a three-week-old 1995 Dodge Caravan in Baltimore, Maryland. The van, traveling at 9.3 miles per hour, struck a car in front of it. The air bag deployed, killing Alison.

Robert Sanders, a business lawyer in Baltimore, was besides himself with grief. He checked himself into a psychiatric hospital for three weeks following the death of his daughter.

Now, Robert Sanders is on a campaign to fix the problem of unsafe air bags. Alison Sanders and more than 90 others, mostly children and women, have been killed by air bags over the past three years.

Sanders is the founder of Parents for Safer Air Bags, a group of parents of children killed by air bags.

Sanders says that some air bags are safer than others. For example, some air bags fire out directly at the occupant. Safer air bags shoot up along the windshield and thus pose less of a risk to the occupant. Many other safety features are also already in vehicles on the road today.

At an April press conference in Washington, D.C., Parents for Safer Air Bags called on the National Highway Traffic Safety Administration (NHTSA) to upgrade its air bag safety tests to prevent front-seat passengers from being killed or seriously injured by poorly designed air bags.

The group petitioned the agency to expand the present tests which currently use only a properly positioned dummy representing a 170-pound male in a 30-mph crash test and do not test for vehicle occupants of other sizes in other positions.

Air bags have saved hundreds of lives and are a major step forward in advancing auto safety—but they have also killed 96 people, including fifty-four children under age 11 and twenty-five women shorter than five feet, four inches.

"Ten children have been killed and six others severely injured in Chrysler mini-vans, yet the company deliberately chose not to test the bags in its family-style mini-vans with child dummies," Sanders said.

Asked why Chrysler didn't test its air bags using child dummies, Chrysler's senior vehicle safety specialist, Howard Willson, testified recently in a deposition in a defective production lawsuit that "you'd destroy the dummy so there was little purpose in testing something where you knew the result was—could be catastrophic as far as the dummy was concerned."

During his deposition, Willson said he "can't say it was a surprise" when he heard that air bags were killing children.

Sanders says he was shocked when he heard about Willson's testimony.

"Chrysler marketed its family-style minivans of the 1990s with photographs of a little leaguer sitting in the front seat of a minivan," Sanders said. "Yet we now learn from the testimony of Howard Willson that Chrysler never crash tested any of its minivans with child-sized dummies, because according to Willson, the company knew that the air bag would 'destroy' the child-sized dummy. By inference, they understood that the air bag would also destroy the child."

In states in which juries are permitted to impose punitive damages, this testimony presents a serious problem for Chrysler, which faces numerous lawsuits from parents who have lost children to Chrysler air bags.

Many manufacturers have deliberately chosen air bag designs that meet the minimum federal standard but which are dangerous for children and women at low-speed collisions.

Now, the auto companies are lobbying Congress and the Department of Transportation to go slow and not set any firm deadlines for setting a proper air bag safety standard.

In September 1996, the National Transportation Safety Board issued an "urgent" safety recommendation that NHTSA "immediately revise" the air bag performance standard to "establish performance requirements that reflect the actual accident environment."

Despite's NHTSA's announcement that it would propose an upgrade in early 1997, no such proposed rule has been issued.

While some manufacturers have incorporated widely available technology in their air bag designs that address real-world crash conditions, many have not.

According to NHTSA data, eight manufacturers—Alfa Romeo, BMW, Honda, Mercedes Benz, Nissan, Porsche, Saab and Subaru—have had no passenger-side air bag deaths or severe injuries. But other companies have installed poorly designed air bags which have resulted in deaths and severe injuries.

To honor the lives of those little ones who have been killed because corporate executives refused to do the right thing, the government must act promptly to require proper testing of these important safety devices. And those corporations responsible for the carnage must be brought to justice.

Discussion Questions

1. Is there anything wrong with having corporate logos and other advertising within public space?

2. Do you feel that advertising and other corporate messages intrude into your "space"?

3. In your opinion, what influence does advertising in schools have on students?

4. What are the hidden costs of "saving" money at a "megastore"?

5. What is "corporate colonialism"?

6. Why didn't Chrysler test airbags with child-sized dummies in its mini-vans?

Writing Suggestion

Investigate or observe your own campus or local community. How pervasive is the intrusion of corporate messages in your "public space"?

Microsoft "Outcells" Competition

Dan Pens

The Celling of America: An Inside Look at the U.S. Prison Industry

Edited by Daniel Burton-Rose, Dan Pens & Paul Wright

Dan Pens, April 1996

In the Seattle area, home to software giant Microsoft, it's not uncommon to hear the phrase "Microsoft Millionaire." There exists a large number of ex-Microsoft employees who made their millions, quit the company, and are now free to enjoy other pursuits. Many of them are quite young, in their thirties or forties.

Not everybody who toils for Microsoft, however, can hope to become a millionaire as a result. Many of Microsoft's products are packaged and shrink-wrapped by prisoners at Washington's Twin Rivers Corrections Center (TRCC).

According to one prisoner who works for Exmark, a company specializing in product packaging, approximately 90 prisoners at TRCC packaged 50,000 units of Windows '95 demo disks and direct-mail promotional packets.

"Those were good times for us," he recalls fondly. "Everybody had plenty of work then." That same worker says he was laid off after the Microsoft contract, and he hasn't worked since. Each day, he says, he checks the bulletin board: Exmark posts a "call-out" list with the names of those workers fortunate enough to have a job the following day. He explains that those prisoners with the least seniority or who have fallen into disfavor—for anything from back-talking to poor work habits—will appear on the call-out list only for the largest contracts.

Exmark is a subsidiary of Pac Services, a Washington company which also employs non-prisoner, or "free world" workers. Steve Curly, a "free world" supervisor at Exmark, denied the company had packed any Windows '95 units. But he said that Exmark's TRCC operation had packed tens of thousands of units of Microsoft Office, and had wrapped and shipped as many as 40,000 Microsoft mice in one week.

Many of Exmark's prison workers are employed mainly—as one prisoner puts it—"when they have a big contract and need the extra workers." When work is plentiful, Exmark's prison workers shift into high gear, often working both day and swing shifts. At other times the crew is called back and most workers remain idle in their cells.

Exmark workers say that Microsoft is not the only beneficiary of Exmark's "flexible" labor force; they also claim to have regularly packaged goods for Costco, Starbucks and JanSport. They also say that Exmark not only packages retail goods, but also stuffs envelopes for mass mailings, something they claim to have often done for telecommunications giant US WEST.

Most people are surprised to learn that private corporations use prison labor. After the initial shock, however, many think it's a terrific new idea. There has been considerable debate as to whether or not it's a "terrific" idea, but rare is the challenge to the premise that it's a "new" one. Most people assume that corporate use of prison labor is a recent innovation. Nothing could be further from the truth.

Beginning in 1817 with New York's Auburn prison, the predominate U.S. prison model was based on a scheme generally referred to as "lease prisons." Sometimes private business entities contracted with states to operate their entire prison system; other times the state would operate the prisons and "lease" the prisoner labor to businesses.

Nineteenth-century prisons were essentially forced labor camps. Prisoners were made to produce a wide array of goods, including shoes, furniture, wagons, and stoves. For the sake of profit they were often housed in squalid conditions, fed spoiled food, and given scant clothing and shoes. Whippings were commonplace, and medical care was non-existent.

Dr. Lewis Wynne, executive director of the Florida Historical Society, says that since states rarely monitored conditions, operators of lease prisons often worked prisoners to death. Mortality rates, Dr. Wynne said, ran as high as 40 percent.

From almost the very start of the lease system, there were scattered protests from manufacturers' associations and organized labor. The states were addicted to the cost savings, however, and refused to dismantle the lease system. Events in Tennessee provide an illustrative example.

In the 1870s competitors of the Tennessee Coal, Iron and Railroad Company charged that convict labor gave that company an unfair competitive advantage. Their protests fell on the deaf ears of state lawmakers, and the lease system continued.

In 1891, the company locked out all of its union workers for refusing to sign a "yellow dog" contract that would have barred them from union membership. The company replaced the locked-out union workers entirely with lease convicts. In what was dubbed the "Coal Creek Rebellion," angry union miners stormed the lease prisons, released over 400 prisoners, and loaded them onto trains headed for the state capitol. The company filled up the work camps with more convicts. The miners released those prisoners, too, and this time they burned the prison stockades to the ground. Shortly thereafter, Tennessee finally dismantled the lease labor system.

By the beginning of this century most other states had followed suit, enacting a patchwork of state laws abolishing or restricting the use of prison labor by private enterprises. Two New Deal-era federal laws, the 1929 Hawes-Cooper Act and the 1935 Ashurst-Sumners Act, effectively ended the private business-convict labor relationship. Hawes-Cooper authorized states to pass legislation prohibiting the entrance of prison-made goods from other states, and Ashurst-Sumners made it a federal offense to move prison-made goods across state boundaries, irrespective of individual state laws. Thus ended this first round of prison labor profiteering.

In the 1970s Chief Justice Warren Burger, born 16 years after the Coal Creek Rebellion, began proselytizing for conversion of U.S. prisons into "factories with fences." Congress was a willing convert. As part of the Justice System Improvement Act of 1979, Congress passed an amendment which established seven Prison Industry Enhancement (PIE) pilot projects which would be exempted from the provisions of Ashurst-Sumners. By 1984, PIE had grown to 20 pilot projects, and the definition of project was changed to encompass not just a single business, but all businesses set up in prisons by either a county or a state. The law was again amended in 1990 to allow up to 50 pilot "projects" (e.g., states) to participate. Today all of the prison products from as many as 50 states or counties may legally enter the stream of interstate commerce. And so begins round two of the prison labor profiteering racket, with a PIE big enough for any business in any state to start grabbing a piece of the action.

For companies like Exmark, it is an attractive proposition. Exmark pays its prison workers the minimum wage ($4.90/hr in Washington), but that figure is misleading. The Department of Corrections deducts twenty percent of prisoners' wages to recover "cost of corrections." (Calculations indicate that the twenty percent deduction from the wages of 100 such prisoner workers is enough to subsidize the salary and benefits of eight guards.) Another ten percent is deducted and placed in a non-interest bearing "mandatory savings account." Five percent is deducted for a "Victims' Compensation Fund" administered by the state. Federal income tax, social security tax, and Medicare tax are also withheld. The DOC can deduct an additional twenty percent to pay court-ordered restitution, court costs, and other debts. When all is said and done prisoners can see a spendable wage of $1.80 to $2.80 per hour. But even this amount is generous, because the law actually authorizes up to eighty percent of a prisoners' wages to be deducted, meaning they could actually "take home" less than one dollar an hour.

Exmark and other private industries operating in Washington's prisons do not have to provide their prison workers with any benefits such as health insurance workers' compensation, or retirement (although the state offers a comprehensive "Three Strikes" retirement plan!). These operations are further subsidized by the state in that they usually pay little or nothing for the factory, office, or warehouse space in the state's prisons.

Exmark has a "lease" (sound familiar?) with Washington state wherein they pay only one dollar per year for an impressive amount of factory and warehouse space. The DOC often subsidizes other overhead expenses (like 24-hour security) that a private company would have to pay in a non-prison setting.

Many of the prisoner workers claim the arrangement offers them tremendous benefits, and these claims are backed up by a waiting list of at least one year for TRCC prisoners hoping to get an Exmark job. Workers say that since they have no real living expenses, most of the money they earn in industry jobs can be sent home to help support their families. Many of them express a fierce sense of pride in the fact that they provide for their families, even while they are imprisoned. Since most prison jobs in Washington state pay 25–42 cents an hour, the prospect of working at Exmark is considered by most prisoners to be a tremendous opportunity.

Some prisoners' rights activists also think that private industry jobs are a boon to prisoners. Charlie Sullivan, Co-Director of Citizens United for the Rehabilitation of Errants (CURE), a national prison reform organization, when asked in a 1995 interview about CURE's accomplishments over the past five years, said:

> I think in general it seems like where we've been successful is concerned with employment. We've been working on prison-based industries, which involves a philosophical argument going on in the prison reform community—particularly the left wing, which is worried about exploitation of prisoners. But I feel very strongly that we should be moving in the direction of supporting the idea, though certainly there should be caution in setting them up... As I've said, the whole goal of the system should be to make prisoners employable upon release.

But what kind of jobs will await these "employable" prisoners when they are released? Many of the jobs that might otherwise be available to them may have moved into prisons. Lockhart Technologies, Inc. is one example of a company which eliminated 130 "free world" jobs. They closed their Austin, Texas, circuit board assembly plant, moved all of their machinery inside of a "private" prison (operated by the Wackenhut Corporation) 30 miles away, and used state prisoners to replace the 130 workers they laid off in Austin. The prison actually designed their factory space to Lockhart Technology's specifications and charges the company one dollar a year rent.

In 1994 the Washington DOC built, with taxpayer money, a 56,000 square foot "industries building" adjacent to the Washington State Reformatory. The state has worked hard to attract private industries to move into the factory space. So far they have attracted Elliot Bay Metal Fabrication, A&I Manufacturing, Inc., and Redwood Outdoors, Inc.[1]

Elliot Bay manufactures micro-brewery vats and commercial fishing equipment such as pans, conveyor belts and storage tanks. They employ eleven highly-skilled welders and metal fabricators, but as with most prison industry jobs, the applicants must bring these skills to the job before they are hired. Elliot Bay does not run a job-training program, and they are not in the business of providing job skills to prisoners. They operate in the prison solely to make a profit.

A&I manufacturing fabricates window blinds, mini-blinds, cell shades (blinds made out of cloth), wire shelving, and are expanding into other window coverings such as curtains. All of their output is sold to De-El Enterprises, Inc., a local company who in turn deals with construction contractors to outfit entire buildings with blinds, shelves, etc.

Redwood Outdoors is a garment manufacturer, employing about twenty prisoners. Prison workers at Redwood say they make clothing for Eddie Bauer, Kelly-Hanson, Planet Hollywood and Brooks, among others. Most Redwood workers are reluctant to talk about their jobs, especially about whose labels they sew into the garments they make. "Eddie Bauer doesn't want anyone to know they use prison labor," one said in a hushed tone.

Considering the cost of the 56,000 square foot building, the salaries of guards and DOC supervisors, maintenance and administrative costs, it is debatable as to whether the DOC makes any money with prison industries, especially considering that they charge a paltry $1 a year to lease out the factory space.

The state legislature is nevertheless committed to expanding private prison industries. In its 1993 session, the Washington legislature passed Senate Bill 5989, codified as RCW 72.09.111. The law mandates that the Washington DOC increase the number of prisoners employed in "Free Venture Industries" by 300 jobs a year, with a net increase of 1,500 new prison industry jobs by the year 2000.

There is language in the statute that alludes to a concern that state prison industry jobs don't displace free workers, stating that the industries shall "provide Washington state manufacturers or business with products or services currently produced by out-of-state or foreign suppliers." The law also says that the DOC is supposed to conduct "an analysis of the potential impact of the proposed products or services on the Washington state business community and labor market."

One could argue that some prison-made goods, like the garments sewn for Redwood Outdoors, may indeed fall into a category of goods "currently produced...by...foreign suppliers," such as the infamous *maquiladora* sweatshops in Mexico and Central America. But what about the micro-brewery and fishing equipment fabricated by Elliot Bay? Are there no Washington state metal fabricators who might produce those goods? What about the blinds and window shades manufactured by A&I? Is there not one Washington state company that could offer those jobs to unemployed free workers?

The law requires the DOC to conduct an analysis of the potential impact of prison industry jobs on the local labor market. But the law is silent about what that analysis might show, or whether the DOC should be prevented from creating prison industry jobs that displace outside workers. The question is: Why should companies like Elliot Bay or A&I Manufacturing offer real-world jobs to unemployed free workers? Not when they can move into factory space provided by the state, and employ a "captive work force" at minimum-wage which they can hire, fire, and lay-off at whim. And how can other local companies compete with these prison industries? The answer is they can't. Companies like Elliot Bay and A&I drive out local jobs and drive down the wages of free workers.

One Elliot Bay worker was talking the other day, boasting that "Elliot Bay is the best program in the joint." He claims that working there allows him to hone his welding skills and prepare for a job on the outside. When it was pointed out to him that Elliot Bay probably takes jobs away from workers in society, he replied, "Fuck society! Society locked me up."

But which segment of society is truly being screwed by prison industry jobs? Those who own stock in Microsoft, US WEST, Costco, and Starbucks are probably satisfied with the arrangement. But unemployed welders, metal fabricators, factory workers, and laborers might see it differently, especially when they realize that the only way they can get a job might be by going to prison.

[*Editors' Note:* Exmark employees report that Microsoft canceled its packaging contract with the prison-based company in December, 1996, ostensibly due to "quality control" issues. The above article, however, was reprinted locally and nationally, and may have been a factor in the termination. Corporations have no qualms about exploiting prison labor, but they don't relish the publicity.]

Notes

1   Boeing, the world's largest civil aviation manufacturer, has also discovered the benefits of captive labor. MicroJet, a small company which makes aircraft components which are sold to Boeing, employs eight prisoners paid significantly less than the outside prevailing wage, at the Washington State Reformatory in Monroe. See: Paul Wright, "Making Slave Labor Fly: Boeing Goes to Prison," *Prison Legal News*, March 1997, p.1.

Discussion Questions

1.   What is your opinion on private industry using prison labor to produce goods and services?

2.   What are the benefits do prisoners get from outside work being brought into prisons? What benefits do corporations get?

3.   What are some of the drawbacks of using prisoners as workers in private corporations?

Writing Suggestion

Research recent controversy surrounding prison labor, including allowing prisoner to take travel and plane reservations over the phone. What is your opinion on the practice?

A Tale of Two Inner Cities

Joanna Cagan & Neil deMause

*Field of Schemes: How the Great Stadium Swindle Turns
Public Money into Private Profit*

"It is simply unconscionable that cities are forced to succumb to blackmail by pro
football and baseball. You should not capitulate to blackmailers. You don't deal
with hostage situations. You don't deal with terrorists. I put these teams in the same
category."

—Maryland state senator Julian Lapides[1]

It was late in the night of March 29, 1984, when a dozen moving vans backed up
to the football training complex in the Maryland suburb of Owings Mills and took
the Baltimore Colts away.

Since 1953 the Colts had been an institution as fundamental to Baltimore's self-
image as crabcakes or Edgar Allan Poe. Now, overnight, this symbol of the city was
to be reborn as something called the Indianapolis Colts, and disappear forever into
an indoor football stadium in the American heartland.

A few spectators gathered in the rain to watch as the worldly belongings of
Baltimore's football team were loaded up for the 600-mile drive west. The movers,
imported from Indianapolis' Mayflower van lines by Colts owner Robert Irsay for the
occasion, packed away helmets and pads, file cabinets and film projectors, as
Pinkerton guards kept onlookers at bay.

"It's unbelievable, the callousness of this man," Colts fan Brian Yaniger told a
crowd of assembled reporters. "Just because he has a couple of bucks, he can tear a
whole city down on his whims."[2]

The Colts' move was hardly the first time a pro sports team switched cities. In
1958, after all, the Dodgers had famously fled Brooklyn, and six of the National
Basketball Association's inaugural eight teams had moved from their original homes
by 1963. The first great era of sports franchise migration ran from 1952 until 1968—
when the Kansas City (née Philadelphia) A's ended their two-decade westward flight
by settling in Oakland. In the interim, more than a dozen sports franchises took up
new residences.

But those were different times. Jet travel had abruptly made bicoastal leagues a reality, and the great population shifts away from the urban centers of the Northeast to the suburbs and the Sunbelt had opened up new markets for pro sports. By the time the Colts took flight, the major sports leagues had already expanded into most of the attractive locations, and franchise shifts had become rare. Before the Oakland Raiders moved to Los Angeles in 1982, no established football team had switched cities in two decades. Baseball hadn't seen a move in 12 years; basketball and hockey had undergone unprecedented expansion but little franchise movement since the early '70s. Sports fans in Baltimore, like their counterparts across the nation, had grown secure in the expectation that their team would still be there to cheer on the following year.

Besides, the team's absentee owner, Robert Irsay, had just been handed $25 million in city-funded stadium improvements to quiet earlier threats to leave town. And the team was moving to Indianapolis of all places, a city no larger than Baltimore, with only a single major-league team to its name, the fledgling Indiana Pacers basketball club—a prototypical hick town derisively nicknamed India-no-place.

The Colts' move, clearly, was something new and frightening: a team leaving its home of three decades not for lack of support (the Colts had continued to attract large crowds in its last years in Baltimore), but solely for the lure of greater profits. "If the Colts can be moved that way," wrote New York Times sports columnist Dave Anderson following the team's midnight flight, "any other franchise area in any sport can wake up some morning to find itself without a team."[3]

They were prophetic words. The Colts' move may have seemed an anomaly at the time, but in retrospect it was the dawn of an era. In 1984, corporations large and small were learning as never before how to supplement profits by extorting money from their hometowns under threat of moving across the country or overseas. The sports industry may have come late to this game of "corporate welfare," as it came to be known, but it soon had adopted the tactic for its own. While a manufacturing plant could win perhaps tens of millions of dollars this way, the final tab for a single sports subsidy could run as high as half a billion dollars.

The Colts' sudden move led to a series of events far beyond anything that could have been imagined that spring night. By the time the dust had settled, another football team had been taken from its diehard fans, and two cities had undertaken the building of four new stadiums, leaving taxpayers in two states to pay close to $1 billion in construction costs. The resulting transfer of public funds into private pockets would lay claim to public schools and fragile urban neighborhoods, leave democratic checks and balances in shambles, and enrich a handful of owners—real estate barons and wealthy industrialists—by hundreds of millions of dollars. The flight of the Baltimore Colts may have seemed like the end of the world for the team's fans, but for sports owners, it was the beginning of a lucrative dream that has yet to end. Before long, Cleveland, another urban center similarly struggling to survive the shifting industrial landscape of the 1970s, would be drawn into the musical-chairs game of relocating sports teams and earmarking public funds for stadium construction. Within a decade, nearly every major city in the nation was being asked to mortgage its future to the sports industry, and Robert Irsay was beginning to look less like a singular demon than the harbinger of a scam of historic proportions.

It all started, inauspiciously enough, with the Hoosier Dome.

Take the Money and Run

The idea was first floated in the mid-1970s by business and political leaders in Indianapolis. The local government had already poured more than $400 million into a decade's worth of downtown office blocks and hotel complexes; a new domed football stadium, they proposed, would complement the city's convention center as the centerpiece of a hub of sports-based tourism.[4] Construction of the Hoosier Dome was under way by 1982, its $78 million price tag financed by a one percent countywide tax on food and beverages and $30 million in grants from two local foundations.[5]

Indianapolis had a state-of-the-art domed stadium rising in its city center, but it still had no team. Dome boosters had assured city leaders that the NFL would place an expansion football team in Indianapolis once construction was complete. By 1982, however, it had become clear that the football league was in no hurry to expand—thanks in part to an ongoing lawsuit over the Raiders' move to Los Angeles the previous year.[6] Furthermore, it was looking more likely that, once expansion did arrive, the NFL would favor booming Sunbelt cities such as Phoenix and Jacksonville over Indianapolis. Articles started appearing in financial publications with such headlines as "Will Indianapolis' Domed Stadium Become a White Elephant?"[7]

This, clearly, would not do. So three-term mayor William Hudnut, sensing political disaster, reestablished an old contact he had made back in 1977, when the dome was still just a set of blueprints: He called Robert Irsay, owner of the Baltimore Colts. And he offered him a deal.

A Chicago industrialist who had made his fortune in sheet metal, Irsay had bought the Colts in 1972 and watched as his new team took an immediate nosedive in the standings. In 1979, with the Colts floundering on the field and in ticket sales, the team's owner demanded that the city pay for $25 million worth of improvements to 25-year-old Memorial Stadium, which the Colts shared with the Baltimore Orioles baseball team. If not, he intimated, he would take his team elsewhere.[8]

The city capitulated to the Colts' owner's demands, but still Irsay's eye wandered. By 1984, his flirtations had focused on Indianapolis, where Hudnut was offering a low-rent lease on the new dome to entice the team to relocate. Baltimore city officials, scrambling to keep the Colts in place, countered with an offer of a $15 million loan and a city-backed guarantee on ticket sales. But even as they held out this lucrative carrot to Irsay, city leaders also readied an unprecedented stick: They asked the state legislature to consider condemning the team via the principle of eminent domain.

Under eminent domain powers, local governments can condemn a private asset and then seize it, paying the former owners fair market value for their property—in this case, the Colts themselves, which would then be sold to a new, local owner. It's a tactic more often used for highway rights-of-way than for football teams; it's also one that had failed two years earlier in Oakland when the Raiders skipped town. But that case had been rejected by an appeals court on very narrow grounds, and legal experts were hopeful that the city of Baltimore would have better luck with its case.

It never got the chance. The Colts, tipped off to the city's plans, hurriedly completed negotiations with Indianapolis.[9] And so, on March 29, 1984, while the Maryland legislature continued to debate the use of eminent domain, in came the moving vans. That afternoon, the bill to place the Colts under state control was passed, but it was a few hours too late: Courts would later rule against the seizure on the grounds that by the time the law was passed, there was nothing left for the state to seize.

The Baltimore Colts were no more. As fans grieved, local politicians plotted to obtain a replacement franchise, either through expansion or by moving an established team. And city officials across the nation braced for a new wave of demands from their own sports teams, under threat of becoming "another Baltimore."

"Mistake on the Lake"

The last thing the city of Cleveland wanted was to become the next Baltimore. It was already the first, and hopefully last, Cleveland, and that was enough of an emotional burden for even the windy town's hardiest souls. Once a thriving industrial center with dominating sports teams, Cleveland had seen its fortunes, its national image, and the reputation of its historic baseball stadium plummet over mere decades.

In 1931, the successful completion of the new sports stadium on the shores of Lake Erie was hailed as the harbinger of great things to come. Cleveland Municipal Stadium, built by the federal Works Project Administration with the hope of luring the 1932 Olympics to downtown Cleveland, was "a monument to the progressive spirit of the city's people," according to the special section of the *Cleveland Plain Dealer* devoted to the new stadium.[10]

The city, not yet crippled under the weight of the Depression, was coming off one of its most successful economic decades ever. Cleveland had become the nation's second largest center for automobile manufacturing, behind only Detroit. Big steel was thriving, as was manufacturing. And the brand-new horseshoe by the lake, built at a cost of some $2.5 million to local taxpayers, was the crown jewel in an economic construction plan designed to give the city even more national attention. When 80,000 fans jammed into Municipal Stadium's wooden seats for the Cleveland Indians' first baseball game there in 1932, headline writers crowed "Depression Given Black Eye."[11] It was there that the team reveled in its glory years of the 1940s and 1950s, when the Indians were one of the most successful teams in baseball and their fans set attendance records that would last for decades.

Fifty years later, the stadium had assumed a very different meaning. Municipal Stadium, and the city itself, became dubbed the "Mistake on the Lake." As Cleveland struggled through a series of national embarrassments in the 1970s—from the Cuyahoga River catching on fire to becoming the first major American city to go into default since the Depression—the dreadful performance of the Indians, and their aging ballpark, seemed horribly symbolic of Cleveland's misfortunes. Year after cellar-dwelling year, the team was considered an embarrassment to professional baseball, and talk escalated that opposing teams dreaded the trip to frigid Cleveland Municipal Stadium, with its bitter winds off Lake Erie and its tiny crowds, cramped locker rooms, and out-of-date scoreboard.[12]

And while many in the city turned critical eyes on the performance of the Indians, Cleveland itself was feeling the uncomfortable burn of a national spotlight that illuminated a shrinking population, deteriorating race relations, escalating poverty, and vanishing industrial jobs. The city, which had lost 23 percent of its population between 1970 and 1980, started the 1980s with its credit suspended by several Wall Street ratings agencies because of its fiscal woes.[13]

When Indians owner Steve O'Neill died in 1983, rumors ran rampant that the financially shaky team would be sold to buyers from another state, most likely Florida. Even before O'Neill's death, league officials had come to town to announce that the Indians were very likely not long for Cleveland. Without a principal owner for the team, its future was suddenly even more precarious. And so in 1984 a new tax initiative to fund a domed stadium (domes were then in fashion, as several cities had followed Indianapolis' lead) was called for, in order, it was claimed, to keep the team in the city.

The campaign for the dome was the brainchild of Cuyahoga County Commissioner Vincent Campanella. Working largely without the organized support of his fellow politicians, Campanella proposed putting a domed stadium in the old Central Market area of downtown Cleveland; the new $150 million, 72,000-seat stadium was to be entirely paid for by a countywide property tax levy.

Emotions ran high among fans and residents throughout the dome debate. The way some locals talked, the threatened move of a sports team would tear the heart out of the city. Yet many Clevelanders questioned the fiscal sanity of forking over public dollars at a time when the town overall was struggling to reverse years of financial woe. Others were reluctant to spend a great deal of tax money on a team that had performed so abysmally for so many years. "Go Browns," a cynical graffitist scrawled on the walk to Municipal Stadium. "And take the Indians with you."

In May 1984, voters resoundingly rejected the proposal. The choice of a property tax to fund the initiative, the poor performance by the Indians on the playing field, and, most important, a lack of consensus among the city's power brokers probably sent the campaign to its defeat.[14] The effort never had the full support of then-Governor Richard Celeste or the city's Republican mayor, George Voinovich. Indeed, Campanella himself would later speculate that the failure of the domed stadium tax killed his political career.[15]

But if Campanella's mishandling of the political situation temporarily doomed the dome, the idea of a new stadium had plenty of support, especially from the city's powerful business community. As would become the national pattern, advertisements by dome supporters promised Cleveland taxpayers that the new stadium would result in magnificent economic dividends for the city as a whole, promises that continued after the referendum went down to a solid defeat. Soon after the initiative lost, the *Washington Post* reported, "Cleveland leaders can't ignore a study that said a dome would result in the construction of three new downtown hotels, an office building and restaurants, that 1,588 full-time construction jobs would be created; that another 6,829 permanent jobs would result; that the total annual spending impact would be $62.2 million."[16] National and local media, the business community and local politicians all firmly pushed the idea that a new stadium was needed for the team and for Cleveland's hopes of re-establishing itself as an important city.

And although their referendum failed, domed stadium backers didn't give up. The Civic Committee to Build a Domed Stadium was formed, chaired by the acting chair of the Greater Cleveland Growth Association, the town's chamber of commerce.[17] The Civic Committee would later become the Greater Cleveland Domed Stadium Corporation, which borrowed $22 million from local banks and the state in order to purchase a site for a new facility.[18] Despite public opposition and construction and financing plans that were sketchy at best, supporters were determined to plunge ahead with the stadium project.

Before Cleveland's power brokers could come up with a new pitch, however, the national sports stadium scene irrevocably shifted—thanks in large part to events taking place back in Baltimore.

"Just Give Me the Tools"

The departure of the Colts in the spring of 1984 had an immediate impact on Baltimore politics. Seeing the outcry over the loss of one sports team, Mayor William Schaefer, who had been a steadfast opponent of spending public money on sports stadiums, abruptly became the biggest booster of a new ballpark for the Baltimore Orioles.

A success on the field and off since relocating from St. Louis in 1954, the Baltimore club ran off seven first-place finishes between 1966 and 1979, and their home at city-owned Memorial Stadium was a pleasant one, nestled in a residential neighborhood of single-family homes whose rooftops were visible beyond the wooden bleachers in right and left fields. In the mid-1980s, a poll of fans ranked Memorial as one of the best ballparks in the major leagues.

But for all its pastoral charm, Memorial was a no-frills ballpark, without such modern-day amenities as luxury boxes or lavish food preparation facilities. As early as 1967, when municipalities across the country were building new concrete "dual-purpose" stadiums to house both their football and baseball teams, the owners of the Colts and Orioles had proposed such a facility for Baltimore, to be situated near the old Camden railyards just west of downtown. In 1972, Orioles exec Frank Cashen upped the ante, proclaiming, "We are not going to be able to do anything in terms of a new long-term lease unless a stadium is built downtown."[19] But as it became clear that no such deal was forthcoming, the Orioles continued to sign short-term leases on Memorial, and no one moved to resurrect the idea of a new facility.

Then, in 1979, local beer magnate Jerrold Hoffberger sold the Orioles to Edward Bennett Williams, a lawyer-to-the-pols from hated rival Washington, D.C. Many in Baltimore suspected Williams of harboring secret plans to move the ballclub to the nation's capital—a suspicion that the new owner wasted no time in using to force the city's hand on his demands for a new stadium. "For as long as the city will support the team," he told the Washington Post, "it will stay here"—leading to rampant speculation that he would take the team south on the pretext of low attendance.[20] When American League President Lee MacPhail followed with a public vow of league support for a new stadium on I-95 between Baltimore and Washington, the pressure built for Baltimore to prevent a repeat of the Colts' betrayal.

By 1986, when Mayor Schaefer was elected governor of Maryland, he was not just a proponent of a new baseball stadium; he had become Williams' greatest ally. The man who as mayor had declared that "unless private enterprise builds it, we won't build it" was now missing no opportunity to stump for a new state-built ball-park.[21] Bill Marker, a local community leader who would play a major role in the stadium battle to come, recalls watching Schaefer's inaugural speech as governor: "I remember saying to friends, 'Well, let's see whether he mentions the stadium, and if so where in his speech.' And it was basically: 'Hi, Marylanders! We've gotta build a stadium!' "

Schaefer knew just where he wanted to build it, too: the same Camden Yards site that had been considered for a multi-sport facility back in the '60s. Ten years earlier, Mayor Schaefer had helped mastermind the reconstruction of Baltimore's inner harbor as the Harborplace mall-and-museum tourist mecca. Now, Governor Schaefer concluded that a stadium could only enhance the attractiveness of the city's rebuilt downtown to out-of-towners and their entertainment dollars.

To keep Williams happy, Schaefer was prepared to build the project entirely with public money, proposing two state-run lotteries with a sports theme to raise the $235 million necessary to condemn the existing industrial park on the site and to fund the construction of separate stadiums for baseball and football. (As it turned out, Schaefer had seriously underestimated the cost of clearing land for the project. The total tab would ultimately reach $410 million, plus an additional $30 million for road improvements, to be paid out of federal transportation funds.)

The plan was cemented at a memorable public hearing of the state senate in March 1987. The star attraction was Williams, who used every bit of his personal charm and political connections to sway the legislators. In attendance that day was Bill Marker, preparing to testify on behalf of his fledgling Marylanders for Sports Sanity (MASS), a hastily organized citizens' group opposing public stadium funding. His hand-drawn placards, detailing alternate proposals that MASS had calculated could keep the team in town for far less money—including having the state buy the team outright for less than the cost of a new stadium—sat unused at his feet as he watched Williams testify at length that a new ballpark was the only solution to the woes of his team, as well as those of Baltimore. The Orioles' owner, recalls Marker, was greeted as an old friend: "It was all these senators saying, 'Oh, you were my professor in law school, and you were so wonderful.' "

While Marker sat, several legislators expressed concerns about spending such a large sum on what was, after all, a private enterprise. When Williams remarked that he needed a stadium that could guarantee sales of 15,000 season tickets, state senator Julian "Jack" Lapides shot back, "It might be cheaper for the state to buy fifteen thousand season tickets." Williams waited for the cheers from the gallery to die down, then replied, "I didn't come here to ask for a subsidy…I can make this thing go in the private sector if I get the tools."[22]

The "tools" Williams wanted—a taxpayer-funded stadium—represented just as much of a subsidy as a direct cash grant, of course, but the state senate didn't let that stand in its way. Four weeks after Williams' testimony, the senate voted to empower the Maryland Sports Authority to build two new stadiums: a baseball park immediately for the Orioles, and a football stadium to follow once a replacement for the Colts could be lined up.

With the governor, state legislature, and mayor united behind a publicly funded ballpark, Marker and his fellow community activists had only one weapon left at their disposal. According to the Maryland state constitution, any government expenditure can be submitted to a binding public referendum. Within two weeks of the state senate decision, MASS had gone door-to-door to gather 28,000 signatures calling for a public vote. The state rejected the petitions on the grounds that the stadium funding bill was not subject to referendum; MASS took the state to court. An initial ruling sided with the neighborhood activists. But that September, the Maryland court of appeals overturned the lower court's ruling, agreeing with the state's argument that the stadium project constituted an "appropriation for maintaining the state government" and so was exempt from public vote.

"I think they lost the distinction that the state was doing it for a private enterprise," Jack Lapides now says of the court's ruling. "If the state were condemning the land, and building the facility for a state football team, or a state road, or a state hospital, or a state school, then there would be justification. But I thought that their rationale was very convoluted."

Opponents screamed long and loud that Schaefer had bullied his way past the democratic process, but the deed was done. The stadium—given the cumbersome appellation "Oriole Park at Camden Yards" at the insistence of Eli Jacobs, who bought the Orioles following Williams' death in 1988—had cleared its final hurdle. On April 6, 1992, five years and $120 million worth of lottery tickets later, the new ballpark opened to a packed house. And the value of Jacobs' team, according to figures compiled by *Financial World* magazine, jumped by nearly $100 million.

At long last, the new stadium had taken its place alongside the other government-sponsored tourist attractions that now crowded the city's Inner Harbor. But as important as it was to Baltimore, Oriole Park at Camden Yards was destined to play a still more pivotal role in the history of pro sports. For the Orioles had insisted on a building that would be not an antiseptic stadium but an intimate ballpark; unlike every other baseball stadium built in recent memory, this one eschewed concrete walls and symmetrical dimensions for a self-consciously quirky design that used steel and brick to sheath its luxury boxes and ad-filled video screens. From the upper-deck seats, fans were treated to vistas not of suburban parking lots but of the city skyline. In a final touch that delighted architectural critics and baseball fans alike, the right-field wall abutted an 87-year-old brick warehouse that was converted into team offices, a baseball museum, and upscale shops.[23]

As Camden Yards biographer Peter Richmond wrote, "Baltimore didn't need a new baseball stadium, but it was more than grateful for the deliverance of a national showpiece."[24] Camden Yards, as the park would soon be known nationwide, caught the attention of every baseball team yearning for a new stadium. As fans flocked through the gates of the new "old-time" park, filling the Orioles' ledgers with unprecedented revenue, the repercussions would be felt nationwide.

"Comeback City"

While the Orioles' new owner was lobbying for a new home in Baltimore, the hapless Indians (helmless as well after O'Neill's death) were about to see their fortunes change. Whether real or imagined, the threat of losing its baseball franchise, no matter how much the Indians had struggled, was of enormous importance to many

Clevelanders. The city had witnessed, as had the rest of the country, what had happened to Baltimore's beloved Colts when another town laid down better terms. So when, two years after the domed stadium went down in defeat at the polls, the Indians were bought by Richard and David Jacobs, there was a collective sigh of relief. The Jacobses (no relation to Orioles owner Eli Jacobs) were local brothers who had made millions in real estate development, especially in shopping mall constructions. Significantly, they had made their fortunes in the Cleveland area and had considerable interest in downtown development projects.[25] "Increasingly they began to make substantial investments in the city of Cleveland," explains David R. Elkins, a professor of political science at Cleveland State University, noting that the brothers purchased building after building in the downtown area. "They made some enormous changes on the physical appearance of the city."

There wouldn't be much of a grace period for Clevelanders, however, because the Jacobs brothers weren't about to give up on the idea of having a new home built for their team. The brothers had made their fortunes in an industry that had benefited tremendously for decades from Cleveland's generous tax abatement policies, and when they bought the Indians, they argued that a central element to their successful rebuilding of the team would have to be a new home. But in a city that had already rejected public funding of a new stadium, it would take masterful manipulation to persuade the populace to fund such a project.

In 1990, the Central Market Gateway Project was formed in order to develop a new downtown stadium for the Indians and arena for the basketball Cavaliers (who had been playing in suburban Richfield) with what was then proposed as a mix of public and private funds. The project got its title from the proposed construction site—28 acres of prime downtown real estate that was home to the city's historic Central Market. The site was one of the city's two old open-air produce and supply markets and was still an active, if somewhat neglected, neighborhood gathering spot when it was demolished in 1989 at the request of the domed stadium supporters. For several years, as stadium backers plotted tactics, the site sat, unused, as Cleveland's inner-city residents were forced to go elsewhere for their shopping needs. Those same taxpayers presumably could take solace, along with the rest of the city, in thinking of the newly razed spot as the centerpiece for what had been dubbed a "comeback city."

With property taxes a proven failure with voters and politicians alike, the principal means of paying off the city bonds that would fund the new stadium project was to be a "sin tax"—a tax on alcoholic beverages and cigarette- and tobacco-related products. The Cuyahoga County commissioners, no doubt fearful of tying their own political futures to such a project, decided to put that decision to the voters—against the wishes of stadium boosters, who desperately wanted to have the county impose the tax without a costly referendum campaign. Raising $1 million from private interests, including $300,000 from both the Indians and the Cavaliers, supporters of the initiative set out to prove to Cleveland voters that a vote for the stadium was a vote for the future of Cleveland.[26]

"Who wins with Issue 2?" blared a newspaper ad just days before the 1990 vote. "We All Do," answered the placards held by a multicultural rainbow of Cleveland schoolchildren. "Gateway will create a development that will generate $33.7 million in public revenues every year and provide: 28,000 good-paying jobs for the jobless;

neighborhood housing development for the homeless; $15 million a year for schools for our children; revenues for city and county clinics and hospitals for the sick; energy assistance programs for the elderly." The ad went on to promise what wouldn't be taken from taxpayers' wallets or given to team owners: "No property tax; no sales tax; no income tax; no tax abatement…Gateway: the next chapter in our future."[27]

The PR campaign was combined with some hardball threats from the Major League Baseball establishment. Two days before the vote, baseball commissioner Fay Vincent paid a visit to the city of Cleveland. "Should this facility not be available in Cleveland, should the vote be a negative one, we may be finding ourselves confronting a subject that we want to avoid," Vincent said. "I say to you, it would be very bad for baseball, and I am opposed to Cleveland losing its team."[28] A *Plain Dealer* columnist laid it out for the public: "Anyone who thinks the Indians will still be playing in [Municipal] Stadium at the end of the century is nuts. They'll either be in a new stadium here or a new stadium elsewhere. Period."[29]

The so-called Gateway initiative won a narrow victory with 51.7 percent of the vote.[30] As with the earlier domed stadium initiative, all but one of the 21 wards located within the city limits voted against the proposal.

The voting reflected a split in the local electorate, explains John Ryan, executive secretary of the Cleveland AFL-CIO. "One is the suburbanites and a couple of wards that have quite a bit of money. The other are low-income people or people that rely on the school systems. And for the most part they are people who don't have much of a voice." The stadium vote had reaffirmed working-class and poor Clevelanders' suspicions that, when it came to matters of public policy and decision-making in the city, their pocketbooks were the first to be raided (via cigarette and liquor taxes, which, like all taxes on the sale of goods, fall disproportionately on those with lower incomes), even though their concerns were the last to be addressed.

Voters had approved the proposal with the understanding that the combined cost of the new stadium and arena would run about $343 million. But that soon turned into a much greater public investment—some estimate the total cost through 1996 to be as high as $462 million, with as much as two-thirds coming from the public. And that cost is still accumulating.[31] It wasn't until late December 1996 that the Gateway Economic Development Corp. signed a contract agreeing to pay, over five years, $1.6 million in overdue taxes—most of it owed to Cleveland schools.[32]

"The arena was the real bugaboo," says Elkins. The Cavaliers played in a nearly new arena in nearby Richfield, he explains, and the team owners, Gordon and George Gund, had just refurbished that arena at their own expense. The Gunds, he recalls, "were constantly saying, 'We don't need to come downtown. We have a fine facility out at Richfield Coliseum, and if we don't have a state-of-the-art facility here in Cleveland, there's no incentive, more or less, for us to come downtown.' "

Cost overruns or not, by the spring of 1994 the Indians had their new home. (Gund Arena, for the Cavaliers, would follow the next year.) Named Jacobs Field after Richard Jacobs offered the highest bid for the naming rights, the new stadium was directly in the Camden Yards mold—intimately sized, constructed out of lime rock to reflect local construction resources, with an asymmetrical seat layout and state-of-the-art scoreboard.

Send in the Browns

Even while some Clevelanders bemoaned a stadium seen as too big, too old, and too drafty for baseball, the town's football team continued to pack in crowds at the same location. The Cleveland Browns, owned since 1961 by multimillionaire GOP fundraiser Art Modell, were as much a symbol of NFL glory as the Indians were a baseball embarrassment. All winter long, Sunday afternoons meant packed Browns games at Municipal Stadium with a boisterous core of working-class fans who'd cheered the team on for decades. The rabid enthusiasm was symbolized by the nationally known "Dawg Pound"—the rowdy crowd of fans in the endzone bleacher seats who painted themselves in the team's orange and brown, often consumed great quantities of alcohol, and usually donned canine masks when the team's defensive secondary took to calling themselves the Dawgs and barking. (Arsenio Hall would immortalize this group by encouraging his late-night national television audience to bark in the same manner.)

By the mid-1980s, when the fate of the Indians was portrayed as being in severe jeopardy, the future of the Browns was never publicly questioned.[33] But on November 4, 1995, Modell stunned the city with the revelation that he had been involved in negotiations with Maryland officials to move his team to Baltimore. Rumors had circulated for months that Modell resented the city finding money to build the Gateway Project and the new Rock and Roll Hall of Fame while not funding renovations of Municipal Stadium. But Modell had also promised the city in 1994 that as long as he owned the team he'd never leave town, and the rumors remained just that—until November 1995.[34]

Modell had long requested renovations to Municipal Stadium, and some were in the works. In fact, the story of his probable exodus broke the day before a scheduled vote to extend the sin tax created to fund the Gateway complex so that it could be used to pay for improvements to the Browns' home. Perhaps not surprisingly (the *Plain Dealer* ran a front-page editorial urging a yes vote), the referendum passed.

But with a lucrative offer from Baltimore in hand, Modell was not about to be placated with stadium renovations. Three days later, the deal was official. Cries of fury came from almost every corner of Cleveland. From carefully orchestrated petition drives by the mayor's office, to spontaneous anti-Modell outbursts (at times lapsing into anti-Semitism—"They killed the wrong Jew," read one memorable home-made sign at a Browns game after Israeli Prime Minister Yitzhak Rabin was slain), the city reacted with passion and outrage to Modell's announcement.

There were several "Save Our Browns" rallies in the months following Modell's announcement—especially after Mayor Michael White urged Clevelanders to let the nation hear their outrage. "No Team, No Peace," was a common slogan in a surreal time in which a city saw its usually moderate mayor tirelessly campaign against one of the town's most famous multimillion-dollar residents. Concerned citizens wore orange armbands and gathered petitions, Cleveland-born comedian Drew Carey spoke at one rally, and a cottage industry blossomed of anti-Modell T-shirts, buttons, and bumper stickers. But the Browns left anyway, and the city reeled. It was perhaps the only time the *New York Times* has ever run a photograph of a grown man wearing a dog mask, smoking a cigar, and weeping.[35]

As for Baltimore, after 12 years the city finally had found its replacement for the Colts, even if the new Baltimore Ravens didn't yet have quite the allure of the old club. The Browns' move also meant that Baltimore would at last have to build the new stadium that it had denied the Colts, a football-only stadium adjacent to Oriole Park at Camden Yards, at a cost of an additional $200 million in state lottery money. For the Ravens, there was no question of paying their own way: their new lease guaranteed the team 30 years of free rent, plus a $50 million cash relocation bonus. "As sweetheart [deals] go, call this one the Demi Moore special," *San Diego Union-Tribune* sportswriter Tom Cushman wrote, noting that a Ravens subsidiary would even rake in half the profits (plus a ten percent "management fee") for rock concerts and other non-football events at the new stadium.[36] The Orioles, noting a parity clause in their lease requiring that they get at least a good a deal as any football team at Camden Yards, immediately demanded free rent, too.

Baltimore had paid dearly to replace its departed football team; now it would be Cleveland's turn to ante up. The city had hoped that the renovation of Municipal Stadium voters had approved in November would be enough to lure a new team. But when Mayor White met with NFL officials in early January 1996, he was told that the league would only consider a replacement team if there was a new stadium in place.[37] White, following negotiations with NFL officials on the city's chances of getting a replacement football team, quickly brokered a deal to tear down Municipal Stadium and replace it with a new $220 million football-only stadium to be paid for primarily with tax money.[38]

A populace that had just been called upon to hand over $175 million in stadium renovation money was now going to have its wallets raided once again. And yet, with the very real specter of a town without football facing Cleveland voters and politicians, local activists calling for a change in fiscal priorities faced an uphill battle.

Marge Misak, a longtime community activist, remembers well her sense of isolation. "There was no outcry. There were no people publicly, no politicians, no groups, that were saying, 'Wait a minute. Let's look at it. Let's question it.' It was astounding, especially in light of the fact that all the cost overruns at Gateway were coming through, and the county was coming up with more and more loans that were obviously not going to be repaid, just to finish that project…It was kind of an astounding juxtaposition, because you would think that there would be questions about, 'Did we learn our lesson here?' "

Six days of debate in the Cleveland City Council culminated in a 13-8 vote in support of funding the new football stadium. The final tally was closer than many had expected. At the council hearings, recalls Misak, "One councilperson got up and talked about his neighborhood and the children, apologizing to the eight-year-olds in his neighborhood who didn't have swings to play on. In the beginning of his speech I thought, 'Oh my gosh. I can't believe this person, who is a total mayor's ally.' I'm thinking he's going to come out against this…" She trails off in a laugh. "But he didn't! He apologized to all the eight-year-olds in his neighborhood and then voted to put the city general fund at risk."

By February 1996, the *Plain Dealer* could boast in its lead editorial, "The best deal possible; Cleveland is rid of Art Modell and his mediocre team, and Mayor White has helped foster a Browns rebirth."[39] It was civic-boostering spin at an all-time peak—what had been painted as tragedy only a few short months before was now seen as the only possible way for the city to hold on to its team name and rid itself of a suddenly unpopular man at the same time. No one dared mention that the city coffers didn't have the money to fund a new stadium—Cleveland's third publicly funded new sports facility in less than a decade—or that acquiring a new team could very well mean enticing a team to bolt from yet another town.

Early reports had the Cincinnati Bengals or, ironically enough, the Indianapolis Colts being brought in to play in the new Cleveland stadium. But the Bengals soon took themselves out of the running by striking a deal for their own new stadium—paid for lock, stock, and luxury box by the citizens of Cincinnati to keep their football team in town. The March 1996 referendum that authorized that football stadium also approved a new stadium for the baseball Reds to keep them from feeling left out. And so, by the spring of 1997, plans had been laid for four stadiums in two states as a consequence of Art Modell's flight from Cleveland, itself a product of the Colts' move from Baltimore over a decade before.

Aftermath

According to today's conventional media wisdom, both Cleveland and Baltimore are cities in the midst of "renaissances," rising from the ashes of '70s decay to stand newly triumphant as urban growth centers. Credit for these rebirths is largely given to the cities' reconstructed downtowns, anchored in each case by a multimillion-dollar sports complex that draws tourists from across the country.

Indeed, it's hard to imagine how the new stadiums could be more successful. Jacobs Field and Camden Yards were virtual sellouts from the day they opened; in 1996 and 1997, the Indians set a new baseball record by selling out the entire season months before opening day, leaving the team's ticket sales staff with little to do for the year but count the money. A study by the city of Baltimore found that the number of fans coming into town from outside the Baltimore-Washington region for Orioles games nearly doubled after the new ballpark was built.

As for the visions of a rising economic tide that would lift all boats, though, the story was more troubling. And so while Cleveland, under the leadership of Mayor White, has been lauded repeatedly by the national media as a classic comeback town—with its beautiful new sports facilities as key ingredients—life remains much the same for the city's still shrinking urban population. In the midst of a decades-long drop in population, the percentage of Clevelanders living in poverty rose from 17 percent in 1970 to over 40 percent by the mid-1990s.[40] The city school system, drained of property taxes, is in shambles—only 38 percent of its students graduate high school, with only seven percent testing at a 12th-grade level—and was placed in state receivership in 1995.[41] In fact, the day before the deal for a new football stadium in Cleveland was approved by the Cleveland city council, the Cleveland public school system announced it would cut $52 million over two years, laying off up to 160 teachers and eliminating interscholastic athletics from a program that Cleveland School Superintendent Richard A. Boyd described as "in the worst financial shape of any school district in the country."[42]

In Baltimore, the toll is harder to quantify. Since the stadiums were built with state money, there is no guarantee that the city would have reaped the benefit of alternative uses for the funds. Still, the Camden Yards complex ultimately drew more than $400 million out of the state treasury, the bulk of it coming from poor Baltimoreans who are the lottery's best customers.[43] That's $400 million, critics charge, that could have been spent on the city's gaping chasm of needs for education or drug treatment. And the vein is now tapped out: With each new sports lottery to meet the stadiums' cost overruns, lottery state officials have seen their yield decline, leading many locals to conclude that the lottery market is simply saturated. In 1997, a plan to legalize limited casino gambling in the city of Baltimore and use the proceeds for education was shot down by Parris Glendening, Schaefer's successor as governor.

As for the neighborhood activists who had opposed Camden Yards, not all of their worst fears were realized. The surrounding neighborhoods, so far at least, have neither been gentrified beyond recognition nor lost in a flood of sports fan amenities. "They did a good job of doing a bad thing," concedes Bill Marker, looking up at the new stadium that literally casts a shadow over his mixed-income row-house neighborhood of Ridgely's Delight. True, the "historic" nature of the ballpark is more cosmetic than real; even the warehouse, without which the baseball field would, in Lapides' words, "just be sort of a blob sitting in the middle of a field," lost its northern end, lopped off to afford better views of the downtown skyline from the seats behind home plate. And the city did lose many of the 1,000 manufacturing jobs provided by the 26 companies that had existed on the Camden Yards site, as well as the property taxes that the food plants and other businesses had generated.[44]

Just across the highway from the new stadiums, the black enclave of Sharp-Leadenhall is less thrilled with its new neighbors, as it continues to plead for money from the city to repair its recreation center and swimming pool amid city cutbacks. "Oh man, the city," sighs Sharp-Leadenhall Planning Committee organizer May Ringold. "It's a pity that the city's there. We need some of that federal money. We're just a small community, but we've been around since the 17th century…If the stadium wanted to come into our neighborhood, I think they should try to help spruce up the neighborhood itself." The Stadium Authority's only offer to date: a new path through the community's playground, so that football fans could walk through more quickly on their way to the games.

Three miles to the north, in Baltimore's old sports center, the picture is more uniformly gloomy. Memorial Stadium now sits empty, save for the eight Sundays a year when the Ravens are in town, occupying the old bowl as they await their new digs at Camden Yards. The residential neighborhoods around the stadium, Waverly and Charles Village, whose modest brick houses provided the backdrop for so many Orioles and Colts games over the years, have started showing the first signs of decline: FOR SALE signs sprout like dandelions along 33rd Street and the shopping drag on nearby Greenmount Avenue is littered with empty storefronts. The Stadium Lounge, on Greenmount and 34th, bears two large signs in its window: "The Stadium Lounge Welcomes the NFL Baltimore Ravens" and "Checks Cashed in a Flash."

Jack Lapides, who is quick to praise the decision to place the new stadiums down-town instead of in the suburbs, is just as quick to point out that Baltimore already had a ballpark that met the same "old-time" criteria that would later draw compliments at Camden Yards. "The old Memorial Stadium was a perfectly valid ballpark," he says. "And it also would have kept up one of the few truly integrated neighborhoods in Baltimore, a nice middle-class neighborhood. People loved having the stadium there—many moved to the neighborhood because the stadium was there. And this was a nice draw in another part of the city, rather than putting everything in the Inner Harbor of Baltimore."

The greatest irony about these new sports palaces is that those who paid the most for them—the buyers of Maryland lottery tickets and Cleveland cigarettes—are the least able to enjoy them. Ticket pricing is steeper than in the old parks, though admittedly not quite as prohibitive as elsewhere in the country. But more important, the facilities often have fewer seats than their older counterparts, and that, coupled with a much greater number of luxury boxes and season tickets, has meant far fewer tickets available for the average fan.

Jacobs Field is beautiful, agrees union activist Ryan. "One of the things that happened though, I've noticed as a lifelong Indians fan, is that the increase in prices and the decrease in low ticket prices has made the crowd much more white. Incredibly much more white.

"And with the special parking and all that, the wealthier people don't mix with the working-class people for the most part. And to me that's disturbing. If you take a look at who's paying for that [with cigarette taxes], it is more the working-class people."

The cost of a game at Camden Yards is "prohibitive for a poor family," agrees Lapides. "You used to be able to go out to Memorial Stadium and sit in a fairly decent seat for three bucks. Three bucks won't even buy you a hot dog now at the new stadium."

If city schools and low-income fans were the losers in the twin stadium deals, the undeniable winners were the owners. The Orioles, bought by Eli Jacobs for $70 million while Camden Yards was still under construction in 1989, were resold in 1993 for $173 million, appreciating a whopping 147 percent in just four years.[45] Art Modell's football team jumped $38 million in value in one year when they left Cleveland for Baltimore. The Indians, whose new stadium coincided with the team's first contending team in 40 years, were the least-valued team in baseball in 1993, the year before Jacobs Field opened, with a value of $81 million; by 1996 the team had appreciated to $125 million, a tidy 54 percent profit in three years for the Jacobs brothers.[46]

Even if the increased attendance abates after the novelty of the new stadiums wears off, team owners can always hit up their hosts for a few renovations or lease improvements, under threat of once again taking their act on the road. "If it's not a personal toy of yours, if you are an owner and you have any fiduciary responsibility to anybody, and you don't demand a new facility, you're probably violating your fiduciary duty, given the way this stuff goes," notes Marker.

Fiduciary duty can rest easy. In the decade since the Colts' flight, not many owners would pass up the opportunity to levy demands on their city, or someone else's. Baltimore and Cleveland would prove to be merely the tip of the sports welfare iceberg.

Notes

1. Peter Richmond, *Ballpark*. New York: Simon & Schuster, 1993, p. 97.
2. Robert McG. Thomas Jr., "Colts' Move to Indianapolis Is Announced." *The New York Times*, March 30, 1984.
3. Dave Anderson, "12 Vans to Indianapolis." *New York Times*, April 1, 1984.
4. Jacob V. Lamar Jr. and Don Winbush, " 'India-no-place' No More; The subject of a joke gains major league attention." *Time*, June 11, 1984.
5. Andrew H. Malcolm, "The Colts' Move: For Indianapolis It's a Boon…But in Baltimore, It Leaves a Void in the Hearts of the Fans." *New York Times*, April 8, 1984. Kent McDill, "Why is Indianapolis building a $75 million domed stadium?" UPI, June 27, 1982.
6. The Raiders' ultimately successful lawsuit challenged the NFL's right to control franchise movement; until it was resolved, the league put its expansion plans on hold. (Mark Fury, "Will Indianapolis' Domed Stadium Become a White Elephant?" *Bond Buyer*, July 28, 1982.)
7. Fury, "Will Indianapolis' Domed Stadium Become a White Elephant?"
8. Charles C. Euchner, *Playing the Field: Why Sports Teams Move and Cities Fight to Keep Them*. Baltimore: Johns Hopkins University Press, 1993, p. 105.
9. According to Hudnut's chief negotiator, the deal was finalized in just three days because of fears of legal entanglements. ("Rushed negotiations for Colts revealed," UPI, April 1, 1984.)
10. "Most Modern Stadium in the World, and One of Most Beautiful." *Plain Dealer*, July 31, 1931.
11. Carol Poh Miller and Robert Wheeler, *Cleveland: A Concise History, 1796–1990*. Bloomington: Indiana University Press, 1990, p. 143.
12. Local baseball fans, desperately searching for explanations for one of the most ignominious reputations in professional sports history, were willing to turn to any explanation. Besides the stadium's inhospitability, Clevelanders pointed to the legendary "curse" of Rocky Colavito, the popular Indians outfielder who was inexplicably traded before the start of the 1960 season. (Terry Pluto, *The Curse of Rocky Colavito*, New York: Simon and Schuster, 1994, p. 47.)
13. Poh Miller and Wheeler, *Cleveland: A Concise History*, pp. 183–184.
14. Mark Rosentraub, *Major League Losers: The Real Cost of Sports and Who's Paying for Them*. New York: BasicBooks, 1997, p. 256.
15. "All it took was a significant proportion of the political elites to contest it," says Elkins, who points out that even Voinovich "had to be persuaded and cajoled." In the course of his own research on the domed saga, Elkins spoke with Campanella and many of the other key figures.
16. Paul Attner, "For Many Cities, There's No Place Like Dome." *Washington Post*, June 8, 1994.
17. Elkins also speculates that there may have been a greater than normal turnout by African-American voters on that day in May 1984—it was the same election day that would see Jesse Jackson score significant numbers in the city of Cleveland in his presidential campaign.
18. Poh Miller and Wheeler, *Cleveland: A Concise History*, p. 189.
19. Richmond, *Ballpark*, p. 49.
20. Richmond, *Ballpark*, p. 58.
21. Euchner, *Playing the Field*, p. 115.

22. Richmond, *Ballpark*, p. 96.
23. That the warehouse was owned by Schaefer's chief fundraiser was, no doubt, merely coincidence. (Euchner, *Playing the Field*, p. 115.)
24. Richmond, *Ballpark*, p. 44.
25. Rosentraub, *Major League Losers*, p. 256. In Rosentraub's extensive look at stadium financing and the cost to local municipalities, he argues that the Jacobs brothers were seen as the ideal new owners of the beleaguered team. Rebuilding the Indians was part of the brothers' plans for redeveloping downtown Cleveland.
26. Ibid., p. 263.
27. Emphasis in original. Newspaper advertisement, *Plain Dealer*, May 3, 1990.
28. Roldo Bartimole, "If you build it." *The Progressive*, June 1994.
29. Rosentraub, *Major League Losers*, p. 261.
30. Ibid., p. 263.
31. Ibid., pp. 269–278.
32. "Gateway agrees to pay taxes on Jacobs Field, Gund Arena." James F. Sweeney, *Plain Dealer*, December 24, 1996.
33. Perhaps it should have been. In *Ballpark*, Peter Richmond mentions, almost in passing, that in 1984 then-Baltimore Mayor William Schaefer "mobilized a secret meeting... between [Orioles owner Edward] Williams, Governor Hughes, Cleveland Browns owner Art Modell, and Larry Lucchino. It was Schaefer's idea: the state would donate the land, private capital would be raised, and Art Modell, a friend of Williams, would buy an NFL team, put it in Cleveland, and move his Browns in." (Richmond, *Ballpark*, p. 65)
34. Stephen Koff, Timothy Heider, and Evelyn Theiss, "How Cleveland lost the Browns." *Plain Dealer*, November 19, 1995.
35. Malcolm Moran, "Hugs, Tears and a Victory: Browns Say Goodbye." *New York Times*, December 18, 1995.
36. Tom Cushman, "Maybe S.D. deal with Chargers is not so bad." *San Diego Union-Tribune*, November 17, 1995.
37. Stephen Koff and Tony Grossi, "City may need new stadium to keep a team, NFL says." *Plain Dealer*, January 5, 1996.
38. Ibid.
39. *Plain Dealer*, February 11, 1996.
40. Norman Krumholtz, "To fund or not to fund?" *Detroit Free Press*, March 12, 1996. W. Dennis Keating, "Cleveland: The Comeback City." Mickey Lauria, ed., *Reconstructing Urban Regime Theory: Regulating Urban Politics in a Global Economy*, Thousand Oaks, Calif.: Sage, 1997, p. 192.
41. Sandra Dallas, ed., "Tackling Football, And Oh, Yes, Education," *Business Week*, December 9, 1996.
42. Scott Stephens, "Cleveland schools to cut sports, teachers," *Plain Dealer*, March 8, 1996.
43. According to Jack Lapides, the poorest 25 percent of the state's population buys 63 percent of all lottery tickets. (Richmond, *Ballpark*, p. 98.)
44. Though the Maryland Stadium Authority would later rent out office space in the warehouse to local companies, as a state agency it pays no property taxes. Jack Lapides reports that over his three decades in the state senate, the portion of city land not paying property taxes had nearly doubled, from 20 percent to 37 percent, as a result of the sports stadiums, university and hospital expansion, and other tax-exempt development.
45. John Helyar, *Lords of the Realm*. New York: Ballantine Books, 1994, pp. 569–572.
46. www.financialworld.com.

Discussion Questions

1. What is your opinion on using public money for private stadiums?
2. Why are sports team owners so successful in getting cities to meet their financial demands?
3. Summarize the history behind the building of Orioles Stadium at Camden Yards. How were voters kept out of the process?
4. Why did Camden Yards' design prompt other cities to desire new stadiums?
5. How did stadium boosters convince Clevelanders to support the Gateway Initiative?
6. How did Art Modell's flight from Cleveland spark the building of four other stadiums?
7. What are the arguments for building stadiums? Do new stadiums ever benefit the average citizen? What are the social costs of building stadiums and arenas?

Writing Suggestion

If you learned that a professional sports team was going to locate in your community, but only if local tax money went to building a stadium, would you support the move? Why or why not?

Disneyland With Dice: Cannibalizing the Economy Under the Guise of Entertainment

Jennifer Vogel

Crapped Out: How Gambling Ruins the Economy and Destroys Lives

In 1995, Americans spent more on gambling than the U.S. government budgeted for defense: around $500 billion in all, or $2,000 for every man, woman and child. From lottery tickets at the corner store to slot machines in a Las Vegas casino, more was spent on gambling than on movies, sporting events, concerts or theater. Large-scale casinos have cropped up from coast to coast: before 1989, they were legal only in Nevada and New Jersey, while 27 states now have them. There are pulltabs and other less blatant forms of gambling in bars and restaurants, lotteries on the Internet, and "video gaming" machines on international flights. Thirty-seven states now operate lotteries, up from a handful just 15 years ago. All told, some form of gambling now operates in every state except Hawaii and Utah. It's clear that gambling has become America's fastest growing industry.

"For the first time," brags a 1996 brochure from Harrah's Entertainment Inc., "more than half of the nation's states each generate more than 1 million household casino trips per year…U.S. households made 154 million visits to casinos in 1995, an increase of 23 percent over the previous year and 235 percent over 1990." The pamphlet goes on to claim that states are benefiting from gambling in terms of job creation and new taxes. Gambling proponents and many politicians would have the public believe that casinos and lotteries are harmless and voluntary fun, doing nothing but economic and social good for the communities that host them. It's often claimed—especially around the time the matter is up for public vote—that a lottery will increase education or environmental spending, that a casino will revitalize a sluggish economy. In fact, these promises often don't come true; in many cases, gambling only makes a bad situation worse. In Texas, elected officials claimed that a lottery would keep taxes down. Citizens, predictably, voted for a lottery and ended up with a hearty tax hike anyway. Gambling itself has enormous hidden costs: increased compulsive gambling, bankruptcies, crime, small business closings. Casinos came to Atlantic City in 1978, but they haven't revitalized the slumping economy there. Retail businesses have closed in droves, replaced by pawnshops. Unemployment has risen. As law professor and gambling expert I. Nelson Rose once told *U.S. News & World Report*: "Atlantic City used to be a slum by the sea. Now it's a slum by the sea with casinos."

The first modern-day casinos opened in Reno, Nevada, in the 1930s, just after the state passed laws legalizing gambling and making it easier to obtain a divorce. The legislation was big news all over America. "Nevada is tired of cactus, alkali wastes, sparse population, hard times and virtue," reported Alabama's *Montgomery Advertiser* at the time. Despite criticism, a new gambling Mecca, Las Vegas, blossomed in the desert throughout the late '40s and early '50s, creating a new world of nonstop dreams and sparkling lights that bore very little resemblance to everyday America. It was constructed by mobsters and other questionable characters like Bugsy Siegel and Lester "Benny" Binion, who left the illegal casino business in Dallas for Nevada legitimacy in a Cadillac packed with suitcases of cash.

Atlantic City contested Nevada's gambling monopoly in 1978, providing the first experiment at bringing casinos into an existing city for the purpose of economic revitalization. Since then, casinos have appeared in places like Black Hawk, Colorado, and Deadwood, South Dakota. Paddleboat casinos, designed to circumvent state laws banning land-based casinos, chug up and down the Mississippi River, stopping at ports in Iowa, Illinois and Mississippi. The Indian Gaming Regulatory Act of 1988 provided Native Americans the right to conduct for profit any form of gambling that states put on for charity. Suddenly, church basement "Las Vegas Nights" became full-fledged 24-hour, tribal-run casinos. Today, they make up only a small part of the overall gambling picture, despite the disproportionate amount of publicity they garner. According to a 1996 issue of *U.S. News & World Report*, non-reservation casinos took in $367.9 billion in bets in 1994, while reservation gambling halls took in only $41.1 billion. Meanwhile, lottery gambling has spread wildly across the country, starting in 1964 with New Hampshire. Thirty years later, all but 12 states were running them, taking in $34.5 billion in wagers.

Gambling's proliferation is, in part, due to its new, more palatable image. Gone are the days of overt mob-control—though examples of involvement in casino management and contracting persist. Today, the Flamingo hotel that Siegel built is owned by the Hilton Hotels Corporation and is traded on the stock market. As David Johnston describes in his book *Temples of Chance*: "In 1989 there were 1,589 Holiday Inns in America. But the Holiday Corporation earned 28 cents of each dollar's profit from a single building in Atlantic City—Harrah's Marina Hotel Casino." Gambling, said one industry executive recently, "has gone through cycles of being prohibited and legalized. But now, for the first time, it is being legitimized. It's coming into the American mainstream."

Powerful investors such as Donald Trump, Merv Griffin and Steve Wynn have done their part to make casinos appear to be good, clean fun. They've built fantasy lands and Ozs with volcanoes, rollercoasters and huge fountains. The strategy today is to attract working class families or "lowrollers." According to a November 1993 issue of *Institutional Investor* magazine, the trend is especially prevalent in Las Vegas, which has found itself competing with casinos across the country: "Mirage Resorts has built a moat and has begun to stage pirate battles. Circus Circus recently opened its 30-story pyramid in the desert. The MGM Grand is putting up a billion-dollar sphinxlike edifice that it boasts will be 'the largest casino in the galaxy' in 'the world's largest hotel.' The Hilton, meanwhile, is erecting a monstrous, 363-foot structure that manager F.M. (Bud) Celey declares will be 'the worlds biggest sign'…The aim in Vegas, once 'sin city', is to create a continuous carnival of spectacles, a 'destination resort' for the whole family. The new Vegas wants to be Disneyland with dice."

That comparison is especially appropriate since staking the future on gambling, economists argue, could only work in a fantasyland. It's an industry that produces no product and no new wealth, and thus makes no genuine contribution to economic development. "Governmental officials are increasingly being enticed to accept and then impose upon the public those discredited economic philosophies which claim that gambling activities increase jobs, foster economic development, and generate new tax revenues—all without raising taxes on the electorate," says University of Illinois economist John Warren Kindt. "In reality, the regional and strategic impacts of legalized gambling almost invariably result in a net loss of jobs, increased taxes, and negative economic spiral which is inherently recessionary…Furthermore, the net creation of jobs claimed by the legalized gambling industry is at best a break-even proposition, and the evidence suggests that net job losses can easily occur—primarily because 'consumer dollars' are drained from the rest of the economy. The literature frequently refers to this process as 'cannibalization.' "

Even some of those who seek to win by running the industry have lost their shirts. According to a March 1992 piece in *Washington Monthly* magazine, the Seneca-Cayuga Indians in Oklahoma hired Wayne Newton Enterprises in October 1990 to run a high-stakes bingo parlor. The tribe had shelled out $300,000 to build the hall and was asked for another $224,000 to get the operation up and running, while Newton was to contribute a never-to-materialize $125,000. By the end of 1991, ledgers reported gross earnings of $12.5 million for the year, yet the parlor recorded a debt of $360,000, which Newton wanted the tribe to pay. Angry tribe members finally gained control of the operation after surrounding the hall with pick-up trucks while Newton's security forces barricaded themselves inside. Though this book [*Crapped Out*] doesn't discuss issues specific to Indian gambling, such as sovereignty, various reports have shown that they face the same problems as other communities when it comes to corruption and social costs. "Wherever it's been tried," the *Washington Monthly* article says, "gambling has been accompanied by a dramatic increase in violent and property crimes, alcoholism, and drug abuse."

Tom Grey, head of the National Coalition Against Legalized Gambling, has become the anointed leader of America's swelling anti-gambling movement. A Methodist minister from Hanover, Illinois, Grey discovered back in 1991 that the local county board had approved docking rights to a riverboat casino without consulting the public. "I remember thinking, what a dumb idea," he says. "Gambling is gambling. It's not the kind of activity you bring into a small rural, conservative community. I thought, gambling makes losers." He discovered that others—housewives, artists—felt the same way. "We invited a state's attorney from Deadwood in for two town meetings. We figured we ought to know what we were getting into. He told us that he wasn't against gambling but that we should be aware that they had wanted only four casinos that would operate during the off season, to maintain a tourist base. He said they wound up with 80 casinos running year round. He said that three car dealerships had closed up. You could have heard a pin drop in that auditorium." Grey and his supporters gathered enough signatures to put the matter on a public ballot, and even though he says casino interests spent $30,000 to counter the campaign, the 21,000 citizens of JoDaviess County voted the proposal down by a huge margin. The vote, it turned out, wasn't enough to convince the state, which approved the necessary licensing anyway. Grey's been fighting gambling ever since, traveling the country organizing and giving speeches.

Grey's efforts, along with the persistence of gambling-related problems, has had an impact on the public consciousness. Casino proliferation slowed to a trickle in 1994 and stringent community opposition to gambling has occurred in a number of locales where expansion was planned. In addition—at the prompting of NCALG—Congress recently passed a bill mandating a national study of the social and economic effects of gambling. (The last such federal study was over 20 years ago, in 1976.) The battle was hard won; the gambling industry reportedly spent millions lobbying against the proposal. But legislators like then-Senator Paul Simon, who co-authored the legislation, made strong arguments. In a July 1995 speech before the Senate, he explained the crucial importance of a large-scale study of "our fastest growing industry." "The gambling elite are not only generous employers of lobbyists, they are multi-million dollar donors to political campaigns, and the combination makes them politically potent," he said. "The unsavory and unhealthy influence of lobbyists and legislators as protectors of this rapidly growing industry means sensible restraint will not be easily achieved." The commission—which will comprise nine appointed members and will have two years to come up with findings—will review gambling policies on a federal, state, local and tribal level and will study gambling's relationship to issues like crime and pathological gambling. It will look at how much money states and tribes make from gambling and explore alternative revenue sources.

Many of the issues and viewpoints the commission will undoubtedly focus on paint a grim picture, one that the gambling industry would rather nobody sees—including compulsive gambling, bankruptcies, increased crime, ongoing mob ties, political corruption and manipulative advertising strategies. Although casinos and lotteries may provide some short-term economic benefits for hard-pressed states and reservations, in the long run they do more harm than good. Kindt estimates that for every dollar gambling contributes in taxes, taxpayers spend at least three dollars on everything from fixing up streets around casinos to increasing police patrols and treating pathological gamblers. The number of compulsive gamblers has been shown to increase in states with legalized gambling, sometimes by 500 percent; the average social cost of a compulsive gambler is estimated to be as high as $53,000 per year.

It's obvious that no matter who is running a casino or a lottery, the issues are the same—a few people get rich while draining money from the rest. Gambling undercuts real economic development, critics point out again and again, while placing citizens' heads on the chopping block.

What are the odds that the gambling movement will be pushed back in favor of meaningful economic activity? Community opposition—along with the often predicted saturation of the market—has the gambling industry on the defensive already. In 1995 it set up the American Gaming Association with the express mission of "creating a better understanding of gaming-entertainment by bringing the facts about the industry to the general public." The AGA's media packet includes a pamphlet called "Gaming Industry Myths and Facts," which refers to gambling as "one of the greatest contributors to our nation's economy" and frets over the fact that "critics still perpetuate old stereotypes." In the end, whether gambling lives or dies will depend heavily on citizen action.

Discussion Questions

1. Why do you think gambling is so popular—the most popular form of entertainment today?

2. What steps have been taken to polish the image of casinos? Why?

3. Have casinos really increased jobs and revitalized communities?

4. What are the hidden social costs of gambling?

5. Have activists been successful in slowing the proliferation of gambling? How so?

Writing Suggestion

Do you support legalized gambling? Why or why not?

From Tiny Tim to Jerry Lewis: Charity and Economic Rights on a Collision Course

Marta Russell

Beyond Ramps: Disability at the End of the Social Contract

"The rich have given to the poor a little food, a little drink, a little shelter and a few clothes. The poor have given to the rich palaces and yachts, and an almost infinite freedom to indulge their doubtful taste for display, and bonuses and excess profits, under which cold and forbidding terms have been hidden the excess labor and extravagant misery of the poor."

—Gilbert Seldes

The U.S. social safety net falls vastly short of humanely aiding those at the bottom of the socio-economic ladder. Large numbers of people remain unemployed, underemployed, and in poverty because our economic system perpetuates high unemployment and the corporate drive for high profits demands low wages. How would the elite address the needs of the "surplus" population, those for whom there are no jobs, those who cannot work, those who work at poverty wages, and those who have no health care? Rather than building a social contract that would provide health care for all and lift everyone to a decent standard of living, the elite would have Americans rely on private sector charity to "help the poor."

What's wrong with charity? Under the best of circumstances, charity becomes oppressive when it is used to buoy inequality, to benefit those "offering" aid, and to mask the greed that forestalls the establishment of economic justice. The mechanics of oppression are in full gear within the Muscular Dystrophy Association (MDA) cure charity, and can be used to illustrate that the charity "solution" really isn't a solution at all.

"Half a Person" Tarnishes Disabled

"As good as gold," said Bob, "and better...He [Tiny Tim] told me, coming home, that he hoped the people saw him in the church, because he was a cripple, and it might be pleasant to them to remember upon Christmas Day, who made lame beggars walk and blind men see." So wrote Charles Dickens in *A Christmas Carol*.

The stereotypical images of "cripples" as patient, saintly Tiny Tims waiting for God to take them home, or as totally distraught inferiors waiting for someone—or some charitable organization—to cure us, have contributed greatly to the oppression of disabled people. In either case, disabled people are good for one thing—to assuage consciences by being the object of charitable pity.

Hey, that's being useful!—for the charities that profit from disablement. The Muscular Dystrophy Association knows Tiny Tim is "as good as gold." The pity ploy theme, the hallmark of the cure charity telethon, has turned the MDA into a multi-million-dollar nonprofit corporation that can afford to pay its top executive $384,000 a year with fringe benefits, deliver a bonus, build a plush new facility in Arizona, cover all of host Jerry Lewis's expenses, and have enough left over to keep some seventy vice-presidents on board.

In the same decade that the Americans with Disabilities Act acknowledges that disabled people are a target of widespread discrimination, Jerry Lewis perpetuates outdated images of disabled persons as leading tragic lives, as homebound victims waiting for cures. Fantasizing about what life would be like if he were disabled, Lewis told *Parade* magazine, "I realize my life is half, so I must learn to do things half way. I must have to learn to try to be good at being *half a person* [italics mine]."[1] What is Lewis's message? There is no life without a cure; disabled people are not capable of working, raising children, or participating in the majority culture in any "whole" sense. Lewis's exhibitions perpetuate the damaging myth that our disabled "half" lives are not worth living.

Lewis was further quoted, "I would put myself in that chair, that *steel imprisonment* that long has been deemed the dystrophic child's plight [italics mine]." To disabled people, the wheelchair is no imprisonment, it means liberty and freedom of movement, it enables us to participate in the majority society. And when Lewis refers to all people with MD as "Jerry's kids," including full-grown adults, how can anyone miss the paternalism? Disabled people do not want to be called "kids" any more than a black man wants to be called "boy."

Disability activists explain that Lewis's tactics tarnish all disabled people. Who is going to hire "half a person"? These paternalistic pity-parade telethons so focused on "cures" sabotage the dignity of the disabled and our acceptance as social equals. These two opposing images of disability, the charity model and the civil rights model, are on a collision course. While disabled people are intent on gaining dignity and equality, Lewis and other charities want to keep us back in Dickens's 19th century.

Now Come The Ungrateful Crips

Dickens's ever-grateful Tiny Tim character (the original poster boy) sets the tone for the behavior of the proper "cripple" who must say, "Thank you, thank you, thank you" for what nondisabled people choose to give. The ungrateful crips, the activists, have gone public to stop the damaging misinformation transmitted to the 250 million viewers of the annual MDA telethon.

- Evan Kemp, former chair of the Equal Employment Opportunity Commission, who has a neuro-muscular condition, wrote in the *New York Times* that society sees disabled people as "helpless, hopeless, nonfunctioning and non-contributing members of society...the Jerry Lewis Muscular Dystrophy Association Telethon with its pity approach to fundraising, has contributed to these prejudices."[2]

- Chris Matthews, a former poster child, wrote to MDA that it was "expert in exploiting the worst side of disability and, with the eager assistance of Lewis, has made us out to be nothing more than pathetic burdens to society, whose only desire is to walk."

- Jerry's Orphans, an anti-telethon group spearheaded by Mike Ervin and Chris Matthews, went on *60 Minutes* to protest Lewis's fundraising tactics.

- Protests (some lasting the length of Lewis's telethon air time) have been ongoing in Los Angeles, Denver, Chicago, Austin, Boston, Nashville, Atlanta, San Francisco, Detroit, Louisville, and other cities for about seven years.

- In an open letter to Lewis called "The Disabled Need Dignity, Not Pity," Harvard graduate and new father Ben Mattlin described his poster boy experience:

> When I was about six years old, I was in a full-page magazine ad for the MDA: big blue eyes peeking though blond curls. The caption read, "If I grow up, I want to be a fireman." I didn't want to be a fireman, and knew then my diagnosis called for a normal life expectancy. Confused, I decided that I wasn't really one of "them" and denied a part of my identity, my connection to the only community where I could learn to feel good about my disability. I didn't know the word "exploitation" yet.[3]

False projections of death and physicalist attitudes are prevalent on the MDA telethon. Encouraged by the on-stage interviewers, the typical parent of a child who uses a wheelchair will usually express the unrelenting sentiment that "I want my kids to run, to jump, to play." Parents who join the MDA in placing so much importance on their children *not* being able to perform these physical acts are essentially saying that their children are what sociologist Erving Goffman has termed "failed normals." The children are getting the message that they are less than OK, that somehow they are a tremendous disappointment and a problem to their family—because they use a wheelchair.

It was interesting to listen to the children (when they were allowed to say something), because they did not reflect the same prejudices as the parents. One particularly offensive interviewer recently asked a young boy, "Ben, is it getting harder for you now that the time is coming?" She meant now that he was getting closer to death (had someone told her this?). Ben sat silent and dignified on the couch, while his father interceded with a reply. But this interviewer did not give up. She asked again, "Benjamin, is it getting harder for you? Does it hurt?" Ben looked at her questioningly and honestly answered, "No, not really." How damaging is it for a child to hear that these adults think they may die any day when, as in Ben Mattlin's earlier case, this is often false projection and many will have average lifespans?

The use of disabled children on the telethon is uncomfortably close to emotional child abuse. Some say you can't make money on a telethon without using the pity ploy. To this we must answer "No, thank you," and replace telethons with universal social policy that promotes dignity and enhances life.

Civil Rights' Head-On Collision with Charity Mentality

Michael Winter and his wife discovered in 1995 that they could not get in the front door of the Planet Hollywood restaurant because there was no ramp. Staff led the Winters to the waiters' entrance and through the kitchen. "It was humiliating and demeaning to be sent to a separate and exceedingly unequal entrance simply because Planet Hollywood couldn't be bothered to comply with the ADA," Winter said. "I ended up with food and garbage in the treads of my wheelchair for hours after."[4]

Ironically, Planet Hollywood, one of the sponsors of the 1995 MDA telethon, was not accessible to those it purported to "help." It was willing to raise money to "help the cripples" but the owners are not willing to take our civil rights seriously. How could the owners—which include Sylvester Stallone, Demi Moore, Bruce Willis, and Arnold Schwarzenegger—claim an "undue hardship" exemption from the ADA accessibility regulations; how could they claim to be unable to afford to build a ramp over three steps?

Leslie Bennetts interviewed Jerry Lewis for *Vanity Fair* and confronted him with disabled activists' concerns about the telethon. Bennetts reported that when Lewis was asked if he thought his detractors made any valid points, he adamantly responded, "Fuck them," then told her to "Do it in caps. FUCK THEM." Bennetts described Lewis's reaction as "so hostile and paranoid it seems almost Nixonian." Lewis told Bennetts, "If you do anything to hurt my kids I'll have you killed, you understand?"[5]

Some of Lewis's supporters react the same way. In 1992 when protestors symbolically blockaded the gates to KTLA in Los Angeles (leaving one back entrance open to get in and out), a group of bikers decided that they would not go around to the open entrance. Screaming profanities at some fifteen people assembled peacefully in wheelchairs, the bikers charged. The *Los Angeles Times* reported that one woman was knocked out of her wheelchair by the bikers.[6] As one biker angrily crashed our demonstrators the hot exhaust pipes came dangerously close to burning my legs. To challenge the charity mentality is to risk collision with those who know little about disability but are filled with self-righteousness.

Who Benefits from the "benefits"?

The question begging to be asked is, who really benefits from the charity business? Research reveals that little of the money donated to MDA is actually spent on direct services or equipment that would assist disabled people in their daily lives. Bill Bolt reported in *In These Times* that:

MDA does not provide the equipment needed to live independently—or, in some cases, to live at all. It does not provide respirators. It does not provide power beds. It does not buy computers, ramps, living-space access modifications, lifts for vans or vans themselves. It refuses to buy power wheelchairs for those not in school or not working—often the more severely disabled who really need a power wheelchair.[7]

So where does the money go? Bolt writes, "The facts are pretty shocking. The Annual Jerry Lewis Muscular Dystrophy Association Telethon raises more than $40 million dollars while MDA brings in a total of more than $100 million each year. Yet, according to the MDA's 1991 annual report, only one MDA dollar in six goes to research awards, grants and fellowships." Bolt further reports, "Another sixth of MDA revenues goes to services purchased for the disabled. The remainder of donations go to overhead, including more than $31 million in salaries, fringes and payroll taxes."

Paul Aziz of *Moving Forward* writes:

The MDA annual report for '91 shows a total of $102 million in revenue from the public. Of that amount, $50 million was spent on "patient services." But the figures are deceiving, because it sounds like the patients are getting half the money the MDA is bringing in.

That is not exactly the case. In their report, only $28 million actually goes to the patients, the remainder of approximately $22 million is spent on salaries, payroll taxes, travel, lodging, office supplies, postage, contract and professional services and other miscellaneous expenses.[8]

When Aziz made several requests for a breakdown of the $28 million going to patients, MDA did not provide it.

The *Disability Rag* reported that more than $800,000 of the first million raised by MDA goes to the top five corporate officers. According to the *Chronicle of Philanthropy*, MDA executive director Robert Ross's 1992 salary was the highest in the "health" category of the not-for-profit organizations—$300,000 per year.[9]

Dianne Piastro, author of the syndicated column "Living with a Disability," asked the director of finance at MDA, "Who used the travel money and what type of travel did they do for the $6.9 million spent in 1990?"[10] Piastro said that MDA did not respond to these questions and failed to supply their tax returns; consequently, she had to file a complaint to get what is supposed to be on file and easily attainable public information.

In fact, charities often do more for nondisabled people. They hire nondisabled employees, appoint nondisabled people to their boards, and contract with nondisabled service organizations who don't employ disabled people. Charities are supposedly set up to do "for" disabled people; in reality they are hierarchies of power in which the socio-economic status quo is perpetuated, with disabled people on the bottom.

Keeping the money and power out of the hands of those "served" and in the hands of the charity's bureaucrats seems to be an MDA priority, evidenced by a series of vitriolic responses to criticisms from disabled activists. Executive director Robert Ross wrote to Dianne Piastro, "We intend to take legal action against Ms. Piastro and her syndicator," and as a result many newspapers felt pressured not to publish her columns even though in the end MDA filed no lawsuit. When Evan Kemp criticized Jerry Lewis's money-raising tactics, Lewis wrote to President Bush accusing Kemp of "misusing the power of his governmental office." (Kemp was then chair of the EEOC.) Activists believed MDA hoped to get Kemp fired. In another instance, MDA threatened to hold Chris Matthews, co-founder of Jerry's Orphans, "personally and financially responsible for any and all losses" that might result from her publicly expressed opinions.

Clearly MDA does not work in partnership with the disabled and therefore can neither meet their clients' needs nor effectively contribute to national disability policy. Would changing the hierarchy solve the inequities? What if charities were forced to appoint disabled people—or members of any group served—to a majority on their boards? Some believe that those affected should make the decisions and set the policies and if they do not, then the tax-exempt status of the charitable organization should be lost. Their hope is that disabled people would direct the organizations to educate and empower disabled people. But despite entitlement-slashing rhetoric, *charities can never build an egalitarian society, simply because they arbitrarily pick and choose whom to serve. No one is entitled to anything from a charity*, rather one must be designated a "deserving" case. Anyone can be denied access to services at any time for any reason. That is not reliable assistance and it is not justice for all.

The Corporate Connection

The corporations that contract with MDA also benefit from the charity business. Since MDA itself is not in the business of health care or research, the dollars raised go to subcontractors: universities, medical providers, equipment companies, social service agencies, and other existing businesses. In 1991, nine million dollars went to "non-medical contract services and professional fees" alone. MDA is an empire that has been built around contracting services, and these businesses have a vested interest in seeing that MDA remains around year after year to renew those contracts.

The Alliance for Research Accountability in Los Angeles, critical of MDA profiteering, writes, "Forty-six years and hundreds of millions of dollars worth of [MDA] research have resulted in nothing but profits for drug companies and research labs. Hundreds, if not thousands, of children have been subjected to futile and dangerous experiments with nothing to show for it beyond giving steroids and immune suppressants for children."[11]

Anyone watching the telethon can see that businesses get a lot of TV advertising for the dollars they donate to MDA. Time and time again corporate representatives are called on stage by Lewis to deliver their checks. The name of each company is prominently placed in the background so viewers cannot possibly miss the connection. Often one donation will be split into several checks so executives come onto the stage several times to mete out their donation one piece at a time—garnering more advertising time.

Busting Altruism: Benefits to the Rich

Dickens's ghost tells Scrooge, "If man you be in heart, not adamant, forbear that wicked cant until you have discovered What the surplus is, and Where it is. Will you decide what men shall live, what men shall die?" In both Dickens's story and the MDA telethon plot, the disabled child [surplus population] will die unless the haves donate money. In the end, Scrooge feels better about himself because he raises the father's salary and Tiny Tim's health improves because he is no longer undernourished. A *Christmas Carol* uses disability to wrench the hearts of the miserly but in the end it is the rich who retain control; they can be generous or they can be stingy, but Dickens leaves no doubt that in nineteenth century capitalist England, the vast majority of the poor and disabled were left to misery and squalor. Similarly, while the Tiny Tim tin cups rattle on the MDA telethon stage, the underlying social issues— poverty and a lack of entitlement to the necessities, like universal health care and living wage employment, that enable a quality life—are not addressed.

The charity system protects the privileged rich who, by donating tax-deductible dollars, appear to be generously concerned about the plight of the poor. However, their "solution" actually serves to keep the wealth, resources, and power in the hands of the few. *Left Business Observer* points out that:

> Altruism was rarely the motivating factor in establishing the large independent foundations—ones like Pew, Ford, MacArthur, Robert Wood Johnson that every NPR listener can name. The Ford Foundation was established to help keep the company in the family without paying estate taxes. John D. MacArthur, founder of Bankers Life and Casualty Company, never made any significant charitable contributions during his lifetime, but left his estate of nearly $1 billion to a foundation rather than to his estranged children. One of the trusts founded by the Sun Oil heirs, the J. Howard Pew Freedom Trust, was established to "acquaint the American people with the evils of bureaucracy...and with the values of a free market...to point out the false promises of Socialism..."[12]

"Nonprofits" also include "educational" organizations like the Kennesaw State College Foundation, which is under investigation for appearing to be a conduit for tax-deductible funds for Newt Gingrich's "Renewing American Civilization" college course, the stated goal of which was to "unseat the Democratic majority in the House."

In addition to serving as fronts for political agendas, nonprofits can create an illusion that they are mending the holes in our social fabric, when behind the benevolent front there is an enormous hoarding of wealth. *LBO* editor Doug Henwood observes, "In economic terms, the larger nonprofits could be thought of as giant stock portfolios, often with marketing operations grafted on." For instance, in 1992, the nonprofits held $1 trillion in financial assets. Nonprofits are managed independently, primarily by the wealthy elite, but they do not pay taxes. In 1991 the nonprofit revenue was $615 billion, or 11 percent of the Gross Domestic Product, none of which was taxed. Forty-two percent of "nonprofit" money is in stocks and 25 percent is in bonds, which means that the nonprofits also have a significant impact on Wall Street.[13]

Because donors to charities are entitled to a tax deduction, roughly one third of every dollar donated is subsidized by the federal government. That means public revenue which could be going to public welfare is lost to nonprofits. Gregory Colvin, an attorney specializing in tax law writes, "...$1.5 million raised and spent through the

Kennesaw State College Foundation…could translate into a Treasury loss of about $500,000 in tax savings by Gingrich's donors."[14]

Arianna Huffington, a constituent of the right-wing Progress and Freedom Foundation, understands this connection. She would have those public tax dollars go into her nonprofit instead. She states, "We are targeting those who think taxes can take care of compassion and ask them to volunteer and to give money [to her Center for Effective Compassion]."[15] Huffington gets it. The law lets rich folks donate stocks to their own foundations, then deduct from income the current stock value, totally avoiding capital gains taxes in the process. Her nonprofit increases her ability (her husband is worth over $25 million) to invest on Wall Street and she determines how the profits are spent.

Jerry Lewis understands the Wall Street connection. When Kemp and other activists criticized MDA, Lewis told then-President Bush to "act to protect and preserve the invaluable American private-sector institution…with a categorical disavowal of Mr. Kemp's assault on MDA."[16]

However, the nonprofits, especially the charities, are rarely challenged. As James Cook put it in *Forbes* magazine, "Most Americans are astonishingly indifferent to how effectively charitable organizations use the money that comes their way. As they tend to see it, the righteousness of their cause assures the integrity of their conduct, and anyone who suggest otherwise had better watch out."[17]

At best, charities postpone societal questions about economic equality. At worst, charities serve as self-serving tax shields and allow right-wing ideologues like Newt Gingrich and Arianna Huffington to assault the "socialist" safety net while claiming that private charities will pick up the pieces. In the process the U.S. Treasury is robbed of dollars that could be put to entitlement programs. Charity, as we know it, is nothing less than an attempt to justify capitalism's inherent injustices, which makes it a euphemism for economic oppression.

Entitlement v. Charity: The 20th Century Beggars

Laura Hershey, former poster child and a disability rights activist who initiated the "Tune Jerry Out" campaign, explains that a shift in thinking about disability is what is called for:

The disability rights approach views disability as a natural phenomenon which occurs in every generation, and always will. It recognizes people with disabilities as a distinct minority group, subject at times to discrimination and segregation…but also capable of taking our rightful place in society.[18]

We need solutions which address reality. The scapegoating of vulnerable populations as costly consumers of tax dollars is reprehensible, and essentially false. The public resources that are distributed to the impoverished and disabled are redistributed in the community—to the pharmaceutical corporations, to the landlords, to the grocery store chains, to the utility companies. The argument that disabled people consume an inordinate amount of our social resources is similarly false; 80 percent of the world's resources are consumed by the wealthiest people.

Why do we still have twentieth century beggars like Jerry Lewis in a so-called civilized nation? The answers lie within the nature of capitalism itself. There is more profit to be made in the construction and equipping of national charity empires than in making public policy fill in the missing gaps. The advertising and contracting opportunities offered by an MDA telethon are more attractive to corporations who can afford the ante of a donation than the wider-spread universal benefit of increases in disability and welfare disbursements.

Just as in Dickens's time, we have not interwoven disability and poverty into the fabric of socio/economic policy so that entitlements replace begging, civil rights replace bigotry, and social justice replaces inequity. The nation needs to eliminate tax-free charity status and return the lost revenues to a democratic government to redistribute wealth in a democratic manner. That, afterall, is what constitutional "promoting the general welfare" is all about. Private and nonprofit charities doling out arbitrary services must be replaced with a sound disability-sensitive universal health care system that allows all citizens to live with dignity, and we must insist on a guaranteed income floor that leaves no one undernourished. Strengthening the social contract means recognizing its deficiences and making health care and sustenance economic rights, not luxuries. The reality is that neither Scrooge nor the disingenuous "thousand points of light" neo-liberal "volunteerism" will be the solution; the public wealth must be distributed more responsibly and a democratic government must be held to the task.

Notes

1. Sept. 2, 1990.
2. Op-ed, Sept. 3, 1981.
3. *Los Angeles Times*, Sept. 1991.
4. *Report on Disability Programs*, Aug. 17, 1995, p. 135.
5. Leslie Bennetts, "Letter From Las Vegas: Jerry vs. the Kids," *Vanity Fair*, Sept. 1993, pp. 87, 82.
6. *Los Angeles Times*, Sept. 8, 1992.
7. Bill Bolte, "Jerry's Kidding and the Joke's on Millions of Disabled People," *In These Times*, Sept. 1992, p. 24.
8. *Moving Forward*, Sept./Oct. 1992, p. 35.
9. *Disability Rag*, Sept./Oct. 1992, p. 12.
10. Dianne Piastro, "The MDA Story That's Not Being Told," *Newspaper Enterprise Association Wire Service*, Aug. 26, 1991.
11. Gary Sifra, *The Daily News*, Sept. 14, 1995.
12. Gina Graham, "Foundation Culture," *Left Business Observer* No. 70, Nov. 4, 1995, p. 4.
13. Doug Henwood, "The Business End," *Left Business Observer* No. 70, p. 5.
14. Gregory Colvin, "Keep Charity Clear of Politics," *Los Angeles Times*, Jan. 8, 1997.
15. National Press Club, Nov. 20, 1995.
16. Lewis letter printed in *Disability Rag*, Sept./Oct. 1992, p. 23.
17. Oct. 28, 1991.
18. *Disability Rag*, Sept./Oct. 1992, p. 7.

Discussion Questions

1. What is wrong with charity, according to Russell?

2. How does the MDA profit from disablement? Do you think what it did was wrong?

3. How have "crips" fought back against society's paternalistic attitudes toward the disabled?

4. Do you think Jerry Lewis and his supporters reacted appropriately when presented with criticism of their fund-raising tactics?

5. Where does most of the money go that the MDA receives?

6. How does the charity system benefit the rich?

7. What does Russell suggest in her conclusion?

Writing Suggestion

What charities do you support and why? How do you evaluate the effectiveness of a charity?

"Rent to Own": The Slick Cousin of Paying on Time

Michael Hudson

Merchants of Misery: How Corporate America Profits from Poverty

Michael Hudson,
The APF Reporter, Alicia Patterson Foundation, 1993

Some people call Larry Sutton "the Reverend of Rent To Own." Sutton preaches the blessings of the rent-to-own business with the enthusiasm of a true believer.

He owns a growing number of Champion Rent-to-own stores in Florida and Georgia: more than 20 so far. They offer televisions, stereos, furniture, washers, you name it, at weekly or monthly rates. If they pay long enough, customers can some-day own these things. If they can't, the store picks the merchandise up and rents it to someone else.

Sutton likes to think of renting-to-own as something like a marriage, with the same mutual debts and duties. The hardest part of the relationship, Sutton once told a seminar of rental dealers, is getting money from customers who are squeezing by from one paycheck or welfare grant to the next. "I had one guy tell me the best close he ever used was: 'If you don't pay, the shit don't stay.' "

Sutton frowns on that approach. Rent-to-own stores have a duty to take care of their customers. "More than anything else," he said, "they are paying us to manage their money."

Advocates for the poor don't see rent-to-own quite so benevolently. They say the industry's phenomenal growth in the past decade has come by exploiting low-income people who have few choices and little political clout. According to the industry's own figures, only about one-fourth of its customers achieve their goal of ownership.

Rent-to-own customers routinely pay two, three, and four times what merchandise would cost if they could afford to pay cash. For example: A Rent-A-Center store in Roanoke, Virginia, recently offered a 20-inch Zenith TV for $14.99 a week for 74 weeks-or $1,109.26. Across town at Sears, the same TV was on sale for $329.99. Putting aside $15 a week, it would take just 22 weeks to save enough to buy it retail.

Iris Green has lived for 20 years in public housing in Paterson, New Jersey. She has no car and has never shopped outside Paterson. She paid Continental Rentals nearly $4,000 toward the purchase of a stereo, a freezer, a washer and other furnishings that had a cash price of less than $2,800. Then she got sick and the paychecks from her job as a nursing home aide stopped coming. She fell behind, and Continental came and took everything. Now she's suing the company.

"My opinion, I thought they was my friends," Green said. "I felt betrayed. I felt disgusted. I felt lonely." She told her sons to stop bringing their girlfriends over. "They had nowhere to sit."

Continental Rentals and other rent-to-own dealers say they offer fair prices and exceptional service to consumers who otherwise couldn't afford to own quality appliances or furniture.

From a business standpoint, the rent-to-own industry has been a success story of the past decade, growing from about 2,000 stores nationwide in 1982 to about 7,000 now. Estimated revenues climbed from $2 billion in 1988 to $3.6 billion in 1991.

"How can we do that by ripping off our customers?" asks Bill Keese, who directs the industry's national trade association. The rapid growth proves the industry treats its customers fairly, he said.

The industry's rise is a story of demographics and salesmanship—and lawsuits and lobbying. Legal Aid lawyers who represent the poor have fought to rein in rent-to-own, but the industry has succeeded in getting laws passed in 30 states that protect it from most legal attacks.

Rent-to-own has prospered in the marketplace by targeting the bottom third of the economic ladder. "Most of our customers are the throwbacks from the retailers that will not deal with them," Continental Rentals owner Michael Schecter said in a court deposition. "...They have limited incomes and they simply can't save money."

The industry got its start during the 1960s. State and federal governments were passing laws to control ghetto merchants who used retail installment contracts to fleece poor people. The rent-to-own industry was born during this time "as a result of the tightening of consumer credit and burgeoning federal consumer protection legislation," its trade group, the Association of Progressive Rental Organizations, says.

Rent to own and retail credit are essentially the same transaction: selling merchandise on time. But rent-to-own dealers have generally managed to escape state and federal credit laws because of one difference: Rent-to-own customers can bring their merchandise back any time with no obligation for the rest of the payments.

The added cost of buying on time from a traditional retailer—the difference between the cash price and the total installment price—is a finance charge regulated by state usury laws. In New Jersey, for example, retailers can charge no more than 30 percent interest each year.

Rent-to-own dealers say they are exempt from usury laws because they do not charge interest. They say the extra price of buying on time from them is a service charge covering their higher costs of doing business, such as making free repairs.

Avoiding retail credit limits has allowed rental dealers to charge much higher prices than retailers. Rent-to-own customers often pay markups that are equal to interest rates of 100 to 200 percent a year. A survey by the New Jersey Public

Advocate, a state agency, turned up a store that was selling a microwave with a markup equal to 440 percent interest.

Such price advantages helped rent-to-own grow steadily in the 1970s and then boom during the uninhibited capitalism of the 1980s, when the industry produced many millionaires and prompted corporate buyouts. In 1987, Thorn EMI PLC, a British conglomerate that owned half the United Kingdom's rental market, purchased the Wichita-based Rent-A-Center chain for $594 million. The American company now has more than 1,200 stores nationwide. It claims, along with its parent, to be the largest buyer of consumer electronics in the world.

Industry officials say the bulk of their customers are working-class families and, increasingly, soldiers and professionals who move from town to town and want only short-term rentals. "The term rent-to-own, in a nutshell, is a marketing concept more than a description of the business," Champion's Sutton said in an interview.

Still, among themselves at least, rent-to-own dealers concede that many of their customers usually struggle to get by.

Sutton told dealers at one how-to seminar that rent-to-own stores should try to work with slow-paying customers—but you can't run a business by letting them get too far behind. You've got to get four payments every month, he advised the dealers.

"We can be good friendly Joes and we can work with 'em til heck freezes over," Sutton said. "But I tell you what, if we're getting three-for-four, sooner or later you'll be out of business. Trust me."

Getting four-for-four takes nurturing, just like a good marriage, he said. You've got to make repairs when the customer asks and keep all your other promises.

"You've got to somehow convince him that you're different than all the rest," Sutton said. "Because John's Finance Company called him about money. Fred from the car company called him about money. Jackson Brown from the clothing store called him about money. You don't want money. You've just got to get an agreement renewed."

Debra Dillard has a great relationship with the manager at the Prime Time Rentals near her home in Trenton, New Jersey. She's even become his son's godmother. Dillard, who runs a day-care business in her home, could shop elsewhere. But she prefers Prime Time's friendliness and convenience. "I pick up the phone. If I have a problem, they're there. It's solved, whether it's a repair or replacement, or I forget how to program my VCR."

She likes the idea of not getting stuck in contracts she can't escape. Also, she doesn't have to lay things away or come up with a big downpayment. "That makes it easier for you to have the things you want in life."

Other customers have fewer choices. Dee Burnett is raising five children and grandchildren on welfare and food stamps in Roanoke, Virginia. For more than a year, she has been paying $220 a month to Magic Rentals for a freezer, refrigerator, stove and bunk beds. Burnett knows she paying more than she would retail, but her divorce left her broke and ruined her credit. Once she pays Magic off, she says, she'll never go back. "From now on, if there's something I want, I don't need it right away. I'll lay it away and pay when I can.

In New Jersey, the Consumers League Education Fund has produced an anti-rent-to-own rap song that's getting some radio airplay as a public-service announcement: *With rent-to-own, your money's blown/You keep on paying til you turn to stone.*

Critics say high prices are only part of the problem. Legal Aid lawyers charge that some unscrupulous dealers sell used goods as new, break into people's homes to repossess merchandise, charge exorbitant insurance and late fees, and use the threat of criminal charges to intimidate late-paying customers. A West Virginia rent-to-own company recently settled lawsuits by four customers who had been jailed on theft charges that were filed by the dealer but later thrown out of court.

Still, the industry has beaten back most lawsuits—either by winning favorable court rulings or by silencing unhappy customers with confidential cash settlements. This March, in Minnesota, the industry defeated its toughest legal challenge to date: a class-action lawsuit filed by Legal Aid and private attorneys charging Rent-A-Center with usury and racketeering against more than 10,000 customers. A legal team from Shook, Hardy & Bacon—a Kansas City firm known for its invincibility as a defender of tobacco companies—convinced a federal jury that rent-to-own transactions are not covered under Minnesota's retail credit act. The jury took just 90 minutes to return with a verdict for Rent-A-Center.

At the same time they've been winning in court, rent-to-own dealers have sideswiped their opponents with an effective legislative strategy: pushing through industry-written laws that provide some state regulation but allow dealers to avoid retail credit limits.

These laws require dealers to reveal basic information such as the total cost of an item and whether it is used. But critics say such laws allow rental dealers to continue charging outrageous prices. "Disclose and anything goes," some Legal Aid attorneys call it.

The industry's trade association has pushed its agenda with well-financed lobbying.

In North Carolina, state Rep. Jeanne Fenner proposed a law in 1983 that would have treated rent-to-own deals like retail sales. The bill eventually was gutted, but the industry took revenge when Fenner came up for reelection two years later. Rent-to-own dealers as far away as Texas gave more than $6,000 to her Republican challenger—accounting for half of his campaign donations. Fenner, who spent $2,000, lost the election. When she ran for the state senate the next year, the industry gave her opponent $15,000. Fenner lost again.

Since then, attempts to regulate rent-to-own prices in North Carolina have failed.

Thirty states have passed laws that require price disclosures but give the industry safe harbor from retail credit regulations. In five of those states, consumer activists managed to win some limits on the total markup that rent-to-own dealers can charge. In Connecticut, for example, the limit is twice the cash price.

The industry has lost outright in only one state. Pennsylvania passed a law in 1989 that defines rent-to-own deals as retail sales and sets an interest limit of 18 percent a year. Pennsylvania's rent-to-own dealers claimed the new law would put them out of business, but many found a way to skirt it. They offer straight rentals—with the promise of a rebate that the customer can use to purchase the item at the end of the contract.

Nationally, rental dealers are pushing Congress to pass a national version of the industry-written state laws. Their trade association also is planning a public-relations campaign that pushes rent-to-own as "an alternative way to get a piece of the American Dream."

Many dealers are diversifying their product lines, offering jewelry and even automobiles. Sutton's Champion stores have been heading upscale, offering personal computers, fax machines and beepers.

All that's fine for business, Sutton says, but you won't make money if all you're doing is peddling merchandise to a faceless public.

In August, at a seminar in New Orleans for fellow dealers, Sutton told a story about one of his store managers in Florida, a country boy with little education.

One day, a customer tried to turn in his portable TV and VCR. He had decided to get something from the Rent-A-Center down the street. The manager—who'd gone out of his way in the past to help the customer—blew up.

He ordered the customer to take his TV and VCR home—and pay his back payments right away.

"Now, two more things," the manager said. "One: Don't never, ever let me catch you taking that TV and VCR out of your room again. No.2: Don't ever let me hear about you going into Rent-A-Center store again. You got it?"

The customer meekly apologized for momentarily straying.

Sutton wouldn't recommend teaching store managers to jump up and down like jealous boyfriends. But he said his manager did teach him an important lesson about dealing with people: "He doesn't rent televisions. He doesn't rent washers…He doesn't sell anything. He develops *relationships* with people." The manager, Sutton noted, was his top money maker.

Discussion Questions

1. How does the rent-to-own industry profit from targeting the poor?
2. What are the advantages and disadvantages to the consumer of rent-to-own?
3. What is meant by the statement that rent-to-own managers don't sell anything but instead "develop relationships"?

Writing Suggestion

Write a persuasive paper in which you try to convince readers who might be tempted to use rent-to-own services to consider alternatives.

The Ideology of Competitiveness: Pitting Worker against Worker

James Rinehart

Corporations Are Gonna Get Your Mama:
Globalization and the Downsizing of the American Dream

Edited by Kevin Danaher

The necessity of competitiveness has been hammered home by governments, corporations, and the media to the point that it is taken for granted, a fact of life that is so obvious that we unthinkingly acquiesce to its dictates. Competitiveness has been elevated to the status of a natural law, like the law of gravity, a force that is useless to question or resist. In part, the seductiveness of the term arises from its roots in the material process of economic competition.

Monopolies and oligopolies notwithstanding, some degree of competition between business firms for markets and profits is an inherent element of capitalism that can be observed and measured. In contrast, competitiveness, or the ideology of competition, is used to justify the decisions and actions of firms, especially when the outcomes adversely affect some people, groups, and classes. Historically, the concept of competitiveness has been used to justify business opposition to: unions, reduced hours of work, wage increases, paid vacations, health and safety regulations and anti-pollution laws.

In recent years, competitiveness has been invoked with increasing frequency and has taken on new usages. We are led to believe that enhancing corporate or national competitiveness is in everyone's interest, a win-win game with no losers, at least in the long run. More and more, competitiveness is used as a form of blackmail.

Corporations and financial capitalists threaten to withhold or relocate investment if workers refuse to grant concessions or if government regulations and spending on social programs are too great. The word competitiveness now is used to justify actions that increase profitability even when firms are not facing declining markets and profits. Finally, the use of competitiveness is no longer restricted to the economic sphere. Increasingly, governments invoke the term to legitimize relaxing regulations on corporations and removing barriers to corporate profitability (most notably enshrined in free trade agreements), such as spending on unemployment compensation, health, education and welfare.

We are told repeatedly that the drive for competitiveness is in the best interests of both employees and employers. Workers are told they must cooperate and become partners with the managers of their companies, they must pull together, do more with less, get lean and mean, to beat out the competition. Only then will their jobs be secure. In this scenario, workers in one country are pitted against those in all others. Canadian workers in one auto, chemical, or insurance company are pitted against Canadian workers in other auto, chemical, and insurance companies in a race for competitive advantage and job security.

Not long ago a rally attended by about 1,000 employees was held in a large tent outside the Ford plant in Oakville, Ontario. The company passed out refreshments and baseball caps with company logos, and managers spoke about the troubled future of the plant. The plant manager said Ford had 6.5 million excess vehicles, that the plant's Topaz and Tempo models didn't measure up to a competitor's model, the Toyota Camry, and that the Oakville plant had higher absenteeism, lower productivity, and more grievances than a sister plant in Kansas City that also produced the Topaz and Tempo. The message being conveyed—that Oakville could be shut down—was a frightening one, a possibility strengthened by these Ford workers having seen plant after plant in southern Ontario shut down, including the Mack Truck plant across the street. A video was shown of a smalltown Pennsylvania football team that produced perennial champions. The message was clear: if you work hard enough, you too can play on a winning team. The speeches had the tone of sermons at a religious revival meeting (also traditionally held in large tents), only in Oakville salvation comes not from faith and good deeds but from working harder, doing more with less, and cooperating with management. The plant manager then made a dramatic announcement. A top manager from Kansas City had just joined the Oakville team. Everyone cheered. The former Kansas City manager appeared on stage and gave a pep talk, assuring the workers that Oakville was a winner. "Watch out, Kansas City," he yelled. "Watch out, Toyota Camry, here comes Oakville." At this point everyone jumped up, threw their hats in the air, clapped, and cheered, as loud rock and roll music with a heavy bass beat filled the tent.

Undoubtedly, Ford workers in Kansas City attended the same kind of pep rally, the only difference being the enemy—Ford Oakville. This same kind of scenario is played out less obviously, but no less destructively, for workers at the community, provincial, state, national and international levels.

While workers compete against each other in a concessions race to the bottom, corporations have found ways of avoiding or cushioning dog-eat-dog competition. Ford owns 25 percent of Mazda and has joint ventures with Volkswagen; General Motors has joint ventures with Toyota, Suzuki, and Fiat; Chrysler allied with Mitsubishi. If you buy a Pontiac Le Mans from GM for, say, $10,000, $3,000 goes to South Korea for assembly labor; $1,750 to Japan for engines, transaxles, and electronics; $750 to Germany for styling and design; $400 to Taiwan, Singapore, and

Japan for small components; $250 to England for advertising and marketing services; and $50 to Ireland and Barbados for data processing.

While workers around the world compete, it is not usually Indonesian, Philippine, or Mexican firms that compete with U.S. or Canadian firms. Instead it is often subsidiaries of General Electric, Northern Telecom, or General Motors, for example, located in one of these countries "competing" against their own plants in North America. Those who are most caught up in the struggle for existence are workers, not major corporations, three hundred of which now own about one-quarter of the productive assets of the world. Of the richest one hundred economies of the world, forty-seven are corporations, not nations.

What these examples suggest is that the ideology of competitiveness greatly exaggerates real levels of interfirm competition among the largest players.

In Adam Smith's eighteenth century vision of economics, competition was undertaken via price cuts of goods and services. But one wonders about the advantage to consumers of competitiveness when a firm like Nike can produce sports shoes in Indonesia for a total cost of $5.60 and sell those same shoes in Europe and North America for anywhere from $70 to $135. Competitiveness now means not cheap prices but which workers, which taxpayers, which provinces, and which countries can give the most to the corporation in exchange for new investment or to insure that work does not move elsewhere.

On July 8, 1992, *Toronto Globe and Mail* business editor Terrance Corcoran praised South Carolina because it was able to lure BMW to build a new auto plant there. The bait? Cheap labor, the lowest corporate taxes in the United States, absence of unions ("right-to-work" state), 40 million tax dollars to upgrade a local airport, a massive infusion of tax dollars for training grants, and a state-run and financed recruitment and training facility at taxpayers' expense. Corcoran concluded his article with this message: "Wake up!" Even if BMW officials had looked at Ontario or other parts of Canada, what would they have found? (Needless to say, Corcoran's vision of an optimally competitive Canada hardly coincides with the kind of country that most of us would want to live in.)

Corporations threaten to withhold or relocate investment (and jobs) to whipsaw workers. They do the same with governments. Restrictions placed on corporations, removal of their tax breaks, increased corporate taxation, laws facilitating unionization, antiscab laws, and so on, are defined as barriers to competitiveness.

For example, in February 1995 the Ontario government announced it might consider limiting overtime in order to create jobs by spreading around the work. The corporate response was immediate. GM of Canada's answer was typical: "Ultimately, it is going to have a negative effect on our bottom line. We would be working at a competitive disadvantage to our southern neighbors who have no restrictions on the amount of overtime they can work."

In the public sector, deficits and debt take on the same function as competitiveness in the private sector. Efforts to fight the debt also are justified by the argument that such action will enhance Canada's competitiveness. We have witnessed more and more cutbacks in public sector jobs and services. In the first five months of 1995, 74,000 public administration jobs (8.2 percent of the total) at the federal, provincial, and municipal levels were chopped; 20,000 more federal jobs were scheduled to disappear in 1995, and by 1998 the total will reach 45,000. To get a sense of the devastation, we must add wage freezes, back-to-work legislation, and the piece by piece dismantling of social programs. All this is undertaken to create, as they say, a level playing field that will enhance Canada's competitiveness.

Corporations have always responded to declining markets and sales by cutting back their workforces and putting pressure on employees to work harder for less. But what is new is that these measures are now being taken by highly secure and profitable companies that justify their actions by the need to remain competitive in the future. Corporate profitability and competitiveness do not guarantee job security. The *Wall Street Journal* reported that during the 1990–1991 recession, laid-off workers were told of a "tough new world" in which global competition and technological change required constant leanness, but most employees assumed that the layoffs would stop when good times returned. They were wrong. While corporate profits soared to record levels in 1994, the number of job cuts approached those seen at the height of the recession. Both in 1991 (a bad year for profits) and 1994 (a good year for profits), U.S. corporations cut between 500,000 and 600,000 jobs. In April 1995, Mobil Corporation announced plans to cut 4,700 jobs, even though its first-quarter earnings had reached record levels. While workers lost their jobs, Mobil stockholders laughed all the way to the bank. Just after the cutback announcement, Mobil stock rose to a one year high. Proctor and Gamble did the same, despite soaring profits. After slashing 13,000 jobs, the P&G chairman said, "We must slim down to stay competitive." He added, "The public has come to think of corporate restructuring as a sign of trouble, but this is definitely not our situation."

Government and business spokespersons maintain that to be competitive Canada should adopt a high-tech development strategy. Since we can't compete with Third World countries on wages, we should encourage industrial growth in sectors where labor costs are a small fraction of total production costs. High-tech industry, we are told, will help restore competitiveness, relieve unemployment, and provide complex, well-paying jobs. The evidence does not bear out this optimism. First, many jobs connected with high-tech (e.g., in the electronics industry) employ a large number of relatively unskilled (mainly women) workers doing light assembly jobs: jobs that are vulnerable to threats to move production off-shore. Second, high-tech firms are slashing their workforces as rapidly as traditional companies. Firms like AT&T, IBM, Xerox, GTE, Ameritech, Apple and other giants in the field are in the process of reducing their workforces by 9 to 22 percent.

Between 1988 and 1992, employment declined by nearly 20 percent in these high-tech industries in Canada: machinery, communications equipment, electrical machinery, aircraft, and office, store and business equipment. Only in pharmaceuticals did high-tech employment grow, and ironically much of this growth was due to job guarantees given in exchange for the Canadian government's extension of patent rights on drugs (i.e., protection against competition from the generic drug producers).

Northern Telecom is a good example of our dubious hightech future. Nortel became a world leader not through fierce competition but through a regulated telecommunications industry that gave its parent, BellCanada, a market monopoly, which was a major consideration in the company's commitment to R&D and expansion in Canada. Nortel now operates in forty countries and is rapidly expanding its foreign (mostly non-union) operations. In 1994 Nortel had profits of $404 million and expected profits of $550 million in 1995, yet it is making massive cutbacks in its Canadian operations. Over the past five years, the company has closed plants in St. John, New Brunswick, and London, Ontario, has put its Kingston, Ontario plant up for sale, and has planned to chop 1,000 full-time jobs from its facility in Bramalea, Ontario.

The continuous implementation of new technology, the small size of the high-tech sector to begin with, and the tendency to disperse production around the world limit high-tech employment opportunities. As micro-technology finds more and more realms of application, the most rapidly growing jobs will require little training and minimal skill. Projections to the year 2005 from the U.S. Bureau of Labor Statistics indicate that of the 30 fastest growing professions (in terms of number of job openings) only systems analysis, computer engineering and science are directly linked to micro or high technology. The greatest demand will be for retail sales clerks, cashiers, truck drivers, health care workers, waiters, waitresses, cooks, janitors and guards.

These projections also reveal that Canada's high unemployment rate and so-called lack of competitiveness cannot be attributed to an under-educated, under-trained labor force. Victim blaming is rife in business circles, but we hear much less about the management—or investor—induced economic problems related to corporate takeovers and mergers, leveraged buy-outs, financial speculation, risky investment in derivatives and other forms of often profitable but nonproductive investment.

As the good jobs disappear, new ones tend to be part-time, temporary or contracted out. In April 1995, Statistics Canada reported a loss of 17,000 full-time jobs, but part-time employment increased by 17,000. This is simply the latest phase of a longer term trend: 46 percent of the jobs created between 1975 and 1993 were part-time, and by 1993 almost one-quarter (23 percent) of all jobs in Canada offered less than thirty hours of work a week.

Competitiveness means not only fewer full-time jobs but also that all jobs are subject to heavy work loads, constant speedup, and overtime. Recently we were warned by Massachusetts Institute of Technology researchers that in this rough and tumble world only manufacturers who adopt the production and management techniques of the Japanese—a system known as lean production—will survive. Lean production is heralded by the MIT group as beneficial to workers and companies. Workers allegedly are well-trained, multi-skilled, perform challenging jobs, and are encouraged to use their knowledge to improve operations.

Research at CAMI, a unionized General Motors-Suzuki auto assembly plant just outside London, Ontario, that uses lean production methods, has revealed a very different picture. At CAMI, as at other lean production plants, most jobs are easily learned, highly standardized, and repetitive, with time cycles ranging from 1.5 to 3 minutes. Workers receive very little training. Much of it is ideological indoctrination, with an emphasis on cultivating the view that all employees, from the president to the production worker, constitute one big team pulling together to beat out the competition. The plant is chronically understaffed, work loads are heavy, rates of repetitive strain injuries are high, and labor management relations are contentious—this is just skimming the surface. We concluded from our research that lean production "the wave of the future"—is a system that strives to operate with minimal labor inputs. It is a system whose objective is to take time out of labor and labor out of production. It is a system that aspires to the elimination of all production buffers save one: workers who will toil harder and longer whenever required. In the Fall of 1992, CAMI workers, members of the Canadian Auto Workers union, struck the plant for five weeks. This first-ever strike of a North American transplant or joint venture shattered illusions about harmonious labor-management relations under Japanese production management.

What are we to conclude from these trends? Corporations and the media bombard us with the message that enhanced competitiveness is the answer to our economic woes, including unemployment. What's missing from these pronouncements is any discussion of exactly how (and when) most of us will benefit from competitiveness. Few would question the competitive capacity of Northern Telecom or Nike, but their competitiveness has not been associated with growing prosperity and employment opportunities, either in their home countries or in the Third World where many of their operations are located. As the connection between corporate success and national prosperity becomes ever more tenuous, the urgent question is: competitiveness for what and for whom? Buying into competitiveness means accepting the right of big business interests to unilaterally determine our future. Competitiveness involves a race to the bottom. There is no end, no stopping point, no time when the corporation will say, "All right, we have reached our targets; now we can increase wages, stop chopping and overloading jobs." This means continuous rounds of cutbacks and concessions, as there will always be workers somewhere in the world who are desperate enough to work more cheaply. Former Canadian Member of Parliament Donald Blenkarn candidly defined competitiveness: "The Canadian worker can either work harder for less money, or not work at all. That's what competitiveness means."

Corporations and governments ask workers to tighten their belts but rarely mention that executive compensation continues to rise, while the incomes of working people stagnate. Those who ask for sacrifices, obviously enough, never impose the same on themselves. Bertolt Brecht made the point well: "Those who take the meat from the table teach contentment. Those for whom taxes are destined demand sacrifice. Those who eat their fill speak to the hungry of wonderful times to come. Those who lead the country into the abyss call ruling too difficult for ordinary people."

Instead of buying into the ideology of competitiveness, we should be searching for ways to combat the corporate agenda, to extend democratic decision-making into all spheres of life, especially the economic sphere, and to develop peoples' intellectual and cooperative capacities. We need a peoples' agenda, not a big business agenda. It has to be a process that starts at home but develops ever broader, more inclusive forms of solidarity and action. Easy to say, tough to do, but it's the only alternative.

Copyright (c) 1996 by MRP. Reprinted by permission of Monthly Review Foundation.

Discussion Questions

1. What is the difference between competition and competitiveness?
2. What do Ford's rallies exemplify?
3. How does competitiveness "greatly exaggerate real levels of interfirm competition"?
4. What is the effect of competitiveness on workers?

Writing Suggestion

In your opinion, what can the average worker do to fight against "competitiveness" as Rinehart defines it?

Writing Suggestions for Chapter Three

1. Using the readings as a starting point, research further the issue of corporate welfare. What is corporate welfare? Do you support it, or are you in favor of eliminating certain forms of corporate welfare?

2. Examine recent issues of major magazines like *Time, Newsweek, Harper's* and so on. Search for ads that are designed to give companies like Exxon, Philip Morris, and Mobil Oil a positive image with regard to the environment and social issues. How are those ads designed? Are they successful, in your opinion?

3. Examine the issue of "socially conscious" investing. What is it? What types of companies do "socially conscious" investment firms avoid? Why? Would you choose to invest your money in such an account?

4. Find out how your college or university invests its endowment. Are they investing in corporations that make products that you believe are harmful to the environment or to our society? Why do they choose to invest in such corporations?

5. If we are what we buy, then who are you? What brands are you loyal to? Why? Do you purposefully avoid certain products because of where they are manufactured or who manufactures them? Why or why not?

Chapter IV

Health and the Environment

In this chapter, the authors expose the hidden, yet real, dangers that we confront each time we purchase certain products or consume certain foods. If we are what we eat, or what we buy, our self-portrait is not a pretty one.

In "The Invisible Threat," from *Toxic Deception: How the Chemical Industry Manipulates Science, Bends the Law and Endangers Your Health*, by Dan Fagin, Marianne Lavelle, and the Center for Public Integrity, the authors report on the toxins found in common products and how industry, using the PR machine, hides information and manipulates science to play down the effects of toxins on our bodies. In "Food Fight," from *Mad Cow U.S.A.: Could the Nightmare Happen Here?*, Sheldon Rampton and John Stauber expose the feeding practices of the cattle industry and investigate how that industry tried to limit free speech by taking legal action against Oprah Winfrey. In the introduction from *Against the Grain: Biotechnology and the Corporate Takeover of Your Food*, Marc Lappé and Britt Bailey raise serious concerns about the growing use of genetically-engineered crops. Liane Clorfene-Casten investigates how toxins and pesticides are raising incidents of breast cancer in "Are You the One in Eight?" from *Breast Cancer: Poisons, Profits, and Prevention*. The chapter concludes with Judi Bari's discussion of how environmentalists often neglect issues of class in "Timber Wars."

The Invisible Threat

Dan Fagin, Marianne Lavelle
& The Center for Public Integrity

Toxic Deception: How the Chemical Industry Manipulates Science,
Bends the Law and Endangers Your Health

David Pinkerton liked to walk inside the skeleton of his family's home-in-progress on Orchard Road in Centralia, Missouri. Two or three nights a week, after his work as a lab technician at the University of Missouri, he and his wife, Mary, checked on the builder's progress. "It was our dream coming true," he would say years later. "The house was going to be ours forever. "[1]

On one visit just a few weeks before moving day, David noticed a health warning printed on the subflooring that had been put in their new house. It noted that the product emitted vapors that could irritate the eyes and upper respiratory system, "especially in susceptible persons."[2] But David trusted the builder. "I figured he's putting this stuff in," Pinkerton recalled thinking. "He makes a living building houses. He wouldn't put anything in there that would hurt anybody."

After the new carpeting went in, David would never see the warning again. He left the house that evening feeling as if he had a cold. He chalked it up to the approach of winter and the stress of getting ready for the move.

The Pinkertons moved their bedroom furniture in first. "The heck with everything else," David said. "We were going to spend the first night in our new house." Soon they had put up their first big Christmas tree in the picture window. And they began to prepare for the December 30 wedding of Joy, the oldest of four daughters from Mary's previous marriage.

It was the second marriage, in fact, for both Mary and David. After Joy left, there were five on Orchard Road: David's 13-year-old daughter, Jacinda; Mary's 13-year-old daughter, Brenda; and seven-year-old Kara, whom they had adopted.

Within a month, the three girls and their parents had grown quite ill.

David would sit in an old overstuffed chair until supper was ready; after dinner, he would usually go right to bed. At one point he missed two weeks of work. Mary could not cook or clean, and Joy would come to help. One night Mary tried to make dinner and David found her leaning against the wall with the skillet in her hand. Dirty clothes began piling up in the basement. All five had bouts of vomiting and diarrhea that would wake them up, almost nightly. Brenda no longer wanted to go to dance classes, even though ballet had been "her big thing in life," Mary later recalled.

"I had horrible headaches," Mary said. "I was tired. I had trouble understanding how I could feel so tired when I should be the happiest person in the world."

A friend invited the Pinkertons to stay at his house at Lake of the Ozarks, in central Missouri, in March. The weather was turning warmer. There was fresh air. Mary told David that she felt good there, better than she had for a long time. She had no headaches, so she started dusting her friend's home. "Hey, you came down here to relax and rest," David recalled their friend saying. "You didn't come down here to clean my house."

When they returned home on a Sunday evening, the Pinkertons had company, some friends from the First Baptist Church's youth group. Within an hour and a half, Mary was leaning on the counter in the kitchen. She felt so worn out that she could not even serve refreshments.

Later that evening, the Pinkertons began to suspect for the first time that the lingering and mysterious sicknesses had something to do with their brand-new home. Their suspicions were borne out a few months later when, at the Pinkertons' request, an inspector from the Missouri Department of Health came to their home. He attached a tiny glass tube to a portable pump and peered closely at the reading. The liquid in the tube turned purple all the way to the top of the scale, at the number 10: ten parts formaldehyde per million parts air—100 times the level at which many people become ill, according to the medical literature. The inspector's readings in other parts of the house showed at least 40 times the danger level.

The health inspector told the Pinkertons to leave the house, the very place they regarded as their dream come true. They were being poisoned slowly by formaldehyde gas.

The Pinkertons are just five of the thousands of people across the nation who fall victim each year to the invisible threats in every corner of the modern home, office, school, or yard. Few manage to trace their problems to one of the many chemical compounds that we breathe, eat, drink, and touch every day. But there has been incontrovertible evidence for some time that our daily use of a panoply of synthetic substances is helping to drive up rates of cancer, sterility, chronic fatigue, and many other diseases and illnesses.

The National Toxicology Program, which is operated by the National Institutes of Health, has designated more than 300 substances and processes as known or possible carcinogens, based on animal testing.[3] And while death rates have been declining because of better nutrition and medical care, more people than ever are contracting many of the cancers that are often associated with exposure to toxic chemicals, including multiple myeloma, non-Hodgkin's lymphoma, skin cancer, and cancers of the lung, prostate, bladder, brain, and breast.[4] Men born in the 1940s, in fact, have had twice as much cancer—and more than twice as much cancer not linked to smoking—as those born from 1888 to 1897, according to a study published in 1994 in the *Journal of the American Medical Association*. The same study found that women born in the 1940s, when compared to women born from 1888 to 1897, had a 50 percent higher cancer rate overall and a 30 percent higher rate for cancers not linked to smoking.[5] Some argue that we have much more cancer partly because people live longer and because we have eliminated many other diseases. But while the average lifespan has increased, age-adjusted analyses of cancer rates have shown that old age cannot account for the 44 percent increase in cancer incidence from 1950 to 1988.[6]

The National Cancer Institute, which has traditionally taken a skeptical view of environmental-related explanations for cancer, suggested recently that higher cancer rates are at least partly attributable to the proliferation of synthetic chemicals since World War II.[7] An article in its journal noted that job-related exposures to toxic chemicals may be responsible for increases in bladder cancer; that hormonally active pollutants may be driving up the incidence of hormone-induced breast tumors; and that some pesticides, hair dyes, and organic solvents may be partly responsible for the rising rates of non-Hodgkin's lymphoma.[8] Even pets are affected. Another study published in the *Journal of the National Cancer Institute* concluded that dogs are 30 percent more likely to get lymphoma if their owners use the weed-killer 2,4-D on their lawns and are more than twice as likely to get lymphoma if their owners apply 2,4-D more than four times a year.[9]

At least twenty peer-reviewed studies have linked various pesticides to cancer in children.[10] A recent study of 474 Denver children, for example, found that they were more than twice as likely to get leukemia if pest strips had been used in their homes and also were significantly more likely to get brain tumors or lymphomas if their homes had been treated by exterminators.[11] And two researchers at the National Cancer Institute, Aaron Blair and Shelia Hoar Zahm, who have conducted at least seven studies of farmers (a population that by most measures is healthier than the rest of us), have found unexpectedly high rates of leukemia, Hodgkin's disease, non-Hodgkin's lymphoma, multiple myeloma, and cancers of the bone, brain, connective tissue, eye, kidney, lip, pancreas, prostate, skin, stomach, and thyroid.[12]

"The patterns themselves suggest that there are some unexplained factors that have been widely introduced into the environment of industrial societies in the past several decades that account for these trends," Davis says. "We know about the farmers, that they die less often of lung cancer and heart disease but more often of non-Hodgkin's lymphoma, skin cancer, brain cancer and prostate cancer...So we believe, my colleagues and I, that this argues for an environmental explanation."

Cancer is not the only serious health problem that has been linked to the proliferation of synthetic chemicals. Multiple chemical sensitivity and sick-building syndromes, though still controversial, have been recognized as conditions that are caused by exposure to toxic compounds.[13] Amazingly, indoor air pollution is now the most common topic of calls to the nationwide workplace-safety hotline operated by the National Institute of Occupational Safety and Health. Asthma rates in the United States have increased at least 30 percent since the 1970s, with the highest increases among children.[14]

Many studies of both humans and animals have found that synthetic chemicals can suppress the immune system by reducing the body's ability to produce antibodies and otherwise kill disease-carrying cells. Some research even suggests that exposure to man-made chemicals may be partly responsible for increases in infectious diseases, especially in children, the elderly, the chronically ill, and others whose immune systems are already weakened.[15]

Hormone-related health effects—especially infertility, breast cancer, and birth defects in the reproductive organs—are of special interest to researchers, because dozens of synthetic chemicals have been shown to perturb the intricate ebb and flow of estrogen, testosterone, and other hormones that guide sexual development in humans and animals. Experiments have shown that even relatively weak hormone disruptors, such as the pesticides dieldrin, endosulfan, and toxaphene, can produce particularly powerful effects when used in combination. A recent study of the effects of those three pesticides on estrogen-sensitive cells in test tubes, for example, found that the pesticides were 1,000 times more potent in combination than individually.[16] The research has especially disturbing implications because in the real world, of course, we all are exposed to a virtually infinite array of chemical combinations.

Today, according to the federal government, at least 70,000 chemicals are in commerce, with nearly six trillion pounds produced annually for plastics, glues, fuels, dyes, and other chemical products.[17] In 1995, the 100 largest U.S.-based chemical manufacturers sold more than $234 billion worth of chemical products—a 17 percent increase over the previous year—and made $35 billion in profits.[18] Their products have become such a pervasive part of American life, in fact, that an estimated 98 percent of all families now use pesticides at least once a year.[19] Every year, more than a billion pounds of pesticides are used in the United States—three-quarters of it on farms.[20]

Why are so many of these toxic chemicals still in our homes and on our lawns? The answer lies in the chemical industry's ability to manipulate the regulatory system to serve its own ends instead of the public's. Most Americans have been taught that the chemical revolution is nothing short of miraculous. Through the science and history films shown in school and the drumbeat of commercial messages at home, we've been told over and over again that we have chemicals to thank for our relatively carefree lifestyles. "Better things for better living" is the message of E. I. du Pont de Nemours and Company, while the catchphrase of Monsanto Company is "Without chemicals, life itself would be impossible."

But there is another side of the chemical revolution that few Americans think about until they—or people they know—are touched by disease or death. Until they have seen shipyard workers die with lungs crippled by asbestos dust. Or until they have watched soldiers carry home from Vietnam the sicknesses caused by their own army's chemical spray, Agent Orange. Or until they have witnessed young girls grow into womanhood sterile because of the synthetic estrogens doled out with abandon to their mothers.

It is not surprising that years after David Pinkerton and his family became ill, when they went public with their problems in a court of law, chemical companies pleaded with the judge in the case to make sure that the lawyers on the other side did not utter the word "asbestos" or the name of any of the other toxic substances that have made headlines in the past 30 years. A chemical manufacturer's success depends, of course, on its ability to maintain the patina of progress that is such a common theme in commercial messages.

When David Pinkerton stumbled on the printed warning on the subfloors of his new home, he could not have known that executives of a half-dozen mammoth corporations had spent five years arguing over those words and, ultimately, crafting them with care. Nor did he know how many millions of dollars they had spent on lawyers, scientists, public relations specialists, and lobbyists—all related, in one way or another, to the problem signaled by the warning notice.

The executives had woven a cloak of secrecy that hid the real dangers of their products as effectively as the carpeting covered the warnings beneath the feet of David, Mary, and the girls. Their companies—Borden, Inc., Celanese Corporation (now Hoechst Celanese), DuPont, Georgia-Pacific Corporation, and others— mapped out a strategy that has allowed them to continue selling dangerous, some-times even lethal, products to millions of Americans every year.

The formaldehyde story is not unique. The same pattern of widespread exposure, documented health threats, and brazen industry manipulation appears again and again in the stories of the hundreds of toxic chemicals that are a virtually ubiquitous presence in our daily lives.

Just as the manufacturers of formaldehyde were able to keep its dangers hidden for so many years, so have the producers of many other toxic products managed to stave off—or at least blunt—efforts to crack down on dangerous products. They have done it by seeking to shape science, influence politicians, and buy publicity. They have alternately cajoled, soothed, and threatened the regulators who are supposed to protect the public. They have stirred up firestorms of "grass-roots'" support from farmers, small-business owners, and others who, ironically, are often hurt the most by the chemicals in question. Behind the scenes, all the while, their lawyers have sparred with tens of thousands of Americans who claim to have been injured by the chemicals—and, in many cases, negotiated secret settlements that keep the rest of us in blissful ignorance.

Manufacturers are not the only interests that try to manipulate the system. Environmental organizations, for example, sometimes misrepresent studies and employ other deceptive tactics to exaggerate the hazards of toxic chemicals. But their efforts are dwarfed by those of chemical manufacturers, who have the most at stake and the bankrolls to get the job done.

Consider the case of Benlate, a fungicide manufactured by DuPont. Although Benlate was supposed to kill molds while leaving plants alone, in 1990 thousands of farmers began reporting that the product was ruining their crops. Faced with a bar-rage of lawsuits alleging that Benlate was tainted with herbicides, DuPont launched a bare-knuckle campaign aimed at suppressing and discrediting scientific evidence that showed the fungicide was indeed contaminated.

Two secret company documents, eventually made public by judicial order, show just how far DuPont was willing to go.[21] A September 1991 letter written by one of DuPont's attorneys called for the company's scientists, who were supposed to be searching for the truth about Benlate, to instead become foot soldiers in DuPont's courtroom wars. "Scientifically, DuPont can maintain that it continues to search for a cause and that it will continue to do so as long as it appears necessary to address the issues raised by customers and regulator," Thomas Burke, an Orlando lawyer, wrote. "[Meanwhile,] in the litigation mode, we will not be forced into admitting that we have found a cause and it is our fault. It is a much better litigation position to state that we have looked, are looking, and will continue to look but have had no success, leaving the issue unresolved, than it is to have to admit that we have isolated the mechanism of injury."

The second DuPont document, written six months later, laid out the details of a secret plan—known internally as "Path Forward"—to fight the contamination claims by applying pressure "via legislators" on administrators at the University of Florida, where researchers were reporting results that contradicted DuPont's claims that Benlate was blameless. The secret plan also called for DuPont to build relationships with politicians and regulators and to move aggressively to undermine scientists who were critical of Benlate. "Cut them off publicly...Don't share information with them...Get intelligence on them so we're not blind-sided...Know your enemies," the Path Forward document said.

However, at least four judges who presided over Benlate lawsuits would later conclude that at the same time DuPont was pushing its public line that Benlate was not contaminated, executives of the company knew otherwise. Noting that company scientists reported directly to DuPont's legal department, one of the judges said that DuPont's conduct "is suggestive of bias." Another fined DuPont $1.5 million for withholding damaging information, and the third slapped DuPont with a staggering $115 million fine for the same offense. The fourth judge didn't stop at a fine. Saying that the company showed "utter disregard" for ethics and legal procedure, she threw out DuPont's defense in a contamination case and awarded victory to a tree farmer.[22] DuPont is appealing all four rulings.

Despite the verdicts, the fines, and the bad publicity, DuPont's aggressive damage-control strategies are paying off. The University of Florida has virtually abandoned its Benlate research, prompting one scientist to retire in disgust. Without admitting guilt, DuPont has ended many of the lawsuits by reaching secret settlements in which the company has paid out more than a half-billion dollars and in return has insisted that farmers and their lawyers sign secrecy agreements and turn over potentially damaging documents. Most important of all, Benlate still has the unrestricted approval of the EPA, even though the agency regards it as a possible carcinogen because it causes liver tumors in lab animals.

DuPont's hardball campaign for Benlate is nothing new. Such efforts have been a staple of the chemical industry since 1962, when manufacturers worked to discredit Rachel Carson after the publication of *Silent Spring* launched the modern environmental movement. Back then, the chemical industry's efforts consisted chiefly of deploying friendly scientists to attack Carson in the press and distributing a sarcastic rebuttal to her book. Today, manufacturers are infinitely more sophisticated, carefully choreographing legions of lobbyists, lawyers, scientists, public relations experts, and mass-marketers for maximum effect.

[*Toxic Deception*] is the story of how the chemical industry has managed to keep so many of its toxic products on the market, even in the face of mounting evidence of their danger and emerging—and safer—alternatives. It is also the story of how the federal agencies that are supposed to be the public's watchdogs have been defanged by the chemical industry's pressure tactics, which include junkets and job offers to government regulators, major contributions to politicians, scorched-earth courtroom strategies, and misleading multimillion-dollar advertising and public relations campaigns.

To tell that story, *Toxic Deception* details the battles over formaldehyde and three other highly toxic chemicals that are in widespread use in the United States.* They are not the most dangerous, or even the most prevalent, chemicals on the market. But these four—all of which have been shown, beyond question, to cause cancer in laboratory animals are emblematic of the thousands of toxic chemicals that are a pervasive yet often overlooked presence in the everyday lives of all Americans.

Atrazine, a farm weed-killer and the nation's most heavily-used pesticide, is a health risk to consumers because it taints drinking water and because small amounts of it are present in corn, milk, beef, and other foods. Whether atrazine causes cancer in humans is still uncertain (the federal government classifies it as a possible human carcinogen), and we may never know for sure because researchers obviously cannot conduct controlled experiments on humans. But scientists can feed atrazine to laboratory animals, and those tests show that atrazine causes cancer in at least one type of rat—a fact that scientists have now known for 20 years. The recent discovery that the weed-killer interferes with the production of sex hormones may explain why laboratory rats have developed atrazine-induced tumors in their mammaries, ovaries, and uteruses. Based on the animal studies, the Environmental Protection Agency has estimated that midwestern corn farmers who mix and apply their own atrazine, get their water from a reservoir, and eat a typical diet face a one in 863 lifetime risk of developing cancer from atrazine; nonfarmers in the Midwest face an estimated cancer risk of one in 20,747. By way of comparison, the EPA generally takes regulatory action when a chemical poses a lifetime cancer risk higher than one in a million. Yet Ciba-Geigy, the Swiss chemical giant that introduced atrazine in the United States, was still selling about $170 million worth of the weed-killer every year in the mid-1990s, according to the National Center for Food and Agricultural Policy, a research group with close ties to agribusiness.

Alachlor, a frequent partner of atrazine in the weed-control arsenals of corn growers, is a risk to consumers and farmers for similar reasons. Best known by the trade name Lasso, alachlor shows up in water wells and reservoirs—and in food, too. The EPA has classified it as a probable human carcinogen, and the agency has estimated that people who get their water from midwestern reservoirs face a one in 250,000 lifetime risk of getting cancer from alachlor. High doses of the chemical have also caused liver degeneration, kidney disease, cataracts, and eye lesions in test animals. Worried about the health risks, a small but increasing number of farmers are employing innovative techniques to grow crops profitably with little or no use of chemical weed-killers. But most farmers never even hear about such innovations. Instead, in a springtime ritual that is as common in the Midwest as baseball games and church picnics, hundreds of thousands of farmers spray alachlor, atrazine, and other herbicides even before weeds begin to sprout. Unsurprisingly, alachlor still generates tens of millions of dollars in annual sales for Monsanto Company, and for many years it was the St. Louis-based agribusiness behemoth's top-selling pesticide.

*The four chemicals are among the most common in the United States and have a long history of government efforts at regulation. All were frequently cited as chemicals that pose significant health concerns in preliminary interviews that the Center for Public Integrity conducted in 1994 with scientists from a cross section of environmental, industrial, government, and research organizations.

Few chemicals have gained such intimate entry into our lives as **pechloroethylene**, the metal degreaser enlisted for use in the dry-cleaning industry in the 1950s. In theory, the solvent is safe within the confines of the tens of thousands of machines in which suits, dresses, and other clothes spin and tumble every day. In reality, it is not easy to contain any liquid as widely used as this one, which is manufactured in the United States by Dow Chemical Company, PPG Industries, Inc., and Vulcan Materials Company and in England by Imperial Chemical Industries Ltd. Perchloroethylene seeps and spills into groundwater, whiles its vapors invade nearby apartments and stores. And tests consistently show that consumers frequently bring "perc" home with them in their dry-cleaned clothes, particularly if their cleaners use old equipment or "short cycle" their machines—removing clothing before it is fully dried—to speed the process. Dry cleaners have always known that too much perc can make them dizzy or "drunk." There is a fierce debate over the effects of long-term exposure to smaller amounts of the chemical, but studies since the 1970s have linked perc not only to cancer but also to a variety of kidney, liver, neurological, and reproductive problems. The International Agency for Research on Cancer has classified perc as a probable human carcinogen, though it has settled on a determination that dry cleaning is only possibly carcinogenic.

Then there is **formaldehyde**, the chemical that invaded the Pinkerton home. A simple substance that actually is manufactured by all living cells in minute quantities, formaldehyde has become so ubiquitous in industry that it is impossible to catalog all of the products through which consumers might bring it into their homes. It is a preservative or binder in some cosmetics, pesticides, cleaners, and adhesives, though it is rarely labeled as such because it is not an "active" ingredient. To create permanent-press fabrics, the apparel industry coats textiles with a formaldehyde resin and bakes them. The primary use of formaldehye—the use that [Toxic Deception] explores in depth—has put it in the cabinets, flooring, walls, or furniture of virtually every American home built or renovated since the post-World War II housing boom. Nearly a dozen U.S. manufacturers produce strong formaldehyde resins, or glues, that are mixed with wood scraps and chips to produce particleboard, plywood, medium-density fiberboard, and other substitutes for solid wood. Few consumers realize they may be bringing formaldehyde into their homes when they install new kitchen cabinets or wood molding or buy furniture that they assemble themselves. Few buyers of mobile homes understand that they have a higher ratio of particleboard, and more formaldehyde gas, than conventional homes. The cheaper the wood, in fact, the more likely that it is a wood "product" held together with formaldehyde. Since the late 1970s, it has been known that formaldehyde causes cancer in rats, and therefore the International Agency for Research in Cancer terms it a probable carcinogen in humans. One of the most irritating gases to be cooked up in a chemistry lab, formaldehyde can gag, sicken, and weaken some people at even extremely low levels. In the worst cases, formaldehyde-sensitive people who have been exposed to high doses of the gas develop severe and debilitating asthmatic symptoms that appear whenever they breathe any chemical—from pesticides to perfumes.

David and Mary Pinkerton had spent their entire lives in the home state of Harry Truman, but in their case, after they discovered formaldehyde in their home, the buck did not stop anywhere. The builder referred them to a wood-products dealer, who advised them to fumigate their home with ammonia. By now, however, David Pinkerton had his doubts.

Georgia-Pacific and a smaller manufacturer, Temple Industries of Texas, would later hire scientists at big universities to say that the tests taken in the Pinkerton house were no good. They hired other testers to check the house—months later—and came out with much lower readings, around two-tenths of a part per million. And they brought other scientists to the witness stand to say that these levels of formaldehyde gas posed no danger.

The scientists conceded that formaldehyde can be "irritating to the eyes and upper respiratory system, especially in susceptible persons"—the words on the warnings underneath the Pinkertons' floor. As for the studies showing that rats that breathed formaldehyde developed cancer—well, they said, rats are not people.

When lawyers for Georgia-Pacific and Temple appeared before a jury in Clay County, Missouri, in 1989—five years after the Pinkertons had abandoned Orchard Street forever—they pointed out that the only federal safety standard for formaldehyde, established by the U.S. Department of Housing and Urban Development for manufactured housing, was no more than four-tenths of a part per million. The lawyers did not mention the industry's high-stakes lobbying campaign to get HUD to set a relatively high level and to block efforts by other federal agencies to regulate formaldehyde.

If the members of the jury did not like the law, the lawyer for Georgia-Pacific and Temple said, they should ask Congress to change it. The lawyer did not let on that his clients knew all about influence on Capitol Hill. The nation's major formaldehyde producers and users, for example, poured nearly $4 million into congressional campaigns from 1979 to 1995.[23]

The lawyer pointed out one more thing. It was about the Pinkertons. If they cared so much about their health, why did both of them smoke? Why was Mary obese, with high blood cholesterol? She had been ill many times in the past, had had her gall bladder removed, and had had a full hysterectomy. Mary's father was an alcoholic and so was her first husband. After her divorce, she had seen a psychiatrist.

The manufacturers had retained a clinical psychologist who rendered the opinion from the stand that Mary had a tendency to blame other people for her problems. It was his assessment that she had adopted a child to avoid closeness with her other children. As for the house on Orchard Road, the Pinkertons simply cared too much about it, said the psychologist hired by the company whose slogan was "See where your dreams and products from Georgia-Pacific can take you."[24]

At least several hundred families have confronted the manufacturers of formaldehyde as the Pinkertons did. But only a handful have ever agreed to stay the searing course of such litigation and to subject themselves, to being "peeled...back to the very core of their soul," as the Pinkerton's lawyer, R. Frederick Walters of Kansas City, put it as their trial drew to a close. Most plaintiffs agree to cash settlements, in which the chemical manufacturer admits no harm, and they promise not to reveal the money they garnered, their stories, or the documents they gathered to bolster their cases.

But the Pinkertons persevered through the longest trial in the history of Clay County. On December 21, 1989, an outraged jury awarded them $140,000 for medical expenses, and $63,000 for property losses; on January 8, 1990, the jury added $16 million in punitive damages. Their story is one of the few on the public record.

Most of their story, that is.

Ever since her six months on Orchard Street, Mary Pinkerton, who had never been very healthy, suffered from a condition known as multiple chemical sensitivity. She grew ill with asthmatic symptoms whenever she was near any chemicals, not just formaldehyde. A year and a half after the verdict, on a family trip, the Pinkertons stayed in a hotel that they later learned had been sprayed with insecticides. Mary became unable to breathe and died on July 1, 1991.

"You know, everybody walks through life and some people carry heavier burdens than others," Walters, the lawyer for the Pinkertons, had said at the trial. "I'm here to tell you [that Mary's] not a strong person. She has had previous problems. But [Georgia-Pacific and Temple] have added to the burden.

"Mary walked into that house thinking her life was going to change, things are going to get better. And six months later, her burden is crushing. You know what? She's never going to get through her burden now."

Notes

1. Pinkerton v. Temple Industries, cv-186-4651-cc, Clay County, Missouri, November 1989.
2. The warning read: "WARNING: IRRITANT. THIS PRODUCT CONTAINS A UREA FORMALDEHYDE RESIN AND MAY RELEASE FORMALDEHYDE VAPORS IN LOW CONCENTRATIONS. FORMALDEHYDE CAN BE IRRITATING TO THE EYES AND UPPER RESPIRATORY SYSTEM, ESPECIALLY IN SUSCEPTIBLE PERSONS SUCH AS THOSE WITH ALLERGIES OR RESPIRATORY AILMENTS. USE WITH ADEQUATE VENTILATION. VENTILATION RATE SHOULD NOT BE LESS THAN ONE (1) AIR CHANGE PER HOUR. IF SYMPTOMS DEVELOP, CONSULT YOUR PHYSICIAN."
3. "IARC & NTP Carcinogen List," compiled by the NTP, http://ntpserver. niehs. nih.gov.
4. Devra Lee Davis, Aaron Blair, and David G. Hoel, "Agricultural Exposures and Cancer Trends in Developed Countries," *Environmental Health Perspectives* 100 (1992): 42–43.
5. Devra Lee Davis, Gregg E. Dinse, and David G. Hoel, "Decreasing Cardiovascular Disease and Increasing Cancer Among Whites in the United States From 1973 Through 1987," *Journal of the American Medical Association* 271, no. 6 (9 February 1994): 431.
6. Samuel S. Epstein, "Evaluation of the National Cancer Program and Proposed Reforms," *American Journal of Industrial Medicine* 24 (1993): 112.
7. Susan Devesa et al., "Recent Cancer Trends in the United States," *Journal of the National Cancer Institute* 87, no. 3 (1 February 1995): 179–80.
8. Ibid.
9. Howard M. Hayes et al., "Case-Control Study of Canine Malignant Lymphoma: Positive Association With Dog Owner's Use of 2,4-Dichlorophenoxyacetic Acid Herbicides," *Journal of the National Cancer Institute* 83 (4 September 1991): 1226–31.
10. Environmental Working Group, Physicians for Social Responsibility, and the National Campaign for Pesticide Policy Reform, *Pesticide Industry Propaganda: The Real Story* (Washington: Environmental Working Group, 1995), 6.
11. Jack K. Leiss and David A. Savitz, "Home Pesticide Use and Childhood Cancer: A Case-Control Study," *American Journal of Public Health* 85, no. 2 (February 1995): 249–52.
12. Aaron Blair and Shelia Hoar Zahm, "Cancer Among Farmers," *Occupational Medicine: State of the Art Reviews* 6, no. 3 (July–September 1991): 3 35; and Aaron Blair, Mustafa Dosemeci,

and Ellen F. Heineman, "Cancer and Other Causes of Death Among Male and Female Farmers From Twenty-Three States," *American Journal of Industrial Medicine* 23 (1993): 729.

13. American Lung Association et al., *Indoor Air Pollution: An Introduction for Health Professionals* (Washington: EPA, 1994); and Leslie Dreyfous, "High-Tech Low: Are We Keeping Up With Our Brave New World?" Associated Press, 20 January 1991.

14. A. Sonia Buist and William M. Vollmer, "Reflections on the Rise in Asthma Morbidity and Mortality," *Journal of the American Medical Association* 264, no. 13 (13 October 1990): 1719-20; and Peter J. Gergen, Daniel I. Mullally, and Richard Evans III, "National Survey of Prevalence of Asthma Among Children in the United States, 1976 to 1980," *Pediatrics* 81, no. I (January 1988): 1–7.

15. Robert Repetto and Sanjay Baligan, *Pesticides and the Immune System: The Public Health Risks* (Washington: World Resources Institute, 1996), 18–56 passim.

16. Steven V. Arnold, "Synergistic Activation of Estrogen Receptor With Combinations of Environmental Chemicals," *Science* 272 (7 June 1996): 1489–91.

17. Inform, Inc., *Toxics Watch 1995*, (New York: Inform, 1995), 4.

18. George Peaff, "Dow Replaces DuPont to Lead Top 100 U.S. Chemical Producers," *Chemical & Engineering News*, 6 May 1996, 15–20.

19. James R. Davis, Ross C. Brownson, and Richard Garcia, "Family Pesticide Use in the Home, Garden, Orchard, and Yard," *Archives of Environmental Contamination and Toxicology* 22 (1992): 260.

20. Statement of Peter F. Guerrero, Associate Director for Environmental Protection Issues of the Resources, Community, and Economic Development Division, GAO, before the House Committee on Government Operations, Subcommittee on Environment, Energy, and Natural Resources, as reprinted in *Pesticides: 30 Years Since Silent Spring—Many Long-Standing Concerns Remain* (Washington: GAO, 1992), 2.

21. Jan Hollingsworth, "Covenant of Silence," *Tampa Tribune*, (18 December 1995), 1.

22. Jan Hollingsworth, "Judge Takes Benlate to Task," *Tampa Tribune*, (22 June 1996), 1.

23. Center for Responsive Politics, National Library on Money and Politics, from Federal Election Commission records.

24. Georgia-Pacific Corporation, pamphlet, n.d.

Discussion Questions

1. What significance does the title of this excerpt hold?
2. Why do the authors begin this chapter with the story of the Pinkertons?
3. Have you or anyone you have known suffered from the effects of household chemicals?
4. Why do the authors choose to focus on just four chemicals?
5. Where do you receive information about potentially hazarded chemicals in common household products? Why aren't the dangers of these chemicals common knowledge?

Writing Suggestion

Do you ever change or alter your buying habits because of the threat of toxins in those products? Why or why not?

Food Fight

Sheldon Rampton & John Stauber

Mad Cow U.S.A.: Could the Nightmare Happen Here?

"Y ou said this disease could make AIDS look like the common cold?" asked TV talk-show host Oprah Winfrey.

"Absolutely," said her guest, Howard Lyman of the Humane Society of the Human Society of the United States.

"That's an extreme statement, you know," Oprah said.

"Absolutely," Lyman said again, "and what we're looking at right now is that we're following exactly the same path that they followed in England. Ten years of dealing with it as public relations rather than doing something substantial about it. A hundred thousand cows per year in the United States are fine at night, dead in the morning. The majority of those cows are rounded up, ground up, fed back to other cows. If only one of them has mad cow disease, it has the potential to affect thousands."

"But cows are herbivores. They shouldn't be eating other cows," Oprah said.

"That's exactly right, and what we should be doing is exactly what nature says. We should have them eating grass, not other cows. We've not only turned them into carnivores, we've turned them into cannibals."[1]

It was easy to see why the National Cattlemen's Beef Association hated Howard Lyman. Many people within the meat industry regarded him as not just a critic but an outright traitor. A fourth-generation rancher, Lyman at age 54 still had a farmer's solid build and temperament. At the peak of the farm boom in the late 1970s, his Montana ranch had been a multi-million-dollar operation with 5,000 feedlot cattle and 1,000 range animals. Later, he had worked for a time as a Washington lobbyist for the National Farmers Union before converting to vegetarianism, organic farming and animal rights activism.

Two events in Lyman's life marked the turning points that led to his conversion. The first was the death of his brother from cancer following exposure to dioxin-con-taminated herbicides. The other event occurred in 1979 when Lyman found himself in a hospital, paralyzed from the waist down. Doctors had found a tumor on the inside of his spine and warned that he would probably never walk again. "As I was lying there in that bed, I found myself remembering what our farm had looked like

when I was a kid. I realized what it had become after twenty years of chemical addiction," Lyman said. "I made a vow that if I was ever able to walk again, I would do
everything I could to make that farm sustainable and chemical-free."

Lyman recovered from the non-malignant tumor and began to make changes in
his life. In 1983 he sold his ranch. He became convinced that excessive meat consumption lay at the heart of his health problems. "If I had not changed my diet, I'd
be dead today," he declared in a 1996 interview. "I've dropped a hundred pounds
since I stopped eating meat. I have more energy than ever before in my life now. I
require less sleep, and my mind is clearer. I think back about a group of friends, ten
of us that used to get together and play cards when I was living on the farm. Only
one of the ten of us has not had heart disease, cancer or died. These were good
friends, hard workers, slim and athletic, dying of heart disease and strokes. They were
dying of a diet of affluence, dying from what they were eating."[2]

In 1992, Lyman signed on as executive director for activist Jeremy Rifkin's
Beyond Beef campaign, which targeted the McDonald's restaurant chain with pick-
eting and leaflets. "The reason I headed up the Beyond Beef campaign is that I
believe factory production of food is an absolute disaster," Lyman said. "I'm still the
greatest supporter in the world of the family farmers, the greatest resource that we
have. The Beyond Beef campaign was not an assault on meat eating. We called for a
50 percent reduction, which seemed to have a greater chance of success than calling
on people to remove all animal products from their diet. Beyond Beef was an impe-
tus for what is happening today, a tremendous consumer awareness of health and diet
issues."

For Lyman, the British government's announcement that mad cow disease could
be linked to human fatalities came as no surprise at all. He had been following developments in England for years and had become convinced that the issue was being
glossed over not only there but in the United States as well. In September 1993, he
had attended a symposium on BSE at the University of Wisconsin-Madison and had
been appalled at the treatment given to Richard Marsh, a UW-Madison professor
whose research suggested that a BSE-like disease might already be infecting U.S. cattle. "It was like they walked him up to the gallows, put the rope around his neck,
sprung the trap," Lyman said. "I believe the entire symposium was orchestrated simply to bring Dick Marsh to heel. I think it broke his heart. I think Marsh is a big
teddy bear, a brilliant researcher, a wonderful human being, but he has no shell
against that kind of attack. The university and industry just destroyed him. Some
people when you pick on them they get tougher, others they wilt."

Marsh had expressed his views in the cautious and often inscrutable language of
a scientist, language that was only dimly understood outside the circle of researchers
who, like himself, specialized in the transmissible spongiform encephalopathies. The
public was unlikely to become concerned by talk of "proteinaceous infectious particles," "heterozygosity at the 129th codon," "infectivity of corneal epithelium" or
"pathogenicity in mink." Lyman, however, was not a scientist. An outspoken, com-
manding speaker with a wry sense of humor and a down-home cowboy-populist style,
he knew how to use words that people understood. The general public might not
understand the significance of proteinaceous infectious particles, but they *did* know
what you meant when you talked about grinding up dead cows and feeding them to

other cows. The chance to appear on Oprah was Lyman's first opportunity to take his message to a national audience, and he was determined to state his case in the simplest, most unmistakable terms.

"How do you know the cows are ground up and fed back to the other cows?" Oprah asked.

"Oh, I've seen it," Lyman said. "These are USDA statistics. They're not something we're making up."

"Now doesn't that concern you all a little bit, right here, hearing that?" Oprah asked her studio audience, which responded with supportive cheers.

"It has just stopped me cold from eating another burger," Oprah said. "I'm stopped!"

"Yeah!" answered the audience, clapping loudly.

Dr. Gary Weber, a policy director for the National Cattlemen's Beef Association, was the man charged with blunting Lyman's attack. Oprah had teamed him up with Will Hueston, a bearded scientist from the USDA. Weber and Hueston found themselves lined up not just against Lyman but also against Vicky Rimmer's grandmother and the father of a boy in the United States who had died of E. coli poisoning from the infamous Jack-in-the-Box hamburger outbreak. It was not the sort of debate that Weber could reasonably expect to win.

"Let me clarify that," Weber began. "There is a reason to be concerned. We've learned from the tragedy in Great Britain and made a decision here…We started taking initiatives ten years ago to make sure this never happened here. Let me go back and correct a couple of things. Number one, we do not have BSE in this country and we have a ten-year history of surveillance to document that based on science. We do not have it. Also, we have not imported any beef in this country since 1985 from Great Britain."

"Are we feeding cattle to the cattle?" Oprah asked.

"There is a limited amount of that done in the United States," Weber admitted, to groans and sighs from the audience. "Hang on just a second now," he said. "The Food and Drug Administration—"

"I have to just tell you, that is alarming to me," Oprah said.

"Now keep in mind that before you view the ruminant animal—the cow was simply vegetarian, remember that they drink milk," Weber said, floundering desperately. "I'm saying we do not have the disease here, we've got ten years of data, the best scientists in the world who are looking for this, over 250 trained technicians and veterinarians around the country. Everyone's watching for this."

"The same thing that we've heard here today is exactly what was heard for ten years in England," Lyman replied. " 'Not to worry, we're on top of this'…If we continue to do what we're doing, feeding animals to animals, I believe we are going to be in exactly the same place…Today we could do exactly what the English did and cease feeding cows to cows. Why in the world are we not doing that? Why are we skating around this and continuing to do it when everybody sitting here knows that would be the safest thing to do? Why is it, why is it? Because we have the greedy that are getting the ear of government instead of the needy and that's exactly why we're doing it," he thundered, again to audience applause.

"We don't want to just alarm you all, but I have to tell you, I'm thinking about the cattle being fed to the cattle and that's pretty upsetting to me," Oprah said.

"I just had one question," said an audience member. "I'm confused about why cattle are being fed lamb, and why are they being fed beef?"

"What it comes down to is about half of the slaughter of animals is nonsellable to humans," Lyman said. "They either have to pay to put it into the dump or they sell it for feed, so they grind it up, turn it into something that looks like brown sugar, add to it all of the animals that died unexpectedly, all of the road kills and the euthanized animals, add it to them, grind it up and feed it back to other animals. It's about as simple as it can be. We are doing something to an animal that was never intended to be done."

"Are the animals tested?" asked another audience member. "All of the animals that are ground into feed that are fed to the cows?"

"There is no test other than analyzing the brains, and since we don't have animals with these symptoms, not every brain is going to be evaluated," Weber admitted. "No animal can enter the plant that has any of these symptoms, by law. And there's veterinarians and...inspection and it doesn't happen, Howard and you know it. it doesn't happen."

"Oh come on, let's get real!" Lyman shot back. "Any animal that is not staggering around goes in there. You know as well as I do. We have a hundred thousand cows per year that die...We ended up feeding downer cows to mink, the mink came down with the disease, transferred it to animals, the animals came down with it, and you're sitting here telling everybody that it's safe. Not true."

Weber sighed. This was *not* going well.

Why not stop feeding cows to cows? If you believed the official propaganda of the Cattlemen, you would think that the practice had already been stopped. Nine days after the British government's alarming admission of a BSE-CJD link, the National Cattlemen's Beef Association had joined other meat industry organizations in announcing a "voluntary ban" to assure that "ruminant-derived protein is not used in ruminant feed products." If you thought about it for a moment, of course, you might realize that a "voluntary ban" is a contradiction in terms, but aside from a few complaining consumer groups, no one bothered to think that hard. "For the most part, the media coverage has focused on the crisis in Great Britain and the media has not tried to import the crisis into the United States," exulted an internal memorandum by Jim Barr, CEO for the National Milk Producers Federation. "Thanks to prompt work on the part of USDA and industry groups, U.S.-focused coverage has talked mainly about the steps taken here since the mid-1980s to keep our country BSE-free."[3]

The Oprah Winfrey Show was the exception to the rule. It aired on Tuesday, April 16—less than a month after the British government's first admission that mad cow disease appeared to be spreading to humans. It was not the first time that U.S. viewers heard about the British troubles, but it was the first time that a major U.S. news program focused on the fact that U.S. cattle breeders were continuing the cannibalistic feeding practices which had created the epidemic in the first place.

The day of the broadcast, livestock traders on the floor of the Chicago Mercantile Exchange scrambled to sell off cattle futures, which fell a penny and a half a pound to 59 cents—the maximum allowable drop for a single day's trading.[4] Spokespersons for the NCBA angrily blasted the TV program, calling it "irresponsible and biased." In a letter to Winfrey, NCBA called the show "one more example of the irresponsible scare tactics with which much of American television has become identified…The show was one of beefbashing—not a reasonable discussion of BSE and the safety of the American beef supply. You took a complex technical issue and turned it into an hour of unjustified scare-mongering."[5] NCBA's Gary Weber complained that the show had selectively edited his comments, cutting out most of his "scientific" rebuttal of Lyman.

At first, Oprah stood her ground. "I am speaking as one consumer for millions of others," she said in a prepared statement. "Cows eating cows is alarming. Americans needed and wanted to know that—I certainly did…I asked the questions that I think the American people deserved to have answered in light of what is happening in Britain. We gave them a chance to respond."[6]

Under pressure, however, Winfrey's staff issued a second statement promising to schedule "another program to address unanswered questions." The follow-up show, which aired a week later, featured a 10-minute one-on-one exchange between a cowed Oprah Winfrey and Gary Weber, who got to have his say this time without any fear of rebuttal from Lyman or other beef industry critics. As Weber issued reassurances, Oprah uttered weak half-apologies that seemed as though they were being forced through gritted teeth, "Our concern was for consumer safety and not about stock prices," she said. "I had no idea the stock prices were going to fall and I wasn't trying to influence them one way or another. You all need to know, you cattle people, that we're just dependent on y'all out there."[7]

Oprah's newfound humility reflected some cold financial realities. In the days following the original show, the beef industry had retaliated by pulling $600,000 in network advertising.[8] Even Oprah's follow-up fluff piece failed to appease. In Texas, State Agriculture Commissioner Rick Perry asked the attorney general to use the state's new "food disparagement law" to file a lawsuit against Lyman and the Oprah show. When the attorney general declined, beef feedlot operator Paul Engler and a company named Cactus Feeders stepped in to shoulder the burden, hiring a powerhouse L.A. attorney to file a lawsuit which sought $2 million in damages plus punitive fines. "We're taking the Israeli action on this thing," Engler said. "Get in there and just blow the hell out of somebody."[9] The lawsuit, filed on May 28, 1996, complained as follows:

The defendants allowed anti-meat activists to present biased, unsubstantiated, and irresponsible claims against beef, not only damaging the beef industry but also placing a tremendous amount of unwarranted fear in the public. Defendant Howard Lyman was negligently allowed to imply that the meat-consuming public should be very afraid of the beef that is produced in this country…Plaintiffs own and operate one of the largest cattle feeding operations in the world…As a direct result of defendants' false, slanderous, and defamatory statements, plaintiffs have endured shame, embarrassment, humiliation, and mental pain and anguish. Additionally, plaintiffs are and will in the future be seriously injured in their good name and reputation in the communi-

ty and exposed to the hatred, contempt, and ridicule of the general public...
Defendants' conduct in making the statements contained herein and allowing those
statements to be aired without verifying the accuracy of such statements goes beyond
all possible bounds of decency and is utterly intolerable in a civilized community.[10]

Interestingly, the lawsuit made no mention of Lyman's main point—the point he
had hammered at repeatedly, and which had triggered the strongest negative reactions from Oprah's audience. Whatever science said about "bovine spongiform
encephalopathy," the thing that stuck hardest in the craw of the audience—and of
Oprah herself—was the simple fact that *cows had been turned into cannibals*. "That in
itself is disturbing to me," Oprah had said. "Cows should not be eating other cows!"

The meat industry's "voluntary ban" was aimed at fooling the public into believing that this practice of "ruminant-to-ruminant" feeding had already ended. It was
misleading, and deliberately so, but from the myopic viewpoint of the Cattlemen,
their own attempt to manipulate the news was simply good public relations. Howard
Lyman's attempt to warn the public, on the other hand, went "beyond all possible
bounds of decency and is utterly intolerable in a civilized community."

Was mad cow disease the threat that Howard Lyman thought it was? Would it
make "AIDS look like the common cold"? Probably not, according to most scientists
who worked in the field of the spongiform encephalopathies—including even
Richard Marsh, from whom Lyman had learned much of what he knew about the disease. In England, on the other hand, failure to recognize the unique nature of the disease *had* enabled BSE to grow into a problem of literally incalculable proportions.

For consumers in the United States, the most important immediate question was,
"Is it safe to eat beef?" The cattle industry was determined to ensure that the answer
they heard would be, "Yes, absolutely." From the industry's point of view, its campaign to silence Oprah Winfrey and Howard Lyman was a battle between "sound science" and "emotional fear-mongering." What the industry missed, or chose to miss,
was that Lyman was raising a different and much more important question: "Are adequate measures being taken to guarantee the safety of our food?"

The lawsuit against Howard Lyman marked the first test case for a new legal standard which the agriculture industry had spent the previous half-decade introducing
into more than a dozen U.S. states. "All agricultural eyes will be watching this one,"
observed one food industry lobbyist. Engler's attorney described the suit as "a historic
case; it serves as a real bellwether. It should make reporters and journalists and enter-
tainers—and whatever Oprah considers herself—more careful."[11]

Known as "agricultural product disparagement laws," the new legislation gave the
food industry unprecedented powers to sue people who criticized their products,
using standards of evidence which dramatically shifted the burden of proof in favor
of the industry. "In them, American agribusiness has its mightiest tool yet against
food-safety activists and environmentalists, whose campaigns can cost industry millions if they affect consumers' buying habits," observed *Village Voice* reporter Thomas
Goetz.[12]

In the past, the food industry had been required to prove that its critics were
deliberately and knowingly circulating false information. Under the new laws, it
didn't matter whether Lyman believed in his statements, or even whether he could
produce scientists who would support him. The industry would be able to convict

him of spreading "false information" if it could convince a jury that his statements on the Oprah show deviated from "reasonable and reliable scientific inquiry, facts, or data"[13]—a standard of proof which gave a clear advantage to the beef industry, particularly in Texas cattle country.

The problem with this standard of proof is not simply that it makes juries comprised of non-scientists responsible for judging the validity of complex scientific theories. The deeper problem is that not even scientists agree on which scientific theories are valid and which are not. Indeed, the scientific method is based on hypothesis and conjecture, on best-guess speculations which change continually as new evidence becomes available. Until the 1950s, for example, smoking tobacco was not only considered safe by many scientists but was recommended as an aid to relaxation, digestion and weight loss. If "agricultural product disparagement laws" had existed in the 1960s, it would have been illegal to criticize pesticides such as DDT, which were believed "safe" for the environment according to data then considered "reasonable and reliable."

Mad cow disease in particular belongs to a class of diseases that have confounded farmers and researchers for more than 250 years. The transmissible spongiform encephalopathies have proven so immune to scientific inquiry that one researcher calls them "god in the guise of a virus"[14]—even though most researchers today do not believe the disease is a virus at all. The history of research into the TSEs has been littered with the bodies of dead theories. In centuries of study, no one has been able even to isolate the agent which causes the illness, let alone explain the remarkable characteristics which set it apart from every other known transmissible disease. In the 20th century alone, the infectious agent has been described at various times as a "sarcosporidia parasite," a "filterable virus," a "slow virus," a "provirus generating RNA," an "unconventional virus," a "replicating protein," "membrane-bound DNA," a "spiroplasma-like organism," a "viroid-like nucleic acid," a "virino," a "replicating polysaccharide," and a "prion."[15] These labels represent differing theories, and none of them has yet been able to explain all of the known evidence about the nature of the disease agent. The leading doctrine today is the "prion theory," which was itself labeled a "heresy" a decade ago because it seemed to violate what biologists consider the "central dogma of modern biology."

In demanding that Lyman and Winfrey confine their remarks about mad cow disease to proven facts, the beef industry was therefore attempting to impose a standard which no one previously had been able to meet—not even scientists, and certainly not the beef industry itself. As Lyman awaited his day in court, the number of theories still swirling left little doubt that scientists, industry and food-safety activists would continue to debate, speculate and disagree for decades to come, and that indeed centuries more might have to pass before they would reach a consensus on what was "reasonable and reliable."

Notes

1. The Oprah Winfrey Show, Apr. 16, 1996.
2. Howard Lyman, interview by John Stauber, Jan. 15, 1997.
3. Jim Barr to General Managers and Communicators, National Milk Producers Federation (memorandum), Apr. 4, 1996.

4. "Oprah Moves World Markets," AP, Apr. 17, 1996.
5. "Cattlemen Condemn Oprah Show," UPI, Apr. 17, 1996.
6. Ibid.
7. "Oprah Says Did Not Intend CME Cattle 'Oprah Crash,' " Reuters, Apr. 23, 1996.
8. "Oprah Causes Beef Industry Flap," *Meet Processing* (Watt Publishing Co., Mount Morris, IL), June 96, p. 8.
9. Thomas Goetz, "After the Oprah Crash," *Village Voice*, Apr. 29, 1997, p. 39.
10. Petition by Paul F. Engler and Cactus Feeders, Inc. against Oprah Winfrey, Harpo Production, Howard Lyman and Cannon Communications, U.S. District Court, Texas Northern District, May 28, 1996.
11. Goetz, op. cit.
12. Ibid.
13. James Grossberg, Seth Berlin and Thomas Newton, "Food Disparagement Bills Defeated in California, Enacted in Oklahoma and Texas," *Libelletter* (New York, NY: Libel Defense Resource Center), June 1995, p. 1.
14. Gary Taubes, "The Game of the Name is Fame. But Is It Science?" *Discover*, Dec. 1986, p. 28.
15. Peter Spencer, "Origins of Spongiform Encephalopathies," presented at the International Symposium on Spongiform Encephalopathies, Georgetown University, Feb. 12–13, 1996.

Discussion Questions

1. Who is Howard Lyman and why did the beef industry consider him an enemy?

2. Why did Howard Lyman become a vegetarian? Do you think his reasoning is sound?

3. What is the danger of feeding cows to other cows?

4. What are agricultural product disparagement laws? Do you believe such laws prohibit freedom of speech?

Writing Suggestion

Whose rights do you support, the cattle industry's or its critics'? Why?

Introduction

Marc Lappé & Britt Bailey

Against the Grain:
Biotechnology and the Corporate Takeover of Your Food

We are on the cusp of a major revolution in the way we grow our crops, a revolution fueled by biotechnology and driven by multinational corporations. This revolution is unique because it entails the first major agricultural transformation of food crops based entirely on genetic engineering. It is also remarkable from a sociological perspective. Many of the key innovations have occurred behind academic and corporate doors with little public input. As a result, the public response in the United States has been strangely muted.

In marked contrast to the American reaction to agricultural biotechnology, the whole concept of genetically engineering food has alarmed many people in Europe, Great Britain, and Australia. A small but vocal group of Americans committed to organic, pesticide-free and genetically untampered foodstuffs has also become increasingly disturbed. Among other issues, many of these proponents of natural foods are upset by the silent intrusion of artificially created commodities into our food supply. Are such concerns simply emotionally driven, or are they undergirded by bona fide issues of scientific uncertainty, health risks, and ecological dangers?

We intend to describe and then get beyond the emotional and political concerns. We are fundamentally interested in the tension between the promise and peril of genetically engineered plants. For many crops, like soybeans and corn, genetic engineering is a *fait accompli*, and issues of health, safety, and nutritional quality are seemingly resolved. From our conversations with corporate representatives, any lingering concerns about safety or health are deemed irrational, overblown, or exaggerated. Corporate scientists point out—correctly—that most transgenic crops are genetically identical to their original progenitors in all but a handful of their tens of thousands of genes. What, then, is there in the construction of new organisms with genes imported from disparate species that warrants concern, you may ask?

Like many others, we are especially concerned about possible health hazards stemming from ingestion of genetically engineered food crops. In researching this issue, we have been frustrated by the lack of good science on which to base a final opinion. So much of the genetically engineered produce has been rushed to market that health effect assessments have been few and far between. What is available deals primarily with the toxicity profile of the herbicides which will come into greater play as genetically engineered crops are commercialized. As we will show, a full spectrum of toxicity can be found. Some of these herbicides, like glyphosate, appear to be relatively benign to their immediate users, while others, like bromoxynil, are quite toxic. Beyond these relatively simplistic assessments lies a disturbingly large universe of uncertainty. Few studies have been performed on ecological impacts of long-term reliance on transgenic cropping methods. And no studies exist that measure the impact of chronic ingestion of finished products containing increased amounts of transgenic crops. Most disturbingly, we may never know these consequences because transgenic food sources are presently marketed cheek-to-jowl with conventional ones. Without any labels to distinguish one from the other, epidemiologists are hamstrung. Should there be a biological effect from ingesting altered soybean by-products (as may result from changes in their estrogenic components), we presently lack any way to identify or track affected populations. As we will show, such an issue is particularly compelling for babies who may drink soy formula or children who increase their ingestion of soy products in candy or diet generally.

We can identify a group of unresolved questions:

- Are there hidden risks in moving genes across species lines in plants?

- Have we missed possible secondary effects of gene transfer across whole crop lineages in assessing the safety of genetically engineered crops?

- Is there a loss of opportunity for genuine progress in choosing certain genes for crop development and not others?

- Are novel ecological risks created from developing monocultures of genetically engineered crops?

- Are special problems of disease resistance and vulnerability posed by transgenic crop types?

- Will new patterns of pesticide use create health risks to farm workers or consumers?

While many of these questions will be answered through review of scientific studies and projections, many other issues raised by genetic engineering of food crops require political and cultural analysis.

The Scope of the Problem

If biotechnology were simply a novel scientific enterprise, it would be fitting to focus our concerns solely on its safety or environmental impacts. Such objections to genetic manipulation preceded the planting of the first genetically engineered crop by at least a decade. In the early 1970s, the first genetically engineered crop was created. The first genetically altered bacteria designed to make strawberries frost resistant were planned for release into a strawberry field in California. Environmental groups concerned about the introduction of new diseases and the possibly catastrophic spread of genetically engineered bacteria to other crops protested loudly—and effectively. The planting was postponed for two seasons.

When it was finally done the results were disappointing. Modest frost protection was achieved, but no great ecological damage ensued. The first wave of opposition to genetically engineered crops was a tempest in a teapot. Neither the bacteria nor their altered genes proved to be a health or environmental hazard—both were short lived and nonpathogenic.

But more robust genes and organisms were planned for testing. The methionine-rich gene from a Brazil nut was slated to be introduced into soybeans to increase their protein level. Fortunately, before the soybeans were commercially released, a group of scientists discovered that the "new" soybeans contained the allergenic properties of the Brazil nut.[1] Some 13 different field trials of transgenic plants have been sabo-taged in Germany in the belief that they posed imminent hazards to the ecosystem. Most recently, a transgenic beet crop planted in Ireland was uprooted, allegedly by activists concerned about the spread of herbicide resistant genes.

Our view, and the focus of [Against the Grain], is that genetically engineered crops pose a much more insidious threat, one that promises to shift our cultural mores and agricultural practices as a whole. It is in their "success" that genetically engineered plants pose the greatest risk. By sidestepping regulatory review and public oversight, arbitrarily chosen genetically engineered plants promise to transform American and—ultimately—world agriculture.

Issues of Scale

The concerns detailed in [Against the Grain] are triggered as much by the scale of present use of transgenic: crops as by its scientific uniqueness. In the last year alone, literally hundreds of new crops have been proposed for field testing. As shown in Figure 1, in the 1996–97 planting season many commodities derived from biotech-nology research have been marketed and planted on over 30 million acres in the United States.[2] These include herbicide resistant field crops such as corn, soybeans, cotton and canola; insecticide resistant crops such as cotton, corn and potatoes; delayed ripening tomatoes; genetically altered soybeans with high-oleic acid oil; alkaline-tolerant corn; and virus resistant squash.

Corporate Dominance

One company in particular has dominated this emerging agriculture/biotechnol-ogy (agbiotech) market (see Figures 1, 2 and 3). Monsanto Company, based in St. Louis, Missouri, has capitalized on its glyphosate herbicide known as Roundup® by selectively engineering crops to be resistant to high levels of this herbicide. Among successfully transformed crops are sugar beets, corn, cotton, rice and soybeans. The particular genetic technique used to convert native strains or cultivars of these crops—or more commonly pre-made hybrids—to an herbicide tolerant state is known as Roundup Ready™ technology. This radical new technology, to be described below, allows plants to withstand high doses of Roundup® that would otherwise destroy them along with their weedy neighbors.

In the four years since its inception in 1994, Roundup Ready™ technology has been applied full force to American seed crops. Barely off the drafting boards in 1997, 15% of the soybean and 14% of the cotton crop was engineered with Roundup

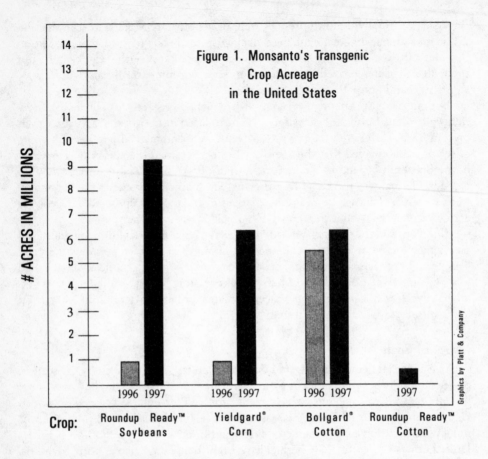

Figure 1. Monsanto's Transgenic Crop Acreage in the United States

Graphics by Platt & Company

Ready™ genes. In 1998, the first corn crops are planned to be engineered with this herbicide resistant gene. According to Hartz Seed Company, a Monsanto subsidiary, Monsanto plans to have half of the United States soybean crop, or some 30 million acres, genetically engineered with Roundup Ready™ genes by 1998. According to the same source, in the year 2000, Monsanto plans to have 100% of soybeans in the United States converted with the Roundup Ready™ gene technology.[3]

An American Perspective

In the United States few people know much about the dramatic events that undergird this transformation of American agriculture. Descriptions of this revolutionary technology in popular publications like *Time*, *Newsweek* or *USA Today* are a rarity. Such media avoidance of crop genetic engineering would be understandable if we were discussing corn or soybean futures on the commodity market or the price of a bushel of wheat. But what we are discussing here promises to affect all our lives. If Monsanto and other primary actors like Dow Chemical, Novartis, and Dupont have their way, within the next four to five years, essentially all of the conventionally grown soy products we consume will be derived from genetically engineered crops. Lest you think you can avoid having to face this growing reality, consider that virtu-

Figure 2. Monsanto's Projected *Roundup Ready*™ Crop Program

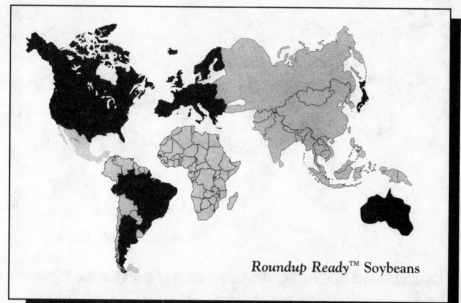

Roundup Ready™ Soybeans

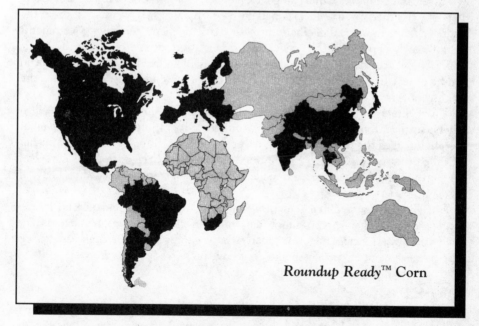

Roundup Ready™ Corn

Graphics by Platt & Company

ally all candy, chocolate bars, ice cream, cookies and salad dressings contain products derived from genetically engineered plants. So too will most of our meat, at least indirectly, as genetically engineered crops like soybeans enter livestock diets in increasing proportions.

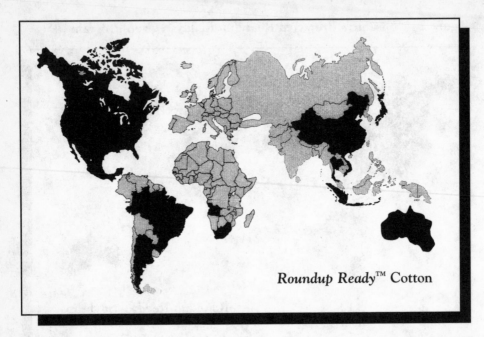

Roundup Ready™ Cotton

Exploring Differences

Given the pending ubiquity of gene-engineered crops in our present and future diet, why has there been so little concern expressed about this transformation in the United States? In marked distinction to our passivity, many European governments are militantly opposed to the production, importation, or sale of transgenic crops. Luxembourg, Austria, France and the United Kingdom head up this revolution in consciousness. Each has taken special steps to ban or limit importation and to require labeling of genetically engineered crops.

The Secretary of the United States Department of Agriculture (USDA), Dan Glickman, has dismissed such actions as misguided and uninformed. In a famous speech, he urged the European Union to recognize the legitimacy and safety of what he called the "Second Green Revolution."[4] Glickman characterized the European reaction to genetically engineered foods as overblown, culturally biased and devoid of scientific merit.

But are the major differences between the United States and Europe in the acceptance of transgenic crops simply cultural artifacts? Are European concerns dictated solely by politics? And is Glickman right to imply genetically engineered crops raise no new scientific or safety issues that have not already been resolved?

Cultural Bias?

From a European perspective, opposition to genetically engineered crops is much more than a cultural artifact. Given the recent Ukrainian experience with Chernobyl and the fresh memories of misuse of German science in WWII, many new scientific manipulations of living things are intrinsically distrusted.

Figure 3. Countries Projected to Use Monsanto's Insect-Resistant Crops

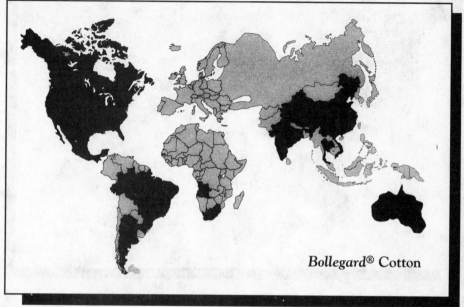

Bollegard® Cotton

Graphics by Platt & Company

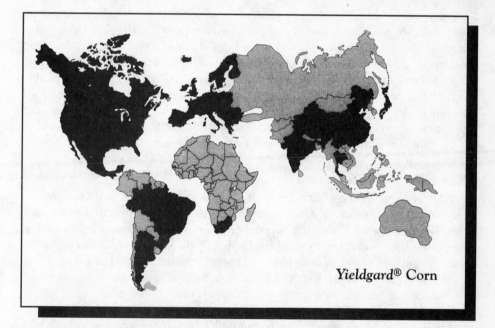

Yieldgard® Corn

Glickman may be missing the deep historical precedent that underlies distrust of genetic science when he admonishes Europeans for their "blind adherence to culture and history." Considering the mass annihilation of whole peoples based on faulty

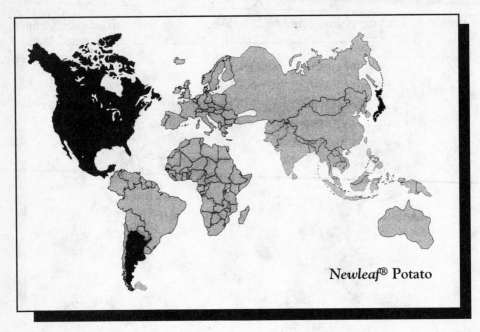

Newleaf® Potato

genetic science, it is understandable if Europeans view a "master race" of food crops skeptically.

Europeans are clearly looking at genetic technologies through a different cultural lens than are Americans. Part of this viewpoint is reflected in the phraseology chosen for genetically altered crops. While the United States government confuses the identity of genetically altered food crops by calling them "transgenic plants," Europeans call them "genetically modified organisms" (GMOs). This semantic distinction may be significant. The European community may find it easier to categorize genetically engineered crops and animals under the GMO rubric than are Americans who may be technically confused by the scientific jargon of "transgenic." At the core of the problem is the distinction between natural and artificial.

"Natural" versus Engineered

What is "natural" and what is artificial is of particular concern to those involved in the organic food movement. For many, this distinction is central to a world view focused on non-chemical means of production, limiting the amount of manipulation of the food chain. New regulations in the United States will permit limited use of the phrase "organic produce" to be applied to genetically modified food crops, on a case by case basis. But for many, the very fact that a "foreign" gene has been interposed in a natural genome is source of concern and disapproval.

Irrespective of their commitment to organic foods, large numbers of Europeans remain skeptical about genetically engineered crops. One survey, conducted by Professor Thomas Hoban at North Carolina State University in Raleigh, North Carolina, in 1995, showed that 49% of Swedes, 70% of Germans and 78% of Austrians would not buy a bioengineered food product. In contrast, an average of 70% of Japanese, American, and Canadian consumers would readily buy such products.[5] At a minimum, this disparity reveals a rift between Japanese and North American versus European attitudes towards genetically engineered crops.

At least part of the explanation for the European distrust of GMOs can be related to the growing environmental movement in Europe. The Green Party has encouraged this trend. In some countries like Germany, some commentators believe the Greens have built on a general antitechnology tendency. It is true that many in the Green Party believe certain technologies are furthering environmental depredations brought about by industry and nuclear energy, but its opposition to genetically engineered crops is more fundamental. The Greens and their supporters believe GMOs represent misuse of genetic power.

Other factors contributing to the antipathy towards genetic engineering have been identified by our correspondent, a social scientist in Sweden, Martin Frid. When we asked his view of the European position, he listed ten major reasons for European distrust of biotechnology (shown in Figure 4). Several of these observations, notably numbers 2–5, are especially salient for European concerns while others (numbers 8–10) characterize American attitudes as well.

From our perspective, at least three factors have fueled the growing malaise with genetic engineering in Europe. First, in Europe the distrust of things genetically engineered *is* clearly emotionally and culturally driven. This reality does not mitigate the

---

Figure 4. Possible Reasons for European Mistrust of Biotechnology

1. A long history of natural, organic agricultural practices.
2. A growing recognition of recent failures of chemically based agriculture.
3. A distrust of scientists and their attempts to subdue nature through overreliance on chemicals like DDT.
4. A fear of monopoly control of European agriculture by non-European corporations.
5. A distrust of American regulatory agencies like the Food and Drug Administration which have given a clean bill of health to many products and chemicals that later proved harmful.
6. The loss of the small family farm.
7. Resistance from women who see American, chemically based, transgenic agriculture as a uniquely male operation.
8. Anger against the imposition of non-labeled crops and products by the United States on the European market.
9. Anger and distrust of the major companies who are developing biotechnology based agricultural commodities.
10. Secrecy and proprietary protections built into the American corporate way of doing business.

Source: Martin J. Frid

depth or legitimacy of popular concern. Ever since the Nazi atrocities, sectors of the European populace have questioned screening or health programs that carry the taint of genetic manipulation. Particularly in Germany, genetic control through in vitro fertilization, genetic engineering and screening, and cloning have all engendered deep misgivings and public anxiety about repeating the Nazi excesses.

In countries like Great Britain and The Netherlands, the public has rejected a previous genetically engineered product, recombinant bovine growth hormone (rBGH) stimulated milk, because of concerns about the safety of the resulting product. In this instance, many Americans shared this concern, while governmental agencies largely downplayed any difference between engineered and non-engineered milk products. The United States FDA asserted that no adverse health effects and no difference in growth hormone levels exist between milk taken from rBGH treated and untreated cows. Opponents pointed out, however, that the FDA failed to consider the secondary effects of forced feeding, higher antibiotic usage in some mastitis-affected cows, and the potentially higher levels of stress hormones in rBGH treated cattle. For others, like the founders of Ben & Jerry's Ice Cream in Vermont, rBGH treated milk is unacceptable simply because it threatens the small farm and is artificially made and engineered. Similar, "irrational" objections to transgenic food crops clearly play a role in the European population's reaction to transgenic crops. The basis for this opposition is instructive.

The European Perspective

European Union countries like Luxembourg, Austria, Germany and Italy have actively resisted the introduction of unlabeled, genetically engineered crops since 1992. The European Council of Ministers first drafted the so-called Novel Food Regulations on December 20, 1996, which specified the conditions for approval and labeling of genetically engineered foods. Three weeks later, these regulations were adopted by the European Parliament. On April 2, 1997, the European Commission voted 407 to 2 to ban the importation of unlabeled, genetically engineered American corn crops. As of July 31, 1997, European Union countries could import genetically engineered crops, but only if they were so labeled. The details of the directive call for a clear notification on the label that the product may contain or may consist of genetically modified organisms. For products consisting of mixtures of both genetically modified and non-modified organisms, the label must disclose the possibility that genetically modified organisms may be present.[6] The fine print of the present policy points up the political difficulties intrinsic in making such a determination: According to Article 8, which describes the scope of the regulation, a given foodstuff or crop is considered genetically modified and novel "if scientific assessment, based on appropriate analysis of existing data" demonstrates that it differs from "conventional food" in a significant way.[7]

According to one of our European contacts, French farmers have resisted novel genetically created crops in part because they simply dislike being told what to plant and how to plant it. This point is not lost to the detail men of major seed providers here and abroad who have been instructed to ensure that they put farmers "in charge" of new genetically engineered crops. But farmers will discover that in most instances they cannot keep or save any seed that is produced by their own crops. As we will discuss below, genetically engineered seed, especially the Roundup Ready™ technology, remains the property of the maker and not the user.

In Germany, in particular, the cultural bias against genetics has greatly reduced governmental and corporate investment in biotechnology, a position decried by Nobel laureate James Watson. In a talk to German politicians given in June 1997, Watson argued that Germany will have to get over its cultural malaise about genetics if it is to join the biotechnology age.[8] Watson asserted that European activist groups, especially those like the Green Party, have undercut genetic research. It is true that the Greens and their affiliates are concerned about domination by the United States-based multinational corporations, an issue brought out in sharp relief by the activities of companies like Monsanto which have extended their global reach to involve Europe, Brazil and Argentina. But, like us, the Greens do not have a single-minded view about a particular science, only concerns about its potential misuses.

Some Scientific Concerns

What merit do such concerns hold? As we will show [in *Against the Grain*], it is likely that genetic modifications made through transgene technology will not always be perfect or ideal. Some early genetic manipulations will of necessity disrupt the balance among the organism's genes needed for normal functioning. This has already proven true in animals where, for instance, inserting genes for human growth hormone in hogs led to misshapen, arthritis-ridden pigs. Similar, albeit less apparent, aberrations are possible in transgenic plants. In fact, many if not most genetically modified plants are the results of thousands of failed experiments. In some instances, transgenic plants were so disrupted by the gene insertion process that successful growth failed. Even where successful, few genetically modified organisms have been precisely modified. Few, if any, genetic agronomists can say where their gene ended up within a given plant genome. As a result, genetically modified plants may be much more of a black box than the pseudoscientific terminology of "transgenic" and implied genetic control connotes.

We will explore other reasons for questioning genetic technology below. Suffice it to say for now that we challenge the orthodox description of such plants as scientifically controlled wonders with stably introduced, balanced genomes.

Another potential problem is that the genes being manipulated are presumed to affect only single traits. But many plant genes produce a variety of effects (called "pleiotropy"), where changes in form and function result from a single gene insertion. Traditional breeding practices take such effects into consideration. In contrast to transgenic crops which are often marketed after only a single test plot is harvested, traditional crop breeding has been much more tedious—and careful. Only after careful breeding, often spanning three to four growing seasons, were novel varieties widely introduced. Norman Borlaug's dwarf wheat is a case in point.

A Pre-Biotech Case Study

Borlaug, a plant breeder at the Center for the Improvement of Maize and Wheat (CIMMYT) outside of Mexico City, bred a remarkable strain of wheat in the 1950s and 1960s through his efforts to increase cereal yields. He found that simple increases in soil nitrogen, while stimulating wheat growth, normally produced an unwieldy plant that was too tall for most combines to harvest and subject to wind damage or "lodging" where the growth-stimulated plant would fall over. Through judicious breeding methods and introgression, Borlaug successfully introduced a "dwarfing gene" from a variety called Norin 10.

Originally isolated by indigenous farmers in Japan in 1873, this gene was introduced into Mexico by native farmers at the turn of the century. Wheat yields increased threefold. Borlaug simply transferred this existing trait (actually a group of closely linked genes) onto a modern wheat variety, giving it the ability to grow in harsher conditions with shorter growth times than before. According to a sign posted at CIMMYT, "100 million lives have been saved by Norin 10."

While this latter statement may be slightly exaggerated, it does reflect the dramatic increase in yields brought about through judicious breeding in the early years of the Green Revolution. The key question about genetically engineered crops is whether or not similar advances could prove attainable through the systematic introduction of single genes. While some, like USDA's Glickman, tout transgenic crops as promising a second Green Revolution, those who control the technology appear less interested in meeting world food needs than in obtaining short term goals. More to the point, would present day genetic engineering science be up to the task?

Literally millions of transgenic plants have already been sown and thousands of gene-altered seeds produced. The genes being chosen for engineering are in the main quite different from Borlaug's Norin 10. Instead of blocks of genes that will increase yield or improve efficiency, geneticists usually inject only one that confers an aesthetic change or makes the plant tolerant to a proprietary chemical. Any increase in yield or nutritional value is usually incidental to a more readily achieved economic advantage. In fact, for Roundup Ready™ crops, some studies indicate *reduced* yields for some strains of genetically engineered crops when compared to the nongenetically engineered crop lines. This point is central to addressing the claim that genetically engineered crops will solve the world's food problems.

World Views Contrasted

Our position is simple: We are skeptical about pronouncements from government officials and optimistic commodity experts that tout genetically modified crops as a panacea for the world's food shortage and a solution to overreliance on pesticides. We see transgenic crops more as an extension of corporate dominance, one centered on short-term gains for shareholders. Of course, the corporate view [documented in *Against the Grain*] is a more sanguine one. While the ultimate truth behind these viewpoints may never be elucidated, one thing is certain: These two world views, one skeptical about our wisdom in modifying life forms, the other highly optimistic about the extension of our technological power, are headed for a collision. Many people, particularly those affiliated with the environmental movement, are profoundly skeptical that we will "get it right" this time. The time honored tradition of subduing nature and remolding it to fit human needs has left thousands of acres in the Sahel region of Africa and our own Southwest region desertified and useless. The initial success and then horrible debacle from overuse of DDT is another example. Even seeming miracles like antibiotics have been despoiled from misuse or overreliance. Some religious figures declare the belief that nature is intended for "Man's [sic] use" engenders a patriarchy of control that misconstrues the purpose of life on earth. Others decry the attitude that casts all living things as intrinsically designed for our exclusive use.

The truth, of course, is that the natural world was never intended or designed for our exclusive use, nor shaped to fit our nutritional needs. Such a realization is belied by our long history of domesticating animals and food crops, a grand experiment that many will cite favorably when considering genetic engineering. But, even as we domesticated plants and animals to reshape them into useful forms, we discovered that many food crops and animals harbored toxins and pathogens that undermined their intrinsic domestic value. The intensification of production that came with the mass growth of livestock in particular has proven ill-advised. Antibiotic resistant bacteria from feed lots, hormone-laced (DES) beef in the 1960s, and bovine spongiform encephalopathy (BSE) today, are all the result of mass production pushed ahead of good science and epidemiology. Mad cow disease is a sobering reminder of the pitfalls of our overreliance on human control to domesticate animals en masse.

Our concern is that the new genetic revolution in agriculture threatens to be similarly disruptive. If pressed ahead at the present accelerating pace, transgenic agriculture may further disrupt our reliance on traditional farming techniques with uncertain ecological impacts. At the core of the problem is the folly of massively substituting human engineered crops for those that were previously selected by natural forces. We do not reject all manipulations as being intrinsically wrong because they alter nature. But we question the blind assurances that the new wave of genetically engineered crops promise unlimited returns at virtually no environmental cost.

Scale and Scope

The very scope and breadth of the revolution to genetically control crops portends radical changes. We are concerned with the vast range of implications of such widely used genetic engineering of our food crops. These concerns span from possible impacts on our health, to wholesale cultural and ecosystem disruption. Are the risks that are being taken commensurate with the benefits we may expect? Will these risks and benefits be distributed equitably? Are we alert to the possibility that as we expand our crop-conversion to novel bioengineered types we may reach a threshold of vulnerability? For instance, many countries like India are right at the balance point between survival and famine. A loss of 15% of the rice crop could endanger as much as 30% of the population. The answers to these problems require answers to a set of prior questions:

1. Are genetically engineered crops simply extensions of a long history of domestication of wild strains of plants, or do they represent a qualitative departure in the way we grow our food?

2. Do genetically engineered crops signal a true revolution in our stewardship of the planet?

3. Will bioengineering offer needed crop productivity at a period of continued population growth?

In the end we must make any decision to proceed in a state of enlightenment rather than in a state of desperation. It is with this view in mind that [*Against the Grain*] was written.

Ultimately, we are challenging the premise that biotechnology will make things better in the long run, not just in terms of the immediate increases in yields or reduced pesticide reliance promised by the innovators, but in terms of the overall sustainability of agriculture as a whole. To fully appreciate the magnitude of the potential problems generated by these new technologies, we clearly need to know the scope of the enterprise. We need to understand how innate cultural resistance to new crops is being overcome by public relations efforts. We need to understand the motives and practices of our major corporations. And we need to be able to anticipate the secondary and often unforeseen consequences of their widespread "success."

In doing this research, we have relied on both corporate documents and major scientific publications. Governmental agencies and their underlying regulations have also been consulted. Hopefully, we have synthesized this information in a form readers will find useful in formulating their own opinions.

Notes

1   Nordlee, J. A., Taylor, Townsend, J. A., Thomas, L. A., Bush, R. IL "Identification of a Brazil-Nut Allergen in Transgenic Soybeans," *The New England Journal of Medicine*, 334: 688–692, 1996.

2   For 1997, this estimate includes 9 million acres in Roundup Ready™ soybeans; 6 million in Yieldgard® Corn; 6 million acres of Bollgard® Cotton; and 2 million in Roundup Ready™ Cotton; an estimated 2–4 million in other genetically engineered crops are known to be planted.

3   Keith Thompson, Vice President General Manager of Hartz' Seeds, personal interview, June 20, 1997.

4   Remarks of Dan Glickman, Secretary of the United States Department of Agriculture, 20 June, 1997.

5   Hoban, T., "Public Perception and Communication of Risk," Raleigh, NC: NC Cooperative Extension Service, 1991.

6   Amended to Annex III of Directive 90/220/EEC of the European Commission of the European Union.

7   See Emma Johnson, "European politicos pass food regulations lacking meat," *Nature Biotechnology* 15: 21, 1997.

8   James Watson, quoted in R. Koenig, "Watson urges 'Put Hitler behind us,'" *Science* 276: 892, 1997.

Discussion Questions

1. What is the authors' thesis in this introduction?

2. Are you aware of genetically engineered crops? Why didn't they initially get much attention in the United States?

3. What is the purpose of genetically engineering crops?

4. How prevalent is the use of soybeans in our food? Why is it nearly impossible to avoid genetically engineered food?

5. Why are Europeans more wary than Americans of genetically engineered crops?

6. Do concerns over biotechnology have merit? What have experiments in the past revealed?

7. What impact does mass farming have on the environment? Do people have a right to control nature?

Writing Suggestion

Are you concerned with "Frankenfoods"? Why or why not?

Are You the One in Eight?

Liane Clorfene-Casten

Breast Cancer: Poisons, Profits and Prevention

Because of the prevalence of cancer in our industrialized society, most people in the United States know of at least one person who has been afflicted with cancer. Many have lost close relatives and friends to the deadly disease, and others have watched neighbors of all ages wither and die from it.

Cancer is a silent disease, stealthily gripping in its lethal claws millions of humans around the world. In the United States, the American Cancer Society (ACS) projected that over 1.2 million new cancer cases in general were diagnosed just in 1994—not including skin cancers, which would add 700,000 more to the statistics.

Over half a million people die from cancer annually in the United States according to ACS's pamphlet *Cancer Facts and Figures—1994*; that translates to 1,400 people a day. Sources differ on the percentage of overall deaths caused by cancer: ACS says one out of every five deaths in the United States is from cancer; the Women's Community Cancer Project states the number is one in four. Devra Lee Davis, former senior advisor to the Assistant Secretary of Health and Human Services and noted cancer researcher (now with the World Resources Institute), wrote in the February 9,1994 issue of JAMA, "Recent birth cohorts of Americans aged 20 years and older are developing higher rates of all forms of cancer compared with those born just before the turn of the century." Since 1950, the overall cancer incidence has increased by 44 percent.

Breast cancer is now at epidemic proportions. One in eight American women has a lifetime risk of the disease. Each year, more than 44,000 women, or nearly one quarter of the 182,000 diagnosed, die from the disease. According to the advocacy group Breast Cancer Fund, an additional 1 million American women probably have the disease and do not know it. This means that, for hundreds of thousands of women, the disease will remain undiagnosed until much later in its development.

Since 1960, more than 950,000 American women have died from breast cancer. To put this in perspective, only 617,000 Americans died in all the wars our country has fought in this century! And shockingly, almost half of these deaths have occurred in the last ten years, according to the 1994 Breast Cancer Health Project Fact Sheet, sponsored by the Massachusetts Department of Public Health. Between 1981 and

1991, about 446,000 women died of breast cancer, according to the Cancer Prevention Coalition; in that decade, annual breast cancer deaths increased by approximately 32 percent.

But these overall numbers mask the dangerous trends that have been developing. The advocacy group Breast Cancer Action states that breast cancer is now the leading cause of death for women between the ages of 32 and 52. (It is a close second to lung cancer for all women.) Studies indicate that tumors in young women tend to be larger and recur more often, and scientists speculate that the cancers of young and old women may be different diseases because the tumors in young women are so much more aggressive. A woman diagnosed with breast cancer in her twenties or thirties is more likely to die from the disease than is a woman in her sixties or seventies.

And when you break the headlining statistics down even farther, the story they tell becomes even more frightening.

- In 1994, ACS stated that while lung cancer has been the leading cause of cancer increase in general, breast cancer leads the statistics in women.

- Breast cancer has become the most common form of cancer in North American women. In 1989, 142,000 women were diagnosed with breast cancer; in that year, 42,836 women died from the disease. In November 1993, *U.S. News and World Report* reported that 2.8 million American women were victims of breast cancer.

- According to ACS, of the approximately 180,000 women diagnosed in 1992, 57.8 percent were between 40 and 70 years old. Women older than 70 make up the next largest group—36 percent.

- From 1940 to 1980, breast cancer rates increased by an average of only 1.2 percent each year. But more recently, rates have skyrocketed, according to ACS. Since 1980, the rate of diagnosis in women has increased about 2 percent a year, reaching a level of about 108 per 100,000 (*Cancer Facts and Figures*, ACS, 1994). From 1980 to 1987 alone, the number of breast cancer cases reported in the U.S. rose by 32 percent.

- Breast cancer incidence is growing rapidly in virtually all of the world's industrialized countries. In 1980, an estimated 500,000 women worldwide died of breast cancer. By the year 2000, that figure is expected to double.

- In 1993, the National Cancer Institute (NCI) had the unpleasant duty to report that breast cancer rates among younger women are rising. Although women under the age of 40 still make up only 6.5 percent of those diagnosed, the long-range effects of this particular increase are devastating. Breast cancer patients under 35 have the poorest survival rate of any age group. And those who do survive live with the constant fear of recurrence and early death.

- NCI researchers state that increases in breast cancer incidence appear to be real—not mere artifacts of improved diagnosis, classification, or recordkeeping. In fact, a growing number of scientists are acknowledging that better screening simply cannot account for the steady increase in incidence.

- Fifty years ago, a woman's chance of getting breast cancer in her lifetime was one in 20. Thirty-five years ago, it was one in 15. A few years ago, when breast cancer began to garner some publicity, the chance was one in nine. Now it is one in eight.

One in eight. In the United States today, there are more than 130 million women of all ages. More than 16 million of them will develop breast cancer.

One in eight. On a typical suburban block with perhaps 25 families, three mothers will develop breast cancer. If each family has two daughters, six of them will develop the disease. In cities, these numbers will be duplicated in just one high-rise.

One in eight. In most elementary schools, the great majority of teachers are women. Assuming two teachers per grade, at least two teachers in any school will develop breast cancer. (In 1994, the American Federation of Teachers reported that teachers have nearly twice the rate of breast cancer deaths as the general population.)

One in eight.

What's behind this explosion in breast cancer incidence? If you listen to the pronouncements that issue from ACS, NCI, the drug companies, and other mainstream agencies, it is our fault. Our family history is to blame, or reproductive/hormonal factors, or fatty diet and alcohol. But the truth is that 70 percent of women with breast cancer are getting their disease from causes other than genetics, chemical imbalances, and lifestyle. For more than 120,000 American women a year, their cancers are caused by environmental poisons—manmade chemicals and radiation that have been produced and distributed worldwide. And the leaders of the "war on cancer" have known this for decades and have refused to deal with this information.

Since the dawn of the chemical age and the production of carcinogenic and hormone-manipulating substances, breast cancer has risen steadily. In 1964, the World Health Organization (WHO) concluded that 80 percent of cancers were due to human-produced carcinogens. In 1979, the National Institutes of Health (NIH) identified environmental factors as the major cause of most cancers. This information is not filtering through to the public.

Annual production rates for synthetic, carcinogenic, and other industrial chemicals exploded from 1 billion pounds in 1940 to more than 500 billion pounds annually during the 1980s. Since cancer has a latency period, it is safe and altogether logical to say the growing incidence corresponds to increased exposure to a variety of carcinogens found nearly everywhere. Despite official denials from NCI and ACS and studies generated by polluting industries, despite the billions of dollars in breast cancer research that ignores the causal connection between our toxic environment and breast cancer, the connection between certain toxins in our environment and the decline of women's health has become more and more obvious.

Industry, farms, and our very own well-kept lawns are the sources of discharges of hundreds of persistent, toxic chemicals into our food, water, and air. Both common chlorine-based organochlorines and low-level radioactive pollution have the potential for compromising the immune system.

The 1994 Environmental Protection Agency (EPA) reassessment of dioxin, another organochlorine, links exposure to this chemical to immune disfunction.

Dioxins (there are actually more than 200 chemical cousins in this family—all of them toxic) are considered the chemical equivalent of nuclear radiation, and they are regularly produced as unwanted waste products of hundreds of industrial processes and products. They are endemic to our environment; they enter our bodies right along with the very elements we need to survive, and go right to work destroying our natural defenses. EPA analysts admit that every person in the United States has a body burden of dioxin that is reaching the potential for a health crisis.

Whatever new statistics each year brings, whatever "breakthrough" drug or treatment plan is ballyhooed in the media, the trend is plain: the epidemic of breast cancer will continue because our exposure to toxins continues.

As more and more women are understanding, a tiny lump in the breast is not the beginning of breast cancer. It is only the first tactile proof of the disease that has been growing for years. Because of the toxins in our environment, we all carry the seeds of our own sorrow.

The conclusion that toxic contaminants are significant (in fact, overriding) causes of breast cancer is one that the cancer establishment is reluctant to address. Industry condemns the studies pointing to environmental causes, and NCI has only recently started to focus on them. Here, according to the Women's Environment and Development Organization (WEDO), the advocacy group founded by Bella Abzug, are some of the conclusions of careful, professional, scientific studies that the cancer establishment is not telling you.

- In a Connecticut study, levels of PCBs and DDT were 50–60 percent higher in the breast tissue of women with breast cancer than in women without breast cancer.

- The EPA found that U.S. counties with waste sites were 6.5 times more likely to have elevated breast cancer rates than counties that did not have such sites.

- A Colorado study reported an association between electromagnetic field (EMF) exposure and female breast cancer. Male breast cancer (an extremely rare disease) may be linked to occupational exposure to EMF.

- Exposure to ionizing radiation can increase the risk of breast cancer, as shown by the increased breast cancer risk among Japanese atomic bomb survivors.

- In Israel, a ban on three carcinogenic pesticides may have been responsible for a 30 percent drop in breast cancer rates from 1976 to 1986.

Other groups have provided evidence from different perspectives. Greenpeace, for instance, in a 1992 release entitled "Breast Cancer and the Environment: The Chlorine Connection," noted several occupations that contribute to the breast cancer epidemic: "Women working in the petroleum, chemical, pharmaceutical, and electrical equipment manufacturing industries had significantly higher rates of breast cancer than the general public...A study of 347 female chemists found breast cancer rates 63 percent higher than expected."

And a 1994 report sponsored by the NAACP and the United Church of Christ offers a geographical connection between breast cancer and environmental carcinogens. "Racial minorities are increasingly more likely than whites to live near hazardous waste sites in America," says Benjamin A. Goldman, co-author of the report. The report contained the following analysis:

> In 1980, 25 percent of the people living in a neighborhood that contained one or more hazardous sites were non-white. By 1993, that figure had risen to 31 percent. Nationally, the average neighborhood is 14.4 percent minority...The situation is getting worse as more people become aware of the controversies surrounding waste facilities. Fewer people want them in their communities, which, in some cases, forces plants to cluster in areas already hosting a facility...Looking at Zip Code plots, the study found that about one-fourth of the 530 commercial hazardous waste treatment, storage, and disposal facilities in the U.S. were in neighborhoods where people of color were in the majority. Some 310 neighborhoods, or close to 60 percent, were above national average in terms of minority populations.

Why is this significant? NCI says the overall increase of 2.7 percent for female breast cancer among all races combined during the period 1973–1989 appears to be primarily due to a nearly 18 percent increase in the disease among black women. And for women younger than 40, blacks are 12 percent more likely than whites to get breast cancer, and 52 percent more likely to die from it. Common sense dictates that geography must be factored into any analysis of breast cancer.

There are many more studies that bring us to the same conclusion: it's the environment. The connection between our toxic, industrialized environment and cancer is compelling. Cancer causing materials have been dumped into the environment and onto people for the past five decades—and today's statistics reflect the long-term development of cancer that exposure to these materials produces.

Accepting this basic principle means our attention must turn to prevention. As Devra Lee Davis stated in *JAMA* "Preventing only 20 percent of all cancers in the United States each year would spare more than 200,000 people and their families from this often disfiguring and disabling disease."

Discussion Questions

1. To what extent have incidents of breast cancer risen since 1960?
2. Why is breast cancer on the rise, according to the author?
3. How can geography be related to cancer?

Writing Suggestion

How well does our society do in informing women of the risk of breast cancer, in your opinion?

Timber Wars

Judi Bari

Timber Wars

Industrial Worker,
October, 1989

"You fucking commie hippies, I'll kill you all!" A shotgun blast went off, and the Earth First!ers scattered. What started as a peaceful logging road blockade had turned violent when a logger sped his truck through our picket line and swerved it towards the demonstrators. The loggers also grabbed and smashed an Earth First!er's camera and, for no apparent reason, punched a 50-year-old protester in the face, knocking her cold and breaking her nose.

The environmental battle in the Pacific Northwest has reached such a level of intensity that even the press now refers to it as the Timber Wars. At stake is the survival of one of the nation's last great forest ecosystems. Our adversaries are giant corporations—Louisiana-Pacific, Georgia-Pacific, and Maxxam in Northern California, where I live.

These companies are dropping trees at a furious pace, clogging our roads no less than 18 hours a day, with a virtual swarm of logging trucks. Even old timers are shocked at the pace and scope of today's strip-logging, ranging from 1000-year-old redwoods, one tree trunk filling an entire logging truck, to six-inch diameter baby trees that are chipped up for the pulp mills and particle-board plants.

One-hundred-forty years ago the county I live in was primeval redwood forest. At the current rate of logging, there will *no* marketable trees left here in 22 years. Louisiana-Pacific President Harry Merlo put it this way in a recent newspaper interview: "It always annoys me to leave anything on the ground when we log our own land. We don't log to a 10-inch top, we don't log to an 8-inch top or a 6-inch top. We log to infinity. It's out there, it's ours, and we want it all. Now."

So the battle lines are drawn. On one side are the environmentalists, ranging from the big-money groups like The Wilderness Society and Sierra Club to the radical Earth First!ers and local mountain people fighting the front-line battles in the woods. Tactics being used include tree-sitting, logging road blockading, and bulldozer dismantling, as well as the more traditional lawsuits and lobbying.

On the other side are the big corporations and the local kulaks who do their bidding. Tactics used by them have included falling trees into demonstrators, suing protesters for punitive damages (and winning), buying politicians, and even attempting to ban the teaching at a local elementary school of a Dr. Seuss book, "The Lorax," which the timber companies say portrays logging in a bad light.

Position of the Workers

But what about the timber workers? Where do they fit into this scenario? Their true interest lies with the environmentalists, because, of course, when the trees are gone, the jobs will be gone too. Logging is listed by the US Labor Department as the most dangerous job in the US, yet the current speed-up has some loggers and millworkers working 10 or more hours a day, six days a week.

Clearcutting is the most environmentally devastating logging method, and also the least labor-intensive. In the long run, the only way to save timber jobs in our area is to change over to sustained yield logging, where logs can only be taken in a manner and at a rate that doesn't destroy the forest. This is exactly what the environmentalists are asking for.

Yet in spite of all this, those timber workers who are organized at all have been organized by the companies *against* the environmentalists. There are a few noteworthy exceptions, but by and large timber workers around here are either doing the companies' dirty work or keeping their mouths shut.

A good example of this is the spotted owl campaign. Scientists and environmentalists have been trying to get the owl listed as an endangered species, as 90–95% of its habitat, the old growth forest, has already been annihilated. The timber companies have responded with a vicious campaign promoting the extinction of the owl so that it would no longer stand in the way of them destroying the last of the old growth. Loggers are the pawns of this game, wearing T-shirts that read: "Save A Logger, Eat An Owl" and "Spotted Owl Tastes Like Chicken." Recently a hearing on the owl's status was held in Redding, CA. The timber companies closed the mills and logging operations for the day and bused 5,000 workers to the hearing, carrying anti-owl banners and cheering as speakers denounced environmentalists.

Then there's the Nazi-like Yellow Ribbon campaign, where workers, their families, and local businesses are asked to fly yellow ribbons to show solidarity with management against the environmentalist "threat." It is dangerous not to fly these ribbons in some timber-dependent small towns. And, of course, there's always the few crazies who harass us face to face, like the logger who came to one of our demos last June, revved a live chainsaw in a peaceful crowd, then sucker-punched and floored an Earth First! organizer.

Why have the companies been so successful at misdirecting the workers' anger? One obvious reason is fear—timber workers can see the end of the forest (and their jobs) in northern California as well as we can. Many of these families have lived and worked in small one-job towns for generations. The environmentalists are often relative newcomers, culturally different and easy to vilify.

But there's another reason not often discussed. That is the utter lack of class consciousness by virtually all of the environmental groups. I have even had an international Earth First! spokesman tell me that there is no difference between the loggers and the logging companies!

I have heard various environmentalists say that working in the woods and mills is not an "honorable" profession, as if the workers have any more control over the corporations' policies (or are gaining any more from them) than we do. As long as people on our side hold these views, it will be easy pickins for the bosses to turn their employees against us.

Potential For Organizing

Into this battleground, our local Earth First! group has tried to bring some class consciousness of the variety prescribed by the Industrial Workers of the World. The first step is to stop blaming the loggers and millworkers for the destruction of the planet. The timber companies treat them the same way they treat the forest—as objects to exploit for maximum profit. We can't form an alliance by saying, "Hey, worker, come help save the trees." We have to recognize that their working conditions are not separate from or subordinate to the rape of the forest. They are part and parcel of the same thing.

With this in mind, it has been surprisingly easy to make contact with timber workers who don't buy the companies' line. The fact that Earth First! is number one on the companies' hit list doesn't seem to faze anyone, and we have managed to meet good, intelligent, and politically astute people working for all three of the big corporations in our area. They have leaked us inside information which has helped us pull off tree-sits, blockades, etc. without getting caught.

But far more important, we have found that conditions among the workers in the woods and mills could mean the opening of a whole new front in the Timber Wars.

Georgia-Pacific (G-P) is a good example. Three years ago they cut wages by 25%, saying they needed the money to "modernize" the mill, and would restore the pay scale in the next contract. G-P is the only unionized outfit around here, but its union (International Woodworkers of America, AFL-CIO) went right along with the pay cut, just like they go along with everything else the company does. So G-P "modernized," eliminating jobs, and raked in record profits with the new low wages. Comes the new contract this year end and, lo and behold, instead of 25% the company offers a 3% wage increase. The millworkers were furious and voted by an 88% margin to strike. But the union, assisted by a federal "mediator," squashed the strike vote by telling the workers they would all just get fired if they went out. They then eliminated the radicals from the vote counting committee, took a re-vote, and passed the contract.

Earlier this year, a G-P millworker was poisoned when a PCB-filled capacitor broke and spilled on his head. The company refused to give the man adequate medical care or close off the area, saying it was just mineral oil. The union, as usual, stuck up for the company. At least 11 more people were contaminated before the workers themselves managed to get OSHA to shut down the plant for three days and fine the company $114,000.

Pacific Lumber is another of the "big three" timber companies in the area. Until recently, it was a locally based, family-run operation paying good wages and amazing benefits. Pacific Lumber also treated the forest better than most and, because of its conservative logging and avoidance of clearcutting, has ended up owning most of the privately owned old-growth redwood that's left in the world.

But in 1986, Pacific Lumber was taken over in a leveraged buyout by Maxxam Corp., a high-finance holding company owned by Texas sleazebag Charles Hurwitz. Hurwitz financed the takeover with junk bonds, and is now liquidating the assets of the company to pay off the debt. But in this case, the assets of the company are the last of the ancient redwoods. Hurwitz has tripled the cut, instituting clearcutting, gutted the pension plan, and started working people overtime.

Employees reacted by attempting to organize an ESOP, or Employee Stock Ownership Plan, so that they could buy the company back and protect their jobs and community. As many as 300 people came to an ESOP meeting at its height. But Hurwitz, of course, refused to sell, and the ESOP plan died. Maxxam expected everyone to just shut up and go back to work at that point. Instead, some of the workers started publishing an underground paper called Timberlyin' (as opposed to the company's paper, Timberline), which lampoons management and, while rejecting the misleadership of both the ESOP and the AFL unions, calls on the workers to organize for self-protection.

The other big timber company around here is Louisiana "We Log To Infinity" Pacific (L-P). This is absolutely the most crass company in the county. They busted the union in 1986, and the workforce is still scattered and disorganized, but they left a vast pool of resentment. Recently, L-P closed down a sawmill which had employed 136 people. They then opened a chipmill nearby which employs 15. Earth First! songwriter Darryl Cherney wrote a song, about the mill closing, called "Potter Valley Mill," which includes two references to sabotage. The song became the most requested song on the local country music station as the millworkers called in for it and sold tapes of it in Potter Valley. Shortly after the mill closed, three men (who were definitely NOT Earth First!ers) tried—unsuccessfully—to torch the new chip mill with a molotov cocktail.

Role of the IWW [Idustrial Workers of the World]

So, while the environmental struggle is raging, and while the public is watching loggers bashing owls, the flames of discontent are slowly igniting among the workers. What's needed is some direction, and it's certainly not coming from the AFL unions. Earth First! is still leading the battle in the woods, but Earth First! can only do so much because it is not a workers' organization.

Historically, it was the IWW who broke the stranglehold of the timber barons on the loggers and millworkers in the nineteen teens. The ruling class fought back with brutality, and eventually crushed the IWW, settling instead for the more cooperative business unions. Now the companies are back in total control, only this time they're taking down not only the workers but the Earth as well. This, to me, is what the IWW-Earth First! link is really about. And if the IWW would like to be more than a historical society, it seems that the time is right to organize again in timber.

Discussion Questions

1. At the time this article was written, at what rate were trees being removed from the Pacific Northwest?
2. What were some of the tactics used by the logging companies to fight protesters?
3. What is sustained yield logging and how would it help loggers?
4. Why is it important to bring class consciousness into discussions of environmentalism?

Writing Suggestion

Which side do you take in the debate over logging, the environmentalists', the loggers' or the logging companies'? Why?

Writing Suggestions for Chapter Four

1. Using some of the readings in this chapter as a basis for your argument, argue for or against adopting a vegetarian diet or limiting one's food consumption to only organically grown foods.

2. Many people respond to the warnings about toxins in food they buy or in the products they use by throwing up their hands and saying "I give up! Everything causes cancer or is going to kill me, so why think about it?" How do you respond to such an attitude? How do you decide what risks you want to take with your health?

3. What are the arguments corporations use to defend the use of pesticides or certain chemicals which may or may not be harmful in their products? Do you agree with their arguments?

4. How are people who protest against certain practices, such as logging, portrayed by the media? Examine recent local or national news. Are protesters ever portrayed in a positive light? Why or why not?

Chapter V

Washington Politics and Religion

Why have many Americans given up on the political process? Why is there such voter apathy? In these readings the authors investigate the uses and abuses of power and money as special interests, including those of the religious right, compete to circumvent the democratic process and buy influence in Washington. In "News That Went Unreported: 'Dollars Per Vote,'" from *The Wizards of Media Oz*, Norman Solomon and Jeff Cohen make clear the connection of dollars to votes in the 1996 presidentail elections. In "Election Day Apathy" and "Campaign Finance: What Future?," from *Red Hot Radio: Sex, Violence and Politics at the End of the American Century*, Saul Landau underscores how it is in politicians' best interests to keep a steady flow of money from special interests, rather than appeal to the common voter. Ken Silverstein goes undercover as a lobbyist in Washington and illustrates how easy it is to buy influence in "Pimps to Power: Lobbyists and the Destruction of Democracy," from *Washington on $10 Million a Day: How Lobbyists Plunder the Nation*. In "School Days, Rule Days," from *Facing the Wrath: Confronting the Right in Dangerous Times*, Sara Diamond exposes the dark side of home schooling. Finally, in "The Devil in the Details," from *Eternal Hostility: The Struggle Between Theocracy and Democracy*, Frederick Clarkson analyzes how the religious right justifies its extremism.

News that Went Unreported: "Dollars Per Vote"

Norman Solomon & Jeff Cohen

Wizards of Media Oz: Behind the Curtain of Mainstream News

By now, many news reports have analyzed the election results in great detail. On television and in print, we've seen lots of charts and graphs showing the breakdown of votes by gender, race, age, income and a whole lot more. But an important aspect of the election has escaped press attention: the cost of each vote.

"Dollars Per Vote" could be a useful category for putting various campaigns into clearer focus. The public ought to know how much the candidates spent for every vote they received.

After the election, we searched for media coverage of Dollars Per Vote. And searched. And searched. No luck.

So, we did the math ourselves. Here's what we discovered:

In the general election campaign, the Dollars Per Vote varied widely among the seven presidential candidates who ran nationwide.

Bill Clinton's campaign spent $61.8 million of taxpayer money to win 45.6 million votes. So, the "DPV" for Clinton was $1.36.

The Bob Dole campaign, which adhered to the same spending limit, garnered 37.9 million votes. That amounted to a DPV of $1.63.

How about Ross Perot? Well, this time around, the pseudo-populist billionaire accepted federal funds with a ceiling of $29 million and captured just under 8 million votes. His DPV: $3.67.

The man who finished fourth in the presidential balloting, Green Party candidate Ralph Nader, opted to cap his campaign expenditures at $5,000. On Election Day, about 581,000 voters chose him. For Nader—alone among the seven candidates—the spending per vote can't be expressed in dollars. He spent about a penny for each vote. In DPV terms, that's $0.01.

In fifth place, Libertarian Party candidate Harry Browne got 471,000 votes. Available reports put his campaign outlays at roughly $3 million. If so, his DPV was $6.37.

The campaigns for the candidates who brought up the rear—the Taxpayers Party's Howard Phillips and the Natural Law Party's John Hagelin—each reportedly spent in the neighborhood of $2 million. For Phillips, who denounces the Republican Party as too liberal, his 179,000 votes cost $11.17 a piece. For Hagelin, who netted 110,000 votes, the DPV was $18.18.

These DPV figures are ballpark measurements that understate the resources behind the major-party candidates, including "soft money." Well-heeled "issue advocacy" groups and unaffiliated boosters were able to skirt the spending limits. In effect, the Clinton and Dole forces expended several dollars for each vote. Meanwhile, the financial gaps were only part of the imbalance. Let's not forget that Clinton and his GOP rival—as well as, to some extent, Ross Perot—enjoyed enormous advantages in the form of profuse media coverage.

No matter how you slice it, the contrast with Ralph Nader is striking. Even if you include all the money that independent committees paid to promote Nader's candidacy—no more than $200,000—the spending per vote on his behalf totaled, at most, one-third of a dollar.

The evident lack of media curiosity about Dollars Per Vote also extends to thousands of other political races—and state ballot initiatives.

The *New York Times* published a prominent post-election story under a sweeping headline: "From California to Maine, Voters Agreed With the Corporate View on Issues." The news article declared that the latest voting on ballot measures "suggests that Americans' on-again, off-again flirtation with anti-business causes is off again."

The article barely mentioned that victorious industries—ranging from high-tech firms to timber companies to health-care conglomerates—had poured huge amounts of money into winning at the ballot box. Instead, the *Times* emphasized the outlooks of analysts like Brookings Institution savant Thomas Mann. "The public is less angry and less willing to identify with populism," he proclaimed, adding that "there's a certain sobriety out there—a new understanding that we need a strong private sector."

Most voters may be sober, but the businesses ponying up millions to get their way at the polls are quite inebriated with their high-rolling power. In state after state, big-money ad campaigns beat back under-funded efforts to protect consumers, medical patients and the environment. A media spotlight on Dollars Per Vote would illuminate the corruption of the initiative process.

As long as news outlets don't provide us with such information, we're going to have to figure it out for ourselves.

November 13, 1996

Discussion Questions

1. What is the "DPV" and how did it differ for various presidential candidates in 1996?

2. What is the authors' purpose in analyzing the "DPV"? What part do you think money plays in elections?

3. Why does the media tend to ignore the "DPV"?

Writing Suggestion

The article mentions presidential candidates from various "outsider" parties. Would you ever vote for a presidential candidate who is not a member of the Democratic or Republican Party? Why or why not?

Election Day Apathy

Saul Landau

Red Hot Radio:
Sex, Violence and Politics at the End of the American Century

November 5, 1996

After casting my ballot I felt nauseated. Will I suffer the moral consequences of voting for people who do not represent my interests, who give new meaning to the word disappointment? Be practical, I said to myself. The other guy's worse. I've always voted for the lesser of two evils, why bitch now?

The nausea abated as I breathed cool autumn air. Outside the polling center, campaign junkies handed out flyers reminding voters of their candidates' names. Nearby, several men and women had outstretched hands.

Stiff them or give each five dollars and get a "bless you"? Are these people preparing to get thrown off welfare; practicing their new occupation? Since Democrats revel over the healthy 5.2% unemployment figure, it makes sense for people to beg—that way they don't cut into the employment rolls and with only several million unemployed, the economy remains robust.

A man stood next to me, waiting for the bus. I assumed by the sour look on his face that he also had just voted.

"No," he said, "I don't vote. It's a matter of principle."

"What principle?" I demanded.

"I pay taxes," he said. "Therefore, I should be represented, but neither party, neither candidate represent my interests as a peace-loving parent and working person. I see Indonesian and Taiwanese businesses represented. Big oil, gas, cars, insurance, booze and tobacco buy the supposed people's representatives."

"Wait a second," I stopped him. "Our system may have a few flaws, but it's still the greatest democracy in the history of the world. Nations throughout Latin America eagerly copy our campaign format. As a result tens of millions of people see their candidates on TV—for a few seconds at a time, except when they debate, which is too boring to watch. But that's freedom, that's our way of life."

He stared at me. "I don't look for candidates with charisma, or that know how to make a speech. I want someone to help address the difficult issues. Millions of poor will receive no help from either party, either candidate. Millions face insecurity over job loss, which means health care loss. Look how the environment continues to suffer as a result of the perpetual growth and development mystique that has gripped us and which politicians don't question."

He was practically in tears. "Get a hold of yourself," I pleaded. "It's not all that bad. The point is we do have a choice and therefore we have to exercise it."

"No," he countered. "There's little meaningful choice in most of our elections. So I don't vote."

"Citizens have an obligation to vote," I lectured. "If the majority acted like you, what kind of country would we have?"

He smiled. "The majority do act as I do. They don't vote."

"What's your name, Mister," I demanded, as the bus came.

"Joe," he said. "Joe Apathy, but you can call me just plain Joe."

Campaign Finance: What Future?

Saul Landau

Red Hot Radio:
Sex, Violence and Politics at the End of the American Century

February 18, 1997

"Mention campaign finance reform and the image emerges of the $2 billion plus donated by corporations and banks to last year's campaigns. Is this why government gives to the rich and not the poor, who cannot afford to make mammoth contributions?" I asked my guru, Dr. Izzy Knowitall.

"You sound naive, or worse, un-American," he said. "Imagine a tobacco chief executive who can't buy political influence! Explain that to the stockholders and Jerry Falwell."

"But in the 1990s," I countered, "PACs and lobbying shouldn't exclude the majority from meaningful participation."

"Please," he said. "The Founding Fathers were terrified that the rabble would rule and take away their ill-gotten wealth. Propertyless people couldn't vote until the 1820s, women until the 1920s and blacks not until the late 1960s."

"Come on," I said. "You believe that a snot-nosed kid who inherits millions of shares of tobacco stock has the right to bribe, I mean contribute, half a million simoleons to Jesse Helms, who will claim that the anti-tobacco campaign is a communist and homosexual plot? Next thing, the tobacco lobby will find doctors who'll say cancer is good for you."

"What's freedom about," said Dr. Knowitall, "if not freedom to buy a member of Congress or even the president himself?"

"How about Chinese businessmen," I said, "who invest in Arkansas natural gas and buy the attorney general and continue influencing him even when he's in the White House?"

"Hey," said Izzy, "foreigners don't have the right to buy Congress and the president. What do you take me for, a one-worlder? But campaign finance reform is a joke."

"Wait," I said. "We proclaim our democracy as the greatest in world history, but our reality has a bunch of rich special interests using that system to get even richer."

"I remember President Warren G. Harding—God rest his soul," he said nostalgically. "Harding played poker with business tycoons who lost money to him every week. He'd let them sleep off their drunks in White House bedrooms. He even kept fancy ladies around for them. That was before these post-modern PACs and manipulation by hocus focus groups."

"What does Bill Clinton have to lose by going for real campaign finance reform?"

"He could lose the guarantee of his pardon, that's what. Clinton doesn't need campaign money, but Gore does and it's Gore who'll have to pardon this Arkansas gonif."

"So, you don't think Clinton or Congress will make campaign finance reform their number one priority?"

"Sure kid, and by December we'll have won the drug war, put Washington on a sound financial basis, forged a lasting Middle East peace, and achieved racial harmony. By the way," he says, "the pharmaceutical industry is throwing a bash for Al Gore tonight, Wanna go?"

"Maybe so," I said. "Will there be some good drugs there? After what you said, I think I need some."

Discussion Questions

1. Do you agree that there is "little meaningful choice in our elections"? Why or why not?

2. How much influence does "special interest" have in politics, in your opinion?

3. Why doesn't Washington make campaign finance reform a central issue?

Writing Suggestion

Do you believe that political contributions should be limited? To what extent?

Pimps to Power: Lobbyists and the Destruction of Democracy

Ken Silverstein

Washington on $10 Million a Day: How Lobbyists Plunder the Nation

When *Fortune* published its 1997 list of the nation's top 500 corporations, the magazine could barely restrain its exuberance. The previous year had been "extraordinary" with regard to profitability, *Fortune* said, as companies "restructured, reengineered, refinanced, downsized, laid off, split up, and merged their way to prosperity." All this had been furthered by "an almost magically favorable economic climate," highlighted by low interest rates and "benign labor costs."

For business and the wealthy, these past few years truly have been the best of times. Profits at Fortune 500 firms rose by 23.3 percent in 1997, after climbing by 13.4 percent the previous year. Salaries for top managers are also soaring. *Business Week*, a publication not normally known for its radical politics, says executive pay is "Out of Control." The magazine reports that the average salary and bonus for CEOs at the nation's biggest firms rose by 39 percent in 1996, to $2.3 million. Total compensation, which includes retirement benefits, incentive plans and stock option packages, was up 54 percent, to $5.7 million. Corporate America's hired help didn't do nearly as well. Workers' salaries rose about 3 percent in 1996, leaving average compensation for CEOs at 209 times higher than that of factory workers.

Meanwhile, the wealthy are paying less and less to the treasury in the form of taxes. Some 2,400 Americans with annual income of $200,000 or more paid no taxes in 1993, compared to just 85 wealthy individuals who escaped paying taxes in 1977. Since Congress in 1997 reduced inheritance taxes and the tax on capital gains, the number of rich Americans who pay little or no taxes is expected to grow in coming years.

Corporations are also avoiding tax payments. Two loopholes Congress provided to companies with operations overseas—the foreign tax credit and tax deferral on foreign income—cost the treasury about $24 billion per year. The bland term "accelerated depreciation" obscures a rule that allows companies to write off the cost of equipment faster than it actually wears out, a gift worth $28.3 billion annually.

Overall, federal corporate income taxes have declined from 30.1 percent of total tax revenues during the 1940s to 12.2 percent in 1996.

Huge corporate profits and low taxes for the wealthy do indeed result from a "favorable economic climate," but there's nothing magical about it, as *Fortune* would have you believe. The policies behind the favorable climate are designed by politicians who are dependent on cash from Corporate America to finance their political careers. The deluge of business dollars—in 1996, the parties and their candidates raised $2.1 billion, an average of $5.75 million every day—means that elected leaders are sure to implement policies designed to fatten their sponsors' bottom lines.

The link between campaign donations and political policy was brought into sharp focus by the campaign finance scandals that erupted during the 1996 campaign. Even jaded observers were startled by the Clinton administration's selling of the Lincoln bedroom to the highest bidder, and its organizing of White House coffee klatsches to reward donors and encourage them to make additional contributions.

But political contributions are only one way that big business wins favors in Washington. The media's focus on who made what phone calls from where, and who gave what funds in exchange for which favors misses a broader picture. Understanding how the capital works, and how business prospers here, requires a trip through the world of beltway lobbying and a review of the vast army of hired guns working at the behest of Corporate America.

Dollar for dollar, lobbying is a better investment than campaign contributions, one reason business spends far more on the former than on the latter. In 1996, Philip Morris coughed up $19.6 million for lobbying programs versus $4.2 million for campaign donations (making it the leader in both categories). The same pattern holds true with other firms. For 1996, Georgia-Pacific spent $8.9 million for lobbying and handed out $527,000 in political money. Corresponding figures for AT&T are $8.4 million versus $1.8 million; for Pfizer, $8.3 million versus $775,000; for Boeing, $5.2 million versus $770,000; for ARCO, $4.3 million versus $1.4 million; for Lockheed, $3.5 million versus $1.26 million; for FedEx, $3.1 million versus $1.9 million; for Dow Chemical $1.5 million versus $578,000.

In addition to in-house efforts, most big corporations spend lavishly for outside lobbying firms. Lockheed, for example, retains at least two dozen beltway lobby shops to supplement its own efforts, while Fedex has an additional 10 firms on retainer. In 1996, Boeing hired seven outside lobby shops for the sole purpose of pushing renewed Most Favored Nation trade status for China, paying them a combined total of at least $160,000 for their efforts.

While corporate lobbying has long been a major force in American politics, it has also been greatly transformed during the past few decades. Today, many efforts involve stealth lobbying—the chief tactic here is mobilizing fake "grassroots" campaigns—or with indirect methods, such as buying research from friendly think tanks in order to influence Congress and public opinion. All of this makes calculating corporate lobbying expenditures nearly impossible, though it's safe to say that lobbying has now become a multi-billion dollar-per-year industry. No one can say whether the figure of $10 million dollars a day in the book's title is accurate. But the trend would suggest it will soon be a very significant understatement—even if weekends and holidays are included.

When you consider the enormous benefits bestowed on Corporate America by the White House and Congress, the big sums companies spend to win favors are revealed as chump change. Lockheed's combined expenditures on lobbying and campaign contributions were about $5 million in 1996. That same year, Lockheed's lobbyists, with help from other arms makers, won approval for the creation of a new $15 billion government fund that will underwrite foreign weapon sales. In 1996, Microsoft spent less than $2 million for its combined lobbying and campaign contribution expenditures (the former accounted for more than two-thirds of that amount). The following year Congress awarded the company tax credits worth hundreds of millions of dollars for the sale of licenses to manufacture its software programs overseas.

Corporate lobbyists don't win every battle (though when they lose it's often because a competing corporate faction bought up even more lobbying firepower). It is indisputable, though, that corporate citizens who retain lobbyists have an enormous advantage in Washington over the regular ones who merely vote. Tommy Boggs, perhaps Washington's best known influence peddler, charges $550 per hour for his services. That's a drop in the bucket to Philip Morris, but Boggs' rate would eat up the average salary earner's entire annual income after a mere 43 hours of lobbying activity.

That lobbying has corrupted the political system is no secret. During his 1992 presidential campaign, Bill Clinton promised to "break the stranglehold the special interests have on our elections and the lobbyists have on our government." Such promises (like many others the president made) were forgotten as soon as the election votes were counted. Clinton picked Vernon Jordan, a top lobbyist and one of Washington's consummate political insiders, to head his presidential transition team. Among those selected for top administration jobs were Ron Brown, a former colleague of Tommy Boggs at the firm of Patton Boggs; Mickey Kantor of the powerhouse firm Manatt, Phelps, & Phillips; and Howard Paster, a former lobbyist for oil companies, banks and weapons makers.

A more recent display of the administration's open door policy to lobbyists came with the White House coffee klatches. Examine the list of the roughly 1,500 people who attended the affairs and one finds that lobbyists were among the most heavily represented.

Republicans criticize Clinton for his coziness with special interests, but they maintain the same intimate relationships with corporate lobbyists. After winning control of Congress in 1994, the GOP House leadership met weekly with "The Thursday Group," a pack of lobbyists and activists who helped plot legislative and media strategy on the Contract With America. Included in this elite troupe were hired guns representing the U.S. Chamber of Commerce, the National Federation of Independent Business, and Americans for Tax Reform.

Washington on Ten Million Dollars A Day tells how monied interests use lobbyists to achieve their goals in Washington, and why no one in the capital seems to want to do anything to change the system. It's also about the woeful ethical standards of Washington lobbyists, most whom will represent any client, from a corporate criminal to a foreign despot, as long as the bills get paid on time.

Fundamentally, though, *Washington on Ten Million Dollars A Day* is about corporate power and the destruction of American democracy. Though the historic vibrancy of this country's democratic system has been vastly inflated by historians and official myth makers, there was a time when the average citizen could make his or her voice heard in the capital. Today, the vast lobbying power of corporations and the wealthy has reduced the collective voice of average citizens to a faint din, barely heard in the corridors of power.

This state of affairs is amply reflected by the political process. Back in 1993, the hottest political issue in Washington was health care. President Clinton called the American system the "costliest and most wasteful" in the world and promised that when he was through, the American people would be able to stand tall and say, "Your government has the courage, finally, to take on the health care profiteers and make health care affordable for every family."

The public would have enthusiastically supported a frontal assault on the health care industry, with polls showing Canada's socialized system being the most popular model for reform. The public, though, was largely excluded from the debate in Washington, which was dominated by the "health care profiteers" that Clinton had pledged to attack. A report from the Center for Public Integrity found that some 660 groups shelled out more than $100 million to thwart reform between 1993 and 1994. About one-quarter of that amount took the form of political donations to members of Congress. A good chunk of the rest was paid to hundreds of lobbying and public relations firms that were hired to influence the health care debate.

At least 80 lobbyists working the issue were former members of Congress or the executive branch. William Gradison was a member of Congress on Sunday and head of the Health Insurers Association of America (HIAA)—a trade group of 270 insurance companies and creator of the infamous "Harry and Louise" TV ads—on Monday. The beltway firm Powell Tate was hired by Bristol-Myers Squibb, RJR Nabisco, T2 Medical Inc., Pharmacia & Upjohn, and Searle. For $2 million, according to an internal memorandum, Powell Tate would "sow doubt" about Clinton's assaults on drug makers and his early calls for price controls on the industry.

The National Federation of Independent Business, one of Washington's most powerful groups with more than 600,000 small business affiliates spread across every congressional district, launched a huge effort to defeat any plan that required employers to help pay for their workers' health care. Over two years, the federation generated two million letters opposing reform and maintained a crew of 10 lobbyists working full time on the issue. "Our structure is very similar to the White House," Federation chieftain John Motley bragged to the Center. "Actually, I've got more people working in the House [of Representatives] than they do...I think they have about four. I've got six."

Consumer and public interest groups also lobbied on health care, but they did not have anywhere near the resources of the business interests. Even Gradison admitted that some groups weren't "well represented" in the debate, saying, "I don't mean there are zero advocates but there aren't a lot of advocates for the poor."

Since average citizens—including nearly 40 million Americans without health care coverage—were not heard from, talk of comprehensive health care reform soon faded. The general public's minuscule influence on political affairs was seen in the fact that a Canadian-style system, while being the single most popular plan with the populace, was swiftly discarded by Clinton and Congress because, said the pundits, it suffered from a lack of political support!

The same divide between public opinion and political power can be seen across the board. People earning less than $22,600 a year outnumber people earning more than $246,000 per year by 40 to 1, but in 1997 Congress passed a plan that reduced the average tax payment for those in the latter category by $16,000, while increasing annual taxes for those in the former by $19. With the end of the Cold War, most Americans hoped for a "peace dividend" in the form of reduced spending for the military and more money for social programs. Yet year after year, Congress and the White House continue to lard the Pentagon with hundreds of billions of dollars while cutting social expenditures to the bone. Welfare programs have been eliminated so that Cold War relics such as Northrop's B-2 bomber can be preserved.

Such outcomes are predictable given the overwhelming influence exerted on the political system by Corporate America's hired guns. Indeed, the American political system is now presided over by lobbyists: they organize fundraisers and otherwise keep lawmakers supplied with campaign cash. They open doors for clients at the White House and government agencies. Because many formerly served in government, they know the rules and how to bend them.

Washington on Ten Million Dollars A Day will tell you—and show you—how lobbyists have bought up the capital and give you the information you need to fight back.

Discussion Questions

1. What is a lobbyist and what does a lobbyist do?
2. Why does Silverstein begin his essay with a discussion of CEOs' salaries?
3. How is lobbying "a better investment than campaign contributions"?
4. How was President Clinton's health care plan destroyed by lobbyists?

Writing Suggestion

Argue the pros and cons of lobbying. Do any lobbying organizations support movements or agendas that are beneficial to working-class people?

School Days, Rule Days

Sara Diamond

Facing the Wrath: Confronting the Right in Dangerous Times

Z Magazine, October 1994

One of the Christian Right's strengths has been its success in attacking secular institutions while simultaneously building an alternative subculture. Education is a case in point. In a number of school districts, from central Florida to San Diego county, Christian rightists have blocked Head Start programs, sex education and multicultural curricula. But public school battles would be even fiercer were it not for the thousands of evangelical families who have dropped out of the system altogether.

Most, though certainly not all, home schoolers are born-again Christians, and estimates of their numbers range widely. The most recent Department of Education study estimates between 248,500 and 353,500 home schooled students, which is less than one percent of the total school-age population. Michael Farris of the Home School Legal Defense Association claims there are 700,000 to one million home school students. Department of Education researcher Patricia Lines says Farris' figures are high because he includes pre-school aged children and an unknown number of students who, though officially enrolled in private Christian academies, spend part of their school week learning at home. Lines also says Farris' figure reflects the growth of home schooling just in the past few years.

Home schooling is common in rural areas, and it's perfectly legal. Most states require only a high school diploma from parents who teach at home. Existing data show that home schooled students perform better than average on achievement tests in basic subjects. And why wouldn't they? Compared with public school classrooms packed with 30 or more students, proper home schooling gives kids one-to-one training in reading, writing, math, etc.

The drive for higher academic achievement is probably the least salient reason why thousands of Christian parents have dropped out of public schools. For the ranks of the Christian Right, home schooling is more than a private choice. It is a trend with profound political implications. Home schooling is one means through which the Right is solidifying a narrow, reactive ideology among parents and their children.

Home schooling advocates reinforce parents' political justifications for the private choice they've made. For example, in one of the movement's most popular books, *The Right Choice*, Home School Legal Defense Association attorney Christopher Klicka urges Christians to break free from the academic, moral and philosophical crises plaguing the public schools. Academically, Klicka claims that "public school history books are filled with pro-Communist propaganda" and that teachers are no longer teaching phonics. Morally, Klicka points to violence, drug abuse and sexual promiscuity, all supposedly promoted by public school teachers who won't teach real values but do teach kids New Age meditation techniques. Philosophically, Klicka writes, the danger lies in the humanist underpinnings of public education since the 19th century. After all, educational philosopher John Dewey was the first president of the American Humanist Association. "Knowing this," Klicka asks, "can we risk sending our children to public school?" And what may happen as more parents decline such a risk? In the coming years, home school graduates will form the backbone for a new generation of Christian Right activists.

Months after the fact, Christian home school activists are still buzzing about their legislative victory last winter. An amendment attached to a Congressional education bill would have required home school teachers to be state-certified in all subjects they teach. But once the bill was publicized on Christian radio stations, home schoolers flooded Congress with faxes and 800,000 constituent phone calls. The amendment was swiftly removed from the bill, and the home schooling movement had its first taste of nationwide lobbying power.

Politics aside, home schooling also spells big bucks for about a dozen leading producers of curricula materials. I got on the mailing lists of a just a few, and was soon deluged with stacks of catalogs, magazines, and free samples, all with a fundamentalist bent. The largest producer of home school materials is called A-Beka School Services, the publishing arm of Pensacola Christian College in Florida. A-Beka sells textbook and educational video sets for 680,000 students each year. Customers include home schoolers plus 24,000 private schools. A-Beka's catalog begins with the advisory that its editorial department "has rejected the humanistic philosophy and methods of the progressive educators and has turned to original sources and the writings of true scholars. Of course, the most original source is always the Word of God, which is the only foundation for true scholarship in any area of human endeavor." From there, the curriculum for grades K to 12 includes Bible study, history, math, science/health, and language skills. For each subject, A-Beka provides age-appropriate books, flash cards, maps, games and workbooks. The math materials are the most straightforward. I don't know what A-Beka's 11th grade "Christian chemistry text" entails. But the 10th grade biology curriculum is called "God's Living Creation," and A-Beka boasts that it is "truly non-evolutionary in philosophy, spirit, and sequence of study." The reading, history and government materials are the most heavily ideological. No multiculturalism here. The early reading textbooks are all about Jesus, the pilgrims, and other famous white guys. The high-school government text is "written from the standpoint of Biblical Christianity and political and economic conservatism...The concepts of private property, free enterprise, profit and capital, and limited government are clearly presented."

A Real Job

I found more evidence of Christian home schooling's links to right-wing politics at a hot August conference entitled "God, Give Us Men: A Gathering for Home-School Fathers and their Wives." Since I am neither a father nor a wife, I felt just a wee bit out of place at the Zion Fellowship Four-Square Gospel church in Danville, one of the Bay area's wealthiest suburbs. (The Four-Square denomination was founded by Aimee Semple McPherson in 1923.) The 300 some-odd men and their wives—paired off like they were headed for Noah's Ark—assembled at the ungodly hour of 8 a.m. for the latest briefings by a few of the home schooling sub-culture's leading figures.

Gregg Harris' Christian Life Workshops organizes dozens of similar conferences all over the country. From his home in Gresham, Oregon, Harris, father of six, is a major distributor of home schooling products in his own right. He spent part of the Saturday conference doing a show-and-tell of new educational products. One was a wall chart to train young children to perform household chores in exchange for paper money, redeemable for toys at the end of each week. Harris was particularly excited about a new board game, "The Richest Christian," a sort of religious version of Monopoly that sells for $23. The goal of the game is for players to "lay up treasures in heaven" by accumulating money that can then be shared charitably with others.

The conferences' main draw, though, was Michael Farris, father of nine and president of the Home School Legal Defense Association. Farris co-founded the HSLDA in 1983, around the same time as he was hired to head the legal department for Concerned Women for America. In the past decade, HSLDA has grown to employ several dozen attorneys, representing some 37,000 member families. For an annual fee of $100, these families rely on HSLDA for legal advice in dealing with local truant officers and school districts. Also in the past decade, home schooling has been recognized as legal in every state, though precise restrictions vary from one place to the next. California's Education Code, for example, requires parents to make attendance records available to school officials and to file an annual private school affidavit with the county superintendent; or to use a public school independent study curriculum; or to enroll as a "satellite program" of an accredited private school. HSLDA helps parents navigate their state's educational codes and represents them in court if need be.

In 1993 Farris made his first bid for public office. He lost his campaign for the lieutenant governorship of Virginia. But he won 46 percent of the vote and is now considered a major power broker in Virginia's Republican Party. It was Farris' supporters who delivered the GOP Senate nomination to Oliver North last spring. Farris has also started a new political action committee, the Madison Project, which will recruit and help bankroll first-time Congressional candidates, not incumbents who already have lists of donors. At the Danville home schooling conference, Farris' Madison Project brochures were stacked high on the entry table, along with a brochure to recruit volunteers for the 1994 reelection campaign of local Congressmember Bill Baker, a darling of the Christian Right. Farris' Saturday morning address was vintage "family values" material. His primary purpose was to instruct fathers on their God-ordained duty to be the spiritual leaders of their families. Farris said that "home schooling is the most effective means of spiritual discipling invented," and he stressed that the real opponent of home schooling is "the enemy of our soul," also known as Satan. To keep the devil at bay, home schooling fathers, not mothers, bear the brunt of the home schooling responsibility. Since dads go to work and moms stay at home, dads have to delegate responsibility to moms. "But when you understand whose job it really is," Farris said, "there's a change in attitude."

Dads should be "deeply grateful" to their wives for performing two full-time jobs, that of homemaker and school teacher. To show their gratitude, husbands should insist that their wives take a daily break—Farris recommended a 30-minute outdoor walk. Husbands should install telephone answering machines so moms won't be pestered by annoying daytime phone calls. Husbands should take wives out to dinner "once in a while," and they should help with the housework. Wow. Farris jokingly clued the audience in on what he calls his "lazy man's" trick: "When you first come home, wash the dishes for the first 30 minutes. Your wife will be so impressed, you can coast for the rest of the night."

Farris continued his litany, all to the effect that moms and dads have rigidly different roles to play in parenting. Moms should be more influential with babies and young kids. Dads are the ones responsible for preparing children for careers, marriage, and political activism. Here things got interesting. Farris explained that children, even teenagers, should not be allowed any boy-girl relationships—not until they are mature enough to consider marriage. To let kids have seemingly cute and harmless friendships with the opposite sex is to encourage teenage sexuality and all the heartbreak that follows. Farris allows no dating, only courtship. Courtship is non-frivolous male-female socializing where the primary goal is to find compatible marriage partners. Courtship must be strictly supervised by both sets of parents and allowed only between fellow believers who are also physically attracted to each other. Farris noted how quickly young men would pass through college or career training programs if they were not allowed to marry (or have sex) until they could support a wife financially.

Everyone in the audience seemed to keep a straight face. We eagerly awaited a break to stretch and go shopping in the church's downstairs exhibit hall. I followed a home schooling father clad in a particularly intriguing T-shirt. The front side said "My wife has a real job," and the back said "...loving me." Downstairs I found the makers of these T-shirts set up in their own booth and wearing the ladies' version. The front says "Get a real job..." The backside reads "...be a wife and mother!" and then lists some of the requisite job skills: arbitrator, nutritionist, chauffeur, nurse, chef, hairdresser, janitor—even lover.

The exhibit hall was filled with a dizzying array of home school product sellers, all doing a brisk business. I looked and fortunately found no materials advocating harsh discipline of children. I found parents loading up on all kinds of books and games for their kids.

One impressive item was a quarterly magazine, *New Attitude*, published by Gregg Harris' son Joshua and a crew of home-schooled teenagers. The magazine is lively and graphically entertaining. It's packed with letters pages, advice columns, features on political campaigns, anti-abortion activism, even a critique of Rush Limbaugh. Editor Joshua Harris, aged 19 and not yet a father, travels around the country preaching teenage sexual abstinence and the virtues of courtship, not dating.

While shopping and snacking on the church lawn, most of the home schoolers seemed to know each other. They'd come from all over northern California. They are well organized, not just in churches, but also through local parents' support groups and the Christian Home Educators' Association, which has chapters in most states.

Stars and Stripes

One of the cornerstones of Christian Right thinking these days is the claim that America's Founding Fathers intended to create a Christian nation. The leading purveyor of this view now is David Barton, who runs a lucrative book and tape sales operation called WallBuilders, Inc. Barton has become ubiquitous on the Christian Right lecture circuit, and he was a featured speaker at the Danville home schooling workshop. I had seen his performance earlier this summer at a meeting of the northern California Christian Coalition. On both occasions I was struck by Barton's popularity with audiences, despite—or maybe because of—his demeanor. Looking like a 30-something cross between Pat Robertson and Ross Perot, Barton wears a big, gawdy stars-and-stripes tie. He never cracks a smile and does not take questions from the floor. He hammers his audiences with a high-speed litany of selected pro-Christian quotes from the leaders of the original thirteen colonies. On an overhead projector, he flashes portraits of the Founders so fast that no one could possibly absorb his "information."

Yet the audiences are riveted by Barton's pitch. With charts and bar graphs, Barton shows a "correlation" between the Supreme Court's 1962 and 1963 decisions removing prayer from public schools and subsequent drastic statistical increases in teenage pregnancies, drug abuse and the like. All of society's problems can be blamed on the fact that Christians did not fight back when the secular humanists pushed God and the Bible out of the public arena. The Founders wanted no such thing as a separation of church and state. On the contrary, Barton selects quotes from people like William Penn to the effect that "only the godly shall rule." For the Christian Coalition meeting, Barton elaborated this point to the effect that *only* Christians should occupy elected offices—and he got a standing ovation.

Barton's pseudo-history and laughable abuse of statistics ought to be an embarrassment to those Christian Right leaders now trying to claim a mainstream mantle. But Barton's popularity should not be dismissed because it points to what motivates much of the movement's following. Here we have a group of people who mix separatism with the belief that Christians—narrowly defined—ought to have dominion over secular society. This is a movement that wants to have its cake and eat it, too.

In *The Right Choice*, Christopher Klicka suggests that conservative Christian parents should stay away from home schoolers of different political and religious persuasions. Yet for the most part, Christian homeschoolers are unwilling to just head for the hills and leave everyone else alone. Some Christian Right activists are fighting to remove liberal educational materials from the public schools while their own kids attend private or home schools. From the safety of their own legally protected churches and private academies, this segment of the Christian Right is training up a new generation to wage what they call "spiritual warfare" all the way into the next millennium.

Discussion Questions

1. What are the advantages and disadvantages of homeschooling?
2. What features characterize the materials used in home schooling?
3. Do you think it is fair that someone with just a high school diploma can teach at home, while public school teachers need to be certified?

Writing Suggestion

If you had children, would you choose to homeschool them? Why or why not?

The Devil in the Details: How the Christian Right's Vision of Political and Religious Opponents as Satanic May Lead to Religious Warfare

Frederick Clarkson

Eternal Hostility: The Struggle Between Theocracy and Democracy

There has been much public discussion and scholarly hand-wringing about the mutual demonization by opposing sides in the so-called culture war. The loaded language, name calling, and "labeling" that drives the direct mail fundraising business and the "sound bites" on television greatly contribute to the corrosion of civil discourse. However, there is a dimension of the problem of demonization that is far more corrosive than direct mail hyperbole. Elements of the Christian Right believe that their opponents are often literally demonic. The worldview of many Christian Right leaders and their followers is, in fact, infused with demons and satanic agents.

Contending with a political movement that sees demons where others see citizens—a movement that characterizes religious, political and sexual diversity as demonic activity—is profoundly different than confronting mere political differences of opinion. If opponents are demons, then shooting people working in abortion clinics—or gays and lesbians—is not a matter of killing people, but ridding the world of evil. Moreover, it is likely that the trend towards seeing people as demons, not just different, fosters the growing view among the Christian Right that religious warfare is on the horizon, if not already underway.

The Gay Movement as the "Lie of Satan"

Rev. Charles McIlhenny of San Francisco, for example, is a leading anti-gay crusader, a friend of R.J. Rushdoony, and a pastor of an Orthodox Presbyterian Church.

In his book, *When the Wicked Seize a City*, he tells of his life as an anti-gay activist in the most openly gay city in the world. McIlhenny concludes that "it is the law of God that must, and ultimately will prevail" against this "demonic trend."[1] He regards as "the lie of Satan" the claims of "the gay movement" that it only seeks "freedom of expression" and that they don't seek "to force themselves on anybody."[2] McIlhenny, who has suffered violent backlash for his views and activities, further writes, "As we see this kind of venomous hatred from gays, lesbians and witches, it becomes more and more obvious that this is not just a political issue, but a religious war. It is a clash between the forces of light and darkness."[3]

A similarly demagogic example is Baptist minister Rick Scarborough, who has mobilized his Pearland, Texas congregation into an electoral force that has taken many of the top offices in this Houston suburb. Scarborough believes that homosexuality is explicitly derived from "Satan," and that "[h]e is not going to stop until he is forced to stop." Satan is also "the father of the lie" of separation of church and state, according to Scarborough.

To battle these "lies," Scarborough has organized a Reconstructionist-oriented political organization called Vision America, whose vision is framed by a violent metaphor: to "cut off the head of the wicked giant" of secular humanism. In this regard, he denounces the "wicked secular humanist lie of feminism." Emblematic of his growing political influence, in 1995 Scarborough administered a "Christian oath of office" to freshman Member of Congress Steve Stockman (R-TX)—who later joined Scarborough's church.[4]

Many believe, like Rev. McIlhenny, that there is no compromise in the "religious war" with the forces of Satan, but that victory is inevitable, if only they persevere. This eternal work ethic of totalitarian Calvinism fuels the war of aggression against democracy and pluralism. Stopping abortion or returning gays and lesbians to the closet is not now, nor has it ever been the primary issue. Waging spiritual warfare against Satan's agents, while preparing for a larger physical showdown, is the actual backdrop to much of the culture war.

The Evil of Halloween

On one side of this "warfare" is Rev. Dick Bernal of Jubilee Christian Center—a megachurch in San Jose, California. Bernal, an activist in the theocratic Coalition on Revival, wages weirdly colorful "spiritual warfare" campaigns against Halloween because he believes it promotes "actual worship of the devil." In Bernal's war on the demons, "prayer warriors" have been dispatched to abortion clinics, New Age organizations, and even the offices of the *San Jose Mercury News*. Bernal was joined in 1990 in his crusade against the "demons" of Halloween by then up-and-coming televangelist Larry Lea, a protégé of faith healer Rev. Oral Roberts, who sometimes wore military fatigues while conducting "spiritual warfare." The *San Francisco Chronicle* reported that "According to Bernal, San Francisco is ruled by the Spirit of Perversion. Oakland is controlled by the Spirit of Murder. San Jose by the Spirit of Greed, Watsonville by the Spirit of Poverty, and Marin County by the New Age Spirit." Peter Wagner, a professor at the evangelical Fuller Theological Seminary in Pasadena, California, coordinates a "spiritual warfare network," which promotes ideas like Bernal's that "territorial spirits" rule certain places. "Satan can't be omnipresent," Wagner claims, "so he has to delegate this to a hierarchy of demons."[5]

Steve Baldwin, a Christian Right politician from El Cajon, California, epitomizes how the contemporary politics of demons plays out. In a demagogic speech during his campaign for the state legislature in 1991, Baldwin raised the specter of satanic forces in public life. "We now have official state witches in certain states," Baldwin claimed. "In Massachusetts we have an official state witch." He further claimed that "in the Air Force, there is an official Air Force witch," and that there are "classes taught in our state schools on witchcraft."[6] Baldwin was widely ridiculed when these claims were reported. He lost that race. However, he made it on the second try, and a combination of the GOP takeover of the state Assembly and the implementation of term limits led to his appointment to the chairmanship of the Education Committee.

Dupes of Satan

Meanwhile, Pat Robertson has long been a general on the front lines of political combat with the demons. At the first national strategy conference of his Christian Coalition in November 1991, Robertson warned his followers that they were arrayed against "satanic forces" and declared: "We are not just coming up against just human beings to beat them in elections. We're going to be coming up against spiritual warfare. And if we're not aware of what we're fighting, we'll lose."[7]

Similarly, Gary North and a colleague stressed in 1983 that in order to "conquer the whole world for Jesus Christ...Christians need an understanding of their God, His law, and their satanic opponents."[8]

Robertson and most others in the Christian Right believe that a Biblically prophesied end-times scenario is being played out, although people disagree about the details and the time frame. As the year 2000 draws near, the numerical and semantic coincidence of the "millennium," and the massive egos and opportunism of aging leaders like Pat Robertson (who has claimed that he will be alive to broadcast the Second Coming of Christ from the Mount of Olives) should combine into an extraordinary political environment. The stakes will not be limited to which social philosophies will prevail, but will include visions of the eternal history of God's Kingdom.

For his part, Robertson foresees a violent struggle with a satanic-backed "New World Order." During a prayer service at the headquarters of his Christian Broadcasting Network, Robertson advised his followers not to fear the coming bloody battle, which will be simultaneously physical and supernatural. "God is going to give us tremendous protection," Robertson predicted. "He is not going to let us get hurt. If somebody's got a machine gun pointing at you, you can just walk right up to it, and it won't hurt you. If there's a fire burning right beside you, you can walk right through it. It's not going to burn you. We shouldn't fear for ourselves, for our lives. We shouldn't fear anything."[9]

In Pat Robertson's book, political opposition is by definition anti-Christian. In fact, in his book *The New World Order*, Robertson describes former presidents Jimmy Carter (a devout Baptist) and George Bush (Episcopal) as unwitting agents of Satan because they support the United Nations: "Indeed, it may well be that...Jimmy Carter, and George Bush, who sincerely want a larger community of nations living at peace in our world, are in reality unknowingly and unwittingly carrying out the mission and mouthing the phrases of a tightly knit cabal whose goal is nothing less than a new order for the human race under the domination of Lucifer and his followers."[10]

Similarly, Robertson sees academics who disagree with him politically as dupes of Satan, although he is less polite about it than when he spoke of the former presidents of the United States. Robertson predicts that his opponents will pay. "The silly so-called intellectuals of academia who are spouting their politically correct foolishness will find themselves considered first irrelevant and then expendable when the real power begins to operate."[11]

Such language is common among the most militant elements of the Christian Right. Randall Terry, the founder of Operation Rescue, has written regarding "Planned Parenthood, Queer Nation and their cohorts from hell," that "[w]e will not put the flawless, eternal Word of God on the same par with godless laws, or the ungodly lies of men and demons."[12] Fr. Paul Marx, the founder of Human Life International (a far-right Catholic group) has written that "After Satan, the principal author of the moral morass in our society today is Margaret Sanger."[13] Sanger, the founder of Planned Parenthood, was long dead when Marx wrote this. Fr. Marx's successor as president of HLI, Fr. Matthew Habiger, found similar evil in a contemporary series of United Nations conferences on Population and Development. Habiger denounced the "hellish forces that are trying to destroy the family" at a conference in Cairo, Egypt. "You don't have to be a prophet to discern the dark forces now at work in the world," he declared.[14]

Operation Rescue co-founder Rev. Joseph Foreman, a pastor in the PCA, denounces as "the doctrines of demons" anything short of all-out opposition to abortion. "Rescue," he writes, "is nothing more than orthodox Christianity transforming Christians in the arena of legalized child murder."[15] Foreman's explanation is a typical example of the integrated theocratic idea in which abortion is seen as a symptom and not the problem itself, and that deviations from Christian political as well as religious orthodoxies are demonic. "Power, when divorced from godly authority, becomes progressively demonic," Rushdoony wrote in *The Institutes of Biblical Law*.[16] Christian Right theorist Gary North sees a permanent religious war in which there is no possible reconciliation, and that "there can never be more than a truce or temporary cease fire..." "*This is a war for the hearts and minds of men,*" he concludes. "*It is also inevitably a war for the lawful control over all of mankind's institutions*" (emphases in the original).[17] Those who oppose the "legitimacy" of the biblical theocracy, according to North, "are affirming the validity of...some variation on the society of Satan."[18] This "political-theological war," he says, has been "going on throughout history."[19]

Religious Cleansing and Fumigation

The cultural base of the politics of demons pervades the charismatic evangelical community, as well as some Catholic congregations. While not all of this culture is explicitly theocratic in orientation, it is slowly being molded to conform to the long-range public policy objectives of the theocrats, which is to institute a Christian Nation, in which other religions are banned, and dissidents from the prevailing orthodoxy are prosecuted and possibly executed.

Since adherents of other religions are often considered by Christian Right leaders to be demonic, there would be many candidates for stoning or forms of mass execution. Pat Robertson complains, for example, that "[I]n Third World countries that practice idolatry, the idols are representatives of demonic power, and their worship often involves actual demon possession."[20] He also identifies the "satanic background of the New Age" religions and "the Buddha."[21]

Robertson has often said that everyone but Christians and Jews are not really qualified for public office. "If anybody understood what Hindus really believe," Robertson ominously declares, "there would be no doubt that they have no business administering government policies in a country that favors freedom and equality."[22] He also insists that "there is absolutely no way that government can operate successfully unless led by godly men and women operating under the laws of the God of Jacob."[23] He claims that Christians built the great institutions of the U.S., but that "the termites are in charge now," and that "the time has arrived for a godly fumigation."[24] The Anti-Defamation League (ADL) has denounced Robertson's profound religious bigotry: "Robertson's repeated references to America as a 'Christian nation' and to American governance as a 'Christian order' insults not merely Jews but all who value religious freedom."[25]

Robertson is not alone in his claims of the demon infestation of the world in the form of other religions. Dr. Lester Sumrall, a prominent author, educator and Pentecostal evangelist based in Indiana, devotes a whole textbook to the problems of demons. In *Demonology & Deliverance: Principalities & Powers*, Sumrall, like Robertson, claims that adherents of other religions are demons or demon influenced.[26] He complains for example, about people who have "curios from foreign lands" such as "idols of Buddha and Confucius" in their homes. "I don't believe they should be there," he explains. "They may not have hurt you yet, but I believe we should clean them out in Jesus' name."[27] What is disturbing about Dr. Sumrall, who epitomizes the pre-millennialist camp, is that his theology, like Pat Robertson's, is moving in a dominionist direction, and is focused on manifestations of demons. Sumrall, like Robertson, believes that the fast-approaching end times will include a "tribulation period of incalculable proportions," a "world of woe masterminded by Satan and his hosts."[28]

Sumrall specifically names contemporary manifestations of demons and evil spirits: Hinduism, Mormonism, Christian Science, Buddhism, Jehovah's Witnesses, Father Divine, Jeanne Dixon, drug pushers, horoscopes, good luck charms, and homosexuals.

Like Dick Bernal, Sumrall believes that certain cities are governed by evil spirits. He names Hollywood and New York City as dominated by evil spirits because "much of the filth on television comes from these two great centers."[29] He also cites the Biblical cities of Sodom and Gomorrah, where "the devil commanded supreme power," and "caused men to make love with men rather than with women," and that because "Sodomy became so dominant...God was obliged to wipe that sinful city off the face of the earth."[30]

Sumrall believes Christians must take "dominion" over the world. "Dominion" he writes however, "implies action."[31] He specifically urges anyone who has a Ouija board at home "to take it out and burn it." If Ouija boards should be burned, what should be done about Mormons and homosexuals, which are of at least comparable concern to Dr. Sumrall? He does not specifically say, but his larger vision is ominously vague. "Demon power is a driving force" behind the "assault of Satan on the human family," he claims. And because time is short on the Biblical time clock, "Satan has unleashed his demon forces to do violence and to take peace from the earth."[32] In preparation for the coming battles, Sumrall urges resistance to evil sprits and satanic manifestations of all kinds. Chillingly he adds, however, that resistance to the devil "is a military action."[33]

Reflecting the widespread nature of such concerns, and the sense of urgency about it, evangelical Christian bookstores are loaded with books on "spiritual warfare"—including lots of fiction. Such books are marketing a philosophy which encourages the Christian Right constituency to see symptoms of demonic activity as opposed to simple religious or political differences among their fellow citizens, or just fellow human beings.

Satanic Conspiracy Nuts or Serious Threat to Democracy?

Significantly, conspiracy theory is integral to the demonology of the Christian Right. Reconstructionism plays a major role in packaging and promoting conspiracy as a matter of doctrine by providing a unifying framework for the many conspiracy theories that drive elements of the right. Gary North explains that, "There is one conspiracy, Satan's, and ultimately it must fail. Satan's supernatural conspiracy is *the* conspiracy; all other visible conspiracies are merely outworkings of this supernatural conspiracy."[34] Robertson makes a similar argument in *The New World Order*.

This conspiracist component of Reconstructionist thought is heavily populated with demonic agents. Rev. Charles McIlhenny explains, for example, that the gay rights movement "is simply one late 20th century event in a long history of little conspiracies down through the ages. We do believe in the grand overall conspiracy of Satan's attempt to destroy the people of God and His Church...but we believe in a much greater conspiracy and that is the triumph of the Kingdom of Jesus Christ, which has been placed over all the world now and forever."[35] Such views are utterly normal, according to Rushdoony. "The view of history as conspiracy..." he explains, "is a basic aspect of the perspective of orthodox Christianity."[36]

A conspiratorial view of history is also a consistent aspect of Christian Right ideology, and is often used to explain the failure of conservative Christian denominations with millennial ambitions to achieve or sustain political power. The blame for this is most often assigned to the Masons, particularly an 18th century Masonic group called the Illuminati, and ultimately to Satan.

Panicked Congregationalist clergy faced with disestablishment of state churches (and thus their political power) in the 18th and 19th centuries fanned the flames of anti-Masonic hatred with conspiracy theory.[37] One of the inheritors of this tradition is Gary North, who declared in 1991 that among the first steps that prospective theocratic churches should take is to "excommunicate anyone who remains a Mason...Churches must publicly break with this covenant with evil." "Bible-believing churches got us into this mess by refusing to cast out Freemasons beginning 250 years ago, [and this]...led to the secularization of the republic." North adds that public schools "are based on the same theology that Masonry promotes: common ground ethics and government. Parents must break with the public schools as surely as churches must excommunicate Freemasons."[38] Meanwhile, an anti-Mason campaign in the 15-million-member Southern Baptist convention has been brewing for several years, led by Dr. James L. Holly of Beaumont, Texas, who casts himself as David fighting the Masonic Goliath. "I believe the philosophy and theology that underlies the Masonic Lodge is Luciferian. That is, satanic," Holly says. Holly wants to oust the million or more Masons from the largest Baptist denomination.[39] Similarly, throughout *The New World Order* Robertson refers to Freemasonry as a satanic conspiracy out to destroy Christianity and thwart Christian rule.

Robertson's conspiracism was well exemplified in one widely publicized episode. In 1992, there was a proposal on the ballot in Iowa to include an Equal Rights Amendment to the state constitution. In a fundraising letter, Robertson claimed that "radical feminists" have a "secret agenda" which "is nothing less than open war on the American family." Then came one of his most famous outbursts of religio-political hyperbole. "The feminist agenda is not about equal rights for women. It is about a socialist, anti-family political movement that encourages women to leave their husbands, kill their children, practice witchcraft, destroy capitalism, and become lesbians."[40] While fundraising letters are not always as representational of the thinking of the leaders of political organizations under whose signature they go out, this letter stands out as one which, in fact, is very much in character.

Exemplifying the political reach of conspiracism is Dr. Stanley Montieth, a member of the Christian Coalition, Coalition on Revival, and a star of the anti-gay propaganda film *The Gay Agenda*.[41] In his book *AIDS, The Unnecessary Epidemic: America Under Siege*, Montieth argues that AIDS is the result of a conspiracy of gays, humanists and other "sinister forces which work behind the scenes attempting to destroy our society."[42] Montieth and others in his movement often work side by side with parallel conspiracy theories. At a 1994 conference of Human Life International, he shared a book table with a book distributor who displayed books claiming to expose the Masonic conspiracy and crude works of anti-Semitism.[43] Dr. Montieth, who insists that he is not anti-Semitic, also chairs the health and human services committee of the California Republican Party.

One of the more disturbing elements is the degree of anti-Semitism present in conspiracy theories driving the millennial ideologies of the Christian Right. In a major, if belated review of *The New World Order* in the *New York Review of Books*, former conservative activist Michael Lind explained the links between Pat Robertson's satanic conspiracy theories, and the "underground literature of far-right populism that purports to interpret world history as dominated by Jews, Freemasons, and 'international bankers.' "

"Not since Father Coughlin or Henry Ford," Lind concludes, "has a prominent white American so boldly and unapologetically blamed the disasters of modern world history on the machinations of international high finance in general and on a few influential Jews in particular."[44]

The ADL concludes that *The New World Order* could be dismissed as largely "harmless kookery," except that Robertson "leads a major movement," and the book has appeared on the *New York Times* best seller list with a half million copies in print. "Robertson's philosophy, in this light, is not merely troubling—it's a national issue."[45]

When they are being particularly frank, Christian Right theorists tend to describe everything they oppose, or all who opposes them, as satanic. For example, R.J. Rushdoony writes of those who he sees as disconnected from Biblical law: "*all* sides of the humanistic spectrum are now, in principle, demonic; communists and conservatives, anarchists and socialists, fascists and Republicans..."[46] (emphasis in the original). Of course, there are few beyond Rushdoony who are frank—or impolitic—enough to declare that biblically incorrect conservatives and Republicans may find themselves on the chopping block, or in the stoning circle, come the Biblical republic.

Moon's Demons

The theocratic Unification Church of Sun Myung Moon is also propelled by the politics of demons. In its indoctrination practices, new members are taught that Satan may be working through their own biological parents. Evil lurks everywhere outside the church.[47] In an interview, former church leader Steve Hassan explained that once in the church, recruits are taught that doubts or questions about faith in Moon are understood as satanic attacks, or evil spirits trying to get in. He learned "thought stopping techniques" to keep out demonic presences. This had the effect of self-imposed totalitarian thought control. As a new member, he was taken to see the film *The Exorcist* (in which a girl is possessed by an evil spirit) and was told that this is what would happen to him if he ever left the church. Later, he was "repeatedly told horror stories" about deprogrammers, who were described as "Satan's elite soldiers committed to breaking people down and destroying their faith in God."[48]

In his book, *Combatting Cult Mind Control*, Hassan tells the horrifying story of how he considered killing his own father while being "deprogrammed." Hassan was a church leader who had gone home in a cast to recuperate after falling asleep at the wheel of a van full of church fundraisers in the 1970s. Hassan's father arranged for a group of people to talk with his son about his involvement in the church. He writes that he "knew" that the "deprogramming team had been sent directly by Satan. In my terror," he wrote, "their faces looked like images of demons. It was very surprising to me then, when they turned out to be warm and friendly." The discussions lasted the better part of a week. On the second day, Hassan writes that while driving down the Long Island Expressway, "my first impulse was to escape by reaching over and snapping my father's neck. I actually thought it was better to die or to kill than to leave the church."

On the fourth day, writes Hassan, the deprogrammers "discussed Hitler and the Nazi movement, comparing Moon and his philosophy of world theocracy to Hitler's global goals for German national socialism. At one point I remember saying, 'I don't care if Moon is like Hitler! I've chosen to follow him and I'll follow him 'til the very end!' When I heard myself say that, an eerie chill went down my spine. I quickly suppressed it." Eventually Hassan decided that he had been had, and left the church.[49]

The conditions that led Steve Hassan to see his parents as demons sent by Satan, are unfortunately not unique to the Unification Church.

From Guatemala to Lebanon: "Religious War" Is Not a Metaphor

One place where the politics of demons was played out in a particularly horrific fashion should serve as a warning. Guatemalan Gen. Efrain Rios Montt seized power in a 1982 military coup that was hailed at the time by U.S. evangelicals who were excited that one of their own (Rios Montt is a member of a U.S.-based Pentecostal sect) was now a head of state. What Pat Robertson refers to as the "enlightened leadership" of the Rios Montt regime,[50] lasted into 1983 when it fell to another military coup. Robertson was and remains a Rios Montt booster, despite, or perhaps because of Rios Montt's scorched earth counter-insurgency campaign that killed as many as 10,000 civilians. This genocidal campaign, ostensibly against a guerrilla insurgency, was often framed in religious terms, according to author Sara Diamond. This episode epitomizes the logical outcome of the politics of demons—what happens when religious intolerance is conflated with the political/military aims of state power. One pastor from Rios Montt's group, the U.S.-based Gospel Outreach, explained: "The Army does not massacre the Indians. It massacres demons, and the Indians are demon possessed; they are communists. We hold Brother Efrain Rios Montt like King David of the Old Testament. He is the King of the New Testament."[51] Gospel Outreach members also reportedly participated in the Montt regime's "espionage and torture-interrogation operations."

Since then Robertson has urged continual preparation for violence in a demon-infested world. The televangelist and power broker fears "the emergence of a New Age world religion," derived from the human potential movement, which he sees as "part of a continuum" which "leads straight to demonic power" and "in turn to a single source of evil identified by the Bible as Satan."[52]

Robertson has repeatedly predicted that the struggle, in which he sees himself engaged, for political control of the world will be violent. On one occasion he lumped together the ACLU, the National Council of Churches and the Communist Party, and declared that the "strategy against the American radical left should be the same as General Douglas MacArthur employed against the Japanese in the Pacific: Bypass their strongholds, then isolate them, bombard them, then blast the individuals out of their power bunkers with hand to hand combat…The battle to regain the soul of America won't be pleasant, but we will win it."[53] In 1992 Robertson wrote that he expected "physically bloody" confrontations in the efforts of "Christians" to win political power.[54]

"Violence is inevitable," he predicts, "it is going to be like Lebanon."[55] Robertson further predicts a "world horror" propelled by "demonic spirits" in which two billion people will die.[56] He is surprisingly frank in his writings, even while the Christian Coalition and Regent University are seeking a more mainstream face.

Meanwhile, the whipping up of fear and hatred of people because of their religious, sexual, or political orientation remains the stock-in-trade of many elements of the Christian Right. This powerful mix of belief in supernatural evil, and ascribing such evil in the form of demons to those with whom they disagree, almost inevitably leads to the kind of violence predicted by Robertson. The *Army of God Manual*, the underground handbook of anti-abortion violence, is a good example. The anonymously written text explains that "This is a manual for those who have come to understand that the battle against abortion is a battle not against flesh and blood, but against the devil and all the evil he can muster among flesh and blood to fight at his side. It is a How-To Manual of means to disrupt and ultimately destroy Satan's power to kill our children, God's children." The manual goes on to describe the U.S. as "a nation under the power of Evil—Satan, who prowls about the world seeking the ruin of the souls of mankind...a nation ruled by a godless civil authority that is dominated by humanism, moral nihilism, and new-age perversion of the high standards upon which a Godly society must be founded, if it is to endure."[57]

That violence would result from such views is unsurprising. Whether this violence emanates only from small bands of anti-abortion guerrilla warriors and militias, and sporadic hate crimes against gays and lesbians, or grows into full blown civil war will depend on whether those who are dedicated to a democratic, pluralist, and just society recognize the growing danger of the contemporary theocratic political movements in time.

Notes

1. Chuck & Donna McIlhenny, *When the Wicked Seize a City: A Grim look at the Future and a Warning to the Church*, Huntington House Publishers, 1993. p. 231.
2. Ibid., p. 127.
3. Ibid., p. 148.
4. Joseph L. Conn, "Bully Pulpit: Baptist Preacher Rick Scarborough Has Driven The Infidels From Pearland, Texas, And He Wants Your Town To Be Next," *Church & State*, May 1996.
5. Don Lattin, " 'God's Green Beret' Plans to Assault S.F. Demons," *San Francisco Chronicle*, September 1, 1990. See also Chip Johnson, "The Devil You Say? San Francisco Faces Halloween Exorcism," *Wall Street Journal*, October 30, 1990; and Don Lattin and David Tuller, "6,500 Christians Attend S.F. 'Exorcism', Gays, Pagans Rally Outside Auditorium," *San Francisco Chronicle*, November 1, 1990.
6. Steve Baldwin, campaign speech, June 20, 1991. Audiotape.
7. Frederick Clarkson, "The Christian Coalition: On The Road To Victory?," *Church & State*, January 1992.
8. Gary North and David Chilton, "Apologetics and Strategy," *Tactics of Christian Resistance*, Geneva Divinity School Press, Tyler, Texas, 1983. p. 107.
9. Skipp Porteous, "The World According to Pat Robertson: The Rev. Pat Robertson Has Mounted a Battle of Biblical Proportions to Rescue America from Satanic Forces," *Reform Judaism*, Spring 1993.
10. Pat Robertson, *The New World Order: It Will Change The Way You Live*, Word Publishing 1991. p. 37.
11. Ibid., p. 253.
12. Randall A. Terry, *Why Does A Nice Guy Like Me Keep Getting Thrown In Jail?*, Huntington House Publishers and Resistance Press, 1993. p. 33.

13. Karen Branan and Frederick Clarkson, "Extremism In Sheep's Clothing: A Special Report on Human Life International," *Front Lines Research*, June 1994.

14. "HLI President Urges Prayer To Combat 'Forces Of Darkness' At Cairo," *The Wanderer*, August 25, 1994.

15. Joseph Lapsley Foreman, *Shattering The Darkness: The Crisis of the Cross in the Church Today*, The Cooling Spring Press, 1992. p. 26.

16. Rousas John Rushdoony, *Institutes of Biblical Law*, Presbyterian and Reformed Publishing, 1973, p. 776.

17. Gary North, *When Justice Is Aborted: Biblical Standards for Non-Violent Resistance*, Dominion Press 1989. p. 20.

18. Gary North, *Unconditional Surrender: God's Program for Victory*, Institute for Christian Economics, 1991. p. 121.

19. North, op. cit.

20. Robertson, op. cit., p. 235.

21. Ibid., p., 254.

22. Ibid., p. 218–219.

23. Ibid., p. 227.

24. David Cantor, *The Religious Right and the Assault on Tolerance, & Pluralism in America*, Anti-Defamation League, 1994, p. 26.

25. Ibid., p. 24.

26. Dr. Lester Sumrall, *Demonology & Deliverance: Principalities & Powers*, LeSEA Publishing Company, 1993.

27. Ibid., p. 103.

28. Ibid., p. 131.

29. Ibid., p. 65.

30. Ibid., p. 63.

31. Ibid., p. 89.

32. Ibid., p. 51.

33. Ibid., p. 112.

34. Gary North, *Conspiracy: A Biblical View*, Dominion Press, 1986. p. 15.

35. Chuck & Donna McIlhenny, op. cit., p. 232.

36. R.J. Rushdoony, *The Nature of the American System*, The Craig Press, Presbyterian and Reformed Publishing Company, p. 156.

37. Seymour Martin Lipset and Earl Raab, *The Politics of Unreason: Right-Wing Extremism in America 1790–1970*, Harper & Row, 1970. p. 42.

38. Gary North, *Political Polytheism: The Myth of Pluralism*, Institute for Christian Economics, 1991. p. 567.

39. Steve Brunsman, "Masonic Campaign Counters Baptist Claims," *Houston Post*, February 20, 1993.

40. Pat Robertson, fundraising letter for the Christian Coalition of Iowa, 1992.

41. For a discussion of this film see Frederick Clarkson, "The Anti-Gay Nineties," *The Freedom Writer*, March–April 1993; reprinted in Frederick Clarkson and Skipp Porteous, *Challenging the Christian Right: The Activists' Handbook*, Institute for First Amendment Studies, 1992, p. 83; see also Laura Flanders, "Hate on Tape: The Video Strategy of the Fundamentalist Right," *Extra!*, June 1993; reprinted in Chip Berlet, ed., *Eyes Right: Challenging the Right-Wing Backlash*, South End Press, 1995. p. 105.

42. Stanley Montieth, *AIDS, The Unnecessary Epidemic: America Under Siege*, Covenant House Books, 1991. p. 383. The publisher is Reconstructionist Dalmar D. Dennis, who is also a member of the National Council of the John Birch Society.

43. Branan and Clarkson, op. cit. See also "Stanley Montieth Replies," *Front Lines Research*, November 1994.

44. Michael Lind, "Rev. Robertson's Grand International Conspiracy Theory," *New York Review of Books*, February 2, 1995.

45. Ibid., p. 25.

46. Rousas John Rushdoony, *Law and Society: Institutes of Biblical Law*, Vol. II, Ross House Books, 1986. p. 167.

47. Robert Boettcher, *Gifts of Deceit: Sun Myung Moon, Tongsun Park and the Korean Scandal*, Holt, Rinehart & Winston, 1980. p. 344.

48. Steve Hassan, *Combatting Cult Mind Control*, Park Street Press, 1988. p. 25

49. Ibid., pp. 26–29. An account of Hassan's experiences also appears in Boettcher, op. cit., pp. 179–180.

50. Robertson, op. cit., p. 228.

51. Sara Diamond, *Roads to Dominion: Right-Wing Movements and Political Power in the United States*, The Guilford Press, 1995. p. 238. See also Kate Cornell, "The Covert Tactics and the Overt Agenda of the New Christian Right," *Covert Action Quarterly*, Winter 1992–93.

52. Robertson, op. cit., p. 168.

53. Quoted in Cornell, op. cit.

54. Skipp Porteous, "The World According to Pat Robertson: The Rev. Pat Robertson has mounted a battle of biblical proportions to rescue America from Satanic forces," *Reform Judaism*, Spring 1993.

55. Ibid.

56. Robertson, op. cit., p. 254.

57. *Army of God*, circa late 1970s. Updated 1992. pp. ii; See also Anne Bower, "Army of God: Still On The March," *The Body Politic*, December 1995.

Discussion Questions

1. Who are the enemies of the Christian Right?

2. Why does the Christian Right use the strategy of defining their enemies as demons?

3. How does the Christian Right justify violence in seeking to advance its agenda?

Writing Suggestion

In your opinion, how prevalent are religious issues in determining national and/or local policy? Do you favor having a system of government with anything other than a clear separation of church and state?

Writing Suggestions for Chapter Five

1. Using personal interviews and/or further research, examine the voting patterns of your peers. How frequently do they vote? For what issues would they vote?

2. Using the readings as a starting point, argue for or against the idea that campaign contributions should be limited to small amounts of money from individuals only.

3. Examine the influence of religion or religious issues in a recent national or local election campaign. How did the candidates position themselves with regard to their own religious backgrounds? How did they attempt to appeal to various religious communities and their concerns?

4. Examine further the political and social issues involved in homeschooling. Under what conditions do you think homeschooling would be successful?

Chapter VI

International Issues

If you were asked to name the nation responsible for producing many of the world's most violent terrorists, you would probably not mention the United States. However, the history of the United States' involvement in other countries, especially in the western hemisphere, is nothing to be proud of. Even when the U.S. supposedly has the best intentions in mind, the effects of intervention—economic or military—can be devastating. This chapter will make you question the role of the U.S. and its motives in intervening in the affairs of other nations. Jean-Bertrand Aristide, the former president of Haiti, underscores the downfalls of unregulated trade in "Globalization: A Choice Between Death and Death," from his book *Eyes of the Heart: Seeking a Path for the Poor in the Age of Globalization*. In the "School of the Terrorists...Near CNN Headquarters in Atlanta" and "Beyond Oklahoma City: A Nation Where Terrorism Rules," from *Wizards of Media Oz*, Norman Solomon and Jeff Cohen expose a college for terrorists that exists in the United States. They also point out our misconceptions about Colombia, a nation more troubled by political killings than drug killings. This point is explored further by Javier Giraldo, S. J., in "Beyond the Stereotype: Human Rights in Colombia," from *Colombia: The Genocidal Democracy*. In "A Guide to Mexican Reality," from *Red Hot Radio*, Saul Landau recounts his visit to Zapatista rebel leader Subcommander Marcos.

In "Poor Journalism South of the Border," from *The Habits of Highly Deceptive Media*, Normon Solomon illustrates how the media ignores the more unpleasant facts about Mexico and the way its people have "benefited" from free trade with America. Finally, the rest of the readings in the chapter focus on the heroism of Guatemalans in fighting against an oppressive regime that was funded and supported by the United States. In "Guatemala 1962 to 1980s: A Less Publicized 'Final Solution,'" from *Killing Hope: U.S. Military and CIA Intervention since World War II*, William Blum looks at the history of CIA involvement in Guatemala. And Jennifer Harbury, a U.S. citizen whose husband was killed by the U.S. supported Guatemalan military, offers some personal testimonies of Guatemalans who fought against their oppressors from her book *Bridge of Courage*.

Globalization: A Choice Between Death and Death

Jean-Bertrand Aristide

Eyes of the Heart:
Seeking a Path for the Poor in the Age of Globalization

> *A morgue worker is preparing to dispose of a dozen corpses. One living soul lifts himself off of the table, shakes his head and declares, "I am not dead!" To which the morgue worker answers, "Yes you are. The doctors say that you are dead, so lie down."*

In today's global marketplace trillions of dollars are traded each day via a vast network of computers. In this market no one talks, no one touches. Only numbers count.

And yet today this faceless economy is already five times larger than the real, or productive, economy.

We know other marketplaces. On a plain high in the mountains of Haiti, one day a week thousands of people still gather. This is the marketplace of my childhood in the mountains above *Port Salut*. The sights and the smells and the noise and the color overwhelm you. Everyone comes. If you don't come you will miss everything. The donkeys tied and waiting in the woods number in the thousands. Goods are displayed in every direction: onions, leeks, corn, beans, yams, cabbage, cassava, and avocados, mangoes and every tropical fruit, chickens, pigs, goats, and batteries, and tennis shoes, too. People trade goods, and news. This is the center; social, political and economic life roll together. A woman teases and coaxes her client. "*Cherie*, the onions are sweet and waiting just for you." The client laughs and teases back until they make a deal. They share trade, and laughter, gossip, politics, and medical and child-rearing tips. A market exchange, and a human exchange.

We are not against trade, we are not against free trade, but our fear is that the global market intends to annihilate our markets. We will be pushed to the cities, to eat food grown on factory farms in distant countries, food whose price depends on the daily numbers game of the first market. "This is more efficient," the economists say. "Your market, your way of life, is not efficient," they say. But we ask, "What is left when you reduce trade to numbers, when you erase all that is human?"

Globalization, the integration of world markets, has promised to "lift all boats", rich and poor, to bring a global culture of entertainment and consumer goods to everyone—the promise of material happiness. And indeed, since 1980 most third world countries have embraced globalization. They have opened their economies to the world, lowered tariffs, embraced free trade, and allowed goods and services from the industrialized world to flow in. It seems the world is brought closer together. In fact the gap between the thumb and the little finger has never been larger.

What happens to poor countries when they embrace free trade? In Haiti in 1986 we imported just 7000 tons of rice, the main staple food of the country. The vast majority was grown in Haiti. In the late 1980s Haiti complied with free trade policies advocated by the international lending agencies and lifted tariffs on rice imports. Cheaper rice immediately flooded in from the United States where the rice industry is subsidized. In fact the liberalization of Haiti's market coincided with the 1985 Farm Bill in the United States which increased subsidies to the rice industry so that 40% of U.S. rice growers' profits came from the government by 1987. Haiti's peasant farmers could not possibly compete. By 1996 Haiti was importing 196,000 tons of foreign rice at the cost of $100 million a year. Haitian rice production became negligible. Once the dependence on foreign rice was complete, import prices began to rise, leaving Haiti's population, particularly the urban poor, completely at the whim of rising world grain prices. And the prices continue to rise.

What lessons do we learn? For poor countries free trade is not so free, or so fair. Haiti, under intense pressure from the international lending institutions, stopped protecting its domestic agriculture while subsidies to the U.S. rice industry increased. A hungry nation became hungrier.

In a globalized economy, foreign investment is trumpeted as the key to alleviating poverty. But in fact, the top beneficiary of foreign investment from 1985–95 was the United States, with $477 billion. Britain ran a distant second at $199 billion, and Mexico, the only third world country in the top ten, received only $44 billion in investment. When the majority of this money fled the country overnight during Mexico's financial meltdown in 1995, we learned that foreign investment is not really investment. It is more like speculation. And in my country, Haiti, it's very hard to find investment statistics. We are still moving from misery to poverty with dignity.

Many in the first world imagine the amount of money spent on aid to developing countries is massive. In fact, it amounts to only .03 % of GNP of the industrialized nations. In 1995, the director of the U.S. aid agency defended his agency by testifying to his congress that 84 cents of every dollar of aid goes back into the U.S. economy in goods and services purchased. For every dollar the United States puts into the World Bank, an estimated $2 actually goes into the U.S. economy in goods and services. Meanwhile in 1995, severely indebted low-income countries paid one billion dollars more in debt and interest to the International Monetary Fund (IMF) than they received from it. For the 46 countries of Subsaharan Africa, foreign debt service was four times their combined governmental health and education budgets in 1996. So, we find that aid does not aid.

The little finger knows that she is sinking deeper into misery each day, but all the while the thumb is telling her that profits are increasing, economies are growing and he is pouring millions of dollars of aid into her country. Whose profit? Whose economy? What aid? The logic of global capitalism is not logical for her. We call this economic schizophrenia.

The history of the eradication of the Haitian Creole pig population in the 1980s is a classic parable of globalization. Haiti's small, black, Creole pigs were at the heart of the peasant economy. An extremely hearty breed, well adapted to Haiti's climate and conditions, they ate readily-available waste products, and could survive for three days without food. Eighty to 85% of rural households raised pigs; they played a key role in maintaining the fertility of the soil and constituted the primary savings bank of the peasant population. Traditionally a pig was sold to pay for emergencies and special occasions (funerals, marriages, baptisms, illnesses and, critically, to pay school fees and buy books for the children when school opened each year in October.)

In 1982 international agencies assured Haiti's peasants their pigs were sick and had to be killed (so that the illness would not spread to countries to the North). Promises were made that better pigs would replace the sick pigs. With an efficiency not since seen among development projects, all of the Creole pigs were killed over period of a thirteen months.

Two years later the new, better pigs came from Iowa. They were so much better that they required clean drinking water (unavailable to 80% of the Haitian population), imported feed (costing $90 a year when the per capita income was about $130), and special roofed pigpens. Haitian peasants quickly dubbed them "*prince à quatre pieds*," (four-footed princes). Adding insult to injury, the meat did not taste as good. Needless to say, the repopulation program was a complete failure. One observer of the process estimated that in monetary terms Haitian peasants lost $600 million dollars. There was a 30% drop in enrollment in rural schools, there was a dramatic decline in the protein consumption in rural Haiti, a devastating decapitalization of the peasant economy and an incalculable negative impact on Haiti's soil and agricultural productivity. The Haitian peasantry has not recovered to this day.

Most of rural Haiti is still isolated from global markets, so for many peasants the extermination of the Creole pigs was their first experience of globalization. The experience looms large in the collective memory. Today, when the peasants are told that "economic reform" and privatization will benefit them they are understandably wary. The state-owned enterprises are sick, we are told, and they must be privatized. The peasants shake their heads and remember the Creole pigs.

The 1997 sale of the state-owned flour mill confirmed their skepticism. The mill sold for a mere $9 million, while estimates place potential yearly profits at $20–30 million a year. The mill was bought by a group of investors linked to one of Haiti's largest banks. One outcome seems certain; this sale will further concentrate wealth—in a country where 1% of the population already holds 45% of the wealth of the country.

If we have lingering doubts about where poor countries fall in this "new" economic order, listen to the World Bank. In September 1996, the *London Guardian* cited a draft World Bank strategy paper that predicted that the majority of Haitian peasants—who make up 70% of Haiti's population—are unlikely to survive bank-advocated free market measures. The Bank concluded: "The small volume of production and the environmental resource constraints will leave the rural population with only two possibilities: to work in the industrial or service sector, or to emigrate."

At present the industrial sector employs only about 20,000 Haitians. There are already approximately 2.5 million people living in *Port-au-Prince*, 70% of them are officially unemployed and living in perhaps the most desperate conditions in the Western Hemisphere. Given the tragic history of Haiti's boat people, emigration, the second possibility, can hardly be considered a real option.

The choices that globalization offers the poor remind me of a story. Anatole, one of the boys who had lived with us at *Lafanmi Selavi**, was working at the national port. One day a very powerful businessman offered him money to sabotage the main unloading forklift at the port. Anatole said to the man, "Well, then I am already dead." The man, surprised by the response, asked, "Why?" Anatole answered, "because if I sneak in here at night and do what you ask they will shoot me, and if I don't, you will kill me." The dilemma is, I believe, the classic dilemma of the poor; a choice between death and death. Either we enter a global economic system, in which we know we cannot survive, or, we refuse, and face death by slow starvation. With choices like these the urgency of finding a third way is clear. We must find some room to maneuver, some open space simply to survive. We must lift ourselves up off the morgue table and tell the experts we are not yet dead.

Discussion Questions

1. What does Aristide mean by the title of this chapter?

2. Why does Aristide begin his chapter with a description of a marketplace from his childhood in Haiti?

3. Which countries benefit the most from a globalized ecomony? Why? What lessons can we learn from Aristide's examples of imported rice and pigs?

Writing Suggestion

Search major newspapers and news internet sites for recent stories concerning trade agreements between nations. Who do you think will benefit most from these agreements, and who may lose out? Do you think the agreements you've researched are a good idea overall? Why or why not?

---

* *Lafanmi Selavi* is the center for street children in *Port-au-Prince* founded by Aristide in 1986.

School of the Terrorists... Near CNN Headquarters in Atlanta

Norman Solomon and Jeff Cohen

Wizards of Media Oz: Behind the Curtain of Mainstream News

Most Americans abhor nations that promote terrorism. We'd be outraged to hear that some country actually maintains a school for many of the world's top kidnappers, torturers and assassins.

If such a school existed, and if it were the subject of intense scrutiny on network TV, it's easy to imagine thousands of aroused citizens demanding that Washington take action to shut the school down.

In fact, such a school does exist. Only it's not on foreign soil. And Washington has not shut it down; Congress keeps it open—with millions of taxpayer dollars yearly.

The U.S. Army's school is located at Fort Benning, Georgia. It's called the School of the Americas, but in Latin America it's known by other names: School of the Assassins; School of the Dictators; School of the Coups.

The school has been mentioned in the news recently because Guatemalan Col. Julio Alpirez—a CIA operative—was implicated in two crimes: the 1990 murder of a U.S. citizen who ran an inn in Guatemala, and the 1992 torture and murder of a Guatemalan leftist guerrilla leader married to an American lawyer.

Col. Alpirez is an alumnus of the School of the Americas. He studied there as a young soldier in 1970, and again 20 years later, when he completed graduate training for senior military officers. A few months after that, Alpirez directed the murder of the American innkeeper.

Alpirez is a small-fry thug compared to some of SOA's other graduates, who include Panama's former dictator Gen. Manuel Noriega and Salvadoran mass murderer Roberto D'Aubuisson.

Listen to the U.S. Army personnel in charge of SOA describe its mission, and you hear rhetoric about training military leaders from Latin America and the Caribbean in democracy and human rights. But action speaks louder than words.

In 1988, the first graduate inducted into SOA's "Hall of Fame" was former Bolivian dictator Hugo Banzer, who seized power in a violent 1971 military coup and brutally suppressed dissent for years.

Other Hall of Famers include Gen. Manuel Antonio Callejas, a Guatemalan intelligence chief who presided over the deaths of thousands; Gen. Policarpio Paz Garcia, a corrupt Honduran dictator; and drug-trafficking suspect Humberto Regalado Hernandez, a Honduran general who took four separate courses at the school.

Framed pictures of these men are proudly displayed in SOA's main foyer. If these are SOA's Hall of Famers, we wonder who's in its Hall of Shame.

"American faculty members readily accepted all forms of military dictatorship in Latin America," asserts Joseph Blair, a U.S. Army instructor at the school from 1986 to 1989.

Occasionally, armies in Latin America have battled each other in border wars. But mostly, they do battle against their own people—especially the poor, peasant groups and labor unions, priests and church activists who work for human rights.

SOA is right in the middle of these dirty wars. Each year, it instructs 2,000 soldiers from the region in counterinsurgency, intelligence, interrogation and psychological warfare.

Martin Almada, a well-known political prisoner under Paraguay's military regime, was researching his own case in that country's "Horror Archives" when he found materials labeled *Instruction at the School of Americas*. They included a torture manual that instructed "interrogators" on how to keep electric-shock victims alive for further questioning.

In 1993, the United Nations released its detailed "Truth Commission Report on El Salvador," identifying the men responsible for atrocities against civilians during the decade-long civil war. Most of the culprits in the major murders were SOA graduates.

Two of the three military officers cited for assassinating Salvadoran Archbishop Oscar Romero in 1980 were SOA graduates. So were three of the five officers involved in the rape and murder of four U.S. church women who worked with Salvador's poor; 10 of 12 officers involved in the El Mozote massacre, which left hundreds of unarmed peasants killed and mutilated; and 19 of 27 officers involved in the massacre of six Jesuit priests, their cook and her daughter on a university campus in 1989.

While the war against Latin America's poor may benefit U.S.-based corporations with plantations or factories in the region, it brings only disgrace to the U.S. citizenry as a whole. Yet we taxpayers heavily fund that war, in part through SOA.

At Fort Benning, Col. Alpirez and others who attended the nine-month Command and General Staff College received up to $25,000 in living allowances (in addition to their regular salaries), and free weekend trips to see Atlanta Braves baseball games or Disney World.

When it comes to federal spending, Newt Gingrich is quite vocal. But he doesn't criticize the millions spent on the school of the assassins in his home state.

Last May [1994], Gingrich and others voted 217-175 to defeat a House measure that would have ended funding for the school. The amendment was sponsored by

Massachusetts Rep. Joe Kennedy, an individual who knows well the horror of polit-ical assassination.

On March 24, 1995—the fifteenth anniversary of Arch-bishop Romero's murder by SOA graduates—religious activists began a fast at the U.S. Capitol to stop SOA funding. The fast is led by Father Roy Bourgeois of SOA Watch, a Maryknoll priest who has served over two years in prison for his protests against the school.

You might ask why the school—located only about 90 minutes from CNN headquarters in Atlanta—has not been subjected to ongoing, hard-hitting TV cov-erage. After all, it's got everything network TV seems to want in a story: Blood, gore, terror.

[In September 1996, a brief flurry of press coverage followed the Pentagon's release of documents acknowledging that School of the Americas training manuals throughout the 1980s advocated torture, executions and false imprisonment.]

March 29, 1995

Beyond Oklahoma City: A Nation Where Terrorism Rules

Norman Solomon and Jeff Cohen

Wizards of Media Oz: Behind the Curtain of Mainstream News

In the painful aftermath of the Oklahoma City tragedy, news coverage has gone to great lengths to convey the humanity of victims and the grief of survivors. As a result, the emotional realities of terrorism now seem much more real to Americans.

What would it be like to live in a country where terrorists struck with impunity on a regular basis, matching the Oklahoma death toll every few weeks?

And what if most of the nation's terrorists—rather than reviling the government—were actually *aligned with* the government, or even part of it?

That's the situation in Colombia, where political killings total 4,000 a year, in a South American nation of 33 million people. If a similar proportion of the population were dying from political violence in the United States, that would add up to about 600 people killed by terrorism *every week*.

When U.S. media outlets mention the Colombian carnage, it's usually in stories blaming drug traffickers for the bloodshed. Yet, as journalist Ana Carrigan pointed out this spring [1995] in the NACLA magazine *Report on the Americas*, "the media's single-minded obsession with drugs" has gotten in the way of telling the truth.

Out of 25,491 politically linked killings of noncombatant Colombian civilians during the last eight years, *less than 3 percent* of the murders were related to the drug trade, according to the Andean Commission of Jurists. Twenty-nine percent of the deaths were attributed to left-wing rural guerrillas and urban insurgents.

Contrary to the impression left by U.S. media accounts, Carrigan reports, nearly 70 percent of the political murders with identified perpetrators "have been committed by the Colombian army and police, or by paramilitary groups and privately financed death squads operating in partnership with state forces."

In effect, the partnership extends to Washington—which keeps sending U.S. taxpayers' money to the Colombian government, despite its horrendous record:

- Each year, hundreds of Colombian children—many of them poor street kids—are killed by death squads engaged in "social cleansing." Human Rights Watch charges that young people arrested by police are regularly beaten, raped and tortured with electric shocks. Special army units also torture children, viewing them as "potential informants on their parents."

- "Political cleansing" goes on daily. In November 1992, for example, eight children associated with a nonviolent, progressive Christian group were massacred in Medellin. The accused include members of a U.S.-trained police intelligence squad.
- After a skirmish with guerrillas near Trujillo a few years ago, soldiers and police rounded up dozens of suspected civilian "sympathizers" in the town. Their mutilated bodies were later found floating in a river. Some had been burned with blowtorches, others had limbs amputated with a chainsaw.

- Paramilitary groups murdered more than 100 labor unionists in Colombia last year.

The U.S. media's favorite plot line—pitting Colombia's noble authorities against nefarious drug traffickers—fits in well with rationales for U.S. government aid, providing Colombian police with about $18 million annually. In addition, Colombia has been a top Latin American buyer of military equipment from the United States; last year's purchases were in the neighborhood of $73 million.

Nine months ago, Manuel Cepeda—a senator leading the left-wing opposition—was gunned down on a Bogota street. A paramilitary group, calling itself "Death to Communists and Guerrillas," quickly claimed responsibility.

Government investigators have tied the murder to Fidel Castano, a well-known paramilitary chieftain, named on seven current arrest warrants related to massacres. Yet he continues to move freely between Colombia and his apartment in Paris.

In the United States, media attention to Colombia's political violence is sparse—and skewed. "The news coverage is completely inadequate because it always seems to focus on so-called drug-related violence," says Mario Murillo of the Pacifica radio network's New York station WBAI, who has reported frequently from Colombia.

"The U.S. aid is supposedly used, and justified, in the name of combating drugs," Murillo told us. But "a majority of U.S. aid is actually being used to combat the guerrillas and the civilian popular sectors struggling for social change."

Most of the victims of Colombian terrorism are peaceable civilians—brutally murdered as surely as the victims in Oklahoma City. No less than the people we have seen so often on our TV screens in recent weeks, their loved ones are left behind to weep and to mourn. But the circumstances of such grief are off the media map.

May 3, 1995

Discussion Questions

1. What is the "School of the Americas" and what is its purpose? Who are some of the graduates of the school?

2. What is the nation "where terrorism rules"?
3. How do you define terrorism?
4. Why does the U.S. continue to pour aid into Columbia?

Writing Suggestion

Research the attempts to defund and/or close the School of the Americas. On which side do you stand and why?

Behind the Stereotype: Human Rights in Colombia

Javier Giraldo, S.J.

Colombia: The Genocidal Democracy

1. The Making of a Stereotype

In the spring of 1986, I was invited by the Catholic Development Committee Against Hunger to take part in the Lenten celebration in France. Before I began to speak, I asked members of the audience what kind of images they associated with my country. Invariably, they associated Colombia with drugs, coffee, cyclists (the annual Tour de France bicycle race is held there) and volcanos (where the November 1985 tragedy of Armero took place, a small town in Colombia that was almost totally buried by an avalanche).

There is no doubt that drugs are the first thing that come to people's minds when they think of Colombia. Some have attributed 80% of the world's drug trade to the Colombian cartels. Although I think the problem has been somewhat blown out of proportion, given the fact that the clandestine nature of the business makes accurate estimates difficult to come by, there is no denying its magnitude. What is important is that this perspective has resulted in the false conclusion that violence in Colombia is linked to drug traffic. Is this simply a result of investigative laziness or are there other factors involved?

Consider the following. On January 30, 1993, a car bomb exploded on a downtown street in Bogota killing 20 people. Almost immediately, news of the bomb, which was attributed to drug traffickers, was circulated worldwide by international press agencies. During the same month of January, 1993, our human rights data bank registered 134 cases of political murder and 16 cases of enforced disappearance in the country.

- In 25 of the murders and 6 of the disappearances all indications suggested that those responsible for the crimes were members of the state (the army, police or government security forces);

- And in 89 of the murders and 10 disappearances, the evidence pointed to paramilitary groups which operate as auxiliaries to the army and police.

In other words, while a crime committed by drug traffickers which claimed 20 lives was widely reported by the international news media, 130 victims of state or para-state violence were ignored outside Colombia; they simply did not exist. Granted, these 130 cases occurred neither on a single day nor in a single place, and thus did not "fit" into the parameters of "international news." But the contrast between what is considered news and reported and what is not, helps explain the way false images are constructed.

Between May, 1989 and June, 1990, the period during which the most drug-related terrorist bombings were carried out, Colombian non-governmental organizations registered 227 drug-related fatalities. During the same period they registered 2,969 politically motivated murders, not counting deaths in combat between the army and guerrillas. Thus drug-related murders were only 7.6% as high as those from political violence.

Indeed, between January 1991 and May 1992, drug-related deaths represented only 0.18% of the total number of violent deaths occurring in the country.

This stereotype linking violence in the country to drugs that the international media have created has served the Colombian government well. On the one hand, it has enabled the government to present itself in international forums as a "victim" of violence outside its control by drug traffickers and the guerrillas, and, on the other, permitted it to neatly conceal crimes of the state which exceed these others many times over but which are so rarely mentioned in the international media.

Between 1988 and 1992, the Colombian armed conflict between the army and guerrillas claimed a total of 6,040 victims, including soldiers, guerrillas and civilians caught in the cross-fire. This figure represents 4.7% of the country's total violent deaths and 30.5% of the politically motivated killings during the same 5 year period. 70% of these latter killings must be explained in some other manner.

2. Counting the Victims: A Painful and Controversial Task

In August, 1986, during its annual assembly, the Conference of Religious Superiors of Colombia approved the following resolution: "To promote, support and encourage the Christian prophetic signs which are present in religious communities, through the creation of a Commission of Justice and Peace which will channel and disseminate information and protests throughout the country."

The board of directors of the Colombian Catholic Conference of Bishops, however, did not approve of this initiative and placed obstacles in its path. Nevertheless, two years later a group of 25 Catholic provincials decided to found the Intercongregational Commission of Justice and Peace, subsequently adopted by the Conference as one of its official commissions. The Commission's first project was to gather and disseminate information about the victims of human rights violations, the right to life, in particular. To this end, we set up a data bank and began registering such cases.

Our first difficulty involved agreeing on categories for the different kinds of violence that we were registering. Convinced as we were that the term "human rights," for historical, philosophical, legal, ethical, political and pragmatic reasons, refers essentially to the relations between citizens and the state, we attempted to classify cases according to the direct or indirect responsibility attributable to government agents. But this proved impossible.

Beginning in the early 1980s, Colombians began to be caught up in what we call a "Dirty War." A vast network of armed civilians began to replace, at least in part, soldiers and policemen who could be easily identified. They also started to employ methods that had been carefully designed to ensure secrecy and generate confusion. Because of this, witnesses and victims of crimes are unsure of the exact identity of the individual(s) responsible for committing them. This problem with identifying the perpetrators is often insurmountable.

At the same time, members of the army and police began to conceal their identities, frequently wearing civilian clothes and hoods, to drive unmarked cars and to take their victims to clandestine torture centers, all in order to forego legal formalities in arrests. What has frequently followed these abductions is intimidation or torture, enforced disappearances and murder. They complement these practices with death threats against family members, witnesses, lawyers and any other individuals likely to denounce their activities. Frequently, members of the state or of paramilitary groups pass themselves off as members of "guerrilla units" when they commit crimes, leaving cryptic communiques at or near the scene of the crime. When reporting such incidents, the media depend almost exclusively on official (government/armed forces) versions of what has happened. This, in turn, reproduces and consolidates the misinformation.

For these reasons, we chose categories which we felt would permit us to differentiate between different kinds of violence that existed in the context of a Dirty War. We began to consider the motives which could be inferred from different characteristics of the crimes: the political and social context of the region where the crime occurred, the characteristics of the victims, their participation in union activities, campesino, community or other kinds of political organizations, and their involvement in denunciations or other kinds of protest activities.

- Cases in which it is possible to infer a political motive (repression of ideological or political beliefs) are classified as political killings.

- Cases in which the available information is not conclusive but still suggestive of such motives are classified as presumed political killings.

- Many other cases are classified as obscure, signifying that there is doubt as to whether or not the crimes were committed by common criminals.

Given the size and geographic complexities of the country and the impossibility of maintaining systematic contact with many of its regions, we obtain initial information of violent deaths from the study of 17 regional and national newspapers, after first attempting to strip accounts of the frequent bias in which they are reported.

Soon, in spite of the repugnance its name caused us, an additional category had to be created: social cleansing killings, referring to the physical elimination of drug addicts, exconvicts, petty thieves and criminals, prostitutes, homosexuals, beggars and street children. Tragically, such killings are a routine practice today, part and parcel of the generalized expansion of violence in the country which began in the 1980s.

Although different interests are involved, indications from a large number of these cases point to members of the national police as being responsible. Anecdotes revealing how accepted this practice is within the police abound. "It's better to eliminate them because if they are arrested and tried, they'll just be freed in no time or there will be nothing to charge them with, and, in a couple of days, they'll be back again, a problem for the police. " Behind this abhorrent practice is a neo-Nazi ideology prevalent within the police which legitimates the taking of human lives.

Beginning in 1988, we began to circulate a quarterly bulletin containing a systematized analysis of the dimensions of the country's political violence. The statistics were, and continue to be, frightening. Consider the following, The Truth and Reconciliation Commission in Chile registered 2,700 cases of political murder and disappearances during 17 years of brutal military dictatorship in that country. This number of cases, horrible as it is, is far less than the number of cases our data bank has registered *annually* in each year since it began operation.

Indeed, a number of religious communities and orders were so horrified when they read the first issues of our bulletin that they sent us letters asking us to stop publishing lists of victims, saying they only depressed them. We didn't heed their request. We feel that there should be a historical record of what has happened and that the victims merit, at the very least, a brief mention documenting their fate as a testament to the failure of so many efforts to relegate them to oblivion and silence. In scores of cases, these few lines are the only written testament to their human dignity.

The Colombian government, for its part, has become more and more uncomfortable with our lists. As I was writing this in June of 1994, the Presidential Counselor for Human Rights invited me to participate in an Indicators Workshop "intended to discuss and share criteria for the elaboration of statistics about violence in general, political violence and human rights violations."

During the workshop's final session, and in front of delegates from all of the government's investigative organizations, the counselor lashed out at our interpretation of political violence. In particular, he objected to the fact that we categorized cases as presumed political killings, and argued that such a category blamed the government for cases where responsibility for the crimes was unclear.

He also criticized us for considering "social cleansing killings" to be the product of a neo-Nazi ideology which prevails within certain government institutions. He insisted, instead, that such practices were carried out by "isolated" individual agents; he was opposed to our registering paramilitary crimes as part of official violence, and so on.

In my talk I attempted to defend our position by insisting that we could not limit ourselves to simply registering cases in which responsibility had been established because the "Dirty War" strategy had, since the early 1980s, been refining and perfecting methods of secrecy, concealment and impunity for those responsible. To register only cases in which the responsibilty was clear would grossly distort the dimensions of what is really going on in the country...

Discussion Questions

1. To what "stereotype" does the title refer?
2. Why is counting victims of murder in Columbia "a painful and controversial task"?
3. What is the "Dirty War"?
4. Why was the Colombian government uncomfortable with the published lists of victims that the author and his organization provided?

Writing Suggestion

Research recent events in Columbia. Have human rights improved?

A Guide to Mexican Reality

Saul Landau

Red Hot Radio:
Sex, Violence and Politics at the End of the American Century

November 7–8, 1995

Do you know where Reality is and how to get there? Fly to Tuxtla Gutierrez, capital of Chiapas, take a *colectivo* to San Cristobal de las Casas, an old colonial city an hour and a half and two mountains away. Go see the person who communicates with the Zapatistas and find out when and where your appointment is.

Early Sunday evening the contact informs me that my filming date was two hours ago, but not to worry because if I arrive there tomorrow morning they will understand. Miraculously, Rebecca, my partner, and I find Carlos Martinez, a cameraman with a camera, charged batteries and tape, and I locate an open rental agency that has a front wheel drive VW Combi. At 11:30 we put our heads on pillows.

At 4 AM Monday morning we depart, south to Comitan, about an hour and a half drive on a pothole-filled, but nevertheless paved road. Head east 20 more miles to Las Margaritas and then continue on a rocky, unpaved road that begins to resemble a mountain trail.

Enjoy magnificent scenery, occasional Indian villages and periodic threats to your life as the vehicle skids down slippery mud slopes with nothing but 200 feet of space between you and the bottom of the canyon. On these steep roads local people tote what look like 100-pound loads of firewood on their backs.

After about three hours of robust kidney exercise you arrive at the village of Guadalupe Tepeyac, a ghost town, the residents driven out by the Federales, the Mexican army, an occupation force. In the village, doctors and nurses sit outside a modern hospital bereft of patients. Armed soldiers amble along the muddy lanes between abandoned houses and a few hookers sit on a rickety bench, waiting for the soldiers to finish their shift.

On the way out of the village, we pass a military camp. A soldier stands in the entrance—a makeshift bamboo gate—snapping a photo of the side of the vehicle as it drives by. Ah, modern security procedures!

We continue east for another half an hour, sliding, literally, down the slippery slopes into Reality. In Spanish, Reality is La Realidad, the name of this village in the

Lacondon jungle, in southeast Chiapas, maybe fifteen miles north of the Guatemalan border, midway between Las Margaritas on the West and San Quintin on the East.

Yes, a wooden sign assures you, this is La Realidad, Reality. Park your vehicle on the side of the road, says a short, dark-skinned man who approaches and asks you in non-syntactical Spanish to write down what you want and give him some ID. He turns out to be the elected village chief. Villagers call him Maxi, which I assume to be short for *maximum jefe*, but is actually an abbreviation for his name, Maximiliano.

I write I had a date with "*el sup*," Subcomandante Marcos. He asks me if I had brought the newspapers or anything else. We had departed before the morning papers arrived, so I gave him a book and some cigars for Comandante Moises, a gift from a friend of his in the city.

He nods, and tells us to park the vehicle in a smidgen of shade offered by a tree near the village classroom, next to the stream that runs through the village.

We wait throughout the morning as colorfully clad, barefooted women and teenage girls return from the mountains carrying formidable loads of wood on their backs with a sling-like affair that reaches around the wood and across their foreheads to absorb and balance the weight. We watched from a crude bench outside the two-room school. Sounds came from the children and teachers inside. The air hangs around us like a cartoon bubble that says "heat and humidity," as the foggy cool of early morning turns furnace-like once the sun burns away the mist. At 11:00 A.M., a dozen lower-grade school school-boys run out of the classrooms, doing somersaults.

Surrounding us, rising precipitously from the valley, green mountains stand like still-life paintings; tropical Vermeers, studded with fir trees, precious wood, banana stalks and, hiding under them, the frail coffee trees—key to the village economy.

The village itself should have posed for a picture postcard. From above one sees a well-ordered pattern of thatched huts, divided by a rapidly-running mountain stream, with women and girls washing corn, beans, clothes and bodies and little kids splashing and frolicking. Firewood is piled neatly in sheds outside the huts and wisps of smoke curl from the kitchens. (Later, we learn that smoke protects villagers from the insect perils of the area). Dogs yap and roosters crow amidst a continual croaking and humming of frogs and bugs, with pigs snorting like bass players in this tropical orchestra of fauna.

Noontime comes and goes and still no word from "*el sup*." Maybe he's in the middle of writing one of his communiqués for the internet or meeting with the other comandantes about political strategy, or reading yesterday's *La Jornada* or this week's *Proceso*, Mexico's best and most progressive newspaper and magazine respectively. Maybe he's in the middle of a hot poker game or hunting an animal or making love to his wife, girlfriend, boyfriend or whomever. Am I feeling a bit frustrated?

The dense humidity begins to hang from everything, especially my clothes and hair. I slug my bottled water both to quench my thirst and temper my hunger pangs. Out of nowhere a buzzing black insect, an image from a gameboy set, circles my head. I wait. It lands on my hand. I slap. Got it! Within seconds a large red spot appears with a black dot in the center. It itches. I resist scratching. It starts to burn. Yeah, I got it all right.

At about three P.M., village men return from the *milpa*, the corn patch. Banal hunger pangs now intrude on any lofty thoughts and feelings I might have. Carlos arranges with the village head to allow us to buy our meals at the house of Jorge's family—for ten pesos a meal, about $1.15. By four, we begin to think *"el sup"* has forgotten us, or the message didn't arrive or he's at an all day prayer meeting.

To hell with him, I say, let's eat.

We wander across the so-called road to Jorge's house. His wife, Gloria, and his kids laugh as we arrive, place hunks of log or kiddie chairs outside the kitchen, plus a small bench, on which a teenage girl, dressed in what looks like her party clothes but which turns out to be traditional women's costume, places a metal bowl of water—for us to wash our hands. She smiles as we fumble with the bowl and try to figure out where to wipe our wet hands. Her jet black hair is perfectly combed, adorned with a bow. She is seventeen, unmarried, one of Jorge and Gloria's eight children. Two others died shortly after birth.

Gloria has cooked us a veritable feast, tepid, flaky corn tortillas, and watery, over-salted beans with pieces of protein—insects and worms—floating in them. She brings a dish with salt, limes and tiny chili peppers. I stuff some beans in my tortilla, jam two tiny peppers in and take a bite. The hair on my ears liquefies, a dentist drills into a nerve on the roof of my mouth.

"We call them look-at-the-sky peppers," says the teenager. As my body temperature reestablishes its equilibrium a small puppy approaches, an animal slightly larger than a mouse, with the pathetic look of a beagle mixed with a tortured rabbit. "She has no name," responds Gloria. I name her *Giganta*, giant, the Saint Bernard of the Lacondon Jungle.

After dinner, about 4:30, I wander over to the village basketball court—every village has one—and the guys invite me to play with them. I have never before, at 5'7" and 155 pounds, been the tallest and heaviest player on the court. The net-less hoops, one of which hangs at a 45 degree angle, present a challenge. A village ref whistles the violations and we change sides after our team scores 20 points.

Our side wins, but I decline my right as member of the winning team to play in a second game and slosh my way off the court. My bloated feet, clad in hiking boots, throb explosively, my clothes cling like freshly glued wallpaper.

Then comes night, the young men still shooting hoops by the full moon, as a chill fills the air, chasing away all but the most determined of people-chewing insects. Wearing sweat pants, sweat shirt and a pair of cotton socks midway up my legs, drenching myself with insect repellent, I curl up in the rear bench of the VW Combi, Rebecca on the middle bench, leaving only a crack of window open—a mistake, as I discover the next morning.

Carlos, the jungle veteran, drapes his hammock with mosquito netting inside the classroom. Roosters crow, frogs and insects chatter away, an occasional whinny comes from a horse, a snort from a pig—Reality's nighttime band.

At about 3:30 Tuesday morning, I awake and notice that some women have begun their trek up the mountainside; others are washing baskets of grain in the nearby stream. I stare at the sky for a couple of hours, then at 5:30 put my boots over the throbbing, itching welts on my ankles and legs and limp toward the communal water tap to throw something cold and wet on my face.

The men begin to file toward the *milpa*, machetes well-filed, faces stoic. Like the women who awoke before them and began their labors two hours earlier, the village men have followed a work-life pattern for centuries. They have relocated when the conquistadors and their descendants drove them into the jungle and obliged them to incorporate Catholicism into their own, far broader and more complex world view.

In La Realidad, some, mostly women, still speak in Tojolabal. The majority speak "Castilla," but haltingly, without evidence of developed vocabularies or syntax. They know what they have learned, however, from their parents, grandparents, and great-grandparents: a culture of order, discipline, respect for Nature and each other—and a democratic, albeit hierarchical, system of government, where the village meets in Assembly to discuss each important decision. Then, a pseudo-military command structure carries out the decisions.

This village is 100 percent Zapatista. In October, elected delegates of Mexico's Congress, along with Bishop Samuel Ruiz and other dignitaries, met here with Zapatista leaders. Many residents of La Realidad prepared for the meetings by slipping bandannas over their mouths and noses and hoisting sticks onto their shoulders, simulating rifles—the Zapatista symbol. The mask identifies the Mayan as a member of the EZLN. He or she takes off the bandanna or ski mask to hide—just another villager who fetches wood, washes corn and hacks the weeds from the *milpa*.

Driven to the inhospitable terrain by progress, cattle ranchers, timber barons and coffee estate owners, by hydroelectric projects and oil drilling, by corrupt and venal political bosses who fostered division inside the Indian communities, by the laws of capital as they have operated for five centuries, these people now face the ultimate threat of annihilation thanks to NAFTA—a subject I was eager to discuss with "*el sup*," if he ever showed up.

I wander with the crew over to Jorge's kitchen where the fire is well stoked, the beans are bubbling, and I pray the coffee water was boiled. Same people, same logs, same pathetic dog, same meal—except this time there's a burned egg thrown on top of the beans, and the chilis are green, not red and burn the roof of my mouth only 85 percent as much as the scarlet killers did.

After breakfast I send another note to "*el sup*"—short of begging, just a polite reminder that we're waiting. We watch the thin, white cover of mist burn away and the jungle sun hurling its daily challenge at the human body.

Antonio, another visitor in waiting, shows us where we can dip our itching, throbbing, sweating bodies into the cool stream. We trudge a quarter of a mile on a mud path and immerse hot flesh in cool mountain water. It is 11 am. Women begin to descend from the mountain with their wood piles. We watch grass, insects, and kids running out of school, trying to figure out who these weirdoes are.

The school teachers chat with us. One of the two young women from Mexico City says that the rebellion of January 1, 1994 gave meaning to her life; the ability to serve in areas that desperately needed teachers. The volunteer nurses had similar explanations. They give Rebecca a list of medicines they need for TB, fungus infections and other common ailments that make villagers miserable—or kill them.

The people of La Realidad suffer a high infant mortality rate, low life expectancy and terrible illnesses while they live. A granny with a kid slung across her back and another in tow told me her daughter-in-law had died and left her with eight orphans. "What am I going to do?" she pleaded. Her son was on his death bed. "A terrible cough," she explained. "It's whattayacallit tuberculosis." All of her kids had died, she said. Not natural. Better she should have died than her daughter-in-law, she whined.

Noon comes and goes. What's time mean when there's no phone to ring, no fax to send? Even cellulars don't function out here. Time in Reality is carried by wind and depends on the speed of the wind on any given day.

Today, the air hangs in place, waiting alongside me in a war of attrition. When hunger pangs develop, I suck on a grapefruit and feel that recurring sensation of worry vibrations tugging at my liver. Could the Zapatista poker game last for more than two days?

At 3:30 in the afternoon I feel like crying, so I smile and force myself into conversation with an eleven-year-old kid who wants to know how much a VW Combi costs and what renting a car means.

Then a young man, wearing blue overalls, strides purposefully toward us. He asks me if I am the *periodista*. I nod. He tells us where to be—a ten minute walk—at four o'clock. We spring into action—camera, tapes, still camera, film, notebook, notes for questions—adrenalin flowing.

At 4:05 two men wearing ski masks and carrying semi-automatic weapons walk into sight. One of them smokes a pipe. "*Buenas tardes*," he says, shaking my hand, smiling through his mud-colored ski mask. He puts his pipe in one hand and cradles his gun in the other. His bodyguard brings two benches for us to sit on and we begin our conversation, which would last until it got dark and then continue the next day.

I finally have my meeting with Subcomandante Insurgente Marcos, Zapatista leader, poet, communicator extraordinaire, from the jungles of Chiapas. We have only an hour of daylight, so we get right into the interview.

I ask Marcos about his thinking at the time of the rebellion, January 1, 1994. He responds in Spanish. "We think that when the uprising took place on the first of January, the globalization process, which coincided with Mexico's formal incorporation into NAFTA, meant the sacrifice of a part of humanity. In our case, it meant the sacrifice of the indigenous, of all the indigenous Mexicans but particularly the indigenous Chiapans," he tells me. "What neo-liberalism has done—the process of world globalization in NAFTA—is to eliminate a part of this population, annihilating them, wiping them from the face of the Earth.

"So, this is what we're looking at when we say, 'Enough already.' Our revolution is a revolution of words, to say, 'Here we are.' Our unique way to make this country and this world remember us, paradoxically, is by hiding ourselves. In order to show who we are, we hide, by wearing ski masks, inside a clandestine organization, using this ambiguous method to tell the country, 'We are many, we are millions, and this country is forgetting about us.'

"This cry begets not so much sympathy, as empathy. We get on the same wavelength as peasant movements and ethnic minorities from other parts of the world. In this sense, without explicitly proposing it, the Zapatista Army's message is converted into a world message, in that the oblivion suffered by the indigenous Chiapans is the same suffered by indigenous or ethnic groups in other parts of the world.

"In one way or another, it's a warning to this globalization process and to the entire world: You cannot forget a part of yourself in each project you make. The project of the future, no matter how modern, has to incorporate its past, has to incorporate its history, and he who forgets his history has to pay for it—like the neo-liberal regimes in Mexico are paying now."

I ask "*el sup*" about the social conditions of the Chiapans prior to the rebellion.

"The Indian wasn't just the citizen relegated to the lowest level. Rather, the indigenous Mexican was sub-human, not even enjoying the possibility of the cellar. In the case of the indigenous, they didn't even have the possibility of beginning to climb the educational staircase, which is the social ladder. They can't even climb the ladder of life. There isn't a family that hasn't lost a quarter or more of its children; dead in the period from birth to age five.

"This is the social-ideological basis that made it possible, on the first of January, 1994, for an army of a thousand indigenous people, poorly armed, badly trained, ill-disciplined, malnourished, poorly-equipped, to challenge a powerful army—a government at the height of its world renown, the government of Salinas de Gortari—and to challenge the entire world in the same way.

"Only a life-or-death perspective could take the indigenous groups to such a radical step—armed insurrection. Maybe if the indigenous people only lacked expectations for educational achievement, or recognized that their social conditions wouldn't allow them to improve their lives, they would have opted for other means, but they didn't have another possibility. Before the uprising, they only had the possibility of not living—of dying and dying needlessly.

"The racism used against the indigenous Chiapans is very similar to apartheid in South Africa. It's just less acknowledged here. Until 1993 a chicken, a hen, was worth more than the life of an indigenous person. Until not long ago, the indigenous in San Cristobal de las Casas couldn't walk on the sidewalk; they had to walk in the street, and they were scorned. They were despised simply because they looked Indian. Anybody not able to speak proper Spanish—meaning able to get proper schooling, besides being dark-skinned, short-statured, and dressed in a particular way—couldn't go into certain places.

"They were treated like animals. And according to what the landowners say, not even like an animal because an animal is worth more. In this sense, the death of an indigenous person didn't even count. If your mule died, you acknowledged it. You had a mule and now you don't. The indigenous people died and no one noticed.

"This is the history of the indigenous in Mexico. They've never been taken into account. On the scale of values in modern Mexico, indigenous people rate zero, lower even than an animal."

At this point, a military spotter plane dives toward us, possibly drawn by the sun reflector we're using.

"Smile," Marcos says, and reminds us that the plane has a camera. Marcos, his bodyguard, and our camera crew move under the eaves of a nearby building. When the plane flies out of sight, we resume.

I ask whether the indigenous can maintain their identity without land.

"No, the concept of land for indigenous people goes beyond what the land produces; or even land as a giver of life itself. It's not the same relationship as it is with a peasant, although his relationship with the land is very similar, in that it gives him a livelihood, roots, a goal in life. For the Indian, land also links him with history. I'm not referring to only the land he works but also the land where he lives, his community and his mountains, his rivers. It is the reference to his historic past that is not limited to something that has already passed, but it is something that is still happening."

Then I ask him about his view of President Clinton and U.S. policy toward Mexico. He answers now in broken and accented English.

"When Clinton supports the Mexican government, Zedillo's government, the U.S. government is supporting its own future problems, because the lack of democracy in Mexico means lack of justice and liberty. This increases the Mexican people's sense of instability, anxiety, and then they must go to another land to find the things they cannot find in their own land.

"I mean, when Mr. Clinton supports the façade of democracy in Mexico, he is supporting the growth of immigration to the United States from Mexico. A lot of people will go across the border because there is no democracy here, no liberty, no justice. The Mexican government doesn't do anything to resolve these problems, only increases repression with the military and police force. The military and police are corrupted by the drug traffic, and the U.S. government knows it.

"What we want in Mexico is democracy, liberty, and justice. The United States can deal with Mexico about immigration, drugs, and crime better by supporting the efforts of the Mexican people for democracy. A better border wall between Mexico and the U.S. is one constructed by democracy, liberty, and justice. We are not looking to threaten or embarrass the United States. We are looking to save our country and tell our story.

"The problem is that the U.S. government has forgotten the story of Mexico, and this is a mistake that all the American people will pay for. When the government of the United State makes a foreign policy mistake, the government doesn't pay the debt; the debt is paid by the American people.

"Each year immigration grows, and each year U.S. taxpayers pay more to solve this problem. But this problem doesn't get solved, because the problem is not in the United States, or on the U.S.-Mexican border. The problem is in Mexico. And the American people's effort to try to solve this should be directed to help the Mexican people, not help the Mexican government.

"When the American government gives money to the Mexican government, that money doesn't go to the Mexican people; it stays in the Mexican government. So poverty remains, and grows and grows and grows."

I wonder whether the Zapatistas represent a threat to the United States.

"Even in spite of our guns, we are not a threat to the United States, not even a threat to the Mexican government. Our guns are only a way of saying, 'Hey, here we are! Remember us? Don't forget us.'

"We are not terrorists. We don't have nuclear bombs. We only have the truth of our words, and we are making one prophecy to you, the American people: Your future problems are in Mexico, and to solve these problems you must help the Mexican people. I repeat, not the Mexican government, but the Mexican people."

Another plane dives down. The sun has dipped behind the Blue Mountain, the wildest part of the jungle, "*el sup*" informs us. We turn the camera off. "We'll finish tomorrow," he says, shaking hands, "between 9 and 10." He and his bodyguard turn and begin their trek from Reality, the village, to their camp. We return to our vehicle, store the camera and tapes and make our way to Jorge's hut for our second meal of the day.

I cannot see by the light of the candles inside the kitchen what else but beans is floating in the bowl. A burned scrambled egg soaked in lemon juice, salt and a hot pepper, wrapped in a flaky tortilla placate my hunger. I dip the dry corn meal cake into the bean juice, hoping not to pick up any cling-ons. I drink the lukewarm, overly sweet coffee, tell the Señora how wonderful everything is and listen to the others converse about Reality.

Just as Marcos said, each family seems to have lost its share of kids, mostly between birth and five years old: fever, cough, diarrhea. With limited vocabulary and poor syntax in Spanish, the villagers nevertheless talk politics. They understand that former President Salinas' revision of Article 27 of the Constitution removed protection from their land—their life, their identity, their future. Under the revised law, there will be no land for their children and their grandchildren.

It is hardly a secret that this village is Zapatista territory. The army sends regular motorized convoys through La Realidad several times a week. Low-flying military planes and helicopters remind the villagers: "We're watching you."

Another cool night, but not cool enough to inhibit the ticks that crawl under my socks and sweat pants to gnaw at my flesh. At four thirty A.M., a horn blows, and I incorporate Yom Kippur into my dream, but when I sit up I hear the sound again. The women have already begun to do their chores. And at six more than a hundred men appear, with machetes, and begin a collective lawn mowing on all the village greenery. They finish within an hour.

Soon after, the ram's horn, called *el cacho*, sounds again and I ask the hornblower if he could repeat the blow so we could film him. He says we must ask permission. Ask Maxi. No, says the head man, the horn blowing calls the assembly; it's not for filming.

By noon, Marcos' advance man shows up and we complete the interview.

I ask him about his reputation as a "post-modern" revolutionary, one who uses drama and a sense of humor—something notably absent in other revolutionary movements.

"Believe me, the only way to survive here in the Lacondon jungle is to laugh. You have to have a well-developed sense of humor or be completely nuts. Or maybe in our case, both of these things. What we tried to do was to be spontaneous, that is to say, don't reflect too much, don't predict things, and I think that is what has given coherence to what we can do."

I ask him whether it's difficult to have a personal life as a guerrilla, or whether he's turned into a different person.

"I've turned into three people. There are three Marcoses: the Marcos of the past who has a past, the Marcos of the mountains before the first of January, and post January 1 Marcos. Of those, the most important one is the Marcos who is the product of all the others up until now. It is the Marcos of after the first of January.

"That's why people say it doesn't matter who Marcos is: Marcos is a symbol, he means something we have constructed. And that's the truth. In reality, the Marcos everyone knows, the Marcos of the ski mask, is someone in turn constructed by this ski mask, and who reflects a mountain of aspirations, and who has nothing to do with the person that is behind the ski mask.

"But someone is behind the ski mask," he laughs, "and that's the truth, and that Marcos is the one who spent twelve years in the mountains before the first of January, who was born out of the corpse of the civilian Marcos."

I mention that Fidel Castro once said there is no life that requires greater sacrifice than guerilla life.

"It was a very tough time, really very difficult. I don't know how to measure deprivation because seeing the indigenous conditions I would say that if anyone lives worse than guerillas it is the indigenous people here.

"But it was a very difficult situation especially for someone from the city. The only thing that allowed you to survive was the hope that something would come from everything we were doing. It was an irrational expectation, totally loony, because there was nothing, absolutely nothing, that would validate what you were doing—not world news, nor anything.

"We are talking about a group of four, five, six people in the mid-1980s, and we kept repeating to ourselves all day, all night, 'We are good. This was what we had to do.' But there was nothing outside of that to confirm that what you were doing made sense.

"Moreover, the mountain was rejecting you. The mountain made you hungry, sick. It pushed rain and cold on you. The aggression of animals, insects, all this was saying, 'Go, go, you have no business here.'

"And the entire world was telling you the same thing. The socialist camp was collapsing, the armed struggle route was completely abandoned, and you were like some nuts clinging to a dream, dreaming because that was the truth.

"You were dreaming that what you were doing was going to be good for something, and we didn't have ambitious dreams. Don't think that we were fantasizing about seizing power and then becoming great presidents or emulating Castro or Lenin or whatever. We were thinking that at least we were going to help the indigenous people transform their lives in a radical and irreversible way so that the past would not return."

He poses for photos with my wife and me. I ask him what size boots he wears, noticing that his are shredded. He says, "Forget it. I have a sentimental attachment to these."

We depart from Reality in late afternoon. I feel mixed emotions. The forty-three red welts and bumps, some with stingers left in them, will remain for only about three weeks, but the other memories will stick.

The road has suffered more rain, thus there is more dangerous, slippery mud. Carlos navigates the Combi, whose steering grows increasingly unresponsive, through perilous pits and caverns. Then, just after we drive through the ghost village of Guadalupe Tepeyac, we meet a road-fixing project—dump trucks loaded with dirt and a giant bulldozer. The army after all, like the Pony Express, has to get through.

A dump truck in front of us tries to turn around and backs its rear wheels into a ditch. It now blocks the entire narrow road. The driver then tries to jump it out by putting the vehicle in low and revving the accelerator. Because of all the weight in the back, he breaks the axle. Behind us is a truckload of village men, presumably Zapatistas, then another dump truck, then an army vehicle with a platoon of soldiers.

I contemplate a variety of scenarios that range from armed confrontation between the soldiers and Zapatistas behind us to slow death by starvation. The soldiers and Zapatistas avert their eyes when the patrol walks by. I note how much alike their young indigenous faces are. Then the bulldozer operator goes into motion, miraculously turns the dump truck and points it downhill, and pushes it onto the shoulder just enough for us to pass. "*Buey*," (Ox) screams Carlos the cameraman as we pass the driver who has broken the truck's axle.

On the road we film an Indian girl, who appears to be no more than 12, carrying a load of wood that a lumber jack would find difficult to hoist. Her stoic young face is a thousand years old. She has been carrying the wood for centuries.

Three hours and much kidney exercise later we arrive at the paved road. We find the phone and call home to ascertain that our kids are alive and well, concerns shared by the people with whom we have spent a few days, who don't have phones, but may have kids living in Los Angeles or Houston, people who cling to a culture that determines life according to Nature's dictates, an organic life style, tough, cruel and Spartan. They and their ancestors have fed themselves and others for over a millennium. Now they face extinction, by what the "*el sup*" calls neo-liberalism.

"Hey," he reminded, "don't forget about us!"

Discussion Questions

1. Why do you think the author uses such vivid detail to describe the environment of the village of Reality?

2. What is the Zapatista Army's message?

3. In response to what event did the Zapatista Army form?

4. How does Subcommander Marcos view U.S. policy toward Mexico?

5. How is Subcommander Marcos a "postmodern" revolutionary?

Writing Suggestion

One of the ways that the Zapatista Army has promoted its message is through the Internet. Search the net for more information concerning Zapatistas and their cause, and then evaluate their ideas.

Poor Journalism
South of the Border

Norman Solomon

The Habits of Highly Deceptive Media:
Decoding Spin and Lies in Mainstream News

Filled with speeches and photo-ops, President Clinton's visit to Mexico [in May 1997] produced a lot of good press back home. Most journalists sang the official tunes about immigration, drugs and corruption. The few off-key notes didn't last long, as when ABC's Peter Jennings reported: "This is where the U.S. gets cheap labor and makes enormous manufacturing profits."

Perhaps you saw TV footage of Mexican people living in dire poverty. But it's unlikely that you heard much about *why* so many are so poor. If the network's roving correspondents knew why, they avoided spilling the beans.

But not all the U.S. reporters arrived and left with Clinton. One of the few who actually lives in Mexico is John Ross, a freelance journalist who has been covering Latin America for sixteen years. He's committed to probing beyond the conventional media wisdom.

When I reached him in Mexico City during Clinton's trip, Ross began by pointing out that "Mexico is a country where 158,000 babies annually do not survive their fifth year due to nutritionally related disease. Two million more infants are seriously harmed by underfeeding."

The crisis, he stressed, is growing more severe. "As many as 40 percent of all Mexicans suffer from some degree of under-nutrition. And a report by Banamex, the nation's top private bank, indicates that half of Mexico's 92 million citizens are eating less than the minimum daily requirement of 1,300 calories as a result of the deepest recession since 1932."

Imagine the human realities behind the dry statistics: "Mexico's basic grain consumption dropped by 29 percent in 1995," Ross says, "and meat and milk consumption has slipped by an alarming 60 percent and 40 percent respectively during the last three years. The price of tortillas, the staple of poor people's diets, has doubled in the past 18 months."

President Clinton's upbeat visit to Mexico is now history. And so is the superficial sheen put on that event by U.S. mass media.

Ross—who wrote the award-winning 1995 book *Rebellion From the Roots: Indian Uprising in Chiapas*—refuses to polish the sheen. Instead, he tells about places like the town of San Agustin Loxicha in southern Mexico, "where poverty is so extreme that babies die in the priests' arms during baptism."

The town is in a region that supplies coffee beans to cafés in my neighborhood and yours.

Those who challenge the conditions in Loxicha face an iron fist, Ross explains: "Fifty of Loxicha's most upstanding citizens, including most of the town government and seven of its teachers, are penned up just outside the Oaxaca state capital, at the riot-scarred Santa Maria Ixcotel penitentiary, behind thick black steel doors in two cramped cells." The pending charge is armed rebellion.

Ross adds that "the prisoners tell of classic torture by authorities—their heads were wrapped in rags and dirty water poured into their mouths; electric wires were attached to their genitals; they were threatened with being hurled from helicopters into the ocean."

Far from media spotlights, the Mexican military—wielding U.S. equipment—is on the march to bolster the status quo, Ross reports. In Oaxaca, the routine includes "forced interrogations, widespread use of torture, secret prisons and kidnappings of prominent citizens, according to a report filed in February [1997] by the Mexican League for the Defense of Human Rights, the state's most active independent human rights group."

Today, at least 60,000 troops are deployed across broad terrain to crush resistance. In Ross's words: "From the Huasteca mountains, an impoverished, coffee-growing range that stretches through five states in eastern Mexico, all the way to the Lacandon jungle on the Guatemalan border, the Mexican army moves through indigenous zones, setting up road blocks, conducting house-to-house searches, arbitrarily beating and incarcerating Indians."

Meanwhile, Ross says, 27 million Mexican people still labor—against worsening odds—to scratch the soil for a living. They do so "despite a decade of decapitalizing the agrarian sector to conform with International Monetary Fund strictures, huge imports of cheap NAFTA grain that is driving small farmers off the land in droves, and forced 'association' with transnational agribusiness that gobbles whole farming communities."

Do you think such information belongs on the evening news?

May 7, 1997

Discussion Questions

1. Why do so many Mexicans live in dire poverty?

2. Who is John Ross, and how is his coverage of Mexican poverty different from that of the mainstream media?

3. Just how extreme are the problems of hunger and malnourishment in Mexico?

Writing Suggestion

Solomon ends his article by offering this question "Do you think such information [about poverty in Mexico] belongs in the news?" Respond to his question.

Guatemala 1962 to 1980s: A Less Publicized "Final Solution"

William Blum

Killing Hope:
U.S. Military and CIA Interventions Since World War II

Indians tell harrowing stories of village raids in which their homes have been burned, men tortured hideously and killed, women raped, and scarce crops destroyed. It is Guatemala's final solution to insurgency: only mass slaughter of the Indians will prevent them joining a mass uprising.[1]

This newspaper item appeared in 1983. Very similar stories have appeared many times in the world press since 1966, for Guatemala's "final solution" has been going on rather longer than the more publicized one of the Nazis.

It would be difficult to exaggerate the misery of the mainly-Indian peasants and urban poor of Guatemala who make up three-quarters of the population of this beautiful land so favored by American tourists. The particulars of their existence derived from the literature of this period sketch a caricature of human life. In a climate where everything grows, very few escape the daily ache of hunger or the progressive malnutrition...almost half the children die before the age of five...the leading cause of death in the country is gastro-enteritis. Highly toxic pesticides sprayed indiscriminately by airplanes, at times directly onto the heads of peasants, leave a trail of poisoning and death...public health services in rural areas are virtually non-existent... the same for public education...near-total illiteracy. A few hundred families possess almost all the arable land...thousands of families without land, without work, jammed together in communities of cardboard and tin houses, with no running water or electricity, a sea of mud during the rainy season, sharing their bathing and toilet with the animal kingdom. Men on coffee plantations earning 20 cents or 50 cents a day, living in circumstances closely resembling concentration camps...looked upon by other Guatemalans more as beasts of burden than humans. A large plantation to sell, reads the advertisement, "with 200 hectares and 300 Indians"...this, then was what remained of the ancient Mayas, whom the American archeologist Sylvanus Morely had called the most splendid indigenous people on the planet.[2]

The worst was yet to come.

We have seen how, in 1954, Guatemala's last reform government, the legally-elected regime of Jacobo Arbenz, was overthrown by the United States. And how, in 1960, nationalist elements of the Guatemalan military who were committed to slightly opening the door to change were summarily crushed by the CIA. Before long, the ever-accumulating discontent again issued forth in a desperate lunge for alleviation—this time in the form of a guerrilla movement—only to be thrown back by a Guatemalan-American operation reminiscent of the Spanish *conquistadores* in its barbarity.

In the early years of the 1960s, the guerilla movement, with several military officers of the abortive 1960 uprising prominent amongst the leadership, was slowly finding its way: organizing peasant support in the countryside, attacking an army outpost to gather arms, staging a kidnapping or bank robbery to raise money, trying to avoid direct armed clashes with the Guatemalan military.

Recruitment amongst the peasants was painfully slow and difficult; people so drained by the daily struggle to remain alive have little left from which to draw courage; people so downtrodden scarcely believe they have the right to resist, much less can they entertain thoughts of success; as fervent Catholics, they tend to believe that their misery is a punishment from God for sinning.

Some of the guerrilla leaders flirted with Communist Party and Trotskyist ideas and groups, falling prey to the usual factional splits and arguments. Eventually, no ideology or sentiment dominated the movement more than a commitment to the desperately needed program of land reform aborted by the 1954 coup, a simple desire for a more equitable society, and nationalist pride vis-à-vis the United States. *New York Times* correspondent Alan Howard, after interviewing guerrilla leader Luis Turcios, wrote:

> Though he has suddenly found himself in a position of political leadership, Turcios is essentially a soldier fighting for a new code of honor. If he has an alter ego, it would not be Lenin or Mao or even Castro, whose works he has read and admires, but Augusto Sandino, the Nicaraguan general who fought the U.S. Marines sent to Nicaragua during the Coolidge and Hoover Administrations.[3]

In March 1962, thousands of demonstrators took to the streets in protest against the economic policies, the deep-rooted corruption, and the electoral fraud of the government of General Miguel Ydigoras Fuentes. Initiated by students, the demonstrations soon picked up support from worker and peasant groups. Police and military forces eventually broke the back of the protests, but not before a series of violent confrontations and a general strike had taken place.

The American military mission in Guatemala, permanently stationed there, saw and heard in this, as in the burgeoning guerrilla movement, only the omnipresent "communist threat." As U.S. military equipment flowed in, American advisers began to prod a less-alarmed and less-than-aggressive Guatemalan army to take appropriate measures. In May the United States established a base designed specifically for counter-insurgency training. (The Pentagon prefers the term "counter-insurgency" to "counter-revolutionary" because of the latter's awkward implications.) Set up in the northeast province of Izabal, which, together with adjacent Zacapa province, constituted the area of heaviest guerrilla support, the installation was directed by a team of U.S. Special Forces (Green Berets) of Puerto Rican and Mexican descent to make the North American presence less conspicuous. The staff of the base was augmented by 15 Guatemalan officers trained in counter-insurgency at the U.S. School of the Americas at Fort Gulick in the Panama Canal Zone.[4]

American counter-insurgency strategy is typically based on a carrot-and-stick philosophy. Accordingly, while the Guatemalan military were being taught techniques of ambush, booby-traps, jungle survival and search-and-destroy warfare, and provided with aircraft and pilot training, a program of "civil action" was begun in the northeast area: some wells were built, medicines distributed, school lunches provided etc., as well as promises of other benefits made, all aimed at stealing a bit of the guerrillas' thunder and reducing the peasants' motivation for furnishing support to them; and with the added bonus of allowing American personnel to reconnoitre guerrilla territory under a non-military cover. Land reform, overwhelmingly the most pressing need in rural Guatemala, was not on the agenda.

As matters were to materialize, the attempt at "winning the hearts and minds" of the peasants proved to be as futile in Guatemala as it was in southeast Asia. When all the academic papers on "social systems engineering" were in, and all the counter-insurgency studies of the RAND Corporation and the other think-tanks were said and done, the recourse was to terror: unadulterated, dependable terror. Guerrillas, peasants, students, labor leaders, and professional people were jailed or killed by the hundreds to put a halt, albeit temporarily, to the demands for reform.[5]

The worst was yet to come.

In March 1963, General Ydigoras, who had been elected in 1958 for a six-year term, was overthrown in a coup by Col. Enrique Peralta Azurdia. Veteran Latin American correspondent Georgie Anne Geyer later reported that "Top sources within the Kennedy administration have revealed the U.S. instigated and supported the 1963 coup." Already in disfavor with Washington due to several incidents, Ydigoras apparently sealed his fate by allowing the return to Guatemala of Juan José Arévalo who had led a reform government before Arbenz and still had a strong following. Ydigoras was planning to step down in 1964, thus leaving the door open to an election and, like the Guatemalan army, Washington, including President Kennedy personally, believed that a free election would reinstate Arévalo to power in a government bent upon the same kind of reforms and independent foreign policy that had led the United States to overthrow Arbenz.[6] Arévalo was the author of a book called *The Shark and the Sardines* in which he pictured the U.S. as trying to dominate Latin America. But he had also publicly denounced Castro as "a danger to the continent, a menace."[7]

The tone of the Peralta administration was characterized by one of its first acts: the murder of eight political and trade union leaders, accomplished by driving over them with rock-laden trucks.[8] Repressive and brutal as Peralta was, during his three years in power U.S. military advisers felt that the government and the Guatemalan army still did not appreciate sufficiently the threat posed by the guerrillas, still were strangers to the world of unconventional warfare and the systematic methods needed to wipe out the guerrillas once and for all; despite American urging, the army rarely made forays into the hills.

Peralta, moreover, turned out to be somewhat of a nationalist who resented the excessive influence of the United States in Guatemala, particularly in his own sphere, the military. He refused insistent American offers of Green Beret troops trained in guerrilla warfare to fight the rebels, preferring to rely on his own men, and he restricted the number of Guatemalan officers permitted to participate in American training programs abroad.

Thus it was that the United States gave its clear and firm backing to a civilian, one Julio Cesar Mendez Montenegro, in the election held in March 1966. Mendez won what passes for an election in Guatemala and granted the Americans the free hand they had been chafing at the bit for. He served another important function for the United States: as a civilian, and one with genuine liberal credentials, Mendez could be pointed to by the Johnson administration as a response to human rights critics at home.

However, whatever social conscience Julio Cesar Mendez may have harbored deep within, he was largely a captive of the Guatemalan army, and his administration far exceeded Peralta's in its cruelty. Yet the army did not trust this former law school professor—in the rarefied atmosphere of Guatemala, some military men regarded him as a communist—and on at least two occasions, the United States had to intervene to stifle a coup attempt against him.

Within days after Mendez took office in July, U.S. Col. John D. Webber, Jr. arrived in Guatemala to take command of the American military mission. *Time* magazine later described his role:

> Webber immediately expanded counterinsurgency training within Guatemala's 5,000-man army, brought in U.S. Jeeps, trucks, communications equipment and helicopters to give the army more firepower and mobility, and breathed new life into the army's civic-action program. Towards the end of 1966 the army was able to launch a major drive against the guerrilla strongholds...To aid in the drive, the army also hired and armed local bands of "civilian collaborators" licensed to kill peasants whom they considered guerrillas or "potential" guerrillas. There were those who doubted the wisdom of encouraging such measures in violence-prone Guatemala, but Webber was not among them. "That's the way this country is," he said. "The communists are using everything they have including terror. And it must be met."[9]

The last was for home consumption. There was never any comparison between the two sides as to the quantity and cruelty of their terror, as well as in the choice of targets; with rare exceptions, the left attacked only legitimate political and military enemies, clear and culpable symbols of their foe; and they did not torture, nor take vengeance against the families of their enemies.

Two of the left's victims were John Webber himself and the U.S. naval attaché, assassinated in January 1968. A bulletin later issued by a guerrilla group stated that the assassinations had "brought to justice the Yanqui officers who were teaching tactics to the Guatemalan army for its war against the people."[10]

In the period October 1966 to March 1968, Amnesty International estimated, somewhere between 3,000 and 8,000 Guatemalans were killed by the police, the mil-

itary, right-wing "death squads" (often the police or military in civilian clothes, carrying out atrocities too bloody for the government to claim credit for), and assorted
groups of civilian anti-communist vigilantes. By 1972, the number of their victims
was estimated at 13,000. Four years later the count exceeded 20,000, murdered or
disappeared without a trace.

Anyone attempting to organize a union or other undertaking to improve the lot
of the peasants, or simply suspected of being in support of the guerrillas, was subject
…unknown armed men broke into their homes and dragged them away to unknown
places…their tortured or mutilated or burned bodies found buried in a mass grave, or
floating in plastic bags in a lake or river, or lying beside the road, hands tied behind
the back…bodies dropped into the Pacific from airplanes. In the Gualán area, it was
said, no one fished any more; too many corpses were caught in the nets…decapitat-
ed corpses, or castrated, or pins stuck in the eyes…a village rounded up, suspected of
supplying the guerrillas with men or food or information, all adult males taken away
in front of their families, never to be seen again…or everyone massacred, the village
bulldozed over to cover the traces…seldom were the victims actual members of a
guerrilla band.

One method of torture consisted of putting a hood filled with insecticide over the
head of the victim; there was also electric shock—to the genital area is the most
effective; in those days it was administered by using military field telephones hooked
up to small generators; the United States supplied the equipment and the instructions for use to several countries, including South Vietnam where the large-scale
counter-insurgency operation was producing new methods and devices for extracting
information from uncooperative prisoners; some of these techniques were finding
their way to Latin America.[11]

The Green Berets taught their Guatemalan trainees various methods of "interrogation," but they were not solely classroom warriors. Their presence in the countryside was reported frequently, accompanying Guatemalan soldiers into battle areas;
the line separating the advisory role from the combat role is often a matter of public
relations.

Thomas and Marjorie Melville, American Catholic missionaries in Guatemala
from the mid-1950s until the end of 1967, have written that Col. Webber "made no
secret of the fact that it was his idea and at his instigation that the technique of
counter-terror had been implemented by the Guatemalan Army in the Zacapa and
Izabal areas."[12] The Melvilles wrote also of Major Bernard Westfall of Iowa City who:

> perished in September 1967 in the crash of a Guatemalan Air Force jet that he was
> piloting alone. The official notices stated that the U.S. airman was "testing" the aero-
> plane. That statement may have been true, but it is also true that it was a common and
> public topic of conversation at Guatemala's La Aurora air base that the Major often
> "tested" Guatemalan aircraft in strafing and bombing runs against guerrilla encamp-
> ments in the Northeastern territory.[13]

F-51(D) fighter planes modified by the United States for use against guerrillas in
Guatemala…after modification, the planes are capable of patrolling for five hours
over a limited area…equipped with six .50-calibre machine guns and wing mount-
ings for bombs, napalm and 5-inch air-to-ground rockets.[14] The napalm falls on vil-

lages, on precious crops, on people…American pilots take off from Panama, deliver loads of napalm on targets suspected of being guerrilla refuges, and return to Panama[15]…the napalm explodes like fireworks and a mass of brilliant red foam spreads over the land, incinerating all that falls in its way, cedars and pines are burned down to the roots, animals grilled, the earth scorched…the guerrillas will not have this place for a sanctuary any longer, nor will they or anyone else derive food from it…halfway around the world in Vietnam, there is an instant replay.

In Vietnam they were called "free-fire zones"; in Guatemala, "*zonas libres*": "Large areas of the country have been declared off limits and then subjected to heavy bombing. Reconnaissance planes using advanced photographic techniques fly over suspected guerrilla country and jet planes, assigned to specific areas, can be called in within minutes to kill anything that moves on the ground."[16]

"The military guys who do this are like serial killers. If Jeffrey Dahmer had been in Guatemala, he would be a general by now."…In Guatemala City, right-wing terrorists machine-gunned people and houses in full light of day…journalists, lawyers, students, teachers, trade unionists, members of opposition parties, anyone who helped or expressed sympathy for the rebel cause, anyone with a vaguely leftist political association or a moderate criticism of government policy…relatives of the victims, guilty of kinship…common criminals, eliminated to purify the society, taken from jails and shot. "See a Communist, kill a Communist," the slogan of the New Anticommunist Organization…an informer with hooded face accompanies the police along a city street or into the countryside, pointing people out: who shall live and who shall die…"this one's a son of a bitch"…"that one…" Men found dead with their eyes gouged out, their testicles in their mouth, without hands or tongues, women with breasts cut off…there is rarely a witness to a killing, even when people are dragged from their homes at high noon and executed in the street…a relative will choose exile rather than take the matter to the authorities…the government joins the family in mourning the victim…[17]

One of the death squads, *Mano Blanca* (White Hand), sent a death warning to a student leader. Former American Maryknoll priest Blase Bonpane has written:

> I went alone to visit the head of the Mano Blanca and asked him why he was going to kill this lad. At first he denied sending the letter, but after a bit of discussion with him and his first assistant, the assistant said, "Well, I know he's a Communist and so we're going to kill him."
> "How do you know?" I asked.
> He said, "I know he's a Communist because I heard him say he would give his life for the poor."[18]

Mano Blanca distributed leaflets in residential areas suggesting that doors of left-wingers be marked with a black cross.[19]

In November 1967, when the American ambassador, John Gordon Mein, presented the Guatemalan armed forces with new armored vehicles, grenade launchers, training and radio equipment, and several HU-1B jet powered helicopters, he publicly stated:

These articles, especially the helicopters, are not easy to obtain at this time since they are being utilized by our forces in defense of the cause of liberty in other parts of the world [i.e., southeast Asia]. But liberty must be defended wherever it is threatened and that liberty is now being threatened in Guatemala.[20]

In August 1968, a young French woman, Michele Kirk, shot herself in Guatemala City as the police came to her room to make "inquiries." In her notebook Michele had written:

It is hard to find the words to express the state of putrefaction that exists in Guatemala, and the permanent terror in which the inhabitants live. Every day bodies are pulled out of the Motagua River, riddled with bullets and partially eaten by fish. Every day men are kidnapped right in the street by unidentified people in cars, armed to the teeth, with no intervention by the police patrols.[21]

The U.S. Agency for International Development (AID), its Office of Public Safety (OPS), and the Alliance for Progress were all there to lend a helping hand. These organizations with their reassuring names all contributed to a program to greatly expand the size of Guatemala's national police force and develop it into a professionalized body skilled at counteracting urban disorder. Senior police officers and technicians were sent for training at the Inter-American Police Academy in Panama, replaced in 1964 by the International Police Academy in Washington, at a Federal School in Los Fresnos, Texas (where they were taught how to construct and use a variety of explosive devices), and other educational establishments, their instructors often being CIA officers operating under OPS cover. This was also the case with OPS officers stationed in Guatemala to advise local police commands and provide in-country training for rank-and-file policemen. At times, these American officers participated directly in interrogating political prisoners, took part in polygraph operations, and accompanied the police on anti-drug patrols.

Additionally, the Guatemala City police force was completely supplied with radio patrol cars and a radio communications network, and funds were provided to build a national police academy and pay for salaries, uniforms, weapons, and riot-control equipment.

The glue which held this package together was the standard OPS classroom tutelage, similar to that given the military, which imparted the insight that "communists," primarily of the Cuban variety, were behind all the unrest in Guatemala; the students were further advised to "stay out of politics," that is, support whatever pro-U.S. regime happens to be in power.

Also standard was the advice to use "minimum force" and to cultivate good community relations. But the behavior of the police and military students in practice was so far removed from this that continued American involvement with these forces over a period of decades makes this advice appear to be little more than a self-serving statement for the record, the familiar bureaucratic maxim: Cover your ass.[22]

According to AID, by 1970, over 30,000 Guatemalan police personnel had received OPS training in Guatemala alone, one of the largest OPS programs in Latin America.[23]

"At one time, many AID field offices were infiltrated from top to bottom with CIA people," disclosed John Gilligan, Director of AID during the Carter administration. "The idea was to plant operatives in every kind of activity we had overseas, government, volunteer, religious, every kind."[24]

By the end of 1968, the counter-insurgency campaign had all but wiped out the guerrilla movement by thwarting the rebels' ability to operate openly and casually in rural areas as they had been accustomed to, and, through sheer terrorization of vil-lagers, isolating the guerrillas from their bases of support in the countryside.

It had been an unequal match. By Pentagon standards it had been a "limited" war, due to the absence of a large and overt U.S. combat force. At the same time, this had provided the American media and public with the illusion of their country's non-involvement. However, as one observer has noted: "In the lexicon of counter-revolutionaries, these wars are 'limited' only in their consequences for the interven-ing power. For the people and country under assault, they are total."[25]

Not until 1976 did another serious guerrilla movement arise, the Guatemalan Army of the Poor (EGP) by name. Meanwhile, others vented their frustration through urban warfare in the face of government violence, which reached a new high during 1970 and 1971 under a "state of siege" imposed by the president, Col. Carlos Arana Osorio. Arana, who had been close to the U.S. military since serving as Guatemalan military attaché in Washington, and then as commander of the counter-insurgency operation in Zacapa (where his commitment to his work earned him the title of "the butcher of Zacapa"), decreed to himself virtually unlimited power to curb opposition of any stripe.[26]

Amnesty International later stated that Guatemalan sources, including the Committee of the Relatives of Disappeared Persons, claimed that over 7,000 persons disappeared or were found dead in these two years. "Foreign diplomats in Guatemala City," reported *Le Monde* in 1971, "believe that for every political assassination by left-wing revolutionaries fifteen murders are committed by right-wing fanatics."[27]

During a curfew so draconian that even ambulances, doctors and fire engines reportedly were forbidden outside…as American police cars and paddy wagons patrolled the streets day and night…and American helicopters buzzed overhead… the United States saw fit to provide further technical assistance and equipment to initiate a reorganization of Arana's police forces to make them yet more efficient.[28]

"In response to a question [from a congressional investigator in 1971] as to what he conceived his job to be, a member of the U.S. Military Group (MILGP) in Guatemala replied instantly that it was to make the Guatemalan Armed Forces as efficient as possible. The next question as to why this was in the interest of the United States was followed by a long silence while he reflected on a point which had apparently never occurred to him."[29]

As for the wretched of Guatemala's earth…in 1976 a major earthquake shook the land, taking over 20,000 lives, largely of the poor whose houses were the first to crumble…the story was reported of the American church relief worker who arrived to help the victims; he was shocked at their appearance and their living conditions;

then he was informed that he was not in the earthquake area, that what he was see-ing was normal.[30]

"The level of pesticide spraying is the highest in the world," reported the *New York Times* in 1977, "and little concern is shown for the people who live near the cot-ton fields"…30 or 40 people a day are treated for pesticide poisoning in season, death can come within hours, or a longer lasting liver malfunction…the amounts of DDT in mothers' milk in Guatemala are the highest in the Western world. "It's very sim-ple," explained a cotton planter, "more insecticide means more cotton, fewer insects mean higher profits." In an attack, guerrillas destroyed 22 crop-duster planes; the planes were quickly replaced thanks to the genius of American industry[31]…and all the pesticide you could ever want, from Monsanto Chemical Company of St. Louis and Guatemala City.

During the Carter presidency, in response to human-rights abuses in Guatemala and other countries, several pieces of congressional legislation were passed which attempted to curtail military and economic aid to those nations. In the years pre-ceding, similar prohibitions regarding aid to Guatemala had been enacted into law. The efficacy of these laws can be measured by their number. In any event, the embar-goes were never meant to be more than partial, and Guatemala also received weapons and military equipment from Israel, at least part of which was covertly underwritten by Washington.[32]

As further camouflage, some of the training of Guatemala's security forces was reportedly maintained by transferring it to clandestine sites in Chile and Argentina.[33]

Testimony of an Indian woman:

My name is Rigoberta Menchú Tum. I am a representative of the "Vincente Menchú" [her father] Revolutionary Christians…On 9 December 1979, my 16-year-old brother Patrocino was captured and tortured for several days and then taken with twenty other young men to the square in Chajul…An officer of [President] Lucas Garcia's army of murderers ordered the prisoners to be paraded in a line. Then he started to insult and threaten the inhabitants of the village, who were forced to come out of their houses to witness the event. I was with my mother, and we saw Patrocino; he had had his tongue cut out and his toes cut off. The officer jackal made a speech. Every time he paused the soldiers beat the Indian prisoners.

When he finished his ranting, the bodies of my brother and the other prisoners were swollen, bloody, unrecognizable. It was monstrous, but they were still alive.

They were thrown on the ground and drenched with gasoline. The soldiers set fire to the wretched bodies with torches and the captain laughed like a hyena and forced the inhabitants of Chajul to watch. This was his objective—that they should be terri-fied and witness the punishment given to the "guerrillas."[34]

In 1992, Rigoberta Menchú Tum was awarded the Nobel Peace Prize.

Testimony of Fred Sherwood (CIA pilot during the overthrow of the Arbenz gov-ernment in 1954 who settled in Guatemala and became president of the American Chamber of Commerce), speaking in Guatemala, September 1980:

Why should we be worried about the death squads? They're bumping off the commies, our enemies. I'd give them more power. Hell, I'd get some cartridges if I could, and everyone else would too...Why should we criticize them? The death squad—I'm for it ...Shit! There's no question, we can't wait 'til Reagan gets in. We hope Carter falls in the ocean real quick...We all feel that he [Reagan] is our saviour.[35]

The Movement for National Liberation (MLN) was a prominent political party. It was the principal party in the Arana regime. An excerpt from a radio broadcast in 1980 by the head of the party, Mario Sandoval Alarcon:

I admit that the MLN is the party of organized violence. Organized violence is vigor, just as organized color is scenery and organized sound is harmony. There is nothing wrong with organized violence; it is vigor, and the MLN is a vigorous movement.[36]

Mario Sandoval Alarcon and former president Arana ("the butcher of Zacapa") "spent inaugural week mingling with the stars of the Reagan inner circle," reported syndicated columnist Jack Anderson. Sandoval, who had worked closely with the CIA in the overthrow of Arbenz, announced that he had met with Reagan defense and foreign-policy advisers even before the election. Right-wing Guatemalan leaders were elated by Reagan's victory. They looked forward to a resumption of the hand-in-glove relationship between American and Guatemalan security teams and businessmen which had existed before Carter took office.[37]

Before that could take place, however, the Reagan administration first had to soften the attitude of Congress about this thing called human rights. In March 1981, two months after Reagan's inaugural, Secretary of State Alexander Haig told a congressional committee that there was a Soviet "hit list...for the ultimate takeover of Central America." It was a "four phased operation" of which the first part had been the "seizure of Nicaragua." "Next," warned Haig, "is El Salvador, to be followed by Honduras and Guatemala."[38]

This was the kind of intelligence information which one would expect to derive from a captured secret document or KGB defector. But neither one of these was produced or mentioned, nor did any of the assembled congressmen presume to raise the matter.

Two months later, General Vernon Walters, former Deputy Director of the CIA, on a visit to Guatemala as Haig's special emissary, was moved to proclaim that the United States hoped to help the Guatemalan government defend "peace and liberty".[39]

During this period, Guatemalan security forces, official and unofficial, massacred at least 2,000 peasants (accompanied by the usual syndrome of torture, mutilation and decapitation), destroyed several villages, assassinated 76 officials of the opposition Christian Democratic Party, scores of trade unionists, and at least six catholic priests.[40]

19 August 1981...unidentified gunmen occupy the town of San Miguel Acatan, force the Mayor to give them a list of all those who had contributed funds for the building of a school, pick out 15 from the list (including three of the Mayor's children), make them dig their own graves and shoot them.[41]

In December, Ronald Reagan finally spoke out against government repression. He denounced Poland for crushing by "brute force, the stirrings of liberty…Our government and those of our allies, have expressed moral revulsion at the police-state tactics of Poland's oppressors."[42]

Using the loopholes in the congressional legislation, both real and loosely interpreted, the Reagan administration, in its first two years, chipped away at the spirit of the embargo: $3.1 million of jeeps and trucks, $4 million of helicopter spare parts, $6.3 million of other military supplies.[43] These were amongst the publicly announced aid shipments; what was transpiring covertly can only be guessed at in light of certain disclosures: Jack Anderson revealed in August 1981 that the United States was using Cuban exiles to train security forces in Guatemala; in this operation, Anderson wrote, the CIA had arranged "for secret training in the finer points of assassination."[44] The following year, it was reported that the Green Berets had been instructing Guatemalan Army officers for over two years in the finer points of warfare.[45] And in 1983, we learned that in the previous two years Guatemala's Air Force helicopter fleet had somehow increased from eight to 27, all of them American made, and that Guatemalan officers were once again being trained at the U.S. School of the Americas in Panama.[46]

In March 1982, a coup put General Efraín Ríos Montt, a "born-again Christian" in power. A month later, the Reagan administration announced that it perceived signs of an improvement in the state of human rights in the country and took the occasion to justify a shipment of military aid.[47] On the first of July, Ríos Montt announced a state of siege. It was to last more than eight months. In his first six months in power, 2,600 Indians and peasants were massacred, while during his 17-month reign, more than 400 villages were brutally wiped off the map.[48] In December 1982, Ronald Reagan, also a Christian, went to see for himself. After meeting with Ríos Montt, Reagan, referring to the allegations of extensive human-rights abuses, declared that the Guatemalan leader was receiving "a bad deal."[49]

Statement by the Guatemalan Army of the Poor, made in 1981 (by which time the toll of people murdered by the government since 1954 had reached at least the 60,000 mark, and the sons of one-time death-squad members were now killing the sons of the Indians killed by their fathers):

The Guatemalan revolution is entering its third decade. Ever since the government of Jacobo Arbenz was overthrown in 1954, the majority of the Guatemalan people have been seeking a way to move the country towards solving the same problems which were present then and have only worsened over time.

The counterrevolution, put in motion by the U.S. Government and those domestic sectors committed to retaining every single one of their privileges, dispersed and disorganized the popular and democratic forces. However, it did not resolve any of the problems which had first given rise to demands for economic, social and political change. These demands have been raised again and again in the last quarter century, by any means that seemed appropriate at the time, and have received each time the same repressive response as in 1954.[50]

Statement by Father Thomas Melville, 1968:

Having come to the conclusion that the actual state of violence, composed of the mal-nutrition, ignorance, sickness and hunger of the vast majority of the Guatemalan pop-ulation, is the direct result of a capitalist system that makes the defenseless Indian compete against the powerful and well-armed landowner, my brother [Father Arthur Melville] and I decided not to be silent accomplices of the mass murder that this system generates.

We began teaching the Indians that no one will defend their rights, if they do not defend themselves. If the government and oligarchy are using arms to maintain them in their position of misery, then they have the obligation to take up arms and defend their God-given right to be men.

We were accused of being communists along with the people who listened to us, and were asked to leave the country by our religious superiors and the U.S. ambassador [John Gordon Mein]. We did so.

But I say here that I am a communist only if Christ was a communist. I did what I did and will continue to do so because of the teachings of Christ and not because of Marx or Lenin. And I say here too, that we are many more than the hierarchy and the U.S. government think.

When the fight breaks out more in the open, let the world know that we do it not for Russia, not for China, nor any other country, but for Guatemala. Our response to the present situation is not because we have read either Marx or Lenin, but because we have read the New Testament.[51]

Postscript, a small sample:

1988: Guatemala continues to suffer the worst record of human-rights abuses in Latin America, stated the Council on Hemispheric Affairs in its annual report on human rights in the Western Hemisphere.[52]

1990: Guatemalan soldiers at the army base in Santiago Atitlán opened fire on unarmed townspeople carrying white flags, killing 14 and wounding 24. The people had come with their mayor to speak to the military commander about repeated harassment from the soldiers.[53]

1990: "The United States, said to be disillusioned because of persistent corruption in the government of President Vinicio Cerezo Arevalo, is reportedly turning to Guatemala's military to promote economic and political stability…even though the military is blamed for human rights abuses and is believed to be involved in drug trafficking."[54]

This was reported in May. In June, a prominent American businessman living in Guatemala, Michael DeVine, was kidnapped and nearly beheaded by the Guatemalan military after he apparently stumbled upon the military's drug trafficking and/or other contraband activities. The Bush administration, in a show of public anger of the killing, cut off military aid to Guatemala, but, we later learned, secretly allowed the CIA to provide millions of dollars to the military government to make up for the loss. The annual payments of $5 to $7 million apparently continued into the Clinton administration.

1992: In March, Guatemalan guerilla leader, Efrain Bamaca Velasquez, was captured and disappeared. For the next three years, his American wife, attorney Jennifer Harbury, waged an impassioned international campaign—including public fasts in Guatemala City (nearly to death) and in Washington—to pressure the Guatemalan and American governments for information about her husband's fate. Both governments insisted that they knew nothing. Finally, in March 1995, Rep. Robert Torricelli of the House Intelligence Committee revealed that Bamaca had been tortured and executed the same year of his capture, and that he, as well as DeVine, had been murdered on the orders of Col. Julio Roberto Alpírez, who had been on the CIA payroll for several years. (Alpírez thus becoming another illustrious graduate of Fort Benning's School of the Americas). The facts surrounding these cases were known early on by the CIA, and by officials at the State Department and National Security Council at least a few months before the disclosure. Torricelli's announcement prompted several other Americans to come forward with tales of murder, rape or torture of themselves or a relation at the hands of the Guatemalan military. Sister Dianna Ortiz, a nun, related how, in 1989, she was kidnapped, burned with cigarettes, raped repeatedly, and lowered into a pit full of corpses and rats. A fair-skinned man who spoke with an American accent seemed to be in charge, she said.[55]

Notes

The details of the events and issues touched upon in this chapter through 1968 were derived primarily from the following sources:

a) Thomas and Marjorie Melville, *Guatemala—Another Vietnam?* (Great Britain, 1971) Chapters 9 to 16; particularly for the conditions of the poor, and U.S. activities in Guatemala. Published in the United States the same year in a slightly different form as *Guatemala: The Politics of Land Ownership.*

b) Eduardo Galeano, *Guatemala, Occupied Country* (Mexico, 1967; English translation: New York, 1969) passim; for the politics of the guerrillas and the nature of the right-wing terror; Galeano was a Uruguayan journalist who spent some time with the guerrillas.

c) Susanne Jonas and David Tobis, editors, *Guatemala* (Berkeley, California, 1974) passim; particularly "The Vietnamization of Guatemala: U.S. Counter-insurgency Programs" pp. 193–203, by Howard Sharckman; published by the North American Congress on Latin America (NACLA, New York and Berkeley).

d) Amnesty International, *Guatemala* (London, 1976) passim; for statistics about the victims of the terror. Other AI reports issued in the 1970s about Guatemala contain comparable information.

e) Richard Gott, *Rural Guerrillas in Latin America* (Great Britain, 1973, revised edition) Chapters 2 to 8; for the politics of the guerrillas.

1. *The Guardian* (London), 22 December 1983, p. 5.
2. The plight of the poor: a montage compiled from the sources cited herein.
3. *New York Times Magazine*, 26 June 1966, p. 8.
4. U.S. counter-insurgency base: *El Imparcial* (Guatemala City conservative newspaper) 17 May 1962 and 4 January 1963, cited in Melville, pp. 163–4.
5. Stephen Schlesinger and Stephen Kinzer, *Bitter Fruit: The Untold Story of the American Coup in Guatemala* (New York, 1982), p. 242.
6. Georgie Anne Geyer: *Miami Herald*, 24 December 1966. Also see: *New York Herald Tribune*, 7 April 1963, article by Bert Quint, section 2, p. 1; Schlesinger and Kinzer, pp. 236–44.
7. Galeano, p. 55.
8. Ibid., pp. 55–6.
9. *Time*, 26 January 1968, p. 23.

10. Ibid.
11. Atrocities and torture: compiled from the sources cited herein; also see A.J. Langguth, *Hidden Terrors* (New York, 1978) pp. 139, 193 for U.S. involvement with the use of the field telephones for torture in Brazil.
12. Melville, p. 292.
13. Ibid., p. 291.
14. *Washington Post*, 27 January 1968, p. A4, testimony of Rev. Blase Bonpane, an American Maryknoll priest in Guatemala at the time.
15. Panama: revealed in September 1967 by Guatemalan Vice-President Clemente Marroquin Rojas in an interview with the international news agency Interpress Service (IPS), reported in *Latin America*, 15 September 1967, p. 159, a weekly published in London. Eduardo Galeano, p. 70, reports a personal conversation he had with Marroquin Rojas in which the vice-president related the same story. Marroquin Rojas was strongly anti-communist, but he apparently resented the casual way in which the American planes violated Guatemalan sovereignty.
16. Norman Diamond, "Why They Shoot Americans," *The Nation* (New York), 5 February 1968. The title of the article refers to the shooting of John Webber.
17. Opening quotation: Clyde Snow, forensic anthropologist, cited in *Covert Action Quarterly*, spring 1994, No. 48, p. 32. Right-wing terrorism: compiled from the sources cited herein.
18. *Washington Post*, 4 February 1968, p. B1. The historic dialogue in Latin America between Christianity and Marxism, begun in the 1970s, can be traced in large measure to priests and nuns like Bonpane and the Melvilles and their experiences in Guatemala in the 1950s and 60s.
19. Galeano, p. 63.
20. *El Imparcial* (Guatemala City), 10 November 1967, cited in Melville, p. 289.
21. Richard Gott, in the Foreword to the Melvilles' book, p. 8.
22. AID, OPS, Alliance for Progress:
    a) "Guatemala and the Dominican Republic," a Staff Memorandum prepared for the U.S. Senate Subcommittee on Western Hemisphere Affairs, Committee on Foreign Relations, 30 December 1971, p. 6;
    b) Jonas and Tobis, pp. 199–200;
    c) Galeano, pp. 72–3;
    d) Michael Klare, *War Without End* (Random House, New York, 1972) pp. 241–69, for discussion of the OPS curriculum and philosophy;
    e) Langguth, pp. 242–3 and elsewhere, for discussion of OPS practices, including its involvement with torture; the author confines his study primarily to Brazil and Uruguay, but it applies to Guatemala as well;
    f) *CounterSpy* magazine (Washington), November 1980–January 1981, pp. 54–5, lists the names of almost 300 Guatemalan police officers who received training in the United States from 1963 to 1974;
    g) Michael Klare and Nancy Stein, "Police Terrorism in Latin America," *NACLA's Latin America and Empire Report* (North American Congress on Latin America, New York), January 1974, pp. 19–23, based on State Department documents obtained by Senator James Abourezk in 1973;
    h) Jack Anderson, *Washington Post*, 8 October 1973, p. C33.
23. AID figure cited in Jenny Pearce, *Under the Eagle: U.S. Intervention in Central America and the Caribbean* (Latin American Bureau, London, updated edition 1982) p. 67.
24. George Cotter, "Spies, strings and missionaries," *The Christian Century* (Chicago), 25 March 1981, p. 321.
25. Eqbal Ahmad, "The Theory and Fallacies of Counter-insurgency," *The Nation* (New York), 2 August 1972, p. 73.

26. Relationship of Arana to U.S. military: Joseph Goulden, "A Real Good Relationship," *The Nation* (New York), 1 June 1970, p. 646; Norman Gall, "Guatemalan Slaughter", *N.Y. Review of Books*, 20 May 1971, pp. 13–17.

27. *Le Monde Weekly* (English edition), 17 February 1971, p. 3.

28. *New York Times*, 27 December 1970, p. 2; *New York Times Magazine*, 13 June 1971, p. 72.

29. U.S. Senate Staff Memorandum, op. cit.

30. *New York Times*, 18 February 1976.

31. Ibid., 9 November 1977, p. 2.

32. Jonathan Marshall, Peter Dale Scott, Jane Hunter, *The Iran-Contra Connection: Secret Teams and Covert Operations in the Reagan Era* (South End Press, Boston, 1987), chapter V, passim; *The Guardian* (London), 9 December 1983; *CounterSpy*, op. cit., p. 53, citing Elias Barahona y Barahona, former press secretary at the Guatemalan Ministry of the Interior who had infiltrated the government for the EGP.

33. *CounterSpy*, op. cit. (Barahona) p. 53.

34. Pearce, p. 278; a book was published later which transcribed Menchú's own account of her life, in which she recounts many more atrocities of the Guatemalan military: Elisabeth Burgos-Debray, ed., *I...Rigoberta Menchú: An Indian Woman in Guatemala* (London, 1984, English translation).

35. Pearce, p. 176; Sherwood's role in 1954: Schlesinger and Kinzer, pp. 116, 122, 128. His statement is partially quoted in Penny Lernoux, *In Banks We Trust* (Doubleday, New York, 1984), p. 238, citing *CBS News Special*, 20 March 1982: "Update: Central America in Revolt."

36. *Washington Post*, 22 February 1981, p. C7, column by Jack Anderson; Anderson refers only to an "official spokesman" of the MLN; the identity of the speaker as Sandoval comes from other places — see, e.g., *The Guardian* (London), 2 March 1984.

37. *Washington Post*, ibid. For a discussion of the many ties between American conservatives and the Guatemalan power structure, see the report of the Council on Hemispheric Affairs (Washington), by Allan Nairn in 1981.

38. *New York Times*, 19 March 1981, p. 10.

39. *Washington Post*, 14 May 1981, p. A16.

40. Ibid.; *New York Times*, 18 May 1981, p. 18; Report issued by the Washington Office on Latin America (a respected human-rights lobby which has worked in liaison with the State Department's human-rights section), 4 September 1981.

41. Washington Office on Latin America report, op. cit. Presumably it was the traditional right-wing fear of the poor being educated which lay behind this incident.

42. *New York Times*, 28 December 1981.

43. Ibid., 21 June 1981; 25 April 1982; *The Guardian* (London), 10 January 1983.

44. *San Francisco Chronicle*, 27 August 1981, p. 57.

45. *Washington Post*, 21 October 1982, p. A1.

46. *The Guardian* (London), 10 January 1983; 17 May 1983.

47. *New York Times*, 25 April 1982. p. 1.

48. Ibid., 12 October 1982, p. 3 (deaths, citing Amnesty International); *Los Angeles Times*, 20 July 1994, p. 11 (villages, citing "human rights organizations"). For the gruesome details of death squads, disappearances, and torture in Guatemala during the early 1980s, see *Guatemala: A Government Program of Political Murder* (Amnesty International, London, 1981) and *Massive Extrajudicial Executions in Rural Areas Under the Government of General Efraín Ríos Montt* (AI, July 1982).

49. *New York Times*, 6 December 1982, p. 14.

50. *Contemporary Marxism* (San Francisco), No. 3, Summer 1981.

51. *National Catholic Reporter* (Kansas City, Missouri weekly), 31 January 1968.

52. *Los Angeles Times*, 25 December 1988.

53. Occurred on 2 December 1990; Report, Summer 1991, from Witness for Peace, Washington, a religious-oriented human rights organization concerned with Central America.
54. *Los Angeles Times*, 7 May 1990.
55. DeVine and Bamaca cases: *New York Times*, 23 March 1995, p. 1; 24 March, p. 3; 30 March, p.1; *Los Angeles Times,* 23 March, p. 4; 2 April, p. M2; *Time* magazine, 10 April 1995, p. 43. Alpírez had actually been linked to the Bamaca case two years earlier in testimony to the OAS, information which the State Department of course had access to. (*Los Angeles Times*, 4 April 1995, letter to the editor from Madeline Rios, editor of *Guatemala Review Magazine*, LA).

Discussion Questions

1. In the introduction to this chapter, how does the author describe conditions in Guatemala?

2. How did the U.S. justify military assistance, terror and torture in Guatemala?

3. How does the use of pesticides affect Guatemalans who live near cotton fields?

4. How did the Reagan administration soften the attitude of congress concerning civil rights abuses in Guatemala?

5. What does Father Tomas Melville mean when he says "I am a communist only if Christ was a communist"?

6. What did Jennifer Harbury learn about the fate of her husband, Guatemalan guerrilla leader Efrain Bamaca Velasquez? What did she have to go through to extract information about her husband from the U.S. government?

Writing Suggestion

Research the current state of human rights in Guatemala. Have conditions improved, in your opinion?

Author's Note

Jennifer Harbury

Bridge of Courage:
Life Stories of the Guatemalan Compañeros and Compañeras

Who are the Guatemalan revolutionaries? What minds and hearts make up the organizations of the entity called the Unidad Revolucionaria Nacional Guatemalteca, the Guatemalan National Revolutionary Union (URNG)? What do they want? What do they think? How do they behave? Do people support them? Magazines, television, and newspapers in the United States reveal little about Guatemala and nothing about the *compañeros** themselves. Not surprisingly, the various Latin American revolutions begin to blur together in the consciousness of the U.S. public. In the absence of concrete information, the image of a guerrilla emerges in foggy and stereotypical form, young and a bit macho, idealistic yet dogmatic, jaunty in a beret and dangerously armed.

In the early 1980s, I began to work with Guatemalan refugees who fled the terror of their country. To find supporting evidence for their political asylum applications, I traveled to Mexico gathering information and testimonies, visiting church organizations, and interviewing people at the refugee camps. Later, I moved to Guatemala itself. The human devastation that I witnessed is well documented in the annals of Amnesty International, in the regular reports of Americas Watch, and the denouncements of the Catholic Church. [*Bridge of Courage*] does not attempt to repeat the documentation. Rather, it attempts to tell a part of the story that, for many reasons, has always been concealed.

During my years in Guatemala, I came to know many people involved in the underground, in the revolution. They were men and women, old and young, professors and peasants, civil rights workers and Mayan villagers. Some are still living but many are now dead, either killed in combat or hunted down in the city streets. In the years since I was forced to leave the country, my contact with these revolutionaries has remained strong. I have come to know more and more of them, as individ-

---

*Compañero(a): Literally friend or companion. In Latin America, the term frequently refers to a person who shares one's ideals. The guerillas use the term to refer to one another.

uals and as friends. To keep them safe from harm, the details of my connections and relationships with them can never be told—at least not until this terrible war has ended. But we know each other well and see each other with great frequency. For me, it has been a privilege.

[*Bridge of Courage*] is an anthology, a collection of oral histories. Throughout the years, there have been many difficult times, but also quiet times, opportunities to talk, swap stories, ask about each other's lives and dreams. I have written down those stories, just as they were told to me. For the sake of accuracy, I have included only accounts that were given to me first hand, and by people I had come to know personally. I have also included excerpts from the journal I kept during my time in Guatemala.

The stories are divided into four categories: Part I gives accounts about how and why people made the difficult and dangerous decision to work for their revolution; Part II describes earlier stages of the war, of conditions, hardships and battles in the early 1980s; Part III includes accounts and descriptions of present day life in the struggle, the changes made and the hopes for the future; Part IV discusses projects people can get involved with to change their plight. I have changed the names and places and other identifying details. I want [*Bridge of Courage*] to cause no deaths. Three of the stories are composites of several similar stories, blended together to avoid repetition. No other changes have been made. None of the people or the events is fictitious.

These are the stories of people I have come, through the years, to love and respect. So many gave their lives with only the hope that their sacrifices would lead to a new and better Guatemala. Some of those whose stories are in this book are now dead. They, and those who still survive, deserve to be known and remembered.

Note

The events described in the following stories took place, for the most part, during the late 1970s and early 1980s. The army unleashed its campaign of terror against all those seeking social change, whether armed revolutionaries or civilians attempting reforms through peaceful and legal means. Mayan civil rights workers died in the Spanish Embassy, cooperatives were destroyed, and rural health and literacy promoters disappeared, never to be seen again. Not even the Church was exempt: progressive priests were assassinated, and catechists were killed and abducted in terrifying numbers. Hardest hit of all were the Mayan villages of the highlands, which the army suspected of supporting the guerrilla movement. The village of San Francisco Nenton was wiped from the map in a single afternoon, leaving some three hundred men, women, and children dead amid the charred debris of the town hall. Hundreds of other villages disappeared as the army assaults against the civilian Mayan population reached genocidal proportions.

The citizens of Guatemala were faced with difficult choices: submission, exile, or struggle. Given the mass destruction of all previous civilian reform efforts, many people chose the path of revolution, despite the personal risks involved. The following stories illustrate how some reached this difficult decision.

Anita

Jennifer Harbury

Bridge of Courage:
Life Stories of the Guatemalan Compañeros and Compañeras

Come on now, don't be shy. I see you are looking at the scars on my face. A big bullet blew off half my jaw about five years ago during an army ambush. As a doctor, I can tell you it was hell to repair all the damage—more than a dozen full-anesthesia surgeries in a Costa Rican hospital. I had family there, so I was lucky. Even though they didn't approve, they provided me with papers and a cover story for the injury. It took years, though. All I really remember from that period is rolling in and out of surgery, and lifting weights and working out in between operations to keep up my strength.

Here, sit down and drink some of this coffee and I'll tell you the whole story. This is good Guatemalan coffee, hard to get here, so I hope you enjoy it. Try this fruit too, from our garden. There's nothing wrong with my jaw now, so we can talk all afternoon, if you like.

My childhood was a little rough and tumble. I never really knew my father. He had abandoned my mother and all of us children, and only came to the house from time to time when he was drunk, to abuse her and take her hard earned money. She never complained much, because she assumed that men were just that way. And besides, she was strong enough to handle anything. She was a tough, beautiful peasant woman who could manage a twenty-hour work day and five small children without even slowing down. And she was smart, too. Even with the meager education she had, she started her own successful business and kept it going. Years later, it was she who saved my life, no questions asked, and got me out of the country to safety. And it was she, no questions asked, who reconnected me to the underground once I was strong enough to go back to war. I know that it is from her example that I developed my opinions on feminism and the role of women.

I joined the underground during my last year of medical school. I had just finished a rotation up in the jungle areas with the peasant cooperatives, and had learned a lot. What an eye opener that year was! It had been very difficult. My school supervisor hated women medical students and had sent me to the most remote regions in hopes that I would give up. Instead, though, I thrived, and came to love the villagers who took me in and cared for me. I loved their gentle ways, and their generosity, and I saw the unfairness and repression that they suffered. I never forgot it, even after I returned to the capital for my last year of study. And with my new awareness, I saw the things in the city that, perhaps, I hadn't wanted to see before.

I lived not far from a small union office, and on the way to the hospital each morning, I saw the fresh black ribbons on the union door, the new photographs, signaling yet another member dragged off to an ugly death in the middle of the night. And I saw the morgues. The tortures that had been inflicted on those poor people, the expressions on those dead faces, I will never forget. It is because of the morgues, I am positive, that so many of us medical students, and yes, even professors, joined up with the underground that year. Look, here is my graduation photo. See the two men handing me my diploma? They are both dead now; they were part of the city underground, but I didn't know it then. The two students next to me? They were with the guerrillas, too. I think they went to the mountains. None of us knew about each other, for security reasons. But I know now, and when I look at this photo, I feel doubly proud. Proud of the diploma and my completed studies, proud of all of us in the group, and proud of the courage represented in this image. It makes me happy to show it to you. I want these people remembered.

At first I worked in the city, with another medical student named Melissa. We had many small tasks: treating a wounded person brought in from the mountains, hiding medicines and passing them on, working in the clandestine clinics. It was all very dangerous. To be caught with medicines outside of the hospital meant death by torture. To be found treating a wounded combatant meant an immediate bullet. We both understood this, but we gave each other so much support, so much love. We were more than sisters. I still weep when I think of Melissa.

I don't know how she was found out, but she was. Things had grown so terrible in the city. Every day, our people were captured and tortured. And under that kind of torture, if people do not die quickly, they will talk. They cannot help it. So perhaps someone spoke of her, described her, gave away her next meeting point. Who knows—it doesn't matter. I found her in the morgue with so many others. She was naked and battered, her face bluish from strangulation, small razor cuts and cigarette burns up and down her arms and legs. Her autopsy report showed vaginal slashes, as if her captors, once finished with her themselves, had raped her with a broken bottle. Her eyes were gone, the sockets filled with mud. Looking down at her, I felt all my physician's arts were useless. It is so strange—it was not her injuries that hurt me the most. She was the same as all the others, there on the metal slabs that day. I had grown used to it. The pain was just from the loss of her, the loss for all of us left living.

That was the day I left for the mountains. I knew they would be coming for me soon. But that wasn't the real reason I left. I knew I could die just as quickly in the mountains. I could have fled the country to safety, but I chose not to. I had made a decision—I had decided to fight. I had decided that when those animals came looking for me, to kill me in that way, by God they were going to find me with a gun in my hands...

The Old Man

Jennifer Harbury

Bridge of Courage:
Life Stories of the Guatemalan Compañeros and Compañeras

Well, yes, certainly I have a favorite story. It's about tall tales, and I'll be glad to tell it to you. I just want to make it clear that this story is not a tall tale itself, just a story about tall tales, or rather, about tales I thought were tall tales, but which turned out to be completely true. You'll probably be thinking the same thing when you hear this, so that's why I'm telling you ahead of time that this really happened.

Well anyway, this started many years ago, in the city. It was back in the early 1980s when things were really, really bad for us. I was in the underground. My older brother had brought me in. I had joined because I would do anything he asked me to do, and because I knew as well as anybody else that things in Guatemala had to change. I had been with the student activists on campus for awhile, until they started being gunned down in the streets, and I had to quit, to cool off. That's when my brother came and talked with me about a real revolution, and I knew he was right. He was killed the next week, but I won't tell you about that. That is not my favorite story.

So anyway, I was young and angry, and I really threw myself into my work with the movement. I was doing very good work, but doing it very maniacally, without balance. This worried my *responsable*, and so one day, as recognition for my efforts and also to give me perspective, he took me to see a very special old man, one of the founders of the movement.

This really was a pretty amazing old man. When I first saw him, I couldn't believe my eyes. He was just a frail old guy dressed in loose work pants and gardening slippers, kneeling over a flower bed with his scruffy old dog at his side. When he stood up, though, he was very straight, with very steady dark eyes over his loose, old man's lips. He walked right up to me and embraced me and led me into the kitchen of his house as if he had known me for many years.

Inside, he made me a big pot of Guatemalan coffee and fed me, and asked me some questions about my work and my life. Then he sat back and started telling me stories, one after the other, some hilarious, some hair-raising, all of them incredible, about his life in the movement. These stories were just too wild, but the old man was so engaging, such a great story-teller, that I couldn't help sitting back, too, relaxing, laughing, and enjoying myself. I was having a really wonderful time, but I knew there was no way, absolutely no way, that all of these stories could be true. Somehow that made me enjoy myself all the more. It was like going to the movies with my grandfather, only the stories were also very inspiring, even though they made me laugh.

I don't remember all of the stories now, but there was one about his carrying a secret military message, very urgent, hidden in a bottle of mayonnaise in a big picnic basket. He ran into an army checkpoint, very bad luck, but almost got through it because he was old and harmless looking. Almost but not quite. At the last minute they grabbed him, and when they didn't like his answers they started torturing him. He insisted on his story though, that he was going to visit a relative with military connections, and finally, they let him go. As if this wasn't enough, he demanded his food back, and kept whining about it until finally the lieutenant yelled "here's your damned food!" and started throwing the stuff at him—the bread, the cheese, the fruit, and yes, the mayonnaise bottle. "Hah!" said the old man "Thank God the bottle didn't break."

"Hah," I thought to myself, "This old man tells the wildest stories I've ever heard." But I loved every minute of it. And by the end of the afternoon, I realized this man had done something really amazing with all his stories. He had pulled me in, opened my eyes, woven me into this incredible web of experiences that all of us in the movement share. All of a sudden I was not alone with my pain and my fear.

Well, finally it was growing late, and I had to leave. The old man followed me out the door and we embraced warmly. I didn't ask if I would ever see him again. As I walked away towards the corner where I was to wait for my ride, he returned to his flowerbed with his trusty mutt. It was then that I heard the sirens, and saw the army trucks come flying up the street towards us. The trucks were full of screaming soldiers, guns at the ready, and I knew they had come for us. I also knew not to run, so I just kept walking towards the corner, and miraculously, they roared past me without so much as a sidewards glance. Then my heart really sank, because I knew they must be coming for the old man. And sure enough, they pulled to a screeching stop on his front lawn. He was still kneeling over the flowerbed when the soldiers began leaping out of the truck.

The neighborhood had gone deadly quiet. I knew I should keep walking and not look back, but I ducked behind a wall and tried to at least see the license plate numbers on the trucks. As if this would make any difference! I was weeping, positive that I was going to see this wonderful human being beaten half to death and then dragged off to die in some secret prison, just like my brother had died. It was unbearable. As I watched, though, the old man rose gently to his feet and faced the group of soldiers racing up the lawn towards him. Most of them ran right past him, straight into the house, but a group of about eight shoved their rifles into his face. The lieutenant was wild-eyed. "Get the fuck out of here old man—things are going to get ugly!" he shrieked. The old man didn't bat an eye. "Sí, *Comandante*, sí." That was all he said. Then he just picked up his little dog and shuffled off down the street without ever even looking back. The rest of the soldiers ran into the house then too, and I could hear them smashing furniture and cursing as I ran off. I guess they were expecting someone who looked more like Che.

It was many years before I would see the old man again. Not long after that things became impossible for me in the city and I had to leave for the mountains. But I saw him once, in a house for the wounded, strengthening the young combatants with his stories and his vision, just as he did for me. You should hear him tell the story about that day. He has everyone spellbound, of course. "*Ocho carabinas! Ocho!*" He tells them all, waving eight fingers in the air. "And they still told me to get lost!" And naturally everyone bursts out laughing, because it really is very funny, even though it didn't seem too funny at the time. And I imagine that a lot of the young ones wonder if this isn't just a tall tale. But I know better now. I realize all those stories he told me that day were true to the last word. I also know it doesn't really matter. Because the gift we all receive from this incredible, brave old man is his vision, and perhaps, most importantly, the ability to see ourselves and our experiences with a sense of humor.

Discussion Questions

1. Why did Harbury gather the testimonies of Guatemalan refugees?
2. What do those testimonies indicate about the conditions they endured in Guatemala?
3. What was the punishment for doctors who attempt to treat patients outside of the hospitals? Why did Anita decide to join the underground despite these risks?
4. How are the stories of the Old Man a gift?

Writing Suggestion

How do you define a hero? Were the actions taken by Harbury, Anita and the Old Man heroic?

Writing Suggestions for Chapter Six

1. Using the readings in this chapter as a basis for your argument, argue for or against the use of U.S. military intervention in the affairs of other countries. Have there been cases in recent history in which military involvement was justified?

2. Examine a week's worth of local or national newspapers for stories on Mexico or Colombia. On what issues are the stories focused?

3. Argue for or against continued military and other forms of aid to Colombia. What issues are at stake? Why are certain members of congress against military aid to Colombia?

4. Argue for or against the idea that consumers should avoid buying products that are grown or manufactured in countries with oppressive governments or governments which neglect the needs of the poor.

About the Authors

Louise Armstrong, author of *Of "Sluts" and "Bastards,"* made her debut as a feminist social critic in the 1970s with the publication of *Kiss Daddy Goodnight*—a groundbreaking book on incest.

Britt Bailey, co-author of *Against the Grain*, holds an advanced degree in Environ-mental Policy and is a research associate at the Center for Ethics and Toxics (CETOS) in northern California.

Judi Bari, author of *Timber Wars*, was active in the environmental and labor movements, serving as an organizer for Earth First! and the Industrial Workers of the World. She was attacked by unknown assailants with a car bomb in 1990, and later died of breast cancer in 1997.

David Barsamian, co-author of *The Future of History* and *Keeping the Rabble in Line*, is the founder and director of *Alternative Radio*. The weekly, award-winning broadcast, heard on radio stations throughout the world, is a radical departure from the nuzak that prevails in the mainstream media.

William Blum, author of *Killing Hope*, left a position in the State Department in 1967 to protest what the U.S. was doing in Vietnam. His latest book is *Rogue State: A Guide to the World's Only Superpower*.

Ginger Ross Breggin, co-author of *The War Against Children of Color*, has done extensive research on the federal youth violence initiative. Jonathan Kozol has called her work "brilliantly controversial and uncomfortably persuasive."

Peter R. Breggin, M.D., author of *Talking Back to Ritalin* and co-author of *The War Against Children of Color*, has been called "the conscience of American psychiatry." A faculty member at John Hopkins University, he currently directs the International Center for the Study of Psychiatry and Psychology.

Daniel Burton-Rose, co-editor of *The Celling of America*, is a freelance journalist and editor of *win: a newsletter on activism at the extremes*.

Joanna Cagan, co-author of *Field of Schemes*, is a writer, editor and lifelong sports fan. Her work has appeared in places like *The Village Voice, In These Times* and *Extra!*

The Center for Public Integrity, co-author of *Toxic Deception*, is a nonpartisan, nonprofit organization well-known for its exposés of corruption in Washington.

Noam Chomsky, author of *Keeping the Rabble in Line*, is Institute Professor of Linguistics at the Massachusetts Institute of Technology. He has written hundreds of articles and dozens of books on a wide range of political issues.

Frederick Clarkson, author of *Eternal Hostility*, is the founding editor of *Front Lines Research*, a bimonthly journal about the Radical Right. He was named a "Media Hero" by the Institute for Alternative Journalism in 1992.

Liane Clorfene-Casten, author of *Breast Cancer*, is an investigative journalist and community activist. She is on the executive committee of Chicago Media Watch and chairs its Environmental Task Force.

Jeff Cohen, co-author of *Wizards of Media Oz*, founded and directed Fairness & Accuracy in Reporting (FAIR), a media watchdog group based in New York City. He currently is continuing his work as a media critic and freelance journalist.

Kevin Danaher, editor of *Corporations Are Gonna Get Your Mama*, is a co-founder of Global Exchange, and currently directs its Public Education Department. His latest book, co-edited with Roger Burbach, is *Globalize This!*

Neil deMause, co-author of *Field of Schemes*, is a longtime investigative journalist and devout Yankees fan. He currently edits the political zine *Here*.

Sara Diamond, author of *Facing the Wrath*, holds a doctorate in sociology from the Univeristy of California. She is one of the foremost authorities on the Christian Right and other right-wing movements.

Dan Fagin, co-author of *Toxic Deception*, is an adjunct professor at New York University. The environmental writer for *Newsday*, he was a 1994 Pulitzer Prize finalist.

Laura Flanders, author of *Real Majority, Media Minority*, is a long-time writer and journalist. She has hosted and produced the nationally-syndicated radio program *CounterSpin*, in addition to reporting for Pacifica Radio, PBS and a variety of newspapers and magazines.

Javier Giraldo, S.J., author of *Colombia*, is a priest who writes extensively on human-rights violations in his country. He has held high-level positions in tribunals investigating crimes against humanity within Latin America.

Kevin Griffith, editor of this book, is an associate professor of English at Capital University. He is the author of two books of poetry and is a two-term member of the National Council of Teachers of English's Committee on Public Doublespeak. He currently lives in Columbus, Ohio with his wife and two children.

Jennifer Harbury, author of *Bridge of Courage*, is an attorney and writer who works very closely with political refugees. After her husband was "disappeared" by the Guatemalan military in the early 1990s, her campaign to find the truth about his death sparked congressional investigations into human-rights abuses sanctioned by the U.S. State Department and CIA.

Michael Hudson, editor of *Merchants of Misery*, has written for the *Washington Post*, *New York Times*, *National Law Journal* and *Utne Reader*. He has won many awards for his coverage of the "poverty industry."

Saul Landau, author of *Red Hot Radio*, is an award-winning writer, filmmaker and political activist. His radio commentaries are aired on *Pacifica Network News*.

Marc Lappé, co-author of *Against the Grain*, holds a doctorate in Experimental Pathology from the University of Pennsylvania and currently directs the Center for Ethics and Toxics (CETOS) in northern California.

Marianne Lavelle, co-author of *Toxic Deception*, is a senior editor at *U.S. News and World Report* and winner of the Polk Award.

Mike A. Males, author of *Framing Youth*, has written extensively on youth and social issues. Once expelled from the second grade, he currently serves on the California Wellness Foundation's Adolescent Health Advisory Board.

Russell Mokhiber, co-author of *Corporate Predators*, is editor of *Corporate Crime Reporter*, a legal weekly based in Washington, DC.

Dan Pens, co-editor of *The Celling of America*, is a Washington-state prisoner and freelance journalist. He co-edits the journal *Prison Legal News* with Paul Wright.

Sheldon Rampton, co-author of *Mad Cow U.S.A.* and *Toxic Sludge is Good for You*, writes and edits the quarterly journal *PR Watch*, together with John Stauber.

James Rinehart, contributor to *Corporations Are Gonna Get Your Mama*, teaches sociology at the University of Western Ontario. He is the author of *Tyranny at Work*.

Marta Russell, author of *Beyond Ramps*, is a journalist, photographer, producer and documentarian whose work has appeared in a wide range of

newspapers and magazines. Her articles have also been reprinted in several anthologies.

Ken Silverstein, author of *Washington on $10 Million a Day*, is an investigative reporter who has published exposés in *Mother Jones*, *Harper's* and the *Nation*.

Norman Solomon, co-author of *Wizards of Media Oz* and author of *The Habits of Highly Deceptive Media* and *The Trouble with Dilbert*, writes a nationally syndicated column called "Media Beat" and is executive director of the Institute for Public Accuracy.

John Stauber, co-author of *Mad Cow U.S.A.* and *Toxic Sludge is Good for You*, is founder and director of the Center for Media & Democracy. He writes and edits the quarterly journal *PR Watch*, together with Sheldon Rampton.

Jennifer Vogel, editor of *Crapped Out*, is online editor at *City Pages*, an alternative weekly newspaper in Minneapolis. She won the *Nation's* I.F. Stone Award for student investigative journalism while in college, and continues to receive accolades for her in-depth reporting and feature writing.

Robert Weissman, co-author of *Corporate Predators*, is editor of the Washington, DC-based *Multinational Monitor* and co-director of the corporate accountability group Essential Action.

Paul Wright, co-editor of *The Celling of America*, co-founded and co-edits the journal *Prison Legal News*. He is a Washington-state prisoner, jailhouse lawyer, activist and reporter.

Matt Wuerker, author of *Meanwhile, In Other News...*, is a political cartoonist whose work has appeared in numerous books, newspapers and magazines and has been hailed as "brilliant" by social commentators and artists alike.

Howard Zinn, author of *The Future of History*, is one of America's most distinguished historians. Professor emeritus at Boston University, his *A People's History of the United States* is considered a classic.

Index